A PLAN FOR THE DICTIONARY OF OLD ENGLISH

a plan for the dictionary of old english

edited by
ROBERTA FRANK
ANGUS CAMERON

Published in association with
the Centre for Medieval Studies, University of Toronto
by University of Toronto Press

© University of Toronto Press 1973
Toronto and Buffalo
Printed in USA
ISBN 0-8020-3303-2
LC 72-97152

The figure on the jacket is the Wyrm from the Slab of Wamphrey

contents

introduction

The tradition of Old English lexicography has been a continuous one since the middle of the sixteenth century when Laurence Nowell compiled his list of Old English words and supplied them with contemporary equivalents.[1] Although the seventeenth and eighteenth centuries saw the publication of Old English dictionaries,[2] the time of greatest activity was the nineteenth century when Joseph Bosworth, and later T.N. Toller, Henry Sweet, C.M.W. Grein, J.R. Clark Hall, and A.S. Napier were at work.[3] More recently we have had specialized dictionaries, glossaries to newly published texts, and supplements to already existing dictionaries.[4]

The *Dictionary of Old English*, for which this volume is a forerunner, will be a scholar's dictionary, designed to replace the Bosworth-Toller *Anglo-Saxon Dictionary*, and to take a place beside the *Middle English Dictionary* in the series of period dictionaries which Sir William Craigie planned as sequels to the *Oxford English Dictionary*.[5] While making full use of the lexicographical work of the past, the *Dictionary of Old English* project will begin with a new and exhaustive collection of materials and will take a fresh look at Old English vocabulary. We are now able to do so because of the intensive work which has been done on Old English manuscripts and texts in recent years, and because of twentieth-century technical innovations such as microfilm, copying machines, and the computer.

The *Dictionary of Old English* is sponsored by the Centre for Medieval Studies at the University of Toronto and work has been underway now for about two years.[6] It is under the editorship of Christopher Ball, Lincoln College, Oxford, and Angus Cameron, the Centre for Medieval Studies. In matters of computer planning the project has the assistance of Richard L. Venezky, the University of Wisconsin; Malcolm Godden, the University of Liverpool, will direct the editing of Old English texts not now in print. The

1 Laurence Nowell, *Vocabularium saxonicum* [ca 1567], ed. Albert H. Marckwardt, University of Michigan Publications in Language and Literature 25, Ann Arbor 1952
2 William Somner, *Dictionarium Saxonico-Latino-Anglicum,* Oxford 1659; reprinted, Scolar Press Facsimile 1970; Thomas Benson, *Vocabularium Anglo-Saxonicum,* Oxford 1701; Edward Lye, *Dictionarium Saxonico et Gothico-Latinum,* ed. Owen Manning, London 1772
3 J. Bosworth, *A Dictionary of the Anglo-Saxon Language*, London 1838; J. Bosworth, *An Anglo-Saxon Dictionary*, ed. T.N. Toller, Oxford 1898; T.N. Toller, *An Anglo-Saxon Dictionary: Supplement*, Oxford 1921; Henry Sweet, *The Student's Dictionary of Anglo-Saxon*, Oxford 1896; Christian M.W. Grein, *Sprachschatz der angelsächsischen Dichter*, Bibliothek der angelsächsischen Poesie 3-4, Cassel 1861-4; Christian M.W. Grein with F. Holthausen, *Sprachschatz der angelsächsischen Dichter*, rev. ed. J.J. Köhler, Heidelberg 1912; J.R. Clark Hall, *A Concise Anglo-Saxon Dictionary*, London 1894; A.S. Napier, 'Contributions to Old English Lexicography,' *Transactions of the Philological Society* [1903-6], 265-358
4 F. Holthausen, *Altenglisches etymologisches Wörterbuch*, Heidelberg 1934; 2nd ed. with revised bibliography by H.C. Matthes, 1963; Jess B. Bessinger, Jr, *A Short Dictionary of Anglo-Saxon Poetry*, Toronto 1960; John C. Pope, ed., *Homilies of Ælfric: A Supplementary Collection*, EETS 259-60, London 1967-8, has a fine glossary which makes a number of contributions to Old English lexicography; J.R. Clark Hall, *A Concise Anglo-Saxon Dictionary,* 4th ed. with supplement by H.D. Meritt, Cambridge 1960. Professor A. Campbell, Pembroke College, Oxford, has recently completed a second supplement to J. Bosworth and T.N. Toller, *An Anglo-Saxon Dictionary.*
5 William A. Craigie, 'New Philological Schemes presented to the Philological Society, 4th April, 1919,' *Transactions of the Philological Society* [1925-30; pub. 1931], 6-11
6 J. Leyerle, 'The Dictionary of Old English: A Progress Report,' *CHum,* 5 [1971], 279-83. This report also appears in an earlier form in *The Old English Newsletter,* 4 [1970-1], 3-9.

editors can call on an International Advisory Committee whose members are Alistair Campbell, Pembroke College, Oxford; Helmut Gneuss, the University of Munich; John Leyerle, the University of Toronto; and Fred C. Robinson, Yale University.

Planning for the *Dictionary of Old English* began at an international conference held at the University of Toronto in March 1969. The proceedings of this first conference were published the following year under the title *Computers and Old English Concordances*.[7] The present volume is the result of a second conference held in Toronto in September 1970. The first chapter summarizes what happened at this gathering when the newly appointed editors put forward a tentative outline of the Dictionary for the criticism and suggestions of the Old English scholars, computer experts, and historical lexicographers present. The meeting was divided into three sessions: the first was on the state of Old English texts, the second on the state of computer concordances to Old English texts, and the third on the form of the *Dictionary of Old English*. Chapters two through five of this volume represent some of the results of these sessions.

Chapter two is a guide for those interested in editing Old English texts in a form suitable for use in the *Dictionary of Old English*. Chapter three is a listing of the corpus of Old English texts, giving manuscript sources and the present state of editorial work for each text. Chapter four contains a set of specific procedures to be followed in preparing Old English texts in computer-readable form for the Dictionary, and outlines a number of ways in which computers can be of assistance to lexicographers. Chapter five is a revised version of 'Some Specimen Entries for the *Dictionary of Old English*,' the paper presented for discussion at the final session of the conference. While the contents of this volume are directly tied to a conference and to a specific dictionary project, we think that they will be more generally useful as reference aids or as contributions to the study of Old English, to the theory of editing, to the use of computers in the humanities, and to historical lexicography.

During the past two years we have assembled the basic materials for the *Dictionary of Old English*, including a set of microfilms of all manuscripts containing Old English texts, and a large collection of printed editions. Work has already begun on putting texts into computer-readable form. We are now well ahead of where we had planned to be in our first two years of work, and we would like to thank all those who have helped to put us in this position: the Canada Council, the Foundation for Education and Social Development of Boston, and the University of Toronto for their financial and material aid; the members of the International Advisory Committee, our colleagues at the Centre for Medieval Studies, the University of Toronto, and the Fellows of Lincoln College, Oxford; the University of Toronto Press and Miss Prudence Tracy; and Mrs Susan Jupp, who has not only prepared the copy for this volume, but who has been of great assistance to all phases of the *Dictionary of Old English* since its beginning.

A.C., C.J.E.B.
August 1972

7 Angus Cameron, Roberta Frank, John Leyerle, eds., *Computers and Old English Concordances*, Toronto 1970

1

the dictionary of old english conference

ROBERTA FRANK

MEMBERS OF THE CONFERENCE

A.J. Aitken *University of Edinburgh*
R.W. Bailey *University of Michigan*
C.J.E. Ball *Oxford University*
J.B. Bessinger, Jr *New York University*
M.W. Bloomfield *Harvard University*
A. Brown *Ohio State University*
R.W. Burchfield *Oxford University*
R.B. Burlin *Bryn Mawr College*
A.F. Cameron *University of Toronto*
A.P. Campbell *University of Ottawa*
F.G. Cassidy *University of Wisconsin*
A.M. Clark *Ball State University*
P.A.M. Clemoes *Cambridge University*
R.L. Collins *University of Rochester*
R.S. Cox *Rice University*
J.E. Cross *University of Liverpool*
L.A. Cummings *St Jerome's College, Waterloo*
D. Fox *University of Toronto*
R. Frank *University of Toronto*
H. Gneuss *University of Munich*
E.B. Irving, Jr *University of Pennsylvania*
J.C. Jamieson *University of Toronto Press*
S.J. Kahrl *Ohio State University*
K.O. Kee *University of Toronto*
J.M. Kirk *University of Colorado*
R.F. Leslie *University of Victoria*
J. Leyerle *University of Toronto*
H.M. Logan *University of Waterloo*
A. McIntosh *University of Edinburgh*
I.M. McKellar *The Canada Council*
B.S. Merrilees *University of Toronto*
R.B. Mitchell *Oxford University*
P.W. Pillsbury *Eastern Michigan University*
J.C. Pope *Yale University*
J. Reidy *University of Michigan*
A.G. Rigg *University of Toronto*
F.C. Robinson *Stanford University*
J.L. Robinson *University of Michigan*
H.A. Roe *University of Toronto*
J.L. Rosier *University of Pennsylvania*
L.K. Shook *Pontifical Institute of Mediaeval Studies*
P.H. Smith, Jr *University of Waterloo*
E.G. Stanley *University of London*
R.D. Stevick *University of Washington*
V.L. Strite *Baylor University*
R.L. Venezky *University of Wisconsin*

... ond ge him syndon ofer sæwylmas
heardhicgende hider wilcuman.
Beowulf 393-4

John Leyerle opened the *Dictionary of Old English* conference by welcoming the
participants to Toronto. He outlined the agenda of the three formal sessions and noted
the several dinners, receptions, and parties in store for the delegates. He also warned of
the presence of two taperecorders which would record the proceedings for posterity and
for this volume. The ensuing discussions and scholarly interchanges were informative,
spirited, and seemed little inhibited by this threat. A summary of some of the conference
highlights follows.

SESSION I: THE STATE OF OLD ENGLISH TEXTS[1]

The chairman listed several topics which he hoped would be discussed: the desirability of
making the Dictionary an exhaustive survey of Old English; the size of the editorial
problem (unpublished manuscripts, inadequate editions of texts, inaccessible editions);
the type of edition required for lexicographical purposes.

   The first issue was disposed of quickly. The delegates agreed that an exhaustive survey
was not only desirable but possible, given the relatively small corpus of Old English texts
and the systematic study granted to these works over the years. In outlining the size of
the editorial problem, the chairman estimated that there were about fifty Old English
homilies, seven glossaries, three interlinear glosses, and a few fugitive pieces still not
edited. There were also inadequate editions to be replaced and inaccessible editions
deserving of wider publication, not only for the convenience of the Dictionary editors
but for the general benefit of Old English scholarship. The chairman asked those present
for advice on what form these new editions might take. Jack Aitken's reply — that for
lexicographical purposes an accurate transcript was all that was necessary — met with
general approval. Such a transcript would be a minimal edition, without introduction,
commentary, or intensive examination of textual cruces. Peter Clemoes directed attention
to the problem of dealing with textual variants in such editions. He asked where the
editors would draw the line between Old and Middle English texts, and how they would
handle twelfth-century copies or modernizations of undoubted Old English works. After
John Reidy had explained the practice of the *Middle English Dictionary* in citing border-
line texts, Eric Stanley expressed to the editors his and the delegates' desire 'to see every
question-marked Old English item which occurs in the *Middle English Dictionary*
appearing as question-marked Middle English in the *Dictionary of Old English*.'

   Turning to an issue of immediate practical import, Helmut Gneuss stated his con-
viction that some sort of organization would be useful to ensure that texts were put
speedily and efficiently into usable form. His appeal for some sort of 'traffic control'
was eloquently supported by Morton Bloomfield and Fred Robinson. Bruce Mitchell
wondered if the two Dictionary editors might act in this capacity. Christopher Ball
announced that the editors were ready and willing to serve as a central post-box, but
thought it inappropriate for them to take over total responsibility for laying down
editorial principles and seeing that such editions were done properly. George Rigg
suggested that the editors of the Dictionary invite a committee to draw up instructions

1 Friday afternoon, 25 September 1970; chairman: Angus Cameron

for editors and to read manuscripts. The question of just who would be willing and able to do the necessary transcripts was discussed at length. Stanley Kahrl observed that scholars might be willing to transcribe a work for the Dictionary as a first stage in their publication of that text.

The chairman then turned the discussion more directly to the question of publication and to the Materials for the Dictionary of Old English, a series proposed and outlined in detail by Eric Stanley after the first DOE conference. The chairman explained that volumes in this series would include editions, bibliographical works, semantic studies, and other tools useful for the Dictionary. Several conference members asked that a preliminary list of hints and/or instructions for editors of Old English texts be drawn up and published as part of this series. (Such a guide forms the second chapter of the present volume.)

The final speaker, John Leyerle, reviewed the major issues debated at this session. He stressed the positive aspects of what had been learned, noting that the vast bulk of material useful for the Dictionary was already adequately edited, and that the unedited, poorly edited, or inaccessible texts made up rather less than ten per cent of the total. Further discussion was checked by the arrival of a fleet of taxis which took the participants to a reception at the home of the president of the University of Toronto. The meeting resumed the following morning.

SESSION II: THE STATE OF COMPUTER CONCORDANCES TO OLD ENGLISH TEXTS[2]

The second session consisted primarily of reports from conference members experienced in the ways of computers and in their use in lexicography. Much valuable information was exchanged in the course of this meeting, and a number of the ideas suggested have been incorporated into the paper which forms chapter four of this volume.

The first report came from the chairman, who described his experience in creating, in partnership with Philip Smith, a 4,000-page concordance to *The Anglo-Saxon Poetic Records* and the recently published *Concordance to Beowulf*.[3] Philip Smith then recounted the lessons he learned from these two projects. Richard Venezky was next and spoke about the work being done on the new *Historical Dictionary of Hebrew* at Jerusalem. He described the use made by that project of advanced computer technology. Mr Venezky then proposed that a computer centre or archive be set up for the DOE. Such a data centre, he suggested, should receive texts encoded for punching according to a specific set of standards, the standards to be determined in advance by the editors and computer programmers and circulated widely. Paul Pillsbury then spoke about his work on the West-Saxon Gospels and the difficulties to be encountered and overcome by an editor of a 'parsed' concordance. He was followed by Jack Aitken who described the concordance procedures used in the *Dictionary of the Older Scottish Tongue*. Mr Aitken questioned the usefulness of sheet concordances for a dictionary editor who needs material in manipulable form (i.e., slips), and noted that a computer program for generating dictionary slips was written for DOST by Paul Bratley. Mr Aitken observed that an archive of the whole corpus of Old English could easily be produced. However,

2 Saturday morning, 26 September 1970; chairman: Jess Bessinger

3 J.B. Bessinger, Jr, and P.H. Smith, Jr, *A Concordance to Beowulf,* Ithaca, New York, 1969

he stressed the need for selectivity in editorial work, and outlined different procedures for tackling low- and high-frequency words by means of the computer. Fred Cassidy was the last speaker in the morning session to report on his experience with computers and lexicography. He described the procedures and progress of the *Dictionary of American Regional English* and underlined the importance of long-term financial security when undertaking such projects as the DOE. The meeting then adjourned for sherry and lunch.

SESSION III: THE FORM OF THE DICTIONARY OF OLD ENGLISH[4]

Discussion in this third and final meeting of the conference was focussed on a paper entitled 'Some Specimen Entries for the *Dictionary of Old English*,' which had been circulated among the participants six weeks earlier. The editors stressed that their proposals in that document were far from final, that many of them were tentative or even speculative. (Chapter five of this volume presents the paper in a revised form which incorporates a number of ideas and proposals worked out at this session.) Christopher Ball's opening remarks included several tentative policy statements on the form of the Dictionary, statements which, he observed, might arouse considerable debate. He asked for criticism on these proposals and on related issues; his request was not turned down.

The first item on the agenda was concerned with the scale of the Dictionary. Jack Aitken noted that, as a large-scale Old English dictionary was justified, work based on a collection of about a million slips would be in order. He and Angus McIntosh remarked on the usefulness of determining the point at which the rate in increase of information (from larger samples) is offset by the rate in increase of time and effort taken to handle that information. Robert Burchfield suggested that Bosworth-Toller could serve as a sensible yardstick; he said he thought it likely that the DOE would turn out to be not that much bigger than Bosworth plus Toller plus Professor Campbell's new supplement. Christopher Ball indicated that Bosworth-Toller used roughly one-third of the available Anglo-Saxon material for entries, while he and Angus Cameron used roughly two-thirds in their 'Specimen Entries.' This would seem to suggest, he continued, that the DOE would be twice as big as Bosworth-Toller, yet it would be published in a more efficient form (i.e., without the doublings or triplings of the headword list required by the two-volume Bosworth-Toller).

The second item on the agenda concerned the contents of a typical dictionary entry. The chairman raised the problem of headwords, noting that the practice followed by the editors was to take the normal Anglo-Saxon form, but with exhaustive cross-references to all divergences from it. John Reidy outlined the procedures of the *Middle English Dictionary* in determining the spelling of a headword. Robert Burchfield noted that all the scholars present seemed to agree that the late West-Saxon form is the one to adopt for the DOE. Fred Cassidy responded to a question put by Christopher Ball in his opening remarks (on the alphabetical treatment of verbs with the 'ge-' prefix) and opted for a completely alphabetical listing throughout for all parts of speech. Christopher Ball pointed out some of the difficulties in listing verbs in a purely alphabetical system: for example, the past participle of 'hiwian' would be automatically listed under 'gehiwian,' as if 'hiwian' had no past participle. Christopher Ball approved the concept of alphabetizing nouns, verbs, adjectives, and adverbs alike, but with the provision that

4 Saturday afternoon, 26 September 1970; chairman: John Leyerle

words prefixed by 'ge-' be alphabetized at the third letter. Fred Cassidy agreed that this would be a workable compromise.

The problem of spellings was discussed next. Jack Aitken objected to the editors' policy statement that the distribution of the various spellings would not be marked, and argued that such a distribution could easily be brought out by a kind of paragraphing. Robert Burchfield concurred with the editors' decision not to distinguish between the spellings þ and ð, yet observed that the more subtle distinctions (raised by Jack Aitken and Eric Stanley) were worth recording.

The problem of grammar words came up next. Eric Stanley expressed concern that an extended treatment of grammar words would vastly increase the scale of the Dictionary and the time needed to complete the project. He was seconded by Helmut Gneuss and Jack Aitken. The chairman reminded the meeting that there would be a final, complete concordance available to scholars on both sides of the Atlantic, and that this concordance could be used to produce the kind of exhaustive grammatical studies which could not be included in the Dictionary.

The chairman next directed the attention of the meeting to the derivational information to be included in the DOE. Bruce Mitchell wondered if this information, along with the frequency and distribution of the lexical items, should not come after the senses and citations rather than before. John Reidy said he preferred the order outlined by the editors.

The problem of ordering citations within a sense gave rise to a lively debate. The editors had tentatively proposed that this ordering could best be done by genre, moving from prose to verse to gloss material. Eric Stanley queried the placing of glosses last. Christopher Ball confessed to possessing a healthy suspicion of glosses as indicators of normal usage. Robert Burchfield asked how Bosworth-Toller ordered their material. Angus Cameron replied that Toller was fairly systematic and frequently ended with gloss material, but that he could discern no pattern in Bosworth's ordering. Victor Strite queried the editors' decision not to translate citations into modern English. Christopher Ball explained that he envisioned the Dictionary as a tool for scholars, not a hand-dictionary for students, and that he wouldn't want to impose his own translations on anyone. Robert Burchfield said that he personally regretted the loss of editorial authority involved in that decision, but thought it inevitable given the twentieth-century con-cordancing habit. There were questions from the conference members on the reasoning behind several sense-orderings in the circulated 'Specimen Entries.' Jack Aitken advised the editors of the advantages of grouping either by sense or by function first, and not by an externally imposed system. Paul Pillsbury asked for the editors' opinions on the dating of texts, and whether such information would be included in the Dictionary. Christopher Ball described the double dating necessary for much of the Old English corpus, noting that the date in which a text is thought to have been composed and the date of the extant version were often far apart. Moreover, he continued, although the manuscripts can be dated fairly accurately, the date of composition given is usually quite insecure. He stated that all available information on the dating would be given in the introduction.

The next issue raised was that of collocations. The editors had proposed that, where words show habitual or typical collocational patterns, these should be listed and the number of occurrences given. Morton Bloomfield questioned the need for information on collocations within the Dictionary, if the complete concordance were to be available. He was supported by Jess Bessinger and Eric Stanley, who remarked that, if a point were reached where economy became desirable, he would be willing to dispense with collocations. Jack Aitken asked if the editors proposed to look for collocations in the selected material, from which they would be editing, or if they would be looking at the full concordance. Christopher Ball said they would have to go to the full entries. Jack Aitken noted that this would be adding quite a burden to the work of the editors, and said he was concerned for much the same reason about the next item on the agenda, sense relations.

Under the heading of sense relations, the editors had proposed to give information, where possible, about the synonyms and antonyms of the entries. Robert Burchfield expressed concern with the amount of time such a study would take, as did Eric Stanley who wondered if such complicated surveys might not be more suitable for monographs. Fred Cassidy saw no reason why the editors should not list synonyms and near-synonyms, antonyms and near-antonyms, as potentially useful information.

The final item on the agenda concerned the exclusion of etymologies, of proper names, and of bibliographical information from the Dictionary, unless they were essential to the establishment of the meaning of the word in Old English. The omissions proposed by the editors generated even more spirited interchanges than the inclusions. There seemed to be a general feeling that, by eliminating etymological and onomastic excurses, the editors would be making the Dictionary too much a product of the twentieth century, 'too stainless steel and precision-ground,' as Denton Fox observed in his analysis of the prevailing mood. Separate pleas for the inclusion of simple etymological state-ments and common personal- and place-name elements were entered by Robert Burchfield, Edward Irving, Eric Stanley, and Helmut Gneuss, who also queried the exclusion of bibliographical information.

Taking each objection in turn, Christopher Ball assured the meeting that when an etymology was the sole or major source of information about a word, it would be given; it was only the 'frivolous' etymology, the one linking Old English 'fot' with Latin 'pedem,' which would be omitted as unimportant and potentially misleading in determining the meaning of the Old English word. Mr Ball agreed that there was great need for both a new etymological dictionary and an Old English onomasticon based on a fresh collection of primary materials, but argued at length that such works should be published in separate volumes by scholars with special expertise in these fields.[5] As for the omission of bibliographical information, he noted that a bibliography of Old English word studies, arranged alphabetically by word and based on the Dictionary headword list, would be ready for publication shortly after 1975. All words included in this bibliography would be marked with a special symbol in the Dictionary; a bibliographical supplement covering the period between 1975 and the date of the final fascicle of the Dictionary would be issued upon completion of the project.

As the chairman noted in drawing the meeting to a close, in the course of two days the conference managed to generate a formidable list of projects: an onomasticon, a revised etymological dictionary, an index of lexical studies, a guide to collocations, and a study of sense relations, among the many other proposals mentioned. The conference ended that afternoon as it began the day before – with a loud and unexpected thunderstorm. Several of the participants interpreted this as an omen from all-judging Jove, perhaps a sign of approval.

R.F.

5 Plans for a new etymological dictionary of Old English have been announced by Alfred Bammesberger, Freiburg im Breisgau, in Fred C. Robinson, 'Old English Research in Progress, 1970-71,' *Neuphilo-logische Mitteilungen*, 72 [1971], 510.

guide to the editing and preparation of texts for the dictionary of old english

HELMUT GNEUSS

1 THE PROJECT

The new *Dictionary of Old English* (DOE) will be produced in three stages.
1 Editing, checking, and preparing the texts
2 Assembling the lexicographical material in alphabetical order, i.e.,
   a/ concording each text
   b/ compiling an alphabetical slip-index from the concordances
3 Editing the Dictionary entries from the material thus concorded and sorted
Stages 1 and 2a are now in progress; they can be carried out concurrently. Stage 2b could start fairly soon, while stage 3 cannot begin before stages 2a and 2b have been completed. The following comments are exclusively concerned with stage 1.

Two principles govern work on the DOE:
A slip-index or concordance containing the complete vocabulary (i.e., all lexemes, with all their forms and occurrences or 'word-tokens')[1] of every literary or non-literary text, of every charter and inscription, must be available to the lexicographers as the basis of their work.
For each of these texts a completely reliable edition must be used in the concording process. Only editions based upon all extant MSS and including in their critical apparatus at least the lexical variants from these MSS (see section 3.5 below) are acceptable.
In order to satisfy the demands listed above, it will be necessary to check the existing editions of all OE texts and to edit or re-edit those found wanting. These texts must then be specially prepared for the concording stage. The steady continuation of work in stage 2 depends on the editorial work in stage 1 being carried out on a large scale and as quickly and reliably as possible.

2 OLD ENGLISH TEXTS

For the present purpose, OE texts[2] may be divided into three categories or groups.
   texts never edited before
   texts published in unsatisfactory editions
   texts edited according to the standards outlined in this chapter

2.1 TEXTS NEVER EDITED BEFORE
There are very few OE texts which have never been edited in any form, and editions of several such texts are now in progress (see section 5 below). Section 3 of this paper is an attempt to outline the methods and problems of editorial work on OE texts, with special reference to the needs of the DOE editors. It is hoped that the hints provided in section 3

---

1 For a small number of lexemes (forms of the personal and of the demonstrative pronouns, forms of 'beon' and 'wesan,' the words 'and' and 'on') the index need not be complete, but this is not relevant to most of the work in stage 1. Cf. the figures given in J.F. Madden and F.P. Magoun, *A Grouped Frequency Word-List of Anglo-Saxon Poetry*, Cambridge, Mass, 1967, 1; in J.B. Bessinger, Jr, and P.H. Smith, Jr, *A Concordance to Beowulf*, Ithaca, New York, 1969, 339, and those quoted by A.J. Aitken, 'Historical dictionaries and the computer,' *The Computer in Literary and Linguistic Research*, ed. R.A. Wisbey, Cambridge 1971, 5 and n 1.
2 For a complete inventory of OE texts in MSS, including charters, see A. Cameron, 'A List of Old English Texts,' below. For inscriptions see E. Okasha, *Hand-list of Anglo-Saxon Non-runic Inscriptions*, Cambridge 1971; a corpus of Anglo-Saxon runic inscriptions is being prepared by R.I. Page.

will as far as possible be taken into consideration by future editors of OE texts. Such editors may have to deal with items not only from the first category listed above, but also from the second, since a number of the available editions cannot be turned into 'standard texts' by mere collating and checking, but must be re-edited. New editions of OE texts can be published in the series to be edited in connection with the DOE, the Materials for the Dictionary of Old English.

2.2 TEXTS PUBLISHED IN UNSATISFACTORY EDITIONS

This group comprises all texts in editions known to be unreliable (such as the glosses to the *Durham Hymnal,* C.18.2 in 'A List of Old English Texts' below, and the OE *Martyrology,* B.19), in editions that do not satisfy present-day standards (such as the *Spelman Psalter*, edited in 1640, C.7.10), in editions that are not based on all the known MSS (such as Alfred's *Cura Pastoralis,* B.9.1), or which offer only a selection of the variant readings (such as the OE *Orosius,* B.9.2). There are other kinds of editorial short-comings: Schröer's edition of the OE *Rule of St. Benedict,* B.10.3.1, gives us a reliable text and a satisfactory critical apparatus, but Schröer missed a complete MS. G.Caro's subsequent collation of the overlooked MS (B.10.3.2) is so full of errors and omissions that it is practically useless.

As was mentioned before, in some cases only a completely new edition will help. In others, a thorough collation must be carried out, based on all the MSS and covering both text and apparatus. The standards and principles of such a collation should correspond to those for new editions outlined below in section 3. Accordingly, if several MSS have to be collated, it is sufficient to record the lexical variants from the non-basic MSS. If the collator has to work with microfilms or photocopies, he should also have the MS or MSS checked for details that may not be visible on a photograph, such as erasures, etc.

The results of a collation should be recorded on an interleaved copy of the text, or on a xerox copy with wide margins; the collator must write very clearly, and must indicate clearly by means of traditional symbols what should stand and what should be added, altered, or deleted in the original printed edition. The collated copy thus produced (or a photocopy of it) should then be put at the disposal of the DOE editors who will xerox the edition and return it or the xerox to the collator. Ideally, the collated edition will have gone through the preparation stage (described in section 5 below) before it is sent to the DOE editors as an actual master-copy.

Collators are also reminded that, in addition to producing a master-copy, they may publish collations not exceeding a certain length in periodicals, thus making them accessible to OE scholars everywhere long before a new edition can appear.

2.3 TEXTS IN SATISFACTORY EDITIONS

A large number of OE printed texts appear to be ready for immediate lexicographical use, provided that they have been properly prepared (see section 5 below). However, not enough is known at present about the accuracy of most of our editions of OE texts, particularly in the case of prose texts, glosses, and glossaries. Since the DOE editors cannot risk having to revise entries in their slip-index or in any other form at a later stage, random checking of nearly every text in the third group should be carried out before these texts reach the concording stage.

The principles underlying this process of checking will be the same as for the second group above. About one tenth of the edited text should be checked, including variant readings and passages taken from various parts of the text. If no misreadings or other serious editorial shortcomings are found, the text so checked should be considered suitable for use in the DOE. If doubts arise as to the reliability of an edition, it should be treated as a member of the second group, that is, the whole text and apparatus will have to be checked.

A great deal of time and labour could be saved if scholars who have information about the trustworthiness of any edition would contact the DOE editors; but such information must always be based on a comparison of the edition with the MS or MSS, or at least with photographs or microfilms.

In the three categories listed above no account has been taken of the fact that there are numerous printed OE texts which are badly in need of comprehensive introductions and explanatory notes. For the time being, in order to give all possible support to the DOE project, all efforts should be concentrated on the textual side of editorial work.

3 EDITING OLD ENGLISH TEXTS

The following notes are not meant as a set of rules and do not hope to offer a solution to every problem. Each text has its individual history, and each demands its specific editorial procedure. What follows is intended:

to draw the prospective editor's attention to some problems he may have to face, and
to offer some suggestions which, on the whole, are based on editorial practice in
standard editions of OE texts printed during the last one hundred years.

A number of books and articles have been written, mainly by classical scholars, on the technique of critical editions, sometimes intended as instructions for editors of a particular text series.[3] So far, however, uniformity of methods and devices in editions of classical, medieval, or modern texts has not been attained and perhaps is not desirable. There are, nevertheless, two aims which an editor should always have in mind: to be absolutely consistent in his methods, and to arrange his text and apparatus in as lucid a form as possible. An edition of an OE text does not only have to satisfy the specialist, who may be spending hours, days, or even years in studying it; it also has to serve the occasional reader, who may just want to see a particular word in its context and who should not be expected to read through a lengthy introduction in order to be able to use the edition.

The editor should personally inspect all the MSS to be edited or collated. Photographs, microfilms, or a facsimile edition may be extremely useful in preparing an edition, but when it comes to erasures, certain types of alterations, and other details, it is only the MS itself that can bring ultimate certainty. The editor should, of course, utilize earlier editions of his text, if there are any, as well as the relevant literature. He should also try to ascertain if copies of such earlier editions with handwritten annotations by their editors or by other leading scholars are still in existence.[4] Finally, the editor must take into account the typographical devices at his disposal. If his edition is a Ph.D. thesis

3   By far the best of these are O. Stählin, *Editionstechnik*, 2d ed., Leipzig 1914, and J. Bidez and A.B. Drachmann, *Emploi des signes critiques: Disposition de l'apparat dans les éditions savantes de textes grecs et latins; Conseils et recommandations*, 2d ed. by A. Delatte and A. Severyns, Brussels 1938. Stählin's book in particular has a great deal of sensible and useful advice.
4   A list of such annotated copies of printed OE texts and of other pertinent modern MS material is a desideratum. Discoveries in this field can still be made; see, e.g., T. Westphalen, *Beowulf 3150-55: Textkritik und Editionsgeschichte*, Munich 1967, 109-24, on Thorpe's collation of the *Beowulf* MS. See also E.G. Stanley in *Archiv für das Studium der neueren Sprachen und Literaturen*, 206 [1970], 459.

which will remain in MS form (and will be available as a xerox or microfilm copy), or if the printed edition will be a photomechanical reproduction of an edition prepared with a standard typewriter (lacking italics, small capitals, boldface type, etc.), the editor must be careful to use what devices he has (such as underlining, spacing) as clearly and economically as possible.

3.1 INTRODUCTORY MATTER

Ideally, every edition of an OE text would be preceded by a comprehensive introduction, which should include a detailed description of the MS or MSS (i.e., their contents, collation, script, decoration, etc.) and of all peculiarities of the OE text (spelling, characteristic mistakes, punctuation, accents). It should also include a discussion of the date, provenance, and history of each MS, and should give information about the history and transmission of the text, post-medieval copies, and earlier editions. The literary and historical significance and influence of the work edited, its metre, style, sources and ante- cedents, authorship, date, dialectal provenance and language (including syntax and, in particular, vocabulary) should also be discussed. All this would be followed by a full bibliography, annotated if possible.

However, an introduction of this kind may take years to prepare. At a time when new or revised editions of many OE texts are urgently needed, a brief introduction with full references to work already published on the particular text will suffice, and not only for the lexicographers working on the DOE. References to research tools which are now available everywhere and which will save the editor a great deal of time and labour — for example, N.R. Ker's *Catalogue of Manuscripts containing Anglo-Saxon* — could some- times take the place of lengthy descriptions and discussions. A complete bibliography will certainly be appreciated by all users of an edition, at least until a comprehensive bibliography of writings on OE literature is in existence.[5]

No edition, however, whether it has a full introduction or not, must be published without certain items which should be placed immediately before the text. I shall call these items the 'textual introduction,' which should not be confused with what the editor has to say about the text in the introduction proper. The textual introduction, or introductory apparatus, should consist of:

An explanation of the editorial principles. Apart from an introduction to the arrange- ment of text and apparatus, this should include the editor's reasons for his choice of the basic MS (on grounds of date, reliability, linguistic interest, etc.), or a reference to the place in the introduction where this information has been given.

A list of all signs, conventions, and abbreviations employed in the text, in the apparatus, and in the explanatory notes, including abbreviated names of former editors of the text. If the editor has a list of abbreviations at the beginning of the book (i.e., preceding the introduction), then this should be complete for introduction and text, so that a reader does not have to look twice for an explanation.

Shortened titles of OE poetical texts should be given according to F.P. Magoun, 'Abbreviated Titles for the Poems of the Anglo-Saxon Poetic Corpus,' *Etudes anglaises*, 8 [1955], 138-46, or to the list of short titles of Old English texts being prepared by Dr Bruce Mitchell, St Edmund Hall, Oxford. Abbreviated titles of scholarly periodicals should always be those used in the annual *MLA Bibliography*. All bibliographical re- ferences here and elsewhere should, of course, be given in conformity with *The MLA*

5 See the bibliographical project announced by S.B. Greenfield and F.C. Robinson in *NM*, 68 [1967], 196.

Style Sheet (2d ed., New York 1970).

A list of all MSS used in the edition, together with their sigla and, if possible, with a brief indication of the date and provenance of each MS. This list is not made superfluous by a detailed treatment of the MSS in the introduction. A reader of the text should not have to search through an introductory chapter to find out what A, B, etc, mean.

3.2 THE TEXT

Editors of OE prose and poetry have hardly ever made an attempt to reconstruct a critical text from the variant readings of several MSS or by means of conjectural emendation, as is feasible and usual in classical texts. Editions of OE texts have generally tended to be very conservative, and quite a number could actually be called diplomatic, that is, they reproduce the text exactly as it stands in the MS. For various reasons — because of the linguistic interest of the texts, because many texts have been transmitted in only one MS, etc — it seems desirable to continue this general policy in future editions and to produce editions of OE texts in a conservative or even diplomatic form.

Consequently, where there is more than one MS for a text, the printed text should follow one MS, the 'base MS' or the basic MS, while the variant readings from the others will appear in the critical apparatus. The choice of the basic MS will often be a difficult task, and no hard and fast rules can be given for this. Usually, the oldest MS or the one with a text believed to be closest to the original will be chosen.

In some cases, the linguistic or textual value of two or more MSS of the same text may justify a different editorial procedure, that of printing two or more versions of a text synoptically (e.g., on facing pages). This seems advisable where there is a considerable number of additions, omissions, and lexical variants in one or more members of a group of MSS.[6] It will often be difficult to decide whether a text should be printed synoptically or from a basic MS together with variant readings. This question is also of utmost importance for the DOE lexicographers, and every editor who is faced with a decision of this kind should get in touch with the Dictionary editors before he starts his work.

This is not the place to discuss the pros and cons of emendation.[7] I would suggest, however, that editorial emendations to OE texts be avoided unless there is an obvious mistake or omission in the MS, and then only if the emendation is based upon sufficient evidence from variant readings in other MSS or upon other reliable criteria. Scribal alterations in the basic MS are to be recorded in the apparatus; they should not normally appear in the text. In some cases, however, an alteration made by the original scribe may have produced alternative authoritative readings from which to choose. Here, the editor can either judge each case on its own merits, or come to a more general decision, printing the original readings only or the secondary readings only in the text.

3.3 SIGNS AND CONVENTIONS

There has never been a uniform system of signs, symbols, and conventions used in editing

6 See, e.g., *Bischof Wærferths von Worcester Übersetzung der Dialoge Gregors des Grossen,* ed. H. Hecht, Bib. ags. Prosa 5, Leipzig and Hamburg 1900-7, repr. Darmstadt 1965, I, 1-174.

7 See George Kane, 'Conjectural Emendation,' *Medieval Literature and Civilization: Studies in Memory of G. N. Garmonsway,* ed. D. A. Pearsall and R. A. Waldron, London 1969, 155-69. It is not possible to deal with the subject of textual criticism here; there is now a great deal of specialized literature in this field, and every editor should be conversant with its methods and problems. For some important bibliographical references see George Kane, *Piers Plowman: The A Version,* London 1960, 53, n 3.

classical or medieval texts. This is particularly true of OE texts. Among more than two dozen standard editions of OE prose and poetry, published by scholars such as S.J. Crawford, E.V.K. Dobbie, B. Fehr, M. Förster, H. Hecht, K. Jost, F. Klaeber, G.P. Krapp, F. Liebermann, A.S. Napier, W.J. Sedgefield, W.W. Skeat, H. Sweet, R. Vleeskruyer, K. Wildhagen, C.L. Wrenn, R.P. Wülcker, and J. Zupitza, no two editions agree in the arrangement of text and apparatus and in the use of square brackets, italics, etc.

A system which has been widely used in editions of classical texts consists of the following four elements:[8]

< >   enclose matter added by the editor (where he conjectures a gap in the MS).
[   ]   enclose matter in the MS which, in the editor's opinion, has to be deleted.
†   †   enclose a *locus desperandus*.
***   stand for what the editor believes to be a gap in the text (which he cannot fill).

This system has never been adopted for OE texts,[9] and it seems in fact doubtful if any satisfactory set of signs could be devised for the various cases of scribal or editorial interference in a text. A brief list of only the most significant of such cases may demonstrate this.

MS reading damaged or illegible
Words or letters erased in MS
Basic MS omits one or more words
Scribal alteration in MS by original scribe, or by a contemporary scribe, or later scribe
Scribal addition; superscript words
MS reading faulty, but not emended by editor
MS reading emended by editor
MS reading omitted by editor
Reading substituted by editor (from other MS)
Words or letters added by editor

This list could easily be expanded. Providing symbols and conventions for all these cases would result in unsightly pages, confusing rather than assisting the reader.[10] It is essential not to overload a page with critical signs or typographical devices such as boldface type or superscript numbers. The latter should never be used to refer the reader to the critical apparatus or to explanatory notes. Details about alterations, emendations, etc, can all be explained in the apparatus. One thing is of chief importance: whenever the editor departs from the text of the MS, he must draw the reader's attention to this fact, preferably by printing in italics all that is not in the MS. Similarly, editorial omissions (which should be rare) could be indicated by italics for the words immediately preceding and following the omitted matter. The editor should also mark words or passages which appear to be corrupt; this could be done by means of an asterisk following each word in question.

8 See the literature referred to in footnote 3 above. A different system has been developed for editions of classical inscriptions. Similarly, there is a set of special signs for OE inscriptions; see E. Okasha, *Hand-list of Anglo-Saxon Non-runic Inscriptions*, 45.

9 But cf. the corresponding use of [ ] and < > in *Die altenglische Version des Halitgar'schen Bussbuches*, ed. J. Raith, Bib. ags. Prosa 13, Hamburg 1933, 2d ed. Darmstadt 1964, vii and *passim*. In most editions of OE texts, however, square brackets enclose what has been omitted in the MS and supplied by the editor.

10 Cf. the typographical devices employed by K. Wildhagen, ed. *Der Cambridger Psalter*, Bib. ags. Prosa 7, Hamburg 1910, repr. Darmstadt 1964, which help us to understand the complex relations between the OE psalter glosses, but which could hardly be employed for a normal prose text.

3.4 SOME TECHNICAL POINTS
The following technical points must be carefully considered when a text is being edited.

Spelling
This should always be that of the MS or basic MS; it should never be normalized or standardized. Normalization may be useful and perfectly legitimate in texts printed for classroom use, but has no place in a standard edition.[11] For corrections of obvious misspellings see above (section 3.2).

Special letter-forms
The printer's type-fount (and, as far as possible, the editor's typewriter) should include þ, ð, æ (and for some texts œ) and their equivalents in capitals. But ʒ instead of g is unnecessary, since we no longer employ the special letter-forms for insular d, f, r, s, t, w, as the early editions and dictionaries do. The use of the runic symbol ƿ for w should be particularly avoided, since even the competent reader may occasionally confuse it with þ.[12]

Capitalization
This should be modernized, so that all sentences and all proper names begin with a capital letter. The editor may choose whether he wants to capitalize words for the deity or not. To indicate in the text each case in which a capital letter was introduced, or in which a MS capital letter was replaced by one in lower case (as is done by Fehr),[13] seems unnecessary.

Vowel quantity
The marking of long vowels is characteristic of readers used in introductory courses. Standard editions, however, with the exception of a few such as Klaeber's *Beowulf*, do not normally mark vowel quantity, and this seems a satisfactory practice; nor do they mark palatalized c and g by means of diacritics.

Abbreviations and contractions
These should be silently expanded; there is no need to print letters supplied by the editor in italics, unless there is doubt about the interpretation of the abbreviation. In this case, the most probable solution could be printed in the text (using italics), while an explanation should be given in the first section of the critical apparatus (see below, 3.5). Similar cases in MSS utilized for section two of the critical apparatus must be treated there accordingly. Except for 7 (= and) and ƀ (= oþþe), signs of abbreviation should not be retained in the text; and 7 and ƀ may be expanded as well.[14] A difficult problem is presented by abbreviated words without abbreviation marks, particularly among glosses;

11 See G.L. Brook, 'The Relation between the Textual and the Linguistic Study of Old English,' *The Anglo-Saxons: Studies in some Aspects of their History and Culture presented to Bruce Dickins*, ed. P. Clemoes, London 1959, 280-91; F.P. Magoun, 'A Brief Plea for a Normalization of Old-English Texts,' *Les Langues Modernes*, 45 [1951], 63-9; F.P. Magoun, *The Anglo-Saxon Poems in Bright's Anglo-Saxon Reader done in a Normalized Orthography*, Cambridge, Mass, 1956, iii-iv.
12 This symbol now seems to have disappeared from editions of OE texts, with the exception of some volumes in Methuen's Old English Library. The situation is different, however, in editions of ME texts.
13 *Die Hirtenbriefe Ælfrics,* ed. B. Fehr, Bib. ags. Prosa 9, Hamburg 1914; repr. with a supplement to the introduction by P. Clemoes, Darmstadt 1966, vii.
14 Cf. A. Campbell, *Old English Grammar,* Oxford 1959, § 24, and the list given by H. Wanley, *Librorum Vett. Septentrionalium Catalogus,* 1705; repr. Hildesheim 1970, Praefatio, sig. a2.

these words ought to be dealt with in the explanatory notes.[15]

MS accents
These are 'generally irregular, and representative of more than one system,' as C. and
K. Sisam have noted.[16] Their value for the reader of an OE text and for the lexicographer
is doubtful, and there seems to be no need to reproduce them in a printed edition. But
the editor would do well to discuss in his introduction the use and frequency of accents
in each of the MSS. It should not be forgotten that accent marks, as well as punctuation
marks, have often been added or altered by a later scribe, and that it is not always easy
to detect this, even in the MS itself.

Word-division
This is a notoriously tricky problem for the editor. Although it is now clear that word-
division in OE MSS is less erratic than it may formerly have seemed,[17] the editor will
always have to divide according to the parts of speech and not according to the rhythmic
units or accentual groups in the MS. A nominal compound, for instance, should be
written as one word. Even so, some difficult categories of words or word-groups remain,
in particular verbs with separable prefixes,[18] and a number of pronouns, adverbs, and
conjunctions: for example, 'aweggewitan': 'aweg gewitan'; 'for ðon ðe': 'forðon ðe':
'for-ðon-ðe'; 'swa swa': 'swaswa.' Editorial practice differs widely in these cases, and it
seems highly desirable that a set of rules for the regulation of word-division in OE
printed texts should be developed. For the time being, four general hints may be useful:
    MS word-division (or lack of such division) should *not* be considered as authoritative.
    Consistency within a text edition should be the guiding principle.
    Hyphens should not be used, so that differences and difficulties are minimized.[19]
    In all doubtful cases, editors are advised to follow the form of entries in J.R. Clark
    Hall and H.D. Meritt, *A Concise Anglo-Saxon Dictionary*. The few hyphenated forms
    in this dictionary should, however, be written as one word.

Punctuation
This should normally be modern and not that of the MS. However, the editor should be

15 For examples, see A.S. Napier, *Old English Glosses*, Oxford 1900, vi; *Ælfric's First Series of Catholic
    Homilies*, ed. N. Eliason and P. Clemoes, EEMF 13, Copenhagen 1966, 29; *Ælfrics Grammatik und
    Glossar*, ed. J. Zupitza, Sammlung englischer Denkmäler 1, Berlin 1880; repr. with intro. by H. Gneuss,
    Berlin 1966, 148: critical apparatus; H. Gneuss, *Hymnar und Hymnen im englischen Mittelalter*, Buch-
    reihe der Anglia 12, Tübingen 1968, 166.
16 *The Salisbury Psalter*, ed. C. and K. Sisam, EETS 242, London 1959, 9. See also K. Sisam, *Studies in
    the History of Old English Literature*, Oxford 1953, 186-8; N.R. Ker, *Catalogue of Manuscripts con-
    taining Anglo-Saxon*, Oxford 1953, xxxv; A. Campbell, *Old English Grammar*, § 26; E. Sievers, K.
    Brunner, *Altenglische Grammatik*, 3rd ed. Tübingen 1965, § 8; T. Westphalen, *Beowulf 3150-55*, 137
    n 211, and the literature quoted by these authors.
17 More work needs to be done on word-division in OE MSS. The first scholar to note the problem seems
    to have been F. Kluge, in *Englische Studien*, 7 [1884], 480-1; see also A. Schröer, *Englische Studien*,
    9 [1886], 292-4. The only detailed treatment, based on a few facsimile editions, is M. Rademacher,
    Die Worttrennung in angelsächsischen Handschriften [Münster Ph.D. thesis, 1921], Münster 1926.
    There are brief but useful notes by W. Keller, *Angelsächsische Paläographie*, Palaestra 48, Berlin 1906,
    I, 51-2, and 'Zur Worttrennung in den angelsächsischen Handschriften,' *Britannica: Max Förster zum
    60. Geburtstag*, Leipzig 1929, 89-90. See also A. Campbell, *Old English Grammar*, § 29.
18 See Campbell, *Old English Grammar*, §§ 78-80; K.D. Bülbring, *Altenglisches Elementarbuch*, Heidel-
    berg 1902, 24-30; T. Perrin Harrison, *The Separable Prefixes in Anglo-Saxon*, Baltimore 1892.
19 For hyphens in OE MSS, see Ker, *Catalogue*, xxxv-xxxvi.

familiar with the principles of medieval punctuation and take the MS into account when preparing and punctuating his edition. The system and peculiarities of punctuation employed in the MS (or MSS) should be briefly discussed in the introduction.[20] As with classical texts, there are as yet no rules as to how far the system of punctuation of the editor's native language (usually Modern English) should be adopted for an OE text.[21] It is the editor's task to help the reader understand the text, and, for this reason, consistency is perhaps less important than clarity.

References

Throughout the text, references to the beginning of the recto and verso of each MS folio should be given (f 81^r, *not* f 81a), either in the text (preferably in square brackets), or in the margin (with a vertical stroke in the text preceding the first word of the MS page). Line numbering should normally be provided for all texts in prose and verse. Where an edition consists of a number of separate prose texts (e.g., a collection of homilies), the lines within each piece may be numbered through; otherwise, lines should be numbered separately for each page. Numbering by fives in the margin is the normal procedure, but fewer errors in references to texts would occur if all editors could be persuaded to number by threes. No line numbers are needed in prose texts which have been divided into small numbered sections (e.g., the *Disticha Catonis* or interlinear versions of psalms). The lineation of the MS should not be preserved, nor is it desirable to indicate the line endings of a MS.

Running titles at the head of each page are often helpful; they should not give the title of the whole book where a psalm number, the number and title of a homily, etc, would be more useful. Whenever an earlier edition of the OE text exists, the editor should make every effort to facilitate reference and to avoid confusion. Line numbers of verse texts, and the numbering for chapters, sections, or paragraphs of prose texts, as found in the earlier edition or editions, should be retained under all circumstances, even if they seem impractical. It is also essential to indicate the beginning of each page of a previous edition, either in the text or in the margin. Such a notation may, for example, help somebody who is looking for the context of a quotation in a dictionary (such as Bosworth-Toller) which used the older edition. A substitute for page-references to earlier editions may be offered in the form of a table of correspondences between the two editions at the beginning or the end of the text,[22] but running references are always preferable.

Glossaries and interlinear glosses

These demand their own editorial methods. Continuous interlinear glosses must always be printed together with the Latin text with each OE gloss word normally printed above its Latin lemma.[23] Gloss-spacing should be regularized and, in order to avoid costly and time-consuming typing and printing, the first letter of the gloss should always stand exactly above the first letter of the lemma. No punctuation should be introduced into the gloss, while that of the lemma should be normalized. The spelling of the lemmata should

---

20 For punctuation in OE MSS, see Ker, *Catalogue*, xxxiii-xxxv; Campbell, *Old English Grammar*, s 28; P. Clemoes, *Liturgical Influence on Punctuation in Late Old English and Early Middle English Manuscripts*, Cambridge 1952; C. G. Harlow, 'Punctuation in some Manuscripts of Ælfric,' *RES*, n.s., 10 [1959], 1-19.

21 See S. Harrison Thomson, 'Editing of Medieval Latin Texts in America,' *Progress of Medieval and Renaissance Studies in the United States and Canada Bulletin*, 16 [1941], 48.

22 See, e.g., *Ælfrics Grammatik und Glossar* [1966], xv-xvi.

23 For a different arrangement, which may be practical in some cases, see H. Gneuss, *Hymnar und Hymnen im englischen Mittelalter*, 266-407.

remain unchanged, and abbreviations of Latin words should be silently expanded. An OE gloss which translates a word or form other than its lemma may be marked with an asterisk and explained in section four of the apparatus.

If a number of OE glosses are found scattered in a Latin text, it seems best to print them in the form of a glossary, but only if each Latin lemma is accompanied by a reference to page, line, or verse in a standard edition of the Latin text.[24]

3.5 THE CRITICAL APPARATUS

It is advisable to divide the apparatus into four separate sections.

> textual notes on the MS or basic MS
> lexical variants from other MSS
> phonological and spelling variants from other MSS
> explanatory notes

Dividing the apparatus like this may at first sight seem awkward and pedantic, yet it will greatly increase the usefulness of the edition for readers and lexicographers. The first section is, of course, indispensable. Sections two and three are only needed for a limited number of OE texts which have been transmitted in more than one MS. Separating the lexical variants from those variants which do not imply any change of wording and meaning has obvious advantages. Section four is not an absolute necessity at a time when reliable editions are needed within a short period, and a great deal of the information usually found in explanatory notes could be published in separate monographs or articles.

Sections one to three should be printed below the corresponding text on the same page (or, in exceptional cases, on the facing page); section four, if it is not too elaborate, should also be placed there. In all sections, references must be to lines or verses of the text, not to superscript numbers, which may spoil the text typographically and which are often difficult to find. All OE readings in the apparatus should be in Roman type; all the rest, including the MS sigla, in italics. Some further details about the individual sections follow.

Section 1: Textual notes on the basic MS
All the peculiarities of the MS text (damaged portions, scribal corrections, alterations, etc) and all changes made by the editor should be recorded here, unless their nature has been made explicit in the printed text. However, lengthy discussions (on why a particular emendation was chosen, etc) belong not here, but in section four. Emendations suggested by previous editors or other scholars, whether the present editor has adopted them or not, may also be recorded in section one.

Line or verse numbers should be typographically prominent (for instance, in bold type) so that reference is facilitated. Signs and symbols such as + (= added), ~ (= transposed), etc, should be avoided, and abbreviations used instead, but *all* abbreviations so used must have been previously explained. The language of the apparatus should be English, not Latin.[25] If the text is accompanied by a considerable number of glosses (OE, ME, or Latin), these may be recorded in an additional section of the apparatus.

As far as possible, scribal alterations and corrections should be identified and dated.

---

24 A more elaborate version of this type of gloss edition has been devised by H.D. Meritt, *The Old English Prudentius Glosses at Boulogne-sur-Mer*, Stanford 1959, esp. xii. Here, in addition to gloss and lemma, the Latin context for each lemma has been supplied.

25 Nor should Latin abbreviations, such as those listed in *Emploi des signes critiques*, 45-6, be employed even though they may seem time-honoured and internationally recognized.

The following use of sigla is recommended.

A   written by original scribe
A^1 altered, added by original scribe
A^2, A^3 ... altered, added by other scribes, contemporary or later
Do not use A^1 for matter clearly not by the original scribe.

    If different individual scribes who have made additions or alterations can be identified, the approximate date of their work should be given in the introduction. The editor may use A^x if it is uncertain whether an alteration is by scribe A or by somebody else; again A^2 may be used for several hands other than those of A, if the hands cannot be clearly distinguished. But this procedure must be explained in the textual introduction.

Section 2: Lexical variants
In this section the editor is to record all lexical variants from all MSS other than the basic MS; this includes all variants affecting sense or grammar, words or passages not in the basic MS, words or passages in the basic MS but missing in one or more of the other MSS, words or sequences of words differing from those of the basic MS, and differences in case, number, person, tense, and mood. All variants which are merely orthographic or phonological (including dialectal) belong in section three of the apparatus.

    The sigla used for the MSS should be single capital letters; in view of the limited transmission of OE texts, there is no need for the use of other letters or combinations of letters (like Ca, C^a, etc). If Greek or other letters are employed, they should be reserved for lost exemplars, archetypes, etc, referred to when discussing the history of a text. Whenever single capital letters have been used as sigla in a previous edition of the text, they should be retained in order to avoid confusion.

    It is essential that individual 'critical units' be carefully constructed and clearly separated from each other. Each critical unit consists of the lemma (i.e., a word or sequence of words as found in the text printed from the basic MS), followed by the variant or variants and their MS sigla. The editor will have to choose between two types of apparatus, positive or negative, and the critical units have to be arranged accordingly. In the *positive apparatus,* whenever there is a variant reading differing from that of the basic MS (or from the reading adopted by the editor), all the readings from all the MSS are recorded. In the *negative apparatus* only the readings differing from the basic MS are recorded. The latter method may save a great deal of space, but has to be employed very carefully. Consider the following example:

MS readings

A (basic MS)	wiðcwedennysse
B and C	wiðcwedennysse
D and F and J	wiðersæce
P	leahtrunge

Positive apparatus
wiðcwedennysse ABC, wiðersæce DFJ, leahtrunge P

Negative apparatus
wiðcwedennysse] wiðersæce DFJ, leahtrunge P

In a negative apparatus, the variant reading should normally be preceded by the lemma, to prevent errors and to facilitate reference. The lemma is to be separated from the variant readings by a square bracket open on the left. Each variant reading should be followed by the MS siglum or sigla. The order of the sigla need not be alphabetical; it will usually be determined by the relations of the MSS. But the order should always be the same, and under no circumstances must expressions like '*cett.*' or 'the rest' be used instead of the sigla. Punctuation, preferably a comma, is required between the variant readings (i.e., after the sigla) within each critical unit. The critical units must be clearly separated from each other. This should not be done simply by spacing (which is of no use if a new critical unit begins a new line), unless each unit begins with a line or verse number. Some editors employ a vertical stroke or a colon to separate critical units, but the use of a full stop or a semicolon seems to be the most practical solution.

4 PREPARING OLD ENGLISH TEXTS FOR CONCORDING

Texts edited, collated, or checked according to the principles outlined in sections 2 and 3 of this paper need further preparation before they can be fed into a data-processing system which will then produce the concordances and the slip index.[26] Part of this preparatory work will have to be left to the DOE editors.

Beyond this, there are two major tasks which must be completed before keypunching occurs or before the text can be retyped in a special fount and then transferred to magnetic tape. One is to indicate in the text certain points about which the lexicographer working with his slips must be informed. The other is to enable the DOE editors to utilize the lexical variants in the critical apparatus of texts extant in more than one MS. This may be done by editors or collators as the final step in the preparation of their mastercopies (see above, section 2) according to the following suggestions.

4.1 PREPARING THE TEXT

The lexicographer working from his slips will often be able to determine the exact meaning of a word and its place in the DOE entry from the context printed on the slip. There will then be no need for him to go back to the edition of the complete text for each occurrence of a word. But this is only practicable if the lexicographer is warned of every case where a quotation departs in any way from the MS reading, or where, in the editor's opinion, the text of the quotation (although taken from the MS) is at any point faulty or corrupt. It is therefore suggested that in all these cases one and the same symbol, a slash, /, should *follow* the relevant words. This symbol would then be recorded by the data-processing system, together with the text, and it would signal to the lexicographer working in stage 3 that, in addition to his slip, he must consult the edition of the text and its critical apparatus.

The slash should follow:
words altered or emended by the editor,
words supplied by the editor (whether from other MSS or not),
words affected by scribal alterations, where both alternative readings (before and after the alteration) make sense,
words or passages that seem meaningless, doubtful, or corrupt.
Where more than one word is involved, each word must be marked by a slash following it. Where long passages requiring frequent marking are involved, the DOE editors should be asked for advice. It will not be sufficient merely to point out such passages by means of symbols at the beginning and end, since on a quotation slip of limited length one or both of these symbols may not appear. Use fine pens for marking.

26 See below, chapter 4, for a description of the data-processing system.

4.2 MARKING LEXICAL VARIANTS

Concording each MS of every OE text for the DOE would be wasteful and would in no
way increase the usefulness of the Dictionary. Such concording will not be done unless
two or more MS versions of an OE text differ considerably from each other. On the other
hand, nothing that could in any way contribute to our knowledge of the vocabulary and
usage of OE should be omitted from the concordances. For this reason, all lexical variants
recorded in critical apparatuses or collations (whether they are alterations in the basic MS,
or variants in the other MSS) will have to be concorded, along with the text of the basic
MS itself. However, all phonological or spelling variants will not be concorded; consequently, those elements in each critical apparatus or collation which ought to be
included in the concording process have to be marked before this stage of the work. This
should be done by means of a single underline; if the edition is in typescript, the underlining must be in red. The following parts of an apparatus or collation will have to be
marked.

all OE words or sequences of words added to the basic MS and only recorded in
the apparatus
all OE words, phrases, or sentences in other MSS differing from the basic MS or
not found in the basic MS in any form at all
all OE words differing from those of the basic MS by their inflexional category (e.g.,
dative instead of accusative), or by belonging to a different inflexional class (e.g.,
the same verb is shown to belong to two different conjugations)
The following parts must not be underlined.

words or sentences of the basic text that have been omitted in other MSS
phonological or spelling variants
dialectal or other variants of inflexional forms
A printed edition of an OE text which has been checked or collated according to the
suggestions in section 2 of this paper (or which has been newly edited), and which has
been prepared for concording in conformity with sections 4.1 and 4.2, will then con-
stitute a true master-copy for all future work on the DOE.

5 CO-ORDINATION OF WORK

In order to prepare for the concording stage of the DOE project, numerous OE texts will
have to be treated in accordance with the plan and requirements outlined above. This
should be done within the next few years, if the Dictionary is to be completed within the
coming twenty or thirty years. Competent scholars who can help are urgently needed.
Individuals willing to edit, re-edit, collate, check, or prepare for concording any OE text
are advised to get in touch with the DOE editors before beginning the task, to avoid
duplication or overlapping of work.

Work in progress on new editions of OE texts has been listed and published for several
years now by F.C. Robinson.[27] However, scholars should keep in mind that listed projects may have been dropped or new projects may have been started since the last 'Old
English Research in Progress' was compiled. The DOE editors should be informed
immediately of any new project in this field. They will then be able to tell the prospective
editor if any specific lexicographical considerations (e.g., the need for a synoptical
edition) must be taken into account for his particular text.

---

27 'Old English Research in Progress,' first published for 1964-5 in *Neuphilologische Mitteilungen*, 66
[1965], 235-50, and since then annually in the same periodical.

Please direct all enquiries to:
    The Editors
    Dictionary of Old English
    Centre for Medieval Studies
    University of Toronto
    Toronto M5S 1A1
    Canada

a list of old english texts

ANGUS CAMERON

This section of *A Plan for the Dictionary of Old English* lists the manuscripts and printed editions on which the Dictionary will be based. The texts are arranged as follows:

A Poetry
B Prose
C Interlinear Glosses
D Glossaries
E Runic Inscriptions
F Inscriptions in the Latin Alphabet

An index of printed editions forms an appendix to the list.

The poetry section follows the order of the poems in G.P. Krapp and E.V.K. Dobbie, *The Anglo-Saxon Poetic Records*, 6 volumes, New York 1931-53, with a few additions at the end.

The prose series is divided into twenty-eight sections, arranged according to the type of text involved. These sections are given at the beginning of the series; they start with the works of Ælfric and Wulfstan, continue through the translations of Alfred and laws and charters, and end with notes and scribbles. There is a certain amount of double listing of texts under different headings, and I have tried to signal these by means of cross-references.

The interlinear gloss series is in two parts: continuous interlinear glosses, followed by occasional interlinear glosses. Within each sequence the listing is alphabetical and follows the names of authors or titles of the work being glossed, as in the 'Index of the Contents of the Manuscripts' in N.R. Ker, *Catalogue of Manuscripts containing Anglo-Saxon*, Oxford 1957, 524-6. The glossary series is listed according to the order in which the manuscripts occur in Ker's *Catalogue*.

The series of runic and Latin alphabet inscriptions are arranged alphabetically according to present location or place of finding. They correspond to the orders given in Hertha Marquardt's *Bibliographie* and Elisabeth Okasha's *Handlist* respectively.

For each text the following information is given:

reference to manuscript by library and catalogue number
reference to facsimiles of manuscripts where these have appeared
reference to printed editions

Generally the most recent printed edition is listed, although references to earlier editions are included when they seem useful, and reviews which include collations or lists of corrections are mentioned. Notices of editions in dissertation form and of editions in progress have been given wherever possible. Abbreviations follow those used in the *MLA International Bibliography* and in Fred C. Robinson, *Old English Literature: A Select Bibliography*, Toronto 1970; a list of additional abbreviations is provided below. The index of printed editions is arranged by editor's surname and date of publication. In the list of texts, full details of a printed edition are given in the first entry, and thereafter in abbreviated form.

For inscriptions I have given the standard place of publication. In cases where the form or meaning of an inscription is disputed, I have tried to give representation to both or all sides of the controversy.

Much of my information comes from N.R. Ker's *Catalogue of Manuscripts containing Anglo-Saxon*; its entries and indices have been invaluable in compiling this list. Other important sources are P.H. Sawyer, *Anglo-Saxon Charters: An Annotated List and Bibliography*, London 1968; H. Marquardt, *Bibliographie der Runeninschriften nach Fundorten I: Die Runeninschriften der Britischen Inseln*, Göttingen 1961; E. Okasha, *Hand-list of Anglo-Saxon Non-runic Inscriptions,* Cambridge 1971; Fred C. Robinson,

'Old English Research in Progress,' which has appeared annually in *Neuphilologische Mitteilungen* beginning with volume 66 for 1965; the *Old English Bibliography* prepared annually by S.B. Greenfield and F.C. Robinson for the Old English Group of the MLA, and a list of editions of Old English texts printed since 1957 prepared by R.B. Mitchell. R.I. Page has very kindly allowed me to check my list of runic inscriptions against the materials he has gathered for his forthcoming corpus of Anglo-Saxon runic inscriptions.

I wish to acknowledge the help of Mrs Susan Jupp and Mr Günter Niemann in preparing this list, and of the following who looked at earlier versions and sent me corrections and suggestions: A.K. Brown, R. Derolez, H. Gneuss, M.R. Godden, J.C. Pope, and E.G. Stanley.

Responsibility for unclear or erroneous listings is my own, and I will be grateful if they are brought to my attention.

A.C.

ABBREVIATIONS

Abbreviations follow those used in the MLA *International Bibliography* and in Fred C. Robinson, *Old English Literature: A Select Bibliography,* Toronto 1970. Only those not found in either list are given here.

ADD	*American Doctoral Dissertations*
AJ	*The Antiquaries Journal*
Bib. ags. Prosa	Bibliothek der angelsächsischen Prosa
BzmV	Beiträge zur mittelalterlichen Volkskunde
JBAA	*The Journal of the British Archaeological Association*
Index	*Index to Theses accepted for Higher Degrees in the Universities of Great Britain and Ireland*
UCO	Umbrae Codicum Occidentalium

A POETRY

1
The Junius Manuscript
MS   Oxford, Bodleian, Junius 11   **Ker 334**
facs   I. Gollancz, *The Caedmon Manuscript of Anglo-Saxon Biblical Poetry,* Oxford 1927
ed   G.P. Krapp, *The Junius Manuscript,* The Anglo-Saxon Poetic Records 1, New York 1931

1.1
Genesis Krapp 1931, 1-87
ed   F. Holthausen, *Die ältere Genesis,* Heidelberg 1914; D.M. Wells, 'A Critical Edition of
the Old English *Genesis A* with a translation' [North Carolina diss.] *DA* 31 [1970] 373A;
B.J. Timmer, *The Later Genesis,* rev. ed. Oxford 1954; J.F. Vickrey, Jr, '*Genesis B*: A
new analysis and edition' [Indiana diss.] *DA* 21 [1961] 3463
proposed eds. Irene Roach, *NM* 67 [1966] 197; A.N. Doane, University of
Wisconsin

1.1.1
Captions for drawings Krapp 1931, xvi-xvii
ed   A.J. Bliss, 'Some unnoticed lines of Old English verse,' *N & Q* 216 [1971] 404

1.2
Exodus Krapp 1931, 90-107
ed   F.A. Blackburn, *Exodus and Daniel, Two Old English Poems,* Belles Lettres Series,
Boston 1907; Edward B. Irving, Jr, *The Old English Exodus,* Yale Studies in English 122,
New Haven 1953
MOEL ed. in prep. Peter J. Lucas, *NM* 71 [1970] 492

1.3
Daniel Krapp 1931, 111-32
ed   Blackburn 1907; F.C. Brennan, 'The Old English *Daniel*' [North Carolina diss.] *DA* 27
[1967] 3421A
MOEL ed. in prep. R.T. Farrell, *NM* 69 [1968] 476

1.4
Christ and Satan Krapp 1931, 135-58
ed   M.D. Clubb, *Christ and Satan, An Old English Poem,* Yale Studies in English 70, New
Haven 1925
proposed eds. Anne Hibbert, University of British Columbia; R.E. Finnegan, University
of Manitoba

2
The Vercelli Book
MS   Vercelli, Biblioteca Capitolare, CXVII   **Ker 394**
facs   M. Förster, *Il Codice Vercellese,* Rome 1913
       EEMF facs. in prep. C. Sisam
ed   G.P. Krapp, *The Vercelli Book,* The Anglo-Saxon Poetic Records 2, New York 1932

2.1
art. 6 Andreas Krapp 1932, 3-51
ed K.R. Brooks, *Andreas and The Fates of the Apostles,* Oxford 1961, 1-55

2.2
art. 7 The Fates of the Apostles Krapp 1932, 51-4
ed Brooks 1961, 56-60

2.3
art. 21 Soul and Body I Krapp 1932, 54-9

2.4
art. 22 Homiletic Fragment I Krapp 1932, 59-60

2.5
art. 23 Dream of the Rood Krapp 1932, 61-5
ed B. Dickins and A.S.C. Ross, *The Dream of the Rood,* MOEL, London 1934, 4th ed. 1954;
Michael Swanton, *The Dream of the Rood,* Manchester 1970

2.6
art. 28 Elene Krapp 1932, 66-102
ed P.O.E. Gradon, *Cynewulf's Elene,* MOEL, London 1958

3
The Exeter Book
MS Exeter, Cathedral, 3501 **Ker 116**
facs R.W. Chambers, M. Förster, R. Flower, *The Exeter Book of Old English Poetry,* London
1933; proposed rev. of intro. P.O.E. Gradon
ed G.P. Krapp and E.V.K. Dobbie, *The Exeter Book,* The Anglo-Saxon Poetic Records 3,
New York 1936

3.1
Christ Krapp-Dobbie 1936, 3-49
ed A.S. Cook, *The Christ of Cynewulf: A Poem in Three Parts,* Boston 1900, reprinted with
pref. by J.C. Pope, 1964; J.J. Campbell, *The Advent Lyrics of the Exeter Book* ll. 1-439,
Princeton 1959; [Christ III] Richard M. Trask, '*The Last Judgment of the Exeter Book:*
A Critical Edition' [Illinois diss.] *DA* 32 [1972] 5753A
proposed ed. Frederick J. Hunt, University of Adelaide

3.2
Guthlac Krapp-Dobbie 1936, 49-88
ed Jane Crawford [Roberts] ,'*Guthlac*: An edition of the Old English prose life, together
with the poems in the *Exeter Book*' [Oxford D.Phil. 1967] *Index* 17 [1966-7] no. 331
proposed eds. [*Guthlac B*] J.L. Rosier, *NM* 69 [1968] 479; Jane Crawford [Roberts] ,
King's College, London, *NM* 70 [1969] 524

3.3
Azarias Krapp-Dobbie 1936, 88-94
MOEL ed. in prep. R.T. Farrell, *NM* 69 [1968] 476

3.4

The Phoenix Krapp-Dobbie 1936, 94-113

ed   N.F. Blake, *The Phoenix,* Manchester 1964; J.B. Trahern, Jr, '*The Phoenix*: A Critical
     Edition' [Princeton diss.] *DA* 25 [1964] 458
     proposed ed. J.B. Trahern, Jr, Illinois, *NM* 69 [1968] 483

3.5

Juliana Krapp-Dobbie 1936, 113-33

ed   R.E. Woolf, *Juliana,* MOEL, London 1955

3.6

The Wanderer Krapp-Dobbie 1936, 134-7

ed   R.F. Leslie, *The Wanderer,* Manchester 1966; T.P. Dunning and A.J. Bliss, *The Wanderer,*
     MOEL, London 1969

3.7

The Gifts of Men Krapp-Dobbie 1936, 137-40

3.8

Precepts Krapp-Dobbie 1936, 140-3

3.9

The Seafarer Krapp-Dobbie 1936, 143-7

ed   I.L. Gordon, *The Seafarer,* MOEL, London 1960

3.10

Vainglory Krapp-Dobbie 1936, 147-9

ed   J.C. Guntner, 'An Edition of Three Old English Poems' [Wisconsin diss.] *DA* 31 [1970]
     2877A
     proposed ed. D.D. Short, North Carolina State University

3.11

Widsith Krapp-Dobbie 1936, 149-53

ed   K. Malone, *Widsith,* Copenhagen 1962

3.12

The Fortunes of Men Krapp-Dobbie 1936, 154-6

     proposed ed. T. Alnaes, Oslo, *NM* 70 [1969] 524

3.13

Maxims I Krapp-Dobbie 1936, 156-63

ed   Blanche C. Williams, *Gnomic Poetry in Anglo-Saxon,* New York 1914; R. MacG. Dawson,
     'An edition of the Gnomic Poems' [Oxford B.Litt. 1953] *Index* 3 [1952-3] no. 128
     proposed ed. John M. Kirk, Brown, *NM* 70 [1969] 528

3.14

The Order of the World Krapp-Dobbie 1936, 163-6

ed   Guntner 1970
     proposed ed. D.D. Short, North Carolina State University

3.15
The Riming Poem Krapp-Dobbie 1936, 166-9
ed F. Holthausen, 'Das altenglische Reimlied' in F. Holthausen and H. Spies, eds. *Festschrift für Lorenz Morsbach,* Studien zur englischen Philologie 50, Halle 1913, 190-200

3.16
The Panther Krapp-Dobbie 1936, 169-71
ed A.S. Cook, *The Old English Physiologus,* Yale Studies in English 63, New Haven 1921, 2-10

3.17
The Whale Krapp-Dobbie 1936, 171-4
ed Cook 1921, 12-20

3.18
The Partridge Krapp-Dobbie 1936, 174
ed Cook 1921, 22-4

3.19
Soul and Body II Krapp-Dobbie 1936, 174-8

3.20
Deor Krapp-Dobbie 1936, 178-9
ed K. Malone, *Deor,* MOEL, London 1933, 4th ed. 1966

3.21
Wulf and Eadwacer Krapp-Dobbie 1936, 179-80

3.22
Riddles 1-59 Krapp-Dobbie 1936, 180-210
ed F. Tupper, *The Riddles of the Exeter Book,* Boston 1910, Darmstadt 1968, 1-43
proposed eds. Leslie Blakeley, Glasgow, *NM* 68 [1967] 204; Craig Williamson, University of Pennsylvania

3.23
The Wife's Lament Krapp-Dobbie 1936, 210-1
ed R.F. Leslie, *Three Old English Elegies,* Manchester 1961 [1966], 47-8

3.24
The Judgment Day I Krapp-Dobbie 1936, 212-5
proposed ed. D.D. Short, North Carolina State University

3.25
Resignation Krapp-Dobbie 1936, 215-8
ed Guntner 1970; T.L. Noronha, 'Five Old English Verse Prayers: An Edition' [Stanford diss.] *DA* 32 [1972] 5748A

3.26
The Descent into Hell Krapp-Dobbie 1936, 219-23

3.27
Alms-Giving Krapp-Dobbie 1936, 223

3.28
Pharaoh Krapp-Dobbie 1936, 223

3.29
The Lord's Prayer I Krapp-Dobbie 1936, 223-4

3.30
Homiletic Fragment II Krapp-Dobbie 1936, 224

3.31
Riddles 30b, 60 Krapp-Dobbie 1936, 224-5
ed Tupper 1910, 23, 43-4
    proposed eds. Blakeley, NM 68 [1967] 204; Williamson, University of Pennsylvania

3.32
The Husband's Message Krapp-Dobbie 1936, 225-7
ed Leslie 1961 [1966], 49-50

3.33
The Ruin Krapp-Dobbie 1936, 227-9
ed Leslie 1961 [1966], 51-2

3.34
Riddles 61-95 Krapp-Dobbie 1936, 229-43
ed Tupper 1910, 44-67
    proposed eds. Blakeley, NM 68 [1967] 204; Williamson, University of Pennsylvania

4
Beowulf and Judith
MS   London, British Museum, Cotton Vitellius A.XV   **Ker 216 arts. 4, 5**
facs [Beowulf] J. Zupitza, *Beowulf,* EETS 77, London 1882, 2nd ed. N. Davis EETS 245,
     London 1959; K. Malone, *The Nowell Codex,* EEMF 12, Copenhagen 1963
ed   E.V.K. Dobbie, *Beowulf and Judith,* The Anglo-Saxon Poetic Records 4, New York 1953

4.1
Beowulf
ed F. Klaeber, *Beowulf and The Fight at Finnsburg,* 3rd ed. with 1st and 2nd supplements,
    Boston 1950; E. von Schaubert, *Heyne-Schückings Beowulf,* 18th ed. Paderborn 1963
    proposed ed. R.F. Leslie, University of Victoria

4.2
Judith
ed B.J. Timmer, *Judith,* MOEL, London 1952, 2nd ed. 1961
    proposed ed. D.K. Fry, NM 69 [1968] 480

5
The Paris Psalter
MS Paris, Bibliothèque Nationale, Lat. 8824 **Ker 367**
facs J. Bromwich et al., *The Paris Psalter,* EEMF 8, Copenhagen 1958
 ed G.P. Krapp, *The Paris Psalter and the Meters of Boethius,* The Anglo-Saxon Poetic
    Records 5, New York 1932, 3-150
    See A.51

6
The Meters of Boethius
MS London, British Museum, Cotton Otho A.VI **Ker 167**
    Oxford, Bodleian, Junius 12 [transcript]
 ed W.J. Sedgefield, *King Alfred's Old English Version of Boethius' De Consolatione
    Philosophiae,* Oxford 1899, Darmstadt 1968, 151-204; Ernst Krämer, *Die altenglischen
    Metra des Boetius,* Bonner Beiträge zur Anglistik 8, Bonn 1902; Krapp 1932, 153-203

7
The Battle of Finnsburh
MS London, Lambeth Palace, 487 [missing] **Ker 282**
    George Hickes, *Linguarum Vett. Septentrionalium Thesaurus,* Oxford 1705, Hildesheim
    and New York 1970, Gramm. part I, 192-3
 ed Klaeber 1950, 245-7; E.V.K. Dobbie, *The Anglo-Saxon Minor Poems,* The Anglo-Saxon
    Poetic Records 6, New York 1942, 3-4; von Schaubert 1963
    proposed ed. Fry, *NM* 69 [1968] 477

8
Waldere
MS Copenhagen, Kongelige Bibliotek, Ny.Kgl.Sam. 167b [4°] **Ker 101**
 ed F. Norman, *Waldere,* MOEL, London 1933, 2nd ed. 1949; Dobbie 1942, 4-6
    proposed ed. A. Zettersten, *NM* 68 [1967] 206

9
The Battle of Maldon
MS London, British Museum, Cotton Otho A.XII [burnt] **Ker 172**
    Oxford, Bodleian, Rawlinson B.203 [Elphinston's transcript]
 ed E.V. Gordon, *The Battle of Maldon,* MOEL, London 1937 [1957]; Dobbie 1942, 7-16

10
The Chronicle Poems
 ed Dobbie 1942, 16-26
facs R. Flower, A.H. Smith, *The Parker Chronicle and Laws,* EETS 208, London 1941 [Ker 39]

10.1
The Battle of Brunanburh
MS Cambridge, Corpus Christi College, 173 **Ker 39**
    London, British Museum, Cotton Tiberius A.VI **Ker 188**
    London, British Museum, Cotton Tiberius B.I **Ker 191**
    London, British Museum, Cotton Tiberius B.IV **Ker 192**
 ed A. Campbell, *The Battle of Brunanburh,* London 1938

10.2
The Capture of the Five Boroughs
MS   Cambridge, Corpus Christi College, 173   **Ker 39**
     London, British Museum, Cotton Tiberius A.VI   **Ker 188**
     London, British Museum, Cotton Tiberius B.I   **Ker 191**
     London, British Museum, Cotton Tiberius B.IV   **Ker 192**

10.3
The Coronation of Edgar
MS   Cambridge, Corpus Christi College, 173   **Ker 39**
     London, British Museum, Cotton Tiberius A.VI   **Ker 188**
     London, British Museum, Cotton Tiberius B.I   **Ker 191**

10.4
The Death of Edgar
MS   Cambridge, Corpus Christi College, 173   **Ker 39**
     London, British Museum, Cotton Tiberius A.VI   **Ker 188**
     London, British Museum, Cotton Tiberius B.I   **Ker 191**

10.5
The Death of Alfred
MS   London, British Museum, Cotton Tiberius B.I   **Ker 191**
     London, British Museum, Cotton Tiberius B.IV   **Ker 192**

10.6
The Death of Edward
MS   London, British Museum, Cotton Tiberius B.I   **Ker 191**
     London, British Museum, Cotton Tiberius B.IV   **Ker 192**

11
Durham
MS   Cambridge, University Library, Ff.i.27   **Ker 14**
     London, British Museum, Cotton Vitellius D.XX [burnt]   **Ker 223**
     Hickes 1705, Gramm. part I, 178
ed   Dobbie 1942, 27

12
The Rune Poem
MS   London, British Museum, Cotton Otho B.X f.165a-165b [missing]   **Ker 179**
     Hickes 1705, Gramm. part I, 135
ed   Dobbie 1942, 28-30; F.G. Jones, Jr, 'The Old English *Rune Poem*: An Edition'
     [Florida diss.] *DA* 29 [1968] 231A

13
Solomon and Saturn
MS   Cambridge, Corpus Christi College, 422   **Ker 70A**

Cambridge, Corpus Christi College, 41 **Ker 32 art. 5**

ed J.M. Kemble, *The Dialogue of Salomon and Saturnus,* Ælfric Society, London 1848;
R.J. Menner, *The Poetical Dialogues of Solomon and Saturn,* MLA Monograph Series 13,
New York 1941; Dobbie 1942, 31-48; R.I. Page, 'A Note on the text of Ms. CCCC 422
[*Solomon and Saturn*] ,' *MÆ* 34 [1965] 36-9

14
The Menologium
MS London, British Museum, Cotton Tiberius B.I **Ker 191 art. 2**
ed Dobbie 1942, 49-55; H.S. Greeson, Jr, 'Two Old English Observance Poems: *Seasons for Fasting* and *The Menologium*: An Edition' [Oregon diss.] *DA* 31 [1971] 3503A

15
Maxims II
MS London, British Museum, Cotton Tiberius B.I **Ker 191 art. 3**
ed Williams 1914, 126-9; Dobbie 1942, 55-7; Dawson 1953
proposed ed. Kirk, Brown, *NM* 70 [1969] 528

16
A Proverb from Winfrid's Time
MS Vienna, Nationalbibliothek, Lat. 751 [Theol. 259] **Ker A.37**
ed Dobbie 1942, 57

17
The Judgment Day II
MS Cambridge, Corpus Christi College, 201 **Ker 49A art. 2a**
ed J.R. Lumby, *Be domes dæge,* EETS 65, London 1876 [1964] , 2-20; H. Löhe, *Be Domes Dæge,* Bonner Beiträge zur Anglistik 22, Bonn 1907; Dobbie 1942, 58-67; L.G. Whit-bread, 'An edition of the Old English Poem *Judgment Day II* with the Latin source and prose adaptation' [London Ph.D.] *Index* 7 [1956-7] no. 170; P.M. Geoghegan, '*Judgment Day II*: An edition' [Illinois diss.] *DA* 30 [1969] 280A; H.M. Chapman, 'An edition of the Old English poem *Judgement Day* [Ms CCCC 201] ' [University of Wales, Aberystwyth, M.A.] *Index* 18 [1967-8] no. 320

18
An Exhortation to Christian Living
MS Cambridge, Corpus Christi College, 201 **Ker 49A art. 2b**
ed Lumby 1876 [1964] , 28-32; Dobbie 1942, 67-9

19
A Summons to Prayer
MS Cambridge, Corpus Christi College, 201 **Ker 49A art. 2c**
ed Lumby 1876 [1964] , 36; Dobbie 1942, 69-70

20
The Lord's Prayer II
MS Cambridge, Corpus Christi College, 201 **Ker 49B art. 57a**
ed Lumby 1876 [1964] , 40-8; Dobbie 1942, 70-4; Noronha 1972

21
The Gloria I
MS Oxford, Bodleian, Junius 121   **Ker 338 art.11**
    Cambridge, Corpus Christi College, 201   **Ker 49B art.57b**
ed Lumby 1876 [1964], 52-5; Dobbie 1942, 74-7; J.M. Ure, *The Benedictine Office,*
    Edinburgh University Publications in Language and Literature 11, Edinburgh 1957, 83-5

22
The Lord's Prayer III
MS Oxford, Bodleian, Junius 121   **Ker 338 art.11**
ed Dobbie 1942, 77-8; Ure 1957, 85-7; Noronha 1972

23
The Creed
MS Oxford, Bodleian, Junius 121   **Ker 338 art.11**
ed Dobbie 1942, 78-80; Ure 1957, 87-9

24
Fragments of Psalms
MS Oxford, Bodleian, Junius 121   **Ker 338 art.11**
ed Dobbie 1942, 80-6; Ure 1957, 89-100

25
The Kentish Hymn
MS London, British Museum, Cotton Vespasian D.VI   **Ker 207 art.c**
ed Dobbie 1942, 87-8

26
Psalm 50
MS London, British Museum, Cotton Vespasian D.VI   **Ker 207 art.e**
ed Dobbie 1942, 88-94

27
The Gloria II
MS London, British Museum, Cotton Titus D.XXVII   **Ker 202 art.i**
ed Dobbie 1942, 94
    See B.23.3.4

28
A Prayer
MS London, British Museum, Cotton Julius A.II   **Ker 159 art.1**
    London, Lambeth Palace, 427   **Ker 280 art.4**
ed Dobbie 1942, 94-6; Noronha 1972

29
Thureth
MS London, British Museum, Cotton Claudius A.III   **Ker 141 art.a**
ed Dobbie 1942, 97

30
Aldhelm
MS Cambridge, Corpus Christi College, 326 **Ker 61 art.a**
 ed Dobbie 1942, 97-8

31
The Seasons for Fasting
MS London, British Museum, Cotton Otho B.XI [missing] **Ker 180 art.10**
London, British Museum, Add. 43703 [Nowell's transcript]
 ed Dobbie 1942, 98-104; Greeson 1971

32
Caedmon's Hymn

32.1
Northumbrian Version
MS Cambridge, University Library, Kk.5.16 f.128b **Ker 25**
Leningrad, Public Library, Lat. Q.v.I.18 f.107a **Ker 122**
Dijon, Bibliothèque Municipale, 574 f.59b **Ker A.8**
Paris, Bibliothèque Nationale, Lat. 5237 f.72b 15th c.
facs P. Hunter Blair, *The Moore Bede,* EEMF 9, Copenhagen 1959 [Ker 25] ; O. Arngart, *The Leningrad Bede,* EEMF 2, Copenhagen 1952 [Ker 122]
 ed A.H. Smith, *Three Northumbrian Poems,* MOEL, London 1933, 2nd ed. 1968, 38-40; E.V.K. Dobbie, *The Manuscripts of Caedmon's Hymn and Bede's Death Song,* Columbia University Studies in English and Comparative Literature 128, New York 1937; Dobbie 1942, 105
MOEL ed. in prep. C.J.E. Ball

32.2
West Saxon Version
MS Oxford, Bodleian, Tanner 10 f.100a **Ker 351**
London, British Museum, Cotton Otho B.XI [missing] **Ker 180**
London, British Museum, Add. 43703 [Nowell's transcript]
Oxford, Corpus Christi College, 279 f.112b **Ker 354**
Cambridge, University Library, Kk.3.18 p.140 **Ker 23**
Cambridge, Corpus Christi College, 41 p.322 **Ker 32**
Winchester, Cathedral, f.81b **Ker 396**
Oxford, Bodleian, Hatton 43 f.129a **Ker 326**
Oxford, Bodleian, Bodley 163 f.152b **Ker 304**
Oxford, Lincoln College, Lat. 31 f.70a **Ker 356**
Oxford, Magdalen College, Lat. 105 f.99a **Ker 357**
Cambridge, Trinity College, R.5.22 f.32b 14th c.
Tournai, Bibliothèque Municipale, 134 f.78b [missing] **Ker 387**
Oxford, Bodleian, Laud Misc. 243 f.82b **Ker 341**
Hereford, Cathedral, P.V.I f.116b **Ker 121**
 ed Dobbie 1937; Dobbie 1942, 106; Smith 1933, 39, 41

33
Bede's Death Song
ed   Smith 1933

33.1
Northumbrian Version
MS   St. Gall, Stiftsbibliothek, 254 f.127a **Ker A.25**
Bamberg, Staatliche Bibliothek, A.I.47 f.21a **Ker A.2**
Admont, Stiftsbibliothek, 225 f.249a **Ker A.1**
Klosterneuburg, 787 f.183a 13th c.
Munich, Bayerische Staatsbibliothek, Lat. 14603 f.138a 16th c.
Klosterneuburg, 708 f.372a 13-14th c.
Heiligenkreuz, Stiftsbibliothek, 12 f.170b **Ker A.13**
Vienna, Nationalbibliothek, 336 f.235a 13th c.
Zwettl, 24 f.182b 13th c.
Admont, 24 f.145a 13th c.
Melk, M.5 f.71b 15th c.
ed   Dobbie 1937; Dobbie 1942, 107; Smith 1933, 42

33.2
The Hague Version
MS   The Hague, Koninklijke Bibliotheek, 70.H.7 f.42b **Ker A.12**
ed   N.R. Ker, 'The Hague Manuscript of the Epistola Cuthberti de obitu Bedae with Bede's
Death Song,' *MÆ* 8 [1939] 40-4; Dobbie 1942, 108

33.3
West Saxon Version
MS   Oxford, Bodleian, Digby 211 f.108a **Ker 321**
Stonyhurst College, 69 f.15b **Ker 386**
Dublin, Trinity College, 492 [E.2.23] f.175b **Ker 104**
Cambridge, Trinity College, R.7.3 f.167a 14th c.
London, British Museum, Arundel 74 f.99a 14th c.
Oxford, Christ Church College, 99 f.113b 14th c.
London, British Museum, Stowe 104 f.112b 13th c. **Ker 273**
Cambridge, St John's College, B.5 14th c.
Cambridge, Trinity College, R.5.22 f.43b 14th c.
Durham, University Library, Bishop Cosin's Library, V.II.6 pp.56-7 **Ker 110***
London, British Museum, Cotton Faustina A.V f.42a **Ker 152**
Oxford, Bodleian, Fairfax 6 f.220a 14th c.
Oxford, Bodleian, Laud Misc. 700 f.28a 14th c.
York, Dean and Chapter Library, XVI.1.12 f.109a 14th c.
Oxford, Lincoln College, Lat. 31 f.99b **Ker 356**
Cambridge, Trinity College, R.7.28 p.26 **Ker 88**
Oxford, Bodleian, Bodley 297 p.281 **Ker 306 art.a**
ed   Dobbie 1937; Dobbie 1942, 108; Smith 1933, 43

34
The Leiden Riddle
MS Leiden, Rijksuniversiteit, Vossianus Lat. 4° 106 f.25v **Ker A.19**
ed Dobbie 1942, 109; Smith 1933, 44, 46; R.W. Zandvoort, 'The Leiden Riddle,' *EGS* 3 [1949-50] 42-56; J. Gerritsen, 'The Text of the Leiden Riddle,' *ES* 50 [1969] 529-44

35
Latin-English Proverbs
MS London, British Museum, Cotton Faustina A.X **Ker 154A art.2**
London, British Museum, Royal 2 B.V **Ker 249 art.b**
ed Dobbie 1942, 109
See also B.7.2, 3 and C.25

36
The Metrical Preface to the Pastoral Care
MS Oxford, Bodleian, Hatton 20 **Ker 324**
London, British Museum, Cotton Otho B.II **Ker 175**
London, British Museum, Cotton Tiberius B.XI [burnt] **Ker 195**
Cambridge, Corpus Christi College, 12 **Ker 30**
Cambridge, Trinity College, R.5.22 **Ker 87**
Cambridge, University Library, Ii.2.4 **Ker 19**
facs N.R. Ker, *The Pastoral Care,* EEMF 6, Copenhagen 1956 [Ker 324]
ed H. Sweet, *King Alfred's West-Saxon Version of Gregory's Pastoral Care,* EETS 45, 50, London 1871 [1958] 8-9; Dobbie 1942, 110
trans. Oxford, Bodleian, Junius 53 [Ker 195]

37
The Metrical Epilogue to the Pastoral Care
MS Oxford, Bodleian, Hatton 20 **Ker 324**
Cambridge, Corpus Christi College, 12 **Ker 30**
facs Ker 1956 [Ker 324]
ed Sweet 1871 [1958], 466-9; Dobbie 1942, 111

38
The Metrical Preface to Wærferth's Translation of Gregory's Dialogues
MS London, British Museum, Cotton Otho C.I vol. 2 **Ker 182**
ed H. Hecht, *Bischof Waerferths von Worcester Uebersetzung der Dialoge Gregors des Grossen,* Bib. ags. Prosa 5, Leipzig and Hamburg 1900-7 [Darmstadt 1965], 2; Dobbie 1942, 112-3

39
The Metrical Epilogue to MS 41, Corpus Christi College, Cambridge
MS Cambridge, Corpus Christi College, 41 pp.483-4 **Ker 32 art.1**
ed Dobbie 1942, 113

40
The Ruthwell Cross [runes]
ed [transliterated] Dickins and Ross 1934 [1954], 25-9; Dobbie 1942, 115
See E.39

41
The Brussels Cross
ed Dickins and Ross 1934 [1954], 26; Dobbie 1942, 115
See F.8

42
The Franks Casket [runes]
ed [transliterated] A.S. Napier, 'Contributions to Old English Literature 2. The Franks
Casket' in *An English Miscellany presented to Dr. Furnivall,* Oxford 1901, 362-81;
Dobbie 1942, 116
See E.2

43
The Metrical Charms

43.1
For Unfruitful Land
MS London, British Museum, Cotton Caligula A.VII ff.176-8   **Ker 137**
ed Dobbie 1942, 116-8; G. Storms, *Anglo-Saxon Magic,* The Hague 1948, no.8

43.2
The Nine Herbs Charm
MS London, British Museum, Harley 585   **Ker 231 art.2**
ed Dobbie 1942, 119-21; Storms 1948, no.9; J.H.G. Grattan and C. Singer, *Anglo-Saxon
Magic and Medicine,* Publications of the Wellcome Historical Medical Museum, n.s. 3,
London 1952, 150-6

43.3
Against a Dwarf
MS London, British Museum, Harley 585   **Ker 231 art.2**
ed Dobbie 1942, 121-2; Storms 1948, no.7; Grattan and Singer 1952, 160-2

43.4
For a Sudden Stitch
MS London, British Museum, Harley 585   **Ker 231 art.2**
ed Dobbie 1942, 122-3; Storms 1948, no.2; Grattan and Singer 1952, 172-6

43.5
For Loss of Cattle
MS London, British Museum, Harley 585   **Ker 231 art.2**
ed Dobbie 1942, 123; Storms 1948, no.14; Grattan and Singer 1952, 182

43.6
For Delayed Birth
MS London, British Museum, Harley 585   **Ker 231 art.2**
ed Dobbie 1942, 123-4; Storms 1948, no.10; Grattan and Singer 1952, 188-90

43.7
For the Water-Elf Disease

MS London, British Museum, Royal 12 D.XVII **Ker 264 art.3**
facs C.E. Wright, *Bald's Leechbook,* EEMF 5, Copenhagen 1955
ed Dobbie 1942, 124-5; Storms 1948, no.5

43.8
For a Swarm of Bees
MS Cambridge, Corpus Christi College, 41 p.182 **Ker 32 art.4**
ed Dobbie 1942, 125; Storms 1948, no.1

43.9, .10
For Loss of Cattle
MS Cambridge, Corpus Christi College, 41 p.206 **Ker 32 art.6**
ed Dobbie 1942, 125-6; Storms 1948, nos.15, 13

43.11
A Journey Charm
MS Cambridge, Corpus Christi College, 41 pp.350-3 **Ker 32 art.16**
ed Dobbie 1942, 126-8; Storms 1948, no.16

43.12
Against a Wen
MS London, British Museum, Royal 4 A.XIV f.106v **Ker 250**
ed Dobbie 1942, 128; Storms 1948, no.4

44
Instructions for Christians
MS Cambridge, University Library, Ii.1.33 **Ker 18 art.44**
ed J.L. Rosier, 'Instructions for Christians,' *Anglia* 82 [1964] 4-22; J.L. Rosier, 'Addenda to "Instructions for Christians," ' *Anglia* 84 [1966] 74; Roland Torkar, 'Textkritische Anmerkungen zum ae. Gedicht *Instructions for Christians,*' *Anglia* 89 [1971] 164-77

45
Cnut's Song
MS Cambridge, Trinity College, O.2.1 f.87v-88 **Ker 93 art.a**
   Ely Cathedral **Ker 113 art.a, Brown-Robbins 2164**
ed E.O. Blake, *Liber Eliensis,* Royal Historical Society, Camden Society 3rd series 92, London 1962, 153

46
Godric's Prayer
MS Cambridge, University Library, Mm.4.28 f.149 **Ker 28**
   Oxford, Bodleian, Laud Misc. 413 f.39v **Ker 342, Brown-Robbins 2988**
ed J. Zupitza, 'Cantus Beati Godrici,' *Englische Studien* 11 [1888] 423; J. Hall, *Selections from Early Middle English,* Oxford 1920, 5

47
The Grave
MS Oxford, Bodleian, Bodley 343 **Ker 310 art.85, Brown-Robbins 3497**

ed R. Buchholz, *Die Fragmente der Reden der Seele an den Leichnam,* Erlanger Beiträge
    zur englischen Philologie 2, Erlangen and Leipzig 1890, 11

48
Distich on Kenelm
MS Cambridge, Pembroke College, 82 f. 1v **Ker 75 art.b, Brown-Robbins 1477.5**
ed N.R. Ker, *Catalogue of Manuscripts containing Anglo-Saxon,* Oxford 1957, 124

49
Distich on the Sons of Lothebrok
MS Cambridge, Pembroke College, 82 f. 1r **Ker 75 art.a, Brown-Robbins 1267.5**
ed Ker 1957, 124

50
Distich, Psalm 17:51
MS London, British Museum, Royal 2 B.V **Ker 249**
ed C. and K. Sisam, *The Salisbury Psalter,* EETS 242, London 1959, 53 footnote

51
Metrical Psalms 90:15-95:2
MS Cambridge, Trinity College, R.17.1 **Ker 91**
facs M.R. James, *The Canterbury Psalter,* London 1935
ed F. Harsley, *Eadwine's Canterbury Psalter,* EETS 92, London 1889, 161-8

52
Genealogical Verse
MS Rochester, Textus Roffensis **Ker 373A art.5**
facs P.H. Sawyer, *Textus Roffensis,* EEMF 7, 11, Copenhagen 1957-62
ed J. Ingram, *The Saxon Chronicle,* Oxford 1823, 375-6
    See B.18.7

53
Sutton Disc Brooch
See F.42

B PROSE

The categories in this list of prose texts are as follows:
  1 Works of Ælfric
  2 Works of Wulfstan
  3 Anonymous Homilies
  4 Prose Romance, Vision Literature
  5 Prose Dialogues
  6 Letters
  7 Proverbs
  8 Biblical Translations
  9 Alfredian and Other Translations
  10 Rules for Monks and Canons
  11 Confessional and Penitential Texts
  12 Liturgical Texts, Creeds, Prayers
  13 Ecclesiastical Laws and Institutes
  14 Laws of England
  15 Charters in English
  16 Records
  17 Chronicles and Historical Texts
  18 Lists of Kings, Saints, and Bishops
  19 Martyrology
  20 Computus
  21 Medical Texts
  22 Other Scientific Texts
  23 Folklore
  24 Notes and Commonplaces
  25 Runic Texts
  26 Cryptograms
  27 Directions to Readers, Scribbles
  28 Colophons, Inscriptions, Names

1
Ælfric

1.1
First Series of Homilies [Catholic Homilies I]
ed B. Thorpe, *The Sermones Catholici or Homilies of Ælfric,* Ælfric Society, London
1844-6, vol. I
proposed EETS ed. P. Clemoes

1.1.1
English Preface
MS Cambridge, University Library, Gg.3.28 **Ker 15 art.2**
Cambridge, Corpus Christi College, 188 [adapted] **Ker 43 art.43**
Cambridge, Corpus Christi College, 178 [adapted] **Ker 41A art.12**
Oxford, Bodleian, Junius 121 [adapted] **Ker 338 art.34**

Oxford, Bodleian, Hatton 115 [adapted]   **Ker 332 art.28**
ed Thorpe 1844-6, I, 2-8

1.1.2
De Initio Creaturae
MS Cambridge, University Library, Gg.3.28   **Ker 15 art.3**
London, British Museum, Royal 7 C.XII   **Ker 257 art.1**
London, British Museum, Cotton Vitellius C.V   **Ker 220 art.2**
Oxford, Bodleian, Bodley 342   **Ker 309 art.33**
Oxford, Bodleian, Bodley 343   **Ker 310 art.6**
Cambridge, Corpus Christi College, 198   **Ker 48 art.66**
Cambridge, Corpus Christi College, 162   **Ker 38 art.1**
London, British Museum, Cotton Vespasian D.XIV   **Ker 209 art.1**
Cambridge, Corpus Christi College, 178   **Ker 41A art.1**
London, British Museum, Cotton Cleopatra B.XIII   **Ker 144 art.3**
London, British Museum, Cotton Otho B.X   **Ker 177 art.1**
Oxford, Brasenose College, Latham M.6.15 [fragment]   **Ker 352**
London, British Museum, Cotton Vespasian A.XXII f.54
facs N. Eliason and P. Clemoes, *Ælfric's First Series of Catholic Homilies*, EEMF 13, Copen-
hagen 1966 [Ker 257 art.1]
ed Thorpe 1844-6, I, 8-28; R.D-N. Warner, *Early English Homilies from the Twelfth Century
Ms Vespasian D.XIV*, EETS 152, London 1917, 1-3 [Ker 209 art.1]; A.S. Napier, 'Fragments of an Ælfric Manuscript,' *MLN* 8 [1893] 398-400 [Ker 352]

1.1.3
Christmas
MS Cambridge, University Library, Gg.3.28   **Ker 15 art.4**
London, British Museum, Royal 7 C.XII   **Ker 257 art.2**
London, British Museum, Cotton Vitellius C.V   **Ker 220 art.3**
Cambridge, Corpus Christi College, 188   **Ker 43 art.2**
Oxford, Bodleian, Bodley 343   **Ker 310 art.34**
Cambridge, Corpus Christi College, 178   **Ker 41A art.21**
Cambridge, Corpus Christi College, 302   **Ker 56 art.6**
Cambridge, University Library, Ii.1.33   **Ker 18 art.3**
London, Lambeth Palace, 489   **Ker 283 art.1**
facs Eliason and Clemoes 1966 [Ker 257 art.2]
ed Thorpe 1844-6, I, 28-44

1.1.4
Stephen
MS Cambridge, University Library, Gg.3.28   **Ker 15 art.5**
London, British Museum, Royal 7 C.XII   **Ker 257 art.3**
London, British Museum, Cotton Vitellius C.V   **Ker 220 art.5**
Cambridge, Corpus Christi College, 188   **Ker 43 art.3**
Oxford, Bodleian, Bodley 340   **Ker 309 art.2**
Oxford, Bodleian, Hatton 113   **Ker 331 art.34**
Cambridge, Corpus Christi College, 198   **Ker 48 art.2**
Cambridge, Corpus Christi College, 302   **Ker 56 art.7**

Cambridge, University Library, Ii.4.6   **Ker 21 art.28**
London, British Museum, Cotton Vitellius D.XVII   **Ker 222 art.11**
Cambridge, University Library, Ii.1.33   **Ker 18 art.21**
London, British Museum, Harley 2110   **Ker 235 art.1**
facs   Eliason and Clemoes 1966 [Ker 257 art.3]
ed   Thorpe 1844-6, I, 44-56; C.E. Wright, 'Two Ælfric Fragments' *MÆ* 7 [1938] 50-5
[Ker 235]

1.1.5
Assumption of St John
MS   Cambridge, University Library, Gg.3.28   **Ker 15 art.6**
London, British Museum, Royal 7 C.XII   **Ker 257 art.4**
London, British Museum, Cotton Vitellius C.V   **Ker 220 art.6**
Cambridge, Corpus Christi College, 188   **Ker 43 art.4**
Oxford, Bodleian, Bodley 340   **Ker 309 art.3**
Oxford, Bodleian, Hatton 113   **Ker 331 art.35**
Cambridge, Corpus Christi College, 198   **Ker 48 art.3**
Cambridge, Corpus Christi College, 302   **Ker 56 art.8**
London, British Museum, Cotton Vitellius D.XVII   **Ker 222 art.3**
Cambridge, University Library, Ii.1.33   **Ker 18 art.11**
London, British Museum, Harley 2110   **Ker 235 art.2**
facs   Eliason and Clemoes 1966 [Ker 257 art.4]
ed   Thorpe 1844-6, I, 58-76; Wright 1938, 50-5 [Ker 235]

1.1.6
Innocents
MS   Cambridge, University Library, Gg.3.28   **Ker 15 art.7**
London, British Museum, Royal 7 C.XII   **Ker 257 art.5**
London, British Museum, Cotton Vitellius C.V   **Ker 220 art.8**
Cambridge, Corpus Christi College, 188   **Ker 43 art.5**
Oxford, Bodleian, Bodley 340   **Ker 309 art.4**
Oxford, Bodleian, Hatton 113   **Ker 331 art.36**
Cambridge, Corpus Christi College, 198   **Ker 48 art.4**
London, British Museum, Cotton Vitellius D.XVII   **Ker 222 art.12**
Cambridge, University Library, Ii.1.33   **Ker 18 art.22**
facs   Eliason and Clemoes 1966 [Ker 257 art.5]
ed   Thorpe 1844-6, I, 76-90

1.1.7
Circumcision
MS   Cambridge, University Library, Gg.3.28   **Ker 15 art.8**
London, British Museum, Royal 7 C.XII   **Ker 257 art.6**
London, British Museum, Cotton Vitellius C.V **Ker 220 art.9**
Cambridge, Corpus Christi College, 188   **Ker 43 art.6**
Oxford, Bodleian, Bodley 340   **Ker 309 art.5**
Oxford, Bodleian, Bodley 343   **Ker 310 art.48**
Oxford, Bodleian, Hatton 113   **Ker 331 art.37**
Cambridge, Corpus Christi College, 198   **Ker 48 art.5**

Cambridge, Corpus Christi College, 178   **Ker 41A art.22**

acs   Eliason and Clemoes 1966 [Ker 257 art.6]
ed   Thorpe 1844-6, I, 90-103

1.1.8
Epiphany

MS   Cambridge, University Library, Gg.3.28   **Ker 15 art.9**
London, British Museum, Royal 7 C.XII   **Ker 257 art.7**
London, British Museum, Cotton Vitellius C.V   **Ker 220 art.10**
Cambridge, Corpus Christi College, 188   **Ker 43 art.7**
Oxford, Bodleian, Bodley 340   **Ker 309 art.6**
Oxford, Bodleian, Hatton 114   **Ker 331 art.38**
Cambridge, Corpus Christi College, 198   **Ker 48 art.6**

acs   Eliason and Clemoes 1966 [Ker 257 art.7]
ed   Thorpe 1844-6, I, 104-20

1.1.9
Third Sunday after Epiphany

MS   Cambridge, University Library, Gg.3.28   **Ker 15 art.10**
London, British Museum, Royal 7 C.XII   **Ker 257 art.8**
London, British Museum, Cotton Vitellius C.V   **Ker 220 art.11**
Cambridge, Corpus Christi College, 188 [additional material]   **Ker 43 art.8**
Oxford, Bodleian, Bodley 340   **Ker 309 art.9**
Oxford, Bodleian, Bodley 343   **Ker 310 art.21**
Cambridge, Corpus Christi College, 303   **Ker 57 art.2**
Cambridge, Corpus Christi College, 198   **Ker 48 art.9**
Cambridge, Corpus Christi College, 162   **Ker 38 art.10**
Cambridge, University Library, Ii.4.6   **Ker 21 art.2**
London, British Museum, Cotton Faustina A.IX   **Ker 153 art.2**

acs   Eliason and Clemoes 1966 [Ker 257 art.8]
ed   Thorpe 1844-6, I, 120-34

1.1.10
Purification

MS   Cambridge, University Library, Gg.3.28   **Ker 15 art.11**
London, British Museum, Royal 7 C.XII   **Ker 257 art.9**
London, British Museum, Cotton Vitellius C.V   **Ker 220 art.12**
Cambridge, Corpus Christi College, 188   **Ker 43 art.9**
Oxford, Bodleian, Bodley 340   **Ker 309 art.10**
Oxford, Bodleian, Bodley 343   **Ker 310 art.36**
Oxford, Bodleian, Hatton 114   **Ker 331 art.39**
Cambridge, Corpus Christi College, 198   **Ker 48 art.10**
Cambridge, Corpus Christi College, 178   **Ker 41A art.24**

acs   Eliason and Clemoes 1966 [Ker 257 art.9]
ed   Thorpe 1844-6, I, 134-50

1.1.11
Quinquagesima

MS Cambridge, University Library, Gg.3.28 **Ker 15 art.12**
London, British Museum, Royal 7 C.XII **Ker 257 art.10**
London, British Museum, Cotton Vitellius C.V **Ker 220 art.13**
Cambridge, Corpus Christi College, 188 **Ker 43 art.10**
Oxford, Bodleian, Bodley 340 **Ker 309 art.17**
Oxford, Bodleian, Bodley 343 **Ker 310 art.27**
Oxford, Bodleian, Hatton 114 **Ker 331 art.41**
Cambridge, Corpus Christi College, 303 **Ker 57 art.6**
Cambridge, Corpus Christi College, 198 **Ker 48 art.17**
Cambridge, Corpus Christi College, 162 **Ker 38 art.13**
London, British Museum, Cotton Vespasian D.XIV **Ker 209 art.53**
Cambridge, Corpus Christi College, 302 **Ker 56 art.16**
Cambridge, University Library, Ii.4.6 **Ker 21 art.6**
London, British Museum, Cotton Faustina A.IX **Ker 153 art.10**
facs Eliason and Clemoes 1966 [Ker 257 art.10]
ed Thorpe 1844-6, I, 152-65; Warner 1917, 149 [Ker 209 art.53]

1.1.12
First Sunday in Lent
MS Cambridge, University Library, Gg.3.28 **Ker 15 art.13**
London, British Museum, Royal 7 C.XII **Ker 257 art.11**
London, British Museum, Cotton Vitellius C.V **Ker 220 art.14**
Cambridge, Corpus Christi College, 188 **Ker 43 art.11**
Oxford, Bodleian, Hatton 114 **Ker 331 art.42**
Cambridge, Corpus Christi College, 303 **Ker 57 art.7**
Cambridge, Corpus Christi College, 198 **Ker 48 art.61**
Cambridge, Corpus Christi College, 162 **Ker 38 art.15**
Cambridge, Corpus Christi College, 302 **Ker 56 art.18**
Cambridge, University Library, Ii.4.6 **Ker 21 art.8**
London, British Museum, Cotton Faustina A.IX **Ker 153 art.11**
London, Lambeth Palace, 489 **Ker 283 art.5**
facs Eliason and Clemoes 1966 [Ker 257 art.11]
ed Thorpe 1844-6, I, 166-80

1.1.13
Mid-Lent Sunday
MS Cambridge, University Library, Gg.3.28 **Ker 15 art.14**
London, British Museum, Royal 7 C.XII **Ker 257 art.12**
London, British Museum, Cotton Vitellius C.V **Ker 220 art.17**
Cambridge, Corpus Christi College, 188 **Ker 43 art.13**
Oxford, Bodleian, Hatton 114 **Ker 331 art.46**
Cambridge, Corpus Christi College, 303 **Ker 57 art.10**
Cambridge, Corpus Christi College, 162 **Ker 38 art.23**
Cambridge, Corpus Christi College, 302 **Ker 56 art.22**
Cambridge, University Library, Ii.4.6 **Ker 21 art.12**
London, British Museum, Cotton Faustina A.IX **Ker 153 art.15**
facs Eliason and Clemoes 1966 [Ker 257 art.12]
ed Thorpe 1844-6, I, 180-92

1.1.14
Annunciation
MS Cambridge, University Library, Gg.3.28 **Ker 15 art.15**
London, British Museum, Royal 7 C.XII **Ker 257 art.13**
London, British Museum, Cotton Vitellius C.V **Ker 220 art.18**
Cambridge, Corpus Christi College, 188 **Ker 43 art.14**
Oxford, Bodleian, Bodley 340 **Ker 309 art.14**
Oxford, Bodleian, Bodley 343 **Ker 310 art.23**
Oxford, Bodleian, Hatton 114 **Ker 331 art.40**
Cambridge, Corpus Christi College, 303 **Ker 57 art.28**
Cambridge, Corpus Christi College, 198 **Ker 48 art.14**
London, British Museum, Cotton Vespasian D.XIV **Ker 209 art.52**
Cambridge, Corpus Christi College, 178 **Ker 41A art.20**
London, British Museum, Cotton Vitellius D.XVII [all lost] **Ker 222 art.36**
acs Eliason and Clemoes 1966 [Ker 257 art.13]
ed Thorpe 1844-6, I, 192-204; Warner 1917, 148-9 [Ker 209 art.52]

1.1.15
Palm Sunday
MS Cambridge, University Library, Gg.3.28 **Ker 15 art.16**
London, British Museum, Royal 7 C.XII **Ker 257 art.14**
London, British Museum, Cotton Vitellius C.V **Ker 220 art.19**
Cambridge, Corpus Christi College, 188 **Ker 43 art.15**
Oxford, Bodleian, Bodley 343 **Ker 310 art.38**
Oxford, Bodleian, Hatton 114 **Ker 331 art.49**
Cambridge, Corpus Christi College, 303 **Ker 57 art.14**
Cambridge, Corpus Christi College, 178 **Ker 41A art.27**
Cambridge, Corpus Christi College, 302 **Ker 56 art.25**
Cambridge, University Library, Ii.4.6 **Ker 21 art.18**
London, British Museum, Cotton Faustina A.IX **Ker 153 art.21**
Oxford, Bodleian, Junius 121 [short passage] **Ker 338 art.33**
London, Lambeth Palace, 487 f.45v
acs Eliason and Clemoes 1966 [Ker 257 art.14]
ed Thorpe 1844-6, I, 206-18
For Ker 338 art.33, see B.3.2.28

1.1.16
Cyrclice þeawas
MS Cambridge, University Library, Gg.3.28 **Ker 15 art.16**
London, British Museum, Royal 7 C.XII **Ker 257 art.14**
London, British Museum, Cotton Vitellius C.V **Ker 220 art.20**
Cambridge, Corpus Christi College, 188 **Ker 43 art.15**
Oxford, Bodleian, Bodley 343 **Ker 310 art.38**
Oxford, Bodleian, Hatton 114 **Ker 331 art.49**
Cambridge, Corpus Christi College, 178 **Ker 41A art.27**
acs Eliason and Clemoes 1966 [Ker 257 art.14]
ed Thorpe 1844-6, I, 218

1.1.17
Easter

MS   Cambridge, University Library, Gg.3.28   **Ker 15 art.17**
     London, British Museum, Royal 7 C.XII   **Ker 257 art.15**
     London, British Museum, Cotton Vitellius C.V   **Ker 220 art.20**
     Cambridge, Corpus Christi College, 188   **Ker 43 art.16**
     Oxford, Bodleian, Bodley 340   **Ker 309 art.27**
     Oxford, Bodleian, Bodley 343   **Ker 310 art.39**
     Oxford, Bodleian, Hatton 114   **Ker 331 art.50**
     Cambridge, Corpus Christi College, 303   **Ker 57 art.16**
     Cambridge, Corpus Christi College, 198   **Ker 48 art.27**
     Cambridge, Corpus Christi College, 178   **Ker 41A art.28**
     Cambridge, University Library, Ii.4.6   **Ker 21 art.19**
     London, British Museum, Cotton Faustina A.IX   **Ker 153 art.25**
     Cambridge, Trinity College, B.15.34   **Ker 86 art.1**
     Cambridge, Corpus Christi College, 367 pt.II   **Ker 63 art.1**
     London, Lambeth Palace, 489   **Ker 283 art.2**
facs   Eliason and Clemoes 1966 [Ker 257 art.15]
  ed   Thorpe 1844-6, I, 220-8

1.1.18
First Sunday after Easter

MS   Cambridge, University Library, Gg.3.28   **Ker 15 art.18**
     London, British Museum, Royal 7 C.XII   **Ker 257 art.16**
     London, British Museum, Cotton Vitellius C.V   **Ker 220 art.21**
     Cambridge, Corpus Christi College, 188*   **Ker 43 art.17**
     Oxford, Bodleian, Bodley 340   **Ker 309 art.28**
     Oxford, Bodleian, Hatton 114*   **Ker 331 art.51**
     Cambridge, Corpus Christi College, 198   **Ker 48 art.28**
     Cambridge, Corpus Christi College, 162   **Ker 38 art.33**
     Cambridge, Corpus Christi College, 178*   **Ker 41A art.29**
     Cambridge, University Library, Ii.4.6   **Ker 21 art.23**
     London, British Museum, Cotton Faustina A.IX*   **Ker 153 art.29**
     Cambridge, Trinity College, B.15.34   **Ker 86 art.4**
facs   Eliason and Clemoes 1966 [Ker 257 art.16]
  ed   Thorpe 1844-6, I, 230-8

1.1.19
Second Sunday after Easter

MS   Cambridge, University Library, Gg.3.28   **Ker 15 art.19**
     London, British Museum, Royal 7 C.XII   **Ker 257 art.17**
     London, British Museum, Cotton Vitellius C.V   **Ker 220 art.22**
     Cambridge, Corpus Christi College, 188*   **Ker 43 art.18**
     Oxford, Bodleian, Bodley 340   **Ker 309 art.29**
     Oxford, Bodleian, Bodley 343   **Ker 310 art.3**
     Cambridge, Corpus Christi College, 198   **Ker 48 art.29**

* these items have passages not edited by Thorpe

Cambridge, Corpus Christi College, 162   **Ker 38 art.34**
Cambridge, Corpus Christi College, 302*   **Ker 56 art.29**
Cambridge, University Library, Ii.4.6*   **Ker 21 art.24**
London, British Museum, Cotton Faustina A.IX*   **Ker 153 art.30**
Cambridge, Trinity College, B.15.34*   **Ker 86 art.5**
London, British Museum, Cotton Cleopatra B.XIII   **Ker 144 art.2**
acs Eliason and Clemoes 1966 [Ker 257 art.17]
 ed Thorpe 1844-6, I, 238-44

1.1.20
In Letania Maiore
MS Cambridge, University Library, Gg.3.28   **Ker 15 art.20**
London, British Museum, Royal 7 C.XII   **Ker 257 art.18**
London, British Museum, Cotton Vitellius C.V   **Ker 220 art.23**
Cambridge, Corpus Christi College, 188   **Ker 43 art.19**
Oxford, Bodleian, Bodley 342   **Ker 309 art.34**
Oxford, Bodleian, Bodley 343   **Ker 310 art.40**
Oxford, Bodleian, Hatton 114   **Ker 331 art.52**
Cambridge, Corpus Christi College, 303   **Ker 57 art.42**
London, British Museum, Cotton Vespasian D.XIV   **Ker 209 art.40**
Cambridge, Corpus Christi College, 302   **Ker 56 art.30**
Cambridge, University Library, Ii.4.6   **Ker 21 arts.29, 36**
Cambridge, Trinity College, B.15.34 [with a marginal alternative]   **Ker 86 art.9**
Cambridge, Corpus Christi College, 421   **Ker 69 art.12**
Cambridge, Jesus College, 15   **Ker 74 art.4**
London, British Museum, Cotton Cleopatra B.XIII   **Ker 144 art.6**
acs Eliason and Clemoes 1966 [Ker 257 art.18]
 ed Thorpe 1844-6, I, 244-58; Warner 1917, 120-1 [Ker 209 art.40]
For Ker 331 art.52, see B.3.2.30

1.1.21
Feria III de dominica oratione
MS Cambridge, University Library, Gg.3.28   **Ker 15 art.21**
London, British Museum, Royal 7 C.XII   **Ker 257 art.19**
London, British Museum, Cotton Vitellius C.V   **Ker 220 art.24**
Cambridge, Corpus Christi College, 188   **Ker 43 art.20**
Oxford, Bodleian, Bodley 342   **Ker 309 art.36**
Oxford, Bodleian, Bodley 343   **Ker 310 art.13**
Oxford, Bodleian, Hatton 113   **Ker 331 art.31**
Cambridge, Corpus Christi College, 162   **Ker 38 art.2**
London, British Museum, Cotton Vespasian D.XIV   **Ker 209 art.50**
Cambridge, Corpus Christi College, 178   **Ker 41A art.5**
Cambridge, Corpus Christi College, 302   **Ker 56 art.32**
Cambridge, University Library, Ii.4.6   **Ker 21 art.37**
Cambridge, Trinity College, B.15.34   **Ker 86 art.10**
Cambridge, Corpus Christi College, 367   **Ker 63 art.3**

* these items have passages not edited by Thorpe

Cambridge, Corpus Christi College, 421   **Ker 69 art. 13**
London, Lambeth Palace, 489   **Ker 283 art. 5**
Cambridge, Jesus College, 15   **Ker 74 art. 5**
Oxford, Bodleian, Hatton 115   **Ker 332 art. 2**
facs Eliason and Clemoes 1966 [Ker 257 art. 19]
 ed Thorpe 1844-6, I, 258-74; Warner 1917, 145-6 [Ker 209 art. 50]

1.1.22
Feria IIII de fide catholica
MS Cambridge, University Library, Gg. 3. 28   **Ker 15 art. 22**
London, British Museum, Royal 7 C.XII   **Ker 257 art. 20**
London, British Museum, Cotton Vitellius C.V   **Ker 220 art. 25**
Cambridge, Corpus Christi College, 188   **Ker 43 art. 21**
Oxford, Bodleian, Bodley 342   **Ker 309 art. 40**
Oxford, Bodleian, Bodley 343   **Ker 310 art. 47**
Cambridge, Corpus Christi College, 162   **Ker 38 art. 3**
London, British Museum, Cotton Vespasian D.XIV [extracts]   **Ker 209 art. 4**
Cambridge, Corpus Christi College, 302   **Ker 56 art. 34**
London, British Museum, Cotton Faustina A.IX **Ker 153 art. 34**
Cambridge, Trinity College, B. 15. 34   **Ker 86 art. 11**
Cambridge, Corpus Christi College, 421   **Ker 69 art. 14**
Cambridge, Magdalene College, Pepys 2981 no. 16   **Ker 243 art. 1**
Oxford, Bodleian, Hatton 115   **Ker 332 art. 3**
facs Eliason and Clemoes 1966 [Ker 257 art. 20]
 ed Thorpe 1844-6, I, 274-94; Warner 1917, 8-9 [Ker 209 art. 4]

1.1.23
Ascension
MS Cambridge, University Library, Gg. 3. 28   **Ker 15 art. 23**
London, British Museum, Royal 7 C.XII   **Ker 257 art. 21**
London, British Museum, Cotton Vitellius C.V   **Ker 220 art. 26**
Oxford, Bodleian, Bodley 342   **Ker 309 art. 42**
Oxford, Bodleian, Bodley 343   **Ker 310 art. 41**
Oxford, Bodleian, Hatton 114   **Ker 331 art. 57**
Cambridge, Corpus Christi College, 303   **Ker 57 art. 48**
Cambridge, Corpus Christi College, 198   **Ker 48 art. 33**
Cambridge, Corpus Christi College, 178   **Ker 41A art. 31**
Cambridge, University Library, Ii. 4. 6   **Ker 21 art. 31**
London, British Museum, Cotton Faustina A.IX   **Ker 153 art. 35**
Cambridge, Trinity College, B. 15. 34   **Ker 86 art. 12**
Cambridge, Corpus Christi College, 421   **Ker 69 art. 15**
facs Eliason and Clemoes 1966 [Ker 257 art. 21]
 ed Thorpe 1844-6, I, 294-310

1.1.24
Pentecost
MS Cambridge, University Library, Gg. 3. 28   **Ker 15 art. 24**
London, British Museum, Royal 7 C.XII   **Ker 257 art. 22**

London, British Museum, Cotton Vitellius C.V   **Ker 220 art. 27**
Cambridge, Corpus Christi College, 188   **Ker 43 art. 22**
Oxford, Bodleian, Bodley 342   **Ker 309 art. 43**
Oxford, Bodleian, Bodley 343   **Ker 310 art. 42**
Oxford, Bodleian, Hatton 114   **Ker 331 art. 58**
Cambridge, Corpus Christi College, 303   **Ker 57 art. 49**
Cambridge, Corpus Christi College, 198   **Ker 48 art. 34**
Cambridge, Corpus Christi College, 162   **Ker 38 art. 39**
Cambridge, Corpus Christi College, 178   **Ker 41A art. 32**
Cambridge, University Library, Ii.4.6   **Ker 21 art. 33**
London, British Museum, Cotton Faustina A.IX   **Ker 153 art. 37**
Cambridge, Trinity College, B. 15.34   **Ker 86 art. 14**
Cambridge, Corpus Christi College, 421   **Ker 69 art. 1**
London, Lambeth Palace, 487 f. 31
Cambridge, Jesus College, 15 f. 9   **Ker 74**
acs Eliason and Clemoes 1966 [Ker 257 art. 22]
ed   Thorpe 1844-6, I, 310-28

1.1.25
Second Sunday after Pentecost
MS Cambridge, University Library, Gg. 3. 28   **Ker 15 art. 25**
London, British Museum, Royal 7 C.XII   **Ker 257 art. 23**
London, British Museum, Cotton Vitellius C.V   **Ker 220 art. 28**
Cambridge, Corpus Christi College, 188   **Ker 43 art. 24**
Oxford, Bodleian, Bodley 342   **Ker 309 art. 44**
Oxford, Bodleian, Bodley 343   **Ker 310 art. 49**
Cambridge, Corpus Christi College, 303   **Ker 57 art. 50**
Cambridge, Corpus Christi College, 198   **Ker 48 art. 35**
Cambridge, Corpus Christi College, 162   **Ker 38 art. 40**
Cambridge, Trinity College, B. 15.34   **Ker 86 art. 19**
acs Eliason and Clemoes 1966 [Ker 257 art. 23]
ed   Thorpe 1844-6, I, 328-38

1.1.26
Fourth Sunday after Pentecost
MS Cambridge, University Library, Gg. 3. 28   **Ker 15 art. 26**
London, British Museum, Royal 7 C.XII   **Ker 257 art. 24**
London, British Museum, Cotton Vitellius C.V   **Ker 220 art. 29**
Cambridge, Corpus Christi College, 188   **Ker 43 art. 25**
Oxford, Bodleian, Bodley 342   **Ker 309 art. 47**
Oxford, Bodleian, Bodley 343   **Ker 310 art. 50**
Cambridge, Corpus Christi College, 303   **Ker 57 art. 53**
Cambridge, Corpus Christi College, 162   **Ker 38 art. 43**
Cambridge, Corpus Christi College, 162 p. 160 and Cambridge, Corpus Christi College,
178 pp. 33-43   **Ker 41A art. 4**
Cambridge, Trinity College, B. 15.34   **Ker 86 art. 21**
London, British Museum, Cotton Vespasian A. XXII f. 59v
acs Eliason and Clemoes 1966 [Ker 257 art. 24]
ed   Thorpe 1844-6, I, 338-50

1.1.27
John the Baptist
MS Cambridge, University Library, Gg. 3. 28   **Ker 15 art. 27**
London, British Museum, Royal 7 C.XII   **Ker 257 art. 25**
London, British Museum, Cotton Vitellius C.V   **Ker 220 art. 37**
Cambridge, Corpus Christi College, 188   **Ker 43 art. 26**
Oxford, Bodleian, Bodley 342   **Ker 309 art. 48**
Oxford, Bodleian, Bodley 343   **Ker 310 art. 43**
Oxford, Bodleian, Hatton 114   **Ker 331 art. 64**
Cambridge, Corpus Christi College, 303   **Ker 57 art. 19**
Cambridge, Corpus Christi College, 198   **Ker 48 art. 38**
London, British Museum, Cotton Vespasian D. XIV   **Ker 209 art. 9**
Oxford, Bodleian, Hatton 116   **Ker 333 art. 2**
London, British Museum, Cotton Otho B.X and Oxford, Bodleian, Rawlinson
Q.e.20   **Ker 177A art. 24**
facs Eliason and Clemoes 1966 [Ker 257 art. 25]
ed Thorpe 1844-6, I, 350-64; Warner 1917, 19-20 [Ker 209 art. 9]

1.1.28
Peter and Paul
MS Cambridge, University Library, Gg. 3. 28   **Ker 15 art. 28**
London, British Museum, Royal 7 C.XII   **Ker 257 art. 26**
London, British Museum, Cotton Vitellius C.V   **Ker 220 arts. 38, 39**
Cambridge, Corpus Christi College, 188   **Ker 43 arts. 27, 28**
Oxford, Bodleian, Bodley 342   **Ker 309 arts. 51, 52**
Oxford, Bodleian, Bodley 343   **Ker 310 arts. 44, 45**
Oxford, Bodleian, Hatton 114   **Ker 331 arts. 65, 66**
Cambridge, Corpus Christi College, 303   **Ker 57 arts. 20, 21**
Cambridge, Corpus Christi College, 198   **Ker 48 arts. 41, 42**
London, British Museum, Cotton Vespasian D.XIV   **Ker 209 art. 10**
Oxford, Bodleian, Hatton 116   **Ker 333 arts. 3, 4**
London, British Museum, Cotton Vitellius D.XVII   **Ker 222 art. 1**
Cambridge, University Library, Ii. 1. 33   **Ker 18 art. 9**
Gloucester, Cathedral, 35 [fragment]   **Ker 117 art. 4**
facs Eliason and Clemoes 1966 [Ker 257 art. 26]
ed Thorpe 1844-6, I, 364-84; Warner 1917, 20 [Ker 209 art. 10]

1.1.29
Paul
MS Cambridge, University Library, Gg. 3. 28   **Ker 15 art. 29**
London, British Museum, Royal 7 C.XII   **Ker 257 art. 27**
London, British Museum, Cotton Vitellius C.V   **Ker 220 arts. 40, 41**
Cambridge, Corpus Christi College, 188   **Ker 43 art. 29**
Oxford, Bodleian, Bodley 342   **Ker 309 art. 53**
Oxford, Bodleian, Bodley 343   **Ker 310 art. 46**
Oxford, Bodleian, Hatton 114   **Ker 331 art. 67**
Cambridge, Corpus Christi College, 303   **Ker 57 art. 22**
Cambridge, Corpus Christi College, 198   **Ker 48 art. 43**

London, British Museum, Cotton Vespasian D.XIV   **Ker 209 art.41**
Oxford, Bodleian, Hatton 116   **Ker 333 art.5**
London, British Museum, Cotton Vitellius D.XVII   **Ker 222 art.44**
Cambridge, University Library, Ii.1.33   **Ker 18 art.7**
The Hague, Koninklijke Bibliotheek, 133.D.22   **Ker 118 art.1**
facs   Eliason and Clemoes 1966 [Ker 257 art.27]
  ed   Thorpe 1844-6, I, 384-400; Warner 1917, 121-2 [Ker 209 art.41]

1.1.30
Eleventh Sunday after Pentecost
MS   Cambridge, University Library, Gg.3.28   **Ker 15 art.30**
London, British Museum, Royal 7 C.XII   **Ker 257 art.28**
London, British Museum, Cotton Vitellius C.V   **Ker 220 art.42**
Cambridge, Corpus Christi College, 188   **Ker 43 art.30**
Oxford, Bodleian, Bodley 342   **Ker 309 art.56**
Oxford, Bodleian, Bodley 343   **Ker 310 art.51**
Cambridge, Corpus Christi College, 303   **Ker 57 art.56**
Cambridge, Corpus Christi College, 162   **Ker 38 art.46**
London, British Museum, Cotton Vespasian D.XIV   **Ker 209 art.14**
Cambridge, Trinity College, B.15.34   **Ker 86 art.28**
The Hague, Koninklijke Bibliotheek, 133.D.22   **Ker 118 art.2**
London, British Museum, Harley 5915   **Ker 243 art.2**
facs   Eliason and Clemoes 1966 [Ker 257 art.28]
  ed   Thorpe 1844-6, I, 402-14; Warner 1917, 28-34 [Ker 209 art.14]

1.1.31
Laurence
MS   Cambridge, University Library, Gg.3.28   **Ker 15 art.31**
London, British Museum, Royal 7 C.XII   **Ker 257 art.29**
London, British Museum, Cotton Vitellius C.V   **Ker 220 art.43**
Cambridge, Corpus Christi College, 188   **Ker 43 art.31**
Oxford, Bodleian, Bodley 343   **Ker 310 art.14**
Cambridge, Corpus Christi College, 303   **Ker 57 art.24**
Cambridge, Corpus Christi College, 198   **Ker 48 art.53**
Oxford, Bodleian, Hatton 116   **Ker 333 art.6**
London, British Museum, Cotton Vitellius D.XVII   **Ker 222 art.23**
Cambridge, University Library, Ii.1.33   **Ker 18 art.24**
The Hague, Koninklijke Bibliotheek, 133.D.22   **Ker 118 art.3**
London, British Museum, Cotton Otho A.XVIII f.131   **Ker 174 art.1**
facs   Eliason and Clemoes 1966 [Ker 257 art.29]
  ed   Thorpe 1844-6, I, 416-36

1.1.32
Assumption of the Virgin
MS   Cambridge, University Library, Gg.3.28   **Ker 15 art.32**
London, British Museum, Royal 7 C.XII   **Ker 257 art.30**
London, British Museum, Cotton Vitellius C.V   **Ker 220 art.47**
Cambridge, Corpus Christi College, 188   **Ker 43 art.32**

Oxford, Bodleian, Bodley 343   **Ker 310 art. 55**
Oxford, Bodleian, Hatton 114   **Ker 331 art. 68**
London, British Museum, Cotton Vespasian D. XIV   **Ker 209 arts. 16, 18**
Oxford, Bodleian, Hatton 116   **Ker 333 art. 7**
London, British Museum, Cotton Vitellius D. XVII   **Ker 222 art. 35**
Cambridge, Corpus Christi College, 367 pt. II   **Ker 63 art. 4**
facs   Eliason and Clemoes 1966 [Ker 257 art. 30]
 ed   Thorpe 1844-6, I, 436-54; Warner 1917, 41-6 and 50-2 [Ker 209 arts. 16, 18]

1.1.33
Bartholomew
MS   Cambridge, University Library, Gg. 3. 28   **Ker 15 art. 33**
London, British Museum, Royal 7 C. XII   **Ker 257 art. 31**
London, British Museum, Cotton Vitellius C. V   **Ker 220 art. 50**
Cambridge, Corpus Christi College, 188   **Ker 43 art. 33**
Oxford, Bodleian, Bodley 343   **Ker 310 art. 15**
Oxford, Bodleian, Hatton 114   **Ker 331 art. 69**
Cambridge, Corpus Christi College, 198   **Ker 48 art. 65**
Oxford, Bodleian, Hatton 116   **Ker 333 art. 8**
London, British Museum, Cotton Vitellius D. XVII   **Ker 222 art. 6**
Cambridge, University Library, Ii. 1. 33   **Ker 18 art. 14**
Cambridge, Corpus Christi College, 367 pt. II   **Ker 63 art. 5**
facs   Eliason and Clemoes 1966 [Ker 257 art. 31]
 ed   Thorpe 1844-6, I, 454-76

1.1.34
Decollation of St John the Baptist
MS   Cambridge, University Library, Gg. 3. 28   **Ker 15 art. 34**
London, British Museum, Royal 7 C. XII   **Ker 257 art. 32**
London, British Museum, Cotton Vitellius C. V   **Ker 220 art. 51**
Cambridge, Corpus Christi College, 188   **Ker 43 art. 34**
Cambridge, Corpus Christi College, 303   **Ker 57 art. 25**
London, British Museum, Cotton Vespasian D. XIV   **Ker 209 art. 19**
Oxford, Bodleian, Hatton 116   **Ker 333 art. 9**
Cambridge, University Library, Ii. 1. 33   **Ker 18 art. 44**
facs   Eliason and Clemoes 1966 [Ker 257 art. 32]
 ed   Thorpe 1844-6, I, 476-90; Warner 1917, 52-8 [Ker 209 art. 19]

1.1.35
Seventeenth Sunday after Pentecost
MS   Cambridge, University Library, Gg. 3. 28   **Ker 15 art. 35**
London, British Museum, Royal 7 C. XII   **Ker 257 art. 33**
London, British Museum, Cotton Vitellius C. V   **Ker 220 art. 52**
Cambridge, Corpus Christi College, 188   **Ker 43 art. 36**
Oxford, Bodleian, Bodley 342   **Ker 309 art. 61**
Oxford, Bodleian, Bodley 343   **Ker 310 art. 52**
Cambridge, Corpus Christi College, 303   **Ker 57 art. 60**
Cambridge, Corpus Christi College, 162   **Ker 38 art. 50**

acs Eliason and Clemoes 1966 [Ker 257 art.33]
 ed Thorpe 1844-6, I, 490-500

1.1.36
Dedicatio ecclesiae sancti Michaelis
MS Cambridge, University Library, Gg.3.28   **Ker 15 art.36**
    London, British Museum, Royal 7 C.XII   **Ker 257 art.34**
    London, British Museum, Cotton Vitellius C.V   **Ker 220 arts.53, 54**
    Cambridge, Corpus Christi College, 188   **Ker 43 art.37**
    Oxford, Bodleian, Bodley 343   **Ker 310 art.74**
    Oxford, Bodleian, Hatton 114   **Ker 331 art.73**
    Cambridge, Corpus Christi College, 303   **Ker 57 art.29**
    Cambridge, Corpus Christi College, 198   **Ker 48 art.55**
    London, British Museum, Cotton Vespasian D.XIV   **Ker 209 art.22**
    Oxford, Bodleian, Hatton 116   **Ker 333 art.11**
    London, British Museum, Cotton Vitellius D.XVII   **Ker 222 art.19**
    Cambridge, Corpus Christi College, 367   **Ker 63 art.9**
acs Eliason and Clemoes 1966 [Ker 257 art.34]
 ed Thorpe 1844-6, I, 502-18; Warner 1917, 61-5 [Ker 209 art.22]

1.1.37
Twenty-first Sunday after Pentecost
MS Cambridge, University Library, Gg.3.28   **Ker 15 art.37**
    London, British Museum, Royal 7 C.XII   **Ker 257 art.35**
    London, British Museum, Cotton Vitellius C.V   **Ker 220 art.55**
    Cambridge, Corpus Christi College, 188   **Ker 43 art.38**
    Oxford, Bodleian, Bodley 342   **Ker 309 art.62**
    Oxford, Bodleian, Bodley 343   **Ker 310 art.53**
    Cambridge, Corpus Christi College, 303   **Ker 57 art.61**
    Cambridge, Corpus Christi College, 162   **Ker 38 arts.51, 52**
acs Eliason and Clemoes 1966 [Ker 257 art.35]
 ed Thorpe 1844-6, I, 520-38

1.1.38
All Saints
MS Cambridge, University Library, Gg.3.28   **Ker 15 art.38**
    London, British Museum, Royal 7 C.XII   **Ker 257 art.36**
    London, British Museum, Cotton Vitellius C.V   **Ker 220 arts.56, 57**
    Cambridge, Corpus Christi College, 188   **Ker 43 arts.39, 40**
    Oxford, Bodleian, Bodley 342   **Ker 309 arts.70, 71**
    Oxford, Bodleian, Bodley 343   **Ker 310 arts.56, 57**
    Oxford, Bodleian, Hatton 114   **Ker 331 arts.74, 75**
    Cambridge, Corpus Christi College, 303   **Ker 57 arts.30, 31**
    London, British Museum, Cotton Vespasian D.XIV   **Ker 209 art.29**
    Oxford, Bodleian, Hatton 116   **Ker 333 arts.12, 13**
    London, Lambeth Palace, 489   **Ker 283 art.3**
acs Eliason and Clemoes 1966 [Ker 257 art.36]
 ed Thorpe 1844-6, I, 538-56; Warner 1917, 73-7 [Ker 209 art.29]

1.1.39
Clement
MS   Cambridge, University Library, Gg.3.28   **Ker 15 art.39**
    London, British Museum, Royal 7 C.XII   **Ker 257 art.37**
    London, British Museum, Cotton Vitellius C.V   **Ker 220 art.58**
    Cambridge, Corpus Christi College, 188   **Ker 43 art.41**
    Oxford, Bodleian, Bodley 342   **Ker 309 art.72**
    Cambridge, Corpus Christi College, 302   **Ker 57 art.32**
    London, British Museum, Cotton Vespasian D.XIV   **Ker 209 art.36**
    Oxford, Bodleian, Hatton 116   **Ker 333 art.14**
    London, British Museum, Cotton Vitellius D.XVII   **Ker 222 art.24**
    Cambridge, University Library, Ii.1.33   **Ker 18 arts.33, 8b**
facs   Eliason and Clemoes 1966 [Ker 257 art.37]
  ed   Thorpe 1844-6, I, 556-76; Warner 1917, 106-9 [Ker 209 art.36]

1.1.40
Andrew
MS   Cambridge, University Library, Gg.3.28   **Ker 15 art.40**
    London, British Museum, Royal 7 C.XII   **Ker 257 art.38**
    London, British Museum, Cotton Vitellius C.V   **Ker 220 arts.59, 60**
    Cambridge, Corpus Christi College, 188   **Ker 43 art.42**
    Oxford, Bodleian, Bodley 342   **Ker 309 arts.78, 79**
    Oxford, Bodleian, Bodley 343   **Ker 310 art.30**
    Cambridge, Corpus Christi College, 303   **Ker 57 art.33**
    Oxford, Bodleian, Hatton 116   **Ker 333 art.15**
    London, British Museum, Cotton Vitellius D.XVII   **Ker 222 art.22**
    Cambridge, University Library, Ii.1.33   **Ker 18 art.10**
facs   Eliason and Clemoes 1966 [Ker 257 art.38]
  ed   Thorpe 1844-6, I, 576-98; K. Sisam, *Studies in the History of Old English Literature,*
    Oxford 1953, 174 [Ker 257 art.38 note]

1.1.41
First Sunday in Advent
MS   Cambridge, University Library, Gg.3.28   **Ker 15 art.41**
    London, British Museum, Royal 7 C.XII   **Ker 257 art.39**
    London, British Museum, Cotton Vitellius C.V   **Ker 220 art.61**
    Cambridge, Corpus Christi College, 188   **Ker 43 art.43**
    Oxford, Bodleian, Bodley 342   **Ker 309 art.73**
    Oxford, Bodleian, Bodley 343   **Ker 310 art.32**
    Cambridge, Corpus Christi College, 162   **Ker 38 art.53**
    Cambridge, Corpus Christi College, 302   **Ker 56 art.2**
    Oxford, Bodleian, Junius 121   **Ker 338 art.31**
facs   Eliason and Clemoes 1966 [Ker 257 art.39]
  ed   Thorpe 1844-6, I, 600-6

1.1.42
Second Sunday in Advent
MS   Cambridge, University Library, Gg.3.28   **Ker 15 art.42**

London, British Museum, Royal 7 C.XII **Ker 257 art.40**
London, British Museum, Cotton Vitellius C.V   **Ker 220 art.62**
Cambridge, Corpus Christi College, 188   **Ker 43 art.44**
Oxford, Bodleian, Bodley 342   **Ker 309 art.74**
Oxford, Bodleian, Bodley 343   **Ker 310 art.33**
Cambridge, Corpus Christi College, 162   **Ker 38 art.54**
London, British Museum, Cotton Vespasian D.XIV   **Ker 209 art.28**
Cambridge, Corpus Christi College, 302   **Ker 56 art.3**
Oxford, Bodleian, Junius 121   **Ker 338 art.32**

facs   Eliason and Clemoes 1966 [Ker 257 art.40]
ed   Thorpe 1844-6, I, 608-18; Warner 1917, 67-72 [Ker 209 art.28]

1.2
Second Series of Homilies [Catholic Homilies II]
ed   Thorpe 1844-6, II
proposed EETS ed. M.R. Godden

1.2.1
English Preface
MS   Cambridge, University Library, Gg.3.28   **Ker 15 art.43**
ed   Thorpe 1844-6, II, 2

1.2.2
Christmas
MS   Cambridge, University Library, Gg.3.28   **Ker 15 art.44**
Oxford, Bodleian, Hatton 113   **Ker 331 art.33**
London, Lambeth Palace, 489 [in catena]   **Ker 283 art.5**
ed   Thorpe 1844-6, II, 4-22

1.2.3
Stephen
MS   Cambridge, University Library, Gg.3.28   **Ker 15 art.45**
London, British Museum, Cotton Vitellius D.XVII   **Ker 222 art.10**
ed   Thorpe 1844-6, II, 24-36
proposed ed. M. Masi, *NM* 71 [1970] 499

1.2.4
Epiphany
MS   Cambridge, University Library, Gg.3.28   **Ker 15 art.46**
Oxford, Bodleian, Bodley 343   **Ker 310 art.35**
Cambridge, Corpus Christi College, 178   **Ker 41A art.23**
ed   Thorpe 1844-6, II, 36-52

1.2.5
Second Sunday after Epiphany
MS   Cambridge, University Library, Gg.3.28   **Ker 15 art.47**
Cambridge, Corpus Christi College, 198   **Ker 48 art.8**
Cambridge, Corpus Christi College, 162   **Ker 38 art.9**

Oxford, Bodleian, Bodley 343   **Ker 310 art.75**
Cambridge, Corpus Christi College, 303   **Ker 57 art.1**
Cambridge, University Library, Ii.4.6   **Ker 21 art.1**
London, British Museum, Cotton Faustina A.IX   **Ker 153 art.1**
ed   Thorpe 1844-6, II, 54-72

1.2.6
Septuagesima
MS   Cambridge, University Library, Gg.3.28   **Ker 15 art.48**
Oxford, Bodleian, Bodley 340 and 342   **Ker 309 arts.15, 77**
Cambridge, Corpus Christi College, 198   **Ker 48 art.15**
Cambridge, Corpus Christi College, 162   **Ker 38 art.11**
Oxford, Bodleian, Bodley 343   **Ker 310 arts.24, 25**
Cambridge, Corpus Christi College, 303   **Ker 57 arts.3, 4**
Cambridge, University Library, Ii.4.6   **Ker 21 art.4**
London, British Museum, Cotton Faustina A.IX   **Ker 153 arts.7, 8**
Cambridge, Corpus Christi College, 302   **Ker 56 arts.13, 14**
Geneva, library of Dr M. Bodmer   **Ker 285**
ed   Thorpe 1844-6, II, 72-88; N.R. Ker, 'The Bodmer Fragment of Ælfric's Homily for Septuagesima Sunday' in N. Davis and C.L.Wrenn, eds. *English and Medieval Studies Presented to J.R.R. Tolkien,* London 1962, 77-83 [Ker 285]

1.2.7
Sexagesima
MS   Cambridge, University Library, Gg.3.28   **Ker 15 art.49**
Oxford, Bodleian, Bodley 340   **Ker 309 art.16**
Cambridge, Corpus Christi College, 198   **Ker 48 art.16**
Cambridge, Corpus Christi College, 162   **Ker 38 art.12**
Oxford, Bodleian, Bodley 343   **Ker 310 art.26**
Cambridge, Corpus Christi College, 303   **Ker 57 art.5**
Cambridge, University Library, Ii.4.6   **Ker 21 art.5**
London, British Museum, Cotton Faustina A.IX   **Ker 153 art.9**
Cambridge, Corpus Christi College, 302   **Ker 56 art.15**
ed   Thorpe 1844-6, II, 88-98

1.2.8
First Sunday in Lent
MS   Cambridge, University Library, Gg.3.28   **Ker 15 art.50**
Oxford, Bodleian, Bodley 340 and 342   **Ker 309 arts.18, 76**
Cambridge, Corpus Christi College, 198   **Ker 48 art.18**
Cambridge, Corpus Christi College, 162   **Ker 38 art.16**
Cambridge, University Library, Ii.4.6   **Ker 21 art.9**
London, British Museum, Cotton Faustina A.IX   **Ker 153 art.12**
Oxford, Bodleian, Hatton 114 [partial]   **Ker 331 art.43**
Cambridge, Corpus Christi College, 302   **Ker 56 art.19**
Cambridge, Corpus Christi College, 178   **Ker 41A art.25**
Oxford, Bodleian, Junius 85 and 86   **Ker 336 art.5**
London, British Museum, Cotton Tiberius A.III [extract]   **Ker 186 art.9h**

ed   Thorpe 1844-6, II, 98-108; H. Wanley, *Catalogus,* [vol. 2 of Hickes, *Thesaurus*] Oxford
     1705, 117 [Ker 38 art. 16, add. passage of 16 ll] ; A.S. Napier, *Wulfstan,* Sammlung
     englischer Denkmäler 4, Berlin 1883, repr. with app., K. Ostheeren 1967, 282-9, no. 55
     [Ker 331 art. 43] ; H. Logeman, 'Anglo-Saxonica Minora,' *Anglia* 12 [1889] 513-5
     [Ker 186 art. 9h]
     See below B.3.4.'44, B.11.10.3

1.2.9
Second Sunday in Lent
MS   Cambridge, University Library, Gg. 3. 28   **Ker 15 art. 51**
     Cambridge, Corpus Christi College, 198   **Ker 48 art. 44**
     Cambridge, Corpus Christi College, 162   **Ker 38 art. 18**
     Cambridge, Corpus Christi College, 303   **Ker 57 art. 8**
     Cambridge, University Library, Ii. 4. 6   **Ker 21 art. 10**
     London, British Museum, Cotton Faustina A. IX   **Ker 153 art. 13**
     Cambridge, Corpus Christi College, 302   **Ker 56 art. 20**
     London, British Museum, Cotton Vitellius C. V   **Ker 220 art. 15**
ed   Thorpe 1844-6, II, 110-6

1.2.10
Gregory
MS   Cambridge, University Library, Gg. 3. 28   **Ker 15 art. 52**
     Oxford, Bodleian, Bodley 340   **Ker 309 art. 11**
     Cambridge, Corpus Christi College, 198   **Ker 48 art. 11**
     London, British Museum, Cotton Vitellius D. XVII   **Ker 222 art. 18**
     Cambridge, University Library, Ii. 1. 33   **Ker 18 art. 25**
     Oxford, Bodleian, Hatton 114   **Ker 331 art. 59**
     London, British Museum, Cotton Faustina A. X   **Ker 154B art. 4**
ed   Thorpe 1844-6, II, 116-32; M. Masi, 'Three Homilies by Ælfric: The Lives of Saints
     Gregory, Cuthbert and Martin: An Edition' [Northwestern diss.] *DA* 29 [1969] 4009A

1.2.11
Cuthbert
MS   Cambridge, University Library, Gg. 3. 28   **Ker 15 art. 53**
     Oxford, Bodleian, Bodley 340   **Ker 309 art. 12**
     Cambridge, Corpus Christi College, 198   **Ker 48 art. 12**
ed   Thorpe 1844-6, II, 132-54; Masi 1969

1.2.12
Benedict
MS   Cambridge, University Library, Gg. 3. 28   **Ker 15 art. 54**
     Oxford, Bodleian, Bodley 340   **Ker 309 art. 13**
     Cambridge, Corpus Christi College, 198   **Ker 48 art. 13**
     London, British Museum, Cotton Vitellius D. XVII   **Ker 222 art. 16**
     Cambridge, University Library, Ii. 1. 33   **Ker 18 art. 5**
ed   Thorpe 1844-6, II, 154-88
     proposed ed. Masi, *NM* 71 [1970] 499

1.2.13
Midlent
MS Cambridge, University Library, Gg. 3.28   **Ker 15 art. 55**
      Cambridge, Corpus Christi College, 162   **Ker 38 art. 7**
      Cambridge, University Library, Ii. 4.6   **Ker 21 art. 13**
      London, British Museum, Cotton Faustina A.IX   **Ker 153 art. 16**
ed   Thorpe 1844-6, II, 188-212

1.2.14
Midlent: secunda sententia
MS Cambridge, University Library, Gg. 3.28   **Ker 15 art. 55**
      Cambridge, Corpus Christi College, 162   **Ker 38 art. 8**
      Cambridge, University Library, Ii. 4.6   **Ker 21 art. 14**
      London, British Museum, Cotton Faustina A.IX   **Ker 153 art. 17**
ed   Thorpe 1844-6, II, 212-24

1.2.15
Fifth Sunday in Lent
MS Cambridge, University Library, Gg. 3.28   **Ker 15 art. 56**
      Cambridge, Corpus Christi College, 198   **Ker 48 art. 45**
      Cambridge, Corpus Christi College, 162   **Ker 38 art. 25**
      Cambridge, Corpus Christi College, 303   **Ker 57 art. 12**
      Cambridge, University Library, Ii. 4.6   **Ker 21 art. 16**
      London, British Museum, Cotton Faustina A.IX   **Ker 153 art. 19**
      Cambridge, University Library, Ii. 1.33   **Ker 18 art. 2**
      Oxford, Bodleian, Hatton 114   **Ker 331 art. 83**
      Cambridge, Corpus Christi College, 302   **Ker 56 art. 23**
ed   Thorpe 1844-6, II, 224-40

1.2.16
Palm Sunday
MS Cambridge, University Library, Gg. 3.28   **Ker 15 art. 57**
      Cambridge, Corpus Christi College, 162   **Ker 38 art. 27**
      Cambridge, Corpus Christi College, 303   **Ker 57 art. 13**
      Cambridge, University Library, Ii. 4.6   **Ker 21 art. 17**
      London, British Museum, Cotton Faustina A.IX   **Ker 153 art. 22**
      Oxford, Bodleian, Hatton 114   **Ker 331 art. 48**
      Cambridge, Corpus Christi College, 302   **Ker 56 art. 26**
      Cambridge, Corpus Christi College, 178   **Ker 41A art. 26**
      London, British Museum, Cotton Tiberius A.III   **Ker 186 art. 16**
ed   Thorpe 1844-6, II, 240-62

1.2.17
Swigdagas
MS Cambridge, University Library, Gg. 3.28 [the notice following the homily]   **Ker 15 art. 57**
      Cambridge, University Library, Ii. 4.6   **Ker 21 art. 17**
ed   Thorpe 1844-6, II, 262

1.2.18
Easter
MS Cambridge, University Library, Gg.3.28 **Ker 15 art.58**
Cambridge, Corpus Christi College, 198 **Ker 48 art.46**
Cambridge, Corpus Christi College, 162 [extracts] **Ker 38 art.32**
Cambridge, University Library, Ii.4.6 **Ker 21 art.20**
London, British Museum, Cotton Faustina A.IX **Ker 153 art.26**
Cambridge, Corpus Christi College, 302 **Ker 56 art.28**
ed Thorpe 1844-6, II, 262-82
For Ker 38 art.32, see B.3.2.27

1.2.19
Easter
MS Cambridge, University Library, Gg.3.28 **Ker 15 art.59**
Cambridge, Corpus Christi College, 198 **Ker 48 art.47**
Cambridge, University Library, Ii.4.6 **Ker 21 art.21**
London, British Museum, Cotton Faustina A.IX **Ker 153 art.27**
Cambridge, Trinity College, B.15.34 **Ker 86 art.2**
Cambridge, Corpus Christi College, 367 pt.II **Ker 63 art.2**
ed Thorpe 1844-6, II, 282-6

1.2.20
Wednesday in Easter Week
MS Cambridge, University Library, Gg.3.28 **Ker 15 art.60**
Cambridge, Corpus Christi College, 198 **Ker 48 art.48**
Cambridge, University Library, Ii.4.6 **Ker 21 art.22**
London, British Museum, Cotton Faustina A.IX **Ker 153 art.28**
Cambridge, Trinity College, B.15.34 **Ker 86 art.3**
Cambridge, Corpus Christi College, 367 pt.II **Ker 63 art.2**
ed Thorpe 1844-6, II, 288-94

1.2.21
Philip and James
MS Cambridge, University Library, Gg.3.28 **Ker 15 arts.61, 62**
Oxford, Bodleian, Bodley 340 **Ker 309 art.30**
Cambridge, Corpus Christi College, 198 **Ker 48 art.30**
London, British Museum, Cotton Vitellius D.XVII **Ker 222 arts.4, 5**
Cambridge, University Library, Ii.1.33 **Ker 18 arts.12, 13**
Oxford, Bodleian, Hatton 114 **Ker 331 arts.60, 61**
ed Thorpe 1844-6, II, 294-302
proposed ed. Masi, *NM* 71 [1970] 499

1.2.22
Invention of the Cross
MS Cambridge, University Library, Gg.3.28 **Ker 15 art.63**
Oxford, Bodleian, Bodley 340 **Ker 309 art.31**
Cambridge, Corpus Christi College, 198 **Ker 48 art.31**
London, British Museum, Cotton Vitellius D.XVII **Ker 222 art.20**

Oxford, Bodleian, Hatton 114 **Ker 331 art.62**
London, British Museum, Cotton Otho B.X [burnt] **Ker 177 art.14**
ed Thorpe 1844-6, II, 302-6

1.2.23
Alexander, Eventius, and Theodolus
MS Cambridge, University Library, Gg.3.28 **Ker 15 art.64**
Oxford, Bodleian, Bodley 340 **Ker 309 art.32**
Cambridge, Corpus Christi College, 198 **Ker 48 art.32**
London, British Museum, Cotton Vitellius D.XVII **Ker 222 art.21**
Oxford, Bodleian, Hatton 114 [cf. art.84: alternative beginning] **Ker 331 art.63**
London, British Museum, Cotton Otho B.X [burnt] **Ker 177 art.15**
ed Thorpe 1844-6, II, 308-12
proposed ed. Masi, *NM* 71 [1970] 499
For Ker 331 art.84, see B.1.4.24

1.2.24
Feria II in Letania Maiore
MS Cambridge, University Library, Gg.3.28 **Ker 15 art.65**
Oxford, Bodleian, Bodley 342 **Ker 309 art.35**
Cambridge, Corpus Christi College, 162 **Ker 38 art.5**
Cambridge, University Library, Ii.4.6 [extracts] **Ker 21 arts.27, 28**
Oxford, Bodleian, Hatton 115 [with 14 unique lines not in Thorpe] **Ker 332 art.7**
Cambridge, Jesus College, 15 [binding leaves] **Ker 74 art.2**
ed Thorpe 1844-6, II, 314-32
For Ker 332 art.7, see B.1.4.25

1.2.25
Feria III in Letania Maiore
MS Cambridge, University Library, Gg.3.28 **Ker 15 art.66**
Oxford, Bodleian, Bodley 342 **Ker 309 art.37**
Oxford, Bodleian, Hatton 115 **Ker 332 art.8**
London, British Museum, Cotton Vespasian D.XIV **Ker 209 art.37**
ed Thorpe 1844-6, II, 332-48; Warner 1917, 109-15 [Ker 209 art.37]

1.2.26
Alia Visio
MS Cambridge, University Library, Gg.3.28 **Ker 15 art.67**
Oxford, Bodleian, Bodley 342 **Ker 309 art.38**
Oxford, Bodleian, Hatton 115 **Ker 332 art.9**
Cambridge, University Library, Ii.1.33 [with altered Incipit] **Ker 18 art.43**
London, British Museum, Cotton Vespasian D.XIV **Ker 209 art.38**
ed Thorpe 1844-6, II, 348-56; Warner 1917, 116-9 [Ker 209 art.38]

1.2.27
Hortatorius sermo
MS Cambridge, University Library, Gg.3.28 **Ker 15 art.68**
Oxford, Bodleian, Bodley 342 **Ker 309 art.39**

Oxford, Bodleian, Hatton 115 **Ker 332 art. 10**
London, British Museum, Cotton Vespasian D.XIV **Ker 209 art.39**
ed Thorpe 1844-6, II, 356-8; Warner 1917, 119-20 [Ker 209 art.39]

1.2.28
Feria IV in Letania Maiore
MS Cambridge, University Library, Gg.3.28 **Ker 15 art.69**
Oxford, Bodleian, Bodley 342 **Ker 309 art.41**
Cambridge, Corpus Christi College, 303 **Ker 57 art.46**
Cambridge, University Library, Ii.4.6 **Ker 21 art.30**
Cambridge, Corpus Christi College, 178 [with 3 passages not in Thorpe] **Ker 41A art.30**
ed Thorpe 1844-6, II, 360-70
For Ker 41A art.30, see B.1.4.26

1.2.29
Third Sunday after Pentecost
MS Cambridge, University Library, Gg.3.28 **Ker 15 art.70**
Oxford, Bodleian, Bodley 342 **Ker 309 art.45**
Cambridge, Corpus Christi College, 198 **Ker 48 art.36**
Cambridge, Corpus Christi College, 162 **Ker 38 art.41**
Cambridge, Corpus Christi College, 303 **Ker 57 art.51**
London, British Museum, Cotton Vitellius C.V **Ker 220 art.30**
Cambridge, Trinity College, B.15.34 **Ker 86 art.20**
ed Thorpe 1844-6, II, 370-8

1.2.30
Third Sunday after Pentecost: alia narratio
MS Cambridge, University Library, Gg.3.28 **Ker 15 art.71**
Oxford, Bodleian, Bodley 342 **Ker 309 art.46**
Cambridge, Corpus Christi College, 198 **Ker 48 art.37**
Cambridge, Corpus Christi College, 162 **Ker 38 art.42**
Cambridge, Corpus Christi College, 303 **Ker 57 art.52**
Cambridge, University Library, Ii.4.6 **Ker 21 art.3**
ed Thorpe 1844-6, II, 378-80
This homily is incorporated in another found only in MS London, British Museum,
Cotton Vitellius C.V. **See B.1.4.18**

1.2.31
Peter and Paul
MS Cambridge, University Library, Gg.3.28 **Ker 15 art.72**
Oxford, Bodleian, Bodley 342 **Ker 309 arts.49, 50**
Cambridge, Corpus Christi College, 198 **Ker 48 arts.39, 40**
Oxford, Bodleian, Bodley 343 **Ker 310 art.58**
London, British Museum, Cotton Vespasian D.XIV **Ker 209 art.13**
Gloucester, Cathedral, 35 **Ker 117 art.5**
ed Thorpe 1844-6, II, 380-94; Warner 1917, 26-7 [Ker 209 art.13]
proposed ed. Masi, *NM* 71 [1970] 499

1.2.32
Eighth Sunday after Pentecost

MS Cambridge, University Library, Gg.3.28 **Ker 15 art.73**
Oxford, Bodleian, Bodley 342 **Ker 309 art.54**
Cambridge, Corpus Christi College, 162 **Ker 38 art.44**
Oxford, Bodleian, Bodley 343 **Ker 310 art.1**
Cambridge, Corpus Christi College, 303 **Ker 57 art.54**
London, British Museum, Cotton Vitellius C.V **Ker 220 art.34**
Cambridge, Trinity College, B.15.34 **Ker 86 art.25**
ed Thorpe 1844-6, II, 394-402

1.2.33
Ninth Sunday after Pentecost

MS Cambridge, University Library, Gg.3.28 **Ker 15 art.74**
Oxford, Bodleian, Bodley 342 **Ker 309 art.55**
Cambridge, Corpus Christi College, 162 **Ker 38 art.45**
Oxford, Bodleian, Bodley 343 **Ker 310 art.2**
Cambridge, Corpus Christi College, 303 **Ker 57 art.55**
London, British Museum, Cotton Vitellius C.V **Ker 220 art.35**
Cambridge, Trinity College, B.15.34 **Ker 86 art.26**
ed Thorpe 1844-6, II, 404-12
Extracts from this homily are found in MSS Cambridge, Corpus Christi College, 178,
and Oxford, Bodleian, Bodley 343, see **B.3.4.4**; and in MS Cambridge, Jesus College, 15,
see **B.1.2.24**

1.2.34
James and the Seven Sleepers

MS Cambridge, University Library, Gg.3.28 **Ker 15 arts.75, 76**
Oxford, Bodleian, Bodley 342 **Ker 309 art.57**
Cambridge, Corpus Christi College, 198 **Ker 48 art.58**
Oxford, Bodleian, Bodley 343 **Ker 310 art.59**
London, British Museum, Cotton Vitellius D.XVII **Ker 222 art.2**
Cambridge, University Library, Ii.1.33 **Ker 18 art.15**
London, British Museum, Cotton Vespasian D.XIV **Ker 209 art.12**
ed Thorpe 1844-6, II, 412-26; Warner 1917, 25-6 [Ker 209 art.12]
proposed ed. Masi, NM 71 [1970] 499

1.2.35
Twelfth Sunday after Pentecost

MS Cambridge, University Library, Gg.3.28 **Ker 15 art.77**
Oxford, Bodleian, Bodley 342 **Ker 309 art.58**
Cambridge, Corpus Christi College, 162 **Ker 38 art.47**
Oxford, Bodleian, Bodley 343 **Ker 310 art.19**
Cambridge, Corpus Christi College, 303 **Ker 57 art.57**
London, British Museum, Cotton Vespasian D.XIV **Ker 209 art.15**
Cambridge, Corpus Christi College, 178 [with 2 passages not in Thorpe] **Ker 41A art.10**
London, British Museum, Cotton Vitellius C.V [with a passage not in Thorpe]
Ker 220 art.44

Cambridge, Jesus College, 15 [binding leaves]   **Ker 74 art.3**
ed Thorpe 1844-6, II, 426-36; Warner 1917, 34-41 [Ker 209 art. 15] , see **B.1.4.22**
     For Ker 41A art.10 and 220 art.44, see B.1.4.27, and 1.4.31

1.2.36
Assumption of the Virgin
MS Cambridge, University Library, Gg.3. 28   **Ker 15 art.78**
     Oxford, Bodleian, Bodley 343   **Ker 310 art.20**
     London, British Museum, Cotton Vespasian D.XIV   **Ker 209 art.17**
     London, British Museum, Cotton Vitellius C.V   **Ker 220 art.48**
     Oxford, Bodleian, Junius 121   **Ker 338 art.35**
ed Thorpe 1844-6, II, 438-44; Warner 1917, 47-50 [Ker 209 art. 17]

1.2.37
First Sunday in September
MS Cambridge, University Library, Gg.3. 28   **Ker 15 art.79**
     Oxford, Bodleian, Bodley 343   **Ker 310 art.11**
     Cambridge, University Library, Ii.1.33   **Ker 18 art.30**
     London, British Museum, Cotton Vespasian D.XIV   **Ker 209 arts.23, 42**
ed Thorpe 1844-6, II, 446-60; Warner 1917, 65 and 123-9 [Ker 209 arts.23, 42]

1.2.38
Sixteenth Sunday after Pentecost
MS Cambridge, University Library, Gg.3. 28   **Ker 15 art.80**
     Oxford, Bodleian, Bodley 342   **Ker 309 art.59**
     Cambridge, Corpus Christi College, 162   **Ker 38 art.48**
     Oxford, Bodleian, Bodley 343   **Ker 310 art.4**
     Cambridge, Corpus Christi College, 303   **Ker 57 art.58**
     London, British Museum, Cotton Vitellius C.V [with a passage not in Thorpe]
     Ker 220 art.46
ed Thorpe 1844-6, II, 460-6
     For Ker 220 art.46, see B.1.4.28

1.2.39
De Maria
MS Cambridge, University Library, Gg.3. 28   **Ker 15 art.81**
     Oxford, Bodleian, Bodley 342   **Ker 309 art.60**
     Cambridge, Corpus Christi College, 162   **Ker 38 art.49**
     Cambridge, Corpus Christi College, 303   **Ker 57 art.59**
ed Thorpe 1844-6, II, 466

1.2.40
Matthew
MS Cambridge, University Library, Gg.3. 28   **Ker 15 art.82**
     Oxford, Bodleian, Bodley 343   **Ker 310 art.17**
     London, British Museum, Cotton Vitellius D.XVII   **Ker 222 art.15**
     Cambridge, University Library, Ii.1.33   **Ker 18 art.16**
     London, British Museum, Cotton Vespasian D.XIV   **Ker 209 art.21**

Cambridge, Corpus Christi College, 367 pt. II **Ker 63 art. 8**

ed Thorpe 1844-6, II, 468-80; Warner 1917, 59-61 [Ker 209 art. 21]
proposed ed. Masi, *NM* 71 [1970] 499

1.2.41
Simon and Jude

MS Cambridge, University Library, Gg. 3. 28 **Ker 15 art. 83**
London, British Museum, Cotton Vitellius D. XVII **Ker 222 art. 7**
Cambridge, University Library, Ii. 1. 33 **Ker 18 art. 17**

ed Thorpe 1844-6, II, 480-98
proposed ed. Masi, *NM* 71 [1970] 499

1.2.42
Martin

MS Cambridge, University Library, Gg. 3. 28 **Ker 15 art. 84**
Cambridge, Corpus Christi College, 198 **Ker 48 art. 56**
London, British Museum, Cotton Vitellius D. XVII **Ker 222 art. 17**

ed Thorpe 1844-6, II, 498-518; Masi 1969

1.2.43
Excusatio dictantis

MS Cambridge, University Library, Gg. 3. 28 **Ker 15 art. 85**
Oxford, Bodleian, Bodley 342 **Ker 309 art. 63**
Cambridge, Corpus Christi College, 198 **Ker 48 art. 57**

ed Thorpe 1844-6, II, 520

1.2.44
Apostle

MS Cambridge, University Library, Gg. 3. 28 **Ker 15 art. 86**
Oxford, Bodleian, Bodley 342 **Ker 309 art. 64**
Cambridge, Corpus Christi College, 303 **Ker 57 art. 35**
Oxford, Bodleian, Hatton 115 **Ker 332 arts. 21, 36**
Cambridge, Corpus Christi College, 421 **Ker 69 art. 2**

ed Thorpe 1844-6, II, 520-8

1.2.45
Apostles

MS Cambridge, University Library, Gg. 3. 28 **Ker 15 art. 87**
Oxford, Bodleian, Bodley 342 **Ker 309 art. 65**
Cambridge, Corpus Christi College, 303 **Ker 57 art. 36**
London, British Museum, Cotton Vitellius D. XVII **Ker 222 art. 39**
Oxford, Bodleian, Hatton 115 **Ker 332 art. 22**
Cambridge, Corpus Christi College, 190 **Ker 45B art. 18**

ed Thorpe 1844-6, II, 528-36

1.2.46
Martyrs

MS Cambridge, University Library, Gg. 3. 28 **Ker 15 art. 88**

Oxford, Bodleian, Bodley 342   **Ker 309 art.66**
Cambridge, Corpus Christi College, 198   **Ker 48 art.49**
Oxford, Bodleian, Bodley 343   **Ker 310 art.60**
Cambridge, Corpus Christi College, 303   **Ker 57 art.37**
Oxford, Bodleian, Hatton 115   **Ker 332 art.23**
Cambridge, Corpus Christi College, 421   **Ker 69 art.3**
ed   Thorpe 1844-6, II, 536-48

1.2.47
Confessor
MS   Cambridge, University Library, Gg.3.28   **Ker 15 art.89**
Oxford, Bodleian, Bodley 342   **Ker 309 art.67**
Cambridge, Corpus Christi College, 198   **Ker 48 art.50**
Oxford, Bodleian, Bodley 343   **Ker 310 art.62**
Cambridge, Corpus Christi College, 303   **Ker 57 art.38**
London, British Museum, Cotton Vitellius D.XVII   **Ker 222 art.40**
Oxford, Bodleian, Hatton 115   **Ker 332 art.24**
Cambridge, Corpus Christi College, 421   **Ker 69 art.4**
ed   Thorpe 1844-6, II, 548-62

1.2.48
Virgins
MS   Cambridge, University Library, Gg.3.28   **Ker 15 art.90**
Oxford, Bodleian, Bodley 342   **Ker 309 art.68**
Cambridge, Corpus Christi College, 198   **Ker 48 art.51**
Oxford, Bodleian, Bodley 343   **Ker 310 art.63**
Oxford, Bodleian, Hatton 115 [with a passage not in Thorpe]   **Ker 332 art.25**
Cambridge, Corpus Christi College, 178   **Ker 41A art.16**
Cambridge, Corpus Christi College, 421 [with a passage not in Thorpe]   **Ker 69 art.5**
Cambridge, University Library, Ii.4.6 [extract]   **Ker 21 art.28**
ed   Thorpe 1844-6, II, 562-74
For Ker 332 art.25 and 69 art.5, see B.1.4.29

1.2.49
Dedicatio ecclesiae
MS   Cambridge, University Library, Gg.3.28   **Ker 15 art.91**
Oxford, Bodleian, Bodley 342   **Ker 309 art.69**
Oxford, Bodleian, Bodley 343   **Ker 310 art.73**
London, British Museum, Cotton Vitellius D.XVII   **Ker 222 art.41**
Oxford, Bodleian, Hatton 115   **Ker 332 art.26**
London, Lambeth Palace, 489 [part of a catena]   **Ker 283 art.6**
ed   Thorpe 1844-6, II, 574-94

1.2.50
Oratio
MS   Cambridge, University Library, Gg.3.28   **Ker 15 art.92**
ed   Thorpe 1844-6, II, 594

1.3
Third Series of Homilies [Lives of Saints]
ed W.W. Skeat, *Ælfric's Lives of Saints,* EETS 76, 82, 94, 114, London 1881-1900, reprinted as 2 vols. 1966

1.3.1
English Preface
MS London, British Museum, Cotton Julius E.VII **Ker 162 art.2**
ed Skeat 1881-1900 [1966], I, 4-6

1.3.2
Nativity of Christ
MS London, British Museum, Cotton Julius E.VII **Ker 162 art.4**
Oxford, Bodleian, Bodley 343 **Ker 310 art.77**
London, British Museum, Cotton Otho C.I vol.2 **Ker 182 art.5**
ed Skeat 1881-1900 [1966], I, 10-24; A.O. Belfour, *Twelfth-century Homilies in Ms.
Bodley 343,* EETS 137, London 1909 [1962], 78-96 [Ker 310 art.77]
See B.1.5.1 and B.1.6.4

1.3.3
Saint Eugenia
MS London, British Museum, Cotton Julius E.VII **Ker 162 art.5**
London, British Museum, Cotton Otho B.X **Ker 177A art.9**
ed Skeat 1881-1900 [1966], I, 24-50

1.3.4
Saint Basil
MS London, British Museum, Cotton Julius E.VII **Ker 162 art.6**
London, British Museum, Cotton Otho B.X and Oxford, Bodleian, Rawlinson Q.e.20
Ker 177A art.3
London, British Museum, Cotton Vitellius D.XVII **Ker 222 art.43**
ed Skeat 1881-1900 [1966], I, 50-90; A.S. Napier, 'A Fragment of Ælfric's *Lives of Saints,*'
MLN 2 [1887] 377-80 [Ker 177A art.3]

1.3.5
Saints Julian and Basilissa
MS London, British Museum, Cotton Julius E.VII **Ker 162 art.7**
London, British Museum, Cotton Otho B.X **Ker 177A art.5**
ed Skeat 1881-1900 [1966], I, 90-114

1.3.6
Saint Sebastian
MS Cambridge, Corpus Christi College, 198 **Ker 48 art.60**
London, British Museum, Cotton Julius E.VII **Ker 162 art.8**
London, British Museum, Cotton Otho B.X **Ker 177A art.6**
London, British Museum, Cotton Vitellius D.XVII **Ker 222 art.13**
ed Skeat 1881-1900 [1966], I, 116-46

1.3.7
Saint Maur
MS London, British Museum, Cotton Julius E.VII **Ker 162 art.9**
     London, British Museum, Cotton Otho B.X [burnt]   **Ker 177A art.4**
ed Skeat 1881-1900 [1966], I, 148-68

1.3.8
Saint Agnes
MS London, British Museum, Cotton Julius E.VII **Ker 162 arts.10, 11**
     London, British Museum, Cotton Otho B.X **Ker 177A arts.7, 8**
     London, British Museum, Cotton Vitellius D.XVII [burnt]   **Ker 222 arts.47, 48**
     London, British Museum, Royal 8 C.VII **Ker 260**
ed Skeat 1881-1900 [1966], I, 170-94

1.3.9
Saint Agatha
MS London, British Museum, Cotton Julius E.VII **Ker 162 art.12**
     London, British Museum, Cotton Vitellius D.XVII [burnt]   **Ker 222 art.49**
     London, British Museum, Royal 8 C.VII **Ker 260**
ed Skeat 1881-1900 [1966], I, 194-208

1.3.10
Saint Lucy
MS London, British Museum, Cotton Julius E.VII **Ker 162 art.13**
     London, British Museum, Cotton Vitellius D.XVII [burnt]   **Ker 222 art.50**
ed Skeat 1881-1900 [1966], I, 210-8

1.3.11
Chair of Saint Peter
MS Cambridge, University Library, Ii.1.33 **Ker 18 art.6**
     London, British Museum, Cotton Julius E.VII **Ker 162 art.14**
     London, British Museum, Cotton Vitellius D.XVII [burnt]   **Ker 222 art.51**
     Oxford, Bodleian, Bodley 343 **Ker 310 art.22**
ed Skeat 1881-1900 [1966], I, 218-38

1.3.12
The Forty Soldiers [Quadraginta Milites]
MS London, British Museum, Cotton Julius E.VII **Ker 162 art.15**
ed Skeat 1881-1900 [1966], I, 238-60; J.T. Algeo, 'Ælfric's *The Forty Soldiers*: An
     Edition' [Florida diss.] *DA* 20 [1961] 4656

1.3.13
Ash-Wednesday
MS Cambridge, University Library, Ii.4.6 [extract]   **Ker 21 arts. 7, 28**
     Cambridge, Corpus Christi College, 162 **Ker 38 art.14**
     Cambridge, Corpus Christi College, 302 **Ker 56 art.17**
     Cambridge, Corpus Christi College, 303 **Ker 57 art.67**
     London, British Museum, Cotton Julius E.VII **Ker 162 art.16**

London, Lambeth Palace, 489 [extract]   **Ker 283 art. 5**
ed   Skeat 1881-1900 [1966], I, 260-82

1.3.14
The Prayer of Moses [De Oratione Moysi]
MS   Cambridge, University Library, Ii.4.6   **Ker 21 art. 15**
Cambridge, University Library, Ii.4.6 [extract]   **Ker 21 art. 28**
Cambridge, Corpus Christi College, 162   **Ker 38 art. 6**
Cambridge, Corpus Christi College, 178 [extract]   **Ker 41A art. 7**
Cambridge, Corpus Christi College, 303   **Ker 57 art. 68**
London, British Museum, Cotton Faustina A.IX   **Ker 153 art. 18**
London, British Museum, Cotton Julius E.VII   **Ker 162 art. 17**
London, Lambeth Palace, 489 [extract]   **Ker 283 art. 6**
Oxford, Bodleian, Hatton 114   **Ker 331 art. 47**
Oxford, Bodleian, Hatton 116 [extract]   **Ker 333 art. 19**
Oxford, Bodleian, Junius 121 [extract]   **Ker 338 art. 26**
ed   Skeat 1881-1900 [1966], I, 282-306

1.3.15
Saint George
MS   Cambridge, University Library, Ii.1.33   **Ker 18 art. 26**
London, British Museum, Cotton Julius E.VII   **Ker 162 art. 18**
London, British Museum, Cotton Otho B.X [burnt]   **Ker 177A art. 22**
London, British Museum, Cotton Vitellius D.XVII   **Ker 222 art. 30**
ed   Skeat 1881-1900 [1966], I, 306-18

1.3.16
Saint Mark
MS   Cambridge, University Library, Ii.1.33   **Ker 18 art. 19**
Cambridge, Corpus Christi College, 198   **Ker 48 art. 59**
London, British Museum, Cotton Julius E.VII   **Ker 162 arts. 19, 20**
London, British Museum, Cotton Vitellius D.XVII   **Ker 222 arts. 8, 9**
ed   Skeat 1881-1900 [1966], I, 320-36

1.3.17
Memory of the Saints
MS   Cambridge, University Library, Ii.1.33   **Ker 18 art. 20**
Cambridge, Corpus Christi College, 178 [extract]   **Ker 41A art. 7**
Cambridge, Corpus Christi College, 303   **Ker 57 art. 62**
London, British Museum, Cotton Julius E.VII   **Ker 162 art. 21**
London, British Museum, Cotton Vespasian D.XIV [extracts]   **Ker 209 arts. 7, 8**
Oxford, Bodleian, Hatton 116   **Ker 333 art. 19**
London, Lambeth Palace, 487 f.37v [extract]
ed   Skeat 1881-1900 [1966], I, 336-62; Warner 1917, 16-9 [Ker 209 arts. 7, 8] ;
R. Morris, *Old English Homilies, First Series,* EETS 29, 34, London 1868, 296-304
[Ker 333 art. 19]
See also B.1.6.2

1.3.18
On Auguries
MS Cambridge, University Library, Ii.1.33   **Ker 18 art.38**
Cambridge, Corpus Christi College, 178   **Ker 41A art.8**
Cambridge, Corpus Christi College, 302   **Ker 56 art.4**
Cambridge, Corpus Christi College, 303   **Ker 57 art.47**
Cambridge, Corpus Christi College, 419   **Ker 68 art.12**
London, British Museum, Cotton Julius E.VII   **Ker 162 art.22**
Oxford, Bodleian, Hatton 115   **Ker 332 art.5**
Oxford, Bodleian, Hatton 116   **Ker 333 art.20**
ed Skeat 1881-1900 [1966], I, 364-82
For Ker 41A art.8 and 333 art.20, see B.1.4.30

1.3.19
From the Book of Kings
MS London, British Museum, Cotton Julius E.VII   **Ker 162 art.23**
Oxford, Bodleian, Hatton 115   **Ker 332 art.33**
ed Skeat 1881-1900 [1966], I, 384-412

1.3.20
Passion of Saint Alban [plus pendant on Acitofel]
MS Cambridge, University Library, Ii.1.33   **Ker 18 arts.27, 28**
Cambridge, Corpus Christi College, 303   **Ker 57 art.70**
London, British Museum, Cotton Julius E.VII   **Ker 162 arts.24, 25**
London, British Museum, Cotton Vitellius D.XVII [burnt]   **Ker 222 arts.52, 53**
London, Lambeth Palace, 489 [extract]   **Ker 283 art.6**
Oxford, Bodleian, Hatton 115   **Ker 332 art.20**
ed Skeat 1881-1900 [1966], I, 414-30

1.3.21
Saint Æthelthryth
MS Cambridge, University Library, Ii.1.33   **Ker 18 art.4**
London, British Museum, Cotton Julius E.VII   **Ker 162 art.26**
London, British Museum, Cotton Otho B.X   **Ker 177A art.23**
London, British Museum, Cotton Vitellius D.XVII [burnt]   **Ker 222 art.54**
ed Skeat 1881-1900 [1966], I, 432-40

1.3.22
Saint Swithun
MS Cambridge, Corpus Christi College, 178 [extract]   **Ker 41A art.8**
Gloucester, Cathedral, 35   **Ker 117 art.1**
London, British Museum, Cotton Julius E.VII   **Ker 162 arts.27, 28**
London, British Museum, Cotton Otho B.X   **Ker 177A art.20**
Oxford, Bodleian, Hatton 116 [extract]   **Ker 333 art.20**
ed Skeat 1881-1900 [1966], I, 440-72; G.I. Needham, *Ælfric: Lives of Three English Saints,* MOEL, London 1966, 60-81

1.3.23
Saint Apollinaris
MS Cambridge, Queens' College, [Horne] 75   **Ker 81 art. 1**
    London, British Museum, Cotton Julius E. VII   **Ker 162 art. 29**
    London, British Museum, Cotton Vitellius D. XVII   **Ker 222 art. 26**
ed Skeat 1881-1900 [1966], I, 472-86

The Seven Sleepers, *Saint Mary of Egypt*, *Saint Eustace*, and *Saint Euphrosyne* homilies are not thought to be by Ælfric: see P. Clemoes, 'The Chronology of Ælfric's Works,' in P. Clemoes, ed., *The Anglo-Saxons: Studies ... presented to Bruce Dickins,* London 1959, 219, and John C. Pope, *Homilies of Ælfric: A Supplementary Collection,* EETS 259, 260, London 1967-8, I, 143 f. 6. They are listed as anonymous homilies **B.3.3.7, 8, 23,** and **34.**

1.3.24
Saints Abdon and Sennes
MS Cambridge, University Library, Ii. 1.33   **Ker 18 art. 37**
    Cambridge, Queens' College, [Horne] 75   **Ker 81 art. 2**
    London, British Museum, Cotton Julius E. VII   **Ker 162 arts. 32, 33**
    London, British Museum, Cotton Vitellius D. XVII [burnt]   **Ker 222 arts. 27, 28**
ed Skeat 1881-1900 [1966], II, 54-66

1.3.25
The Maccabees
MS Cambridge, University Library, Ii. 1.33   **Ker 18 arts. 35, 36**
    Cambridge, Corpus Christi College, 178   **Ker 41A art. 14**
    Cambridge, Corpus Christi College, 198   **Ker 48 art. 52**
    Cambridge, Corpus Christi College, 303   **Ker 57 arts. 71, 72**
    Cambridge, Queens' College, [Horne] 75   **Ker 81 art. 3**
    London, British Museum, Cotton Julius E. VII   **Ker 162 arts. 34, 35, 36**
    London, British Museum, Cotton Vitellius D. XVII [art. 45 remains in part; art. 46 was burnt]   **Ker 222 arts. 45, 46**
    Oxford, Bodleian, Hatton 115   **Ker 332 art. 11**
ed Skeat 1881-1900 [1966], II, 66-124

1.3.26
Saint Oswald
MS Cambridge, University Library, Ii. 1.33   **Ker 18 art. 31**
    London, British Museum, Cotton Julius E. VII   **Ker 162 art. 37**
    London, British Museum, Cotton Vitellius D. XVII   **Ker 222 art. 31**
ed Skeat 1881-1900 [1966], II, 124-43; Needham 1966, 27-42

1.3.27
The Exaltation of the Holy Cross
MS Cambridge, University Library, Ii. 1.33   **Ker 18 art. 39**
    Cambridge, Corpus Christi College, 367 pt. II   **Ker 63 art. 7**
    London, British Museum, Cotton Julius E. VII   **Ker 162 art. 38**
    London, British Museum, Cotton Vitellius D. XVII   **Ker 222 art. 37**
ed Skeat 1881-1900 [1966], II, 144-58

1.3.28
Saint Maurice and his Companions
MS London, British Museum, Cotton Julius E.VII **Ker 162 art.39**
    London, British Museum, Cotton Vitellius D.XVII [burnt] **Ker 222 art.33**
ed Skeat 1881-1900 [1966], II, 158-68

1.3.29
Passion of Saint Denis and his Companions
MS Cambridge, University Library, Ii.1.33 **Ker 18 art.32**
    London, British Museum, Cotton Julius E.VII **Ker 162 art.40**
    London, British Museum, Cotton Vitellius D.XVII [burnt] **Ker 222 art.34**
ed Skeat 1881-1900 [1966], II, 168-90

1.3.30
Saint Martin
MS London, British Museum, Cotton Caligula A.XIV **Ker 138 art.1**
    London, British Museum, Cotton Julius E.VII **Ker 162 art.42**
    Oxford, Bodleian, Bodley 343 **Ker 310 art.18**
ed Skeat 1881-1900 [1966], II, 218-312

1.3.31
Passion of Saint Edmund
MS Cambridge, University Library, Ii.1.33 **Ker 18 art.29**
    London, British Museum, Cotton Julius E.VII **Ker 162 art.43**
    London, British Museum, Cotton Otho B.X **Ker 177A art.21**
    London, British Museum, Cotton Vitellius D.XVII **Ker 222 art.42**
    Oxford, Bodleian, Bodley 343 **Ker 310 art.31**
ed Skeat 1881-1900 [1966], II, 314-34; Needham 1966, 43-59

1.3.32
Passion of Saint Cecilia
MS London, British Museum, Cotton Julius E.VII **Ker 162 art.45**
    London, British Museum, Cotton Vitellius D.XVII **Ker 222 art.25**
ed Skeat 1881-1900 [1966], II, 356-76

1.3.33
Passion of Saint Chrysanthus and his Wife Daria
MS London, British Museum, Cotton Julius E.VII **Ker 162 art.46**
ed Skeat 1881-1900 [1966], II, 378-98

1.3.34
Passion of Saint Thomas the Apostle
MS Cambridge, University Library, Ii.1.33 **Ker 18 art.18**
    London, British Museum, Cotton Caligula A.XIV **Ker 138 art.2**
    London, British Museum, Cotton Julius E.VII **Ker 162 art.47**
    London, British Museum, Cotton Vitellius D.XVII [burnt] **Ker 222 art.32**
ed Skeat 1881-1900 [1966], II, 398-424

1.3.35
The Martyrdom of Saint Vincent
MS Cambridge, University Library, Ii.1.33 **Ker 18 art.23**
ed Skeat 1881-1900 [1966], II, 426-42;
See **B.1.5.9** and Clemoes **1959, 236**

1.4
Homilies of Ælfric
ed J.C.Pope, *Homilies of Ælfric: A Supplementary Collection,* 2 vols., EETS 259, 260,
London 1967-8

1.4.1
Nativitas Domini
MS London, British Museum, Cotton Vitellius C.V **Ker 220 art.4**
ed Pope 1967-8, I, 196-216

1.4.2
Feria VI in Prima Ebdomada Quadragesimae
MS Cambridge, Corpus Christi College, 162 **Ker 38 art.17**
London, British Museum, Cotton Vitellius C.V **Ker 220 art.63**
ed Pope 1967-8, I, 230-42

1.4.3
Feria VI in Secunda Ebdomada Quadragesimae
MS Cambridge, Corpus Christi College, 162 **Ker 38 art.20**
London, British Museum, Cotton Vitellius C.V **Ker 220 art.64**
ed Pope 1967-8, I, 248-56

1.4.4
Dominica III in Quadragesima
MS Cambridge, Corpus Christi College, 303 **Ker 57 art.9**
Cambridge, Corpus Christi College, 198 **Ker 48 art.63**
Cambridge, Corpus Christi College, 162 [rubric only] **Ker 38 art.21**
London, British Museum, Cotton Vespasian D.XIV **Ker 209 art.20**
London, British Museum, Cotton Vitellius C.V **Ker 220 art.16**
Cambridge, University Library, Ii.4.6 **Ker 21 art.11**
London, British Museum, Cotton Faustina A.IX **Ker 153 art.14**
Cambridge, Corpus Christi College, 302 **Ker 56 art.21**
Cambridge, Corpus Christi College, 188 **Ker 43 art.12**
Oxford, Bodleian, Hatton 114 **Ker 331 art.45**
ed Pope 1967-8, I, 264-80; Warner 1917, 58-9 [Ker 209 art.20]

1.4.5
Feria VI in Tert[i]a Ebdomada Quadragesimae
MS Cambridge, Corpus Christi College, 162 **Ker 38 art.22**
London, British Museum, Cotton Vitellius C.V **Ker 220 art.65**
ed Pope 1967-8, I, 288-300

1.4.6
Feria VI in Quarta Ebdomada Quadragesimae
MS Oxford, Bodleian, Bodley 343 **Ker 310 art. 83**
    Cambridge, Corpus Christi College, 303 **Ker 57 art. 11**
    Cambridge, Corpus Christi College, 162 **Ker 38 art. 24**
    London, British Museum, Cotton Vitellius C.V **Ker 220 art. 66**
    Oxford, Bodleian, Hatton 115 **Ker 332 art. 12**
    Oxford, Bodleian, Hatton 116 **Ker 333 art. 25**
ed Pope 1967-8, I, 311-29; Belfour 1909, 136-40 [Ker 310 art. 83]
    See B.1.5.3

1.4.7
Dominica IV Post Pascha
MS Cambridge, University Library, Ii.4.6 **Ker 21 art. 25**
    London, British Museum, Cotton Faustina A.IX **Ker 153 art. 32**
    Cambridge, Trinity College, B.15.34 **Ker 86 art. 7**
ed Pope 1967-8, I, 340-50

1.4.8
Dominica V Post Pascha
MS Oxford, Bodleian, Bodley 343 **Ker 310 art. 8**
    London, British Museum, Cotton Cleopatra B. XIII **Ker 144 art. 8**
    Cambridge, University Library, Ii.4.6 **Ker 21 art. 26**
    London, British Museum, Cotton Faustina A.IX **Ker 153 art. 33**
    Cambridge, Trinity College, B.15.34 **Ker 86 art. 8**
ed Pope 1967-8, I, 357-68; Belfour 1909, 12-22 [Ker 310 art. 8]

1.4.9
Dominica Post Ascensionem Domini
MS Cambridge, University Library, Ii.4.6 **Ker 21 art. 32**
    London, British Museum, Cotton Faustina A.IX **Ker 153 art. 36**
    Oxford, Bodleian, Junius 121 **Ker 338 art. 29**
    Cambridge, Trinity College, B.15.34 **Ker 86 art. 13**
ed Pope 1967-8, I, 378-89

1.4.10
Dominica Pentecosten
MS Cambridge, University Library, Ii.4.6 **Ker 21 art. 34**
    London, British Museum, Cotton Faustina A.IX **Ker 153 art. 38**
    Cambridge, Trinity College, B.15.34 **Ker 86 art. 15**
ed Pope 1967-8, I, 396-405

1.4.11
Sermo ad Populum, in Octavis Pentecosten Dicendus
MS Cambridge, Corpus Christi College, 303 **Ker 57 art. 41**
    Cambridge, University Library, Ii.4.6 **Ker 21 art. 27**
    Cambridge, Corpus Christi College, 188 **Ker 43 art. 23**

Cambridge, Corpus Christi College, 178   **Ker 41A art.6**
Oxford, Bodleian, Hatton 113   **Ker 331 art.32**
Cambridge, Trinity College, B.15.34   **Ker 86 art.17**
Cambridge, Corpus Christi College, 421   **Ker 69 art.6**
Cambridge, Jesus College, 15 [binding leaves]   **Ker 74 art.1**
ed   Pope 1967-8, I, 415-47

1.4.12
De Sancta Trinitate et de Festis Diebus Per Annum
MS   London, British Museum, Cotton Vitellius C.V   **Ker 220 art.1**
ed   Pope 1967-8, I, 463-72
See also B.1.6.1 and B.1.8.6

1.4.13
Dominica I Post Pentecosten
MS   Oxford, Bodleian, Bodley 343   **Ker 310 art.7**
Cambridge, University Library, Ii.4.6   **Ker 21 art.35**
Cambridge, Trinity College, B.15.34   **Ker 86 art.18**
ed   Pope 1967-8, I, 479-89; Belfour 1909, 2-12 [Ker 310 art.7]

1.4.14
Dominica V Post Pentecosten
MS   London, British Museum, Cotton Vitellius C.V   **Ker 220 art.31**
Cambridge, Trinity College, B.15.34   **Ker 86 art.22**
ed   Pope 1967-8, II, 497-507

1.4.15
Dominica VI Post Pentecosten
MS   London, British Museum, Cotton Vitellius C.V   **Ker 220 art.32**
Cambridge, Trinity College, B.15.34   **Ker 86 art.23**
ed   Pope 1967-8, II, 515-25

1.4.16
Dominica VII Post Pentecosten
MS   London, British Museum, Cotton Vitellius C.V   **Ker 220 art.33**
Cambridge, Trinity College, B.15.34   **Ker 86 art.24**
ed   Pope 1967-8, II, 531-41

1.4.17
Dominica X Post Pentecosten
MS   London, British Museum, Cotton Vitellius C.V   **Ker 220 art.36**
Cambridge, Trinity College, B.15.34   **Ker 86 art.27**
ed   Pope 1967-8, II, 547-59

1.4.18
Dominica XII Post Octavas Pentecosten
MS   London, British Museum, Cotton Vitellius C.V   **Ker 220 art.45**
ed   Pope 1967-8, II, 567-80
See B.1.2.30

1.4.19
Sermo de Die Iudicii
MS Oxford, Bodleian, Hatton 115   **Ker 332 art.4**
      Cambridge, Corpus Christi College, 188   **Ker 43 art.46**
      Cambridge, Corpus Christi College, 178   **Ker 41A art.9**
ed   Pope 1967-8, II, 590-609; W.J. Swan, '*Sermo de die iudicii*: An Ælfrician Homily'
      [Florida diss.]*DA* 29 [1968] 1221A

1.4.20
De Doctrina Apostolica
MS Cambridge, Corpus Christi College, 303   **Ker 57 art.64**
      London, British Museum, Cotton Faustina A.IX   **Ker 153 art.31**
      Oxford, Bodleian, Hatton 115   **Ker 332 art.6**
      Cambridge, Corpus Christi College, 419   **Ker 68 art.15**
ed   Pope 1967-8, II, 622-35; W. Braekman, 'Ælfric's Old English Homily *De Doctrina
      Apostolica*: An Edition,' *SGG* 5 [1963] 141-73

1.4.21
De Populo Israhel
MS Oxford, Bodleian, Hatton 115   **Ker 332 art.29**
      London, British Museum, Cotton Otho C.I vol.2   **Ker 182 art.7**
ed   Pope 1967-8, II, 641-60

1.4.22
De Falsis Diis
MS Cambridge, Corpus Christi College, 303   **Ker 57 art.65**
      London, British Museum, Cotton Vespasian D.XIV   **Ker 209 art.15**
      Cambridge, University Library, Ii.1.33   **Ker 18 art.34**
      Cambridge, Corpus Christi College, 178   **Ker 41A art.18**
      Oxford, Bodleian, Hatton 116   **Ker 333 art.21**
      Oxford, Bodleian, Hatton 113   **Ker 331 art.16**
      London, British Museum, Cotton Julius E.VII   **Ker 162 art.49**
      Paris, Bibliothèque Nationale, Lat. 7585   **Ker 366 art.a**
ed   Pope 1967-8, II, 676-712; Warner 1917, 34-41 [Ker 209 art.15]
      See B.2.2.10 for Wulfstan revision

1.4.23
Wyrdwriteras us secgað ... [excerpt]
MS Oxford, Bodleian, Hatton 115   **Ker 332 art.17**
ed   Pope 1967-8, II, 728-32; W. Braekman, '*Wyrdwriteras*: An Unpublished Ælfrician Text
      in Manuscript Hatton 115,' *RBPH* 44 [1966] 959-70

1.4.24
Addition to Catholic Homilies II no.20: Sanctorum Alexandri ...
MS Oxford, Bodleian, Hatton 114   **Ker 331 art.84**
ed   Pope 1967-8, II, 737-46
      See B.1.2.23

1.4.25
Addition to Catholic Homilies II no.21: Se þe gelome sweraδ
MS Oxford, Bodleian, Hatton 115   **Ker 332 art.7**
    Cambridge, Jesus College, 15 [binding leaves]   **Ker 74 art.2**
ed Pope 1967-8, II, 752
    See B.1.2.24

1.4.26
Three Additions to Catholic Homilies II no.25: In Letania Maiore, Feria IV
MS Cambridge, Corpus Christi College, 178   **Ker 41A art.30**
    Cambridge, Jesus College, 15 [binding leaves]   **Ker 74 art.2**
ed Pope 1967-8, II, 755-7
    See B.1.2.28

1.4.27
Addition to Catholic Homilies II no.33: Dominica XII Post Pentecosten
MS London, British Museum, Cotton Vitellius C.V   **Ker 220 art.44**
    Cambridge, Corpus Christi College, 178   **Ker 41A art.10**
ed Pope 1967-8, II, 762-9
    See B.1.2.35

1.4.28
Addition to Catholic Homilies II no.36: Dominica XVI Post Pentecosten
MS London, British Museum, Cotton Vitellius C.V   **Ker 220 art.46**
ed Pope 1967-8, II, 775-9
    See B.1.2.38

1.4.29
Addition to Catholic Homilies II no.44: In Natale Sanctarum Virginum
MS Oxford, Bodleian, Hatton 115   **Ker 332 art.25**
    Cambridge, Corpus Christi College, 421   **Ker 69 art.5**
ed Pope 1967-8, II, 784
    See B.1.2.48

1.4.30
Addition to Lives of Saints no.17: De Auguriis
MS Cambridge, Corpus Christi College, 178   **Ker 41A art.8**
    Oxford, Bodleian, Hatton 116   **Ker 333 art.20**
    London, British Museum, Cotton Julius E.VII   **Ker 162 art.28**
ed Pope 1967-8, II, 790-6
    See B.1.3.18

1.4.31
Passages from De Virginitate
MS Cambridge, Corpus Christi College, 178   **Ker 41A art.10**
    Cambridge, Corpus Christi College, 419   **Ker 68 art.15**
ed Pope 1967-8, II, 804-8
    See B.1.2.35

1.5
Remaining Homilies by Ælfric

1.5.1
Christmas Day
MS Oxford, Bodleian, Bodley 343   **Ker 310 art. 77**
ed Belfour 1909, 78-96
    See B.1.3.2

1.5.2
Wednesday in the Fourth Week of Lent [Secundum Iohannem]
MS Oxford, Bodleian, Bodley 343   **Ker 310 art. 54**
ed Belfour 1909, 58-74
    proposed ed. Michael Williams, Liverpool

1.5.3
Friday in the Fourth Week of Lent
MS Oxford, Bodleian, Bodley 343   **Ker 310 art. 83**
ed Belfour 1909, 136-40
    See B.1.4.6

1.5.4
Homily for Friday after the Fifth Sunday in Lent
MS Cambridge, Corpus Christi College, 162   **Ker 38 art. 26**
    Cambridge, Corpus Christi College, 302   **Ker 56 art. 24**
    London, British Museum, Cotton Faustina A. IX   **Ker 153 art. 20**
    [London, British Museum, Cotton Vitellius C. V, missing   **Ker 220**]
ed B. Assmann, *Angelsächsische Homilien und Heiligenleben,* Bib. ags. Prosa 3, Kassel
    1889, reprinted with introduction by P. Clemoes, Darmstadt 1964, 65-72

1.5.5
Homily for the Third Sunday after Easter
MS Cambridge, Trinity College, B. 15.34   **Ker 86 art. 6**
ed Assmann 1889, 73-80

1.5.6
Twenty-Second Sunday after Pentecost
MS Oxford, Bodleian, Bodley 343   **Ker 310 art. 9**
ed Belfour 1909, 22-30
    proposed ed. Michael Williams, Liverpool

1.5.7
Twenty-Third Sunday after Pentecost
MS Oxford, Bodleian, Bodley 343   **Ker 310 art. 10**
ed Belfour 1909, 30-40
    proposed ed. Michael Williams, Liverpool

1.5.8
Homily for the Nativity of the Blessed Virgin Mary

MS Cambridge, Corpus Christi College, 188 **Ker 43 art. 35**
Cambridge, Corpus Christi College, 303 **Ker 57 art. 27**
Oxford, Bodleian, Hatton 116 **Ker 333 art. 10**
London, British Museum, Cotton Vitellius C.V **Ker 220 art. 49**
ed Assmann 1889, 24-48

1.5.9
On a Martyr's Day
MS Oxford, Bodleian, Bodley 343 **Ker 310 art. 61**
ed Belfour 1909, 74-6; Clemoes 1959, 236
proposed ed. Michael Williams, Liverpool
See B.1.3.35

1.5.10
Assumption of the Virgin [De Sancta Virginitate, vel de tribus ordinibus castitatis]
MS London, British Museum, Cotton Vitellius C.V **Ker 220 art. 49**
See B.1.5.8 and B.1.8.5

1.5.11
Homily for the Common of a Confessor
MS Cambridge, Corpus Christi College, 188 **Ker 43 art. 45**
Cambridge, Corpus Christi College, 178 **Ker 41A art. 11**
Oxford, Bodleian, Hatton 114 **Ker 331 art. 76**
Oxford, Bodleian, Hatton 116 **Ker 333 art. 16**
Oxford, Bodleian, Bodley 343 **Ker 310 art. 84**
London, British Museum, Cotton Vitellius D.XVII **Ker 222 art. 38**
Kansas University, Y 104 [originally a leaf from Oxford, Bodleian, Hatton 115]
See B. Colgrave and A. Hyde, 'Two Recently Discovered Leaves from Old English
Manuscripts,' *Speculum* 37 [1962] 60-78
ed Assmann 1889, 49-64

1.5.12
Dedication of a Church
MS Paris, Bibliothèque Nationale, Lat. 943 **Ker 364 art. a**
London, Lambeth Palace, 489 **Ker 283 art. 8**
Oxford, Bodleian, Hatton 114 **Ker 331 art. 77**
ed R. Brotanek, *Texte und Untersuchungen zur altenglischen Literatur und Kirchen-
geschichte,* Halle 1913, 3-15

1.5.13
Hexameron
MS Oxford, Bodleian, Hatton 115 **Ker 332 art. 1**
Oxford, Bodleian, Hatton 116 **Ker 333 art. 17**
Cambridge, Corpus Christi College, 178 [162] **Ker 41A art. 2**
Cambridge, Corpus Christi College, 188 **Ker 43 art. 1**
Cambridge, Corpus Christi College, 302 **Ker 56 art. 1**
London, British Museum, Cotton Otho B.X **Ker 177 art. 2**
London, British Museum, Cotton Otho C.I **Ker 182 art. 5**
ed S.J. Crawford, *Exameron Anglice or The Old English Hexameron,* Bib. ags. Prosa 10,

Hamburg 1921, reprinted Darmstadt 1968
proposed ed. G.B. Niemann, Toronto, *NM* 70 [1969] 519
For Ker 182 art.5, see B.1.6.4

1.5.14
Esther
MS Oxford, Bodleian, Laud Misc. 381 [17th c transcript]   **Ker 410**
ed Assmann 1889, 92-101

1.5.15
Judith
MS Cambridge, Corpus Christi College, 303   **Ker 57 art.73**
London, British Museum, Cotton Otho B.X ff.29-30   **Ker 178 art.1**
ed Assmann 1889, 102-16

1.6
Tracts

1.6.1
Interrogationes Sigewulfi in Genesin
MS Cambridge, Corpus Christi College, 178 [162]   **Ker 41A art.3**
Cambridge, Corpus Christi College, 303   **Ker 57 art.66**
London, British Museum, Cotton Julius E.VII   **Ker 162 art.48**
London, British Museum, Harley 3271   **Ker 239 art.7**
Oxford, Bodleian, Hatton 114   **Ker 331 art.38**
Oxford, Bodleian, Hatton 115   **Ker 332 art.32**
Oxford, Bodleian, Hatton 116   **Ker 333 art.18**
d G.E. MacLean, 'Ælfric's Version of *Alcuini Interrogationes Sigeuulfi in Genesin,*'
Anglia 7 [1884] 1-59
For Ker 239 art.7, see B.24.12.3; see also B.1.4.12

1.6.2
De Duodecim Abusivis
S Cambridge, Corpus Christi College, 178   **Ker 41A art.7**
Cambridge, Corpus Christi College, 303   **Ker 57 art.63**
London, British Museum, Cotton Vespasian D.XIV   **Ker 209 arts.6, 7, 8**
Oxford, Bodleian, Hatton 115   **Ker 332 art.31**
Oxford, Bodleian, Hatton 116   **Ker 333 art.19**
London, Lambeth Palace, 487 f.37v
d Morris 1868, 296-304; Warner 1917, 11-9 [Ker 209 arts.6, 7, 8]
proposed eds. Jacqueline A. Yerbury, London, *NM* 70 [1969] 519; Michael Williams,
Liverpool
See also B.1.3.17

1.6.3
De Septiformi Spiritu [Be þam halgan gaste]
S Cambridge, Trinity College, B.15.34   **Ker 86 art.16**
London, British Museum, Cotton Faustina A.IX   **Ker 153 art.31**

London, British Museum, Cotton Tiberius C.VI **Ker 199 art.b**
London, British Museum, Harley 3271 **Ker 239 art.20**
Oxford, Bodleian, Bodley 343 **Ker 310 art.69**
Oxford, Bodleian, Hatton 115 **Ker 332 art.16**
Oxford, Bodleian, Hatton 116 **Ker 333 art.22**
ed Napier 1883 [1967], 56-60; H. Logeman, 'Anglo-Saxonica Minora,' *Anglia* 11 [1889]
107-10 [Ker 199 art.b]
See Wulfstan's version **B.2.2.6**

1.6.4
De Creatore et Creatura
MS London, British Museum, Cotton Otho C.I vol.2 [additions to Crawford's text of the
Hexameron] **Ker 182 art.5**
ed Clemoes 1959, 214 n.2
See B.1.3.2, 1.5.13

1.6.5
De Sex Etatibus Mundi
MS London, British Museum, Cotton Otho C.I vol.2 **Ker 182 art.6**
proposed ed. P. Clemoes, Clemoes 1959, 214 n.2

1.6.6
De cogitatione [portion]
See B.3.4.52 and Pope 1967-8, I, 55

1.6.7
De infantibus
See B.3.4.51 and Pope 1967-8, I, 55-6

1.7
Non Liturgical Old Testament Narrative Pieces

The Old English Heptateuch
See B.8.1 for complete listing. For discussion of the Ælfrician parts of the translation,
see Clemoes 1959, 218, and Pope 1967-8, I, 143. The sections they accept are Genesis
1-3, 6-9, 12-4; 22; Numbers 13-31; Joshua 1:16 to 11, 21-24; Judges.

1.8
Letters

1.8.1
Letter to Wulfsige
MS Cambridge, University Library, Gg.3.28 **Ker 15 art.97**
Cambridge, Corpus Christi College, 190 **Ker 45B art.17**
Oxford, Bodleian, Junius 121 **Ker 338 art.26**
ed B. Fehr, *Die Hirtenbriefe Ælfrics,* Bib. ags. Prosa 9, Hamburg 1914, reprinted with
supplement by P. Clemoes, Darmstadt 1966, 1-34 [corrections, 267]

1.8.2
First Old English Letter for Wulfstan
MS   Cambridge, Corpus Christi College, 190   **Ker 45B art. 2**
Cambridge, Corpus Christi College, 201   **Ker 49B art. 17**
Oxford, Bodleian, Bodley 343   **Ker 310 art. 67**
London, British Museum, Cotton Vespasian D. XIV [extract]   **Ker 209 art. 25**
ed   Fehr 1914 [1966], 68-145 [corrections, 269]; Warner 1917, 65-6 [Ker 209 art. 25]

1.8.3
Second Old English Letter for Wulfstan
MS   Cambridge, Corpus Christi College, 190   **Ker 45B art. 3**
Oxford, Bodleian, Junius 121   **Ker 338 art. 27**
Oxford, Bodleian, Bodley 343   **Ker 310 art. 68**
London, British Museum, Cotton Tiberius A. III   **Ker 186 art. 29**
London, British Museum, Cotton Vespasian D. XIV [extract]   **Ker 209 art. 5**
ed   Fehr 1914 [1966], 146-221; Warner 1917, 9-11 [Ker 209 art. 5]

1.8.4
Letter to Sigeweard ['On the Old and New Testament']
MS   London, British Museum, Cotton Vitellius C. V [extract]   **Ker 220 art. 7**
London, British Museum, Harley 3271 [extracts]   **Ker 239 arts. 21, 22**
Oxford, Bodleian, Bodley 343   **Ker 310 art. 65**
Oxford, Bodleian, Laud Misc. 509 and London, British Museum, Cotton Vespasian
D. XXI ff. 18-40   **Ker 344 art. 4**
ed   S.J. Crawford, *The Old English Version of the Heptateuch*, EETS 160, London 1922,
reprinted with additions by N.R. Ker 1969, 15-75; M.I. Mann, 'Ælfric's *De Veteri
Testamento et Novo*' [Birmingham MA thesis] *Index* 13 [1962-3] no. 153; Assmann
1889, 81-91 [Ker 310 art. 65]

1.8.5
Letter to Sigefyrth
MS   London, British Museum, Cotton Vespasian D. XIV   **Ker 209 art. 2**
London, British Museum, Cotton Faustina A. IX   **Ker 153 art. 3**
Cambridge, Corpus Christi College, 302   **Ker 56 art. 9**
London, British Museum, Cotton Vitellius C. V   **Ker 220 art. 49**
Cambridge, Corpus Christi College, 419   **Ker 68 art. 15**
ed   Assmann 1889, 13-23; Warner 1917, 3 [Ker 209 art. 2]
See B.1.5.10 [Ker 220 art. 49]; 1.4.31 [Ker 68 art. 15]

1.8.6
Letter to Wulfgeat
MS   Oxford, Bodleian, Hatton 115   **Ker 332 art. 27**
Oxford, Bodleian, Junius 121   **Ker 338 art. 28**
Oxford, Bodleian, Laud Misc. 509 and London, British Museum, Cotton Vespasian
D. XXI ff. 18-40   **Ker 344 art. 3**
London, British Museum, Cotton Vitellius C. V ff. 1r and 4-5v; also 2-3r   **Ker 220 art. 1**
ed   Assmann 1889, 1-12; Pope 1967-8, I, 463-5 [Ker 220 art. 1]
See B.1.4.12

1.8.7
De Sanguine [an excerpt]

MS Oxford, Bodleian, Hatton 115 **Ker 332 art.15**
Cambridge, Corpus Christi College, 178 **Ker 41A art.13**
Oxford, Bodleian, Hatton 116 **Ker 333 art.23**

ed F. Kluge, 'Fragment eines angelsächsischen Briefes,' *Englische Studien* 8 [1885] 62-3

1.9
Other Texts

1.9.1
Grammar

MS Cambridge, University Library, Hh.1.10 **Ker 17**
Cambridge, Corpus Christi College, 449 **Ker 71**
Cambridge, Trinity College, R.9.17 **Ker 89 art.1**
Durham, Cathedral, B.III.32 **Ker 107B**
London, British Museum, Cotton Faustina A.X **Ker 154A art.1**
London, British Museum, Cotton Julius A.II **Ker 158**
London, British Museum, Harley 107 **Ker 227 art.1**
London, British Museum, Harley 3271 **Ker 239 art.5**
London, British Museum, Harley 5915 ff.8-9 [fragments] **Ker 242**
Bloomington, Indiana, Lilly Add. 1000 **Ker 384**
London, British Museum, Royal 12 G.XII ff.2-9 and Oxford, All Souls College, 38 ff.1-12 **Ker 265**
London, British Museum, Royal 15 B.XXII **Ker 269**
Oxford, St John's College, 154 **Ker 362 art.1**
Paris, Bibliothèque Nationale, Anglais 67 **Ker 363**
Worcester, Cathedral, F.174 **Ker 398 art.1**
London, British Museum, Cotton Vitellius C.IX ff.213-5 [16th c transcript] **Ker 406**

ed J. Zupitza, *Ælfrics Grammatik und Glossar,* Sammlung englischer Denkmäler 1, Berlin 1880, reprinted with introduction by H. Gneuss 1966, 1-296

1.9.2
Glossary

MS Cambridge, University Library, Hh.1.10 **Ker 17**
Cambridge, Corpus Christi College, 449 **Ker 71**
London, British Museum, Cotton Faustina A.X **Ker 154A art.1**
London, British Museum, Cotton Julius A.II **Ker 158**
London, British Museum, Harley 107 **Ker 227 art.1**
Oxford, Bodleian, Barlow 35 [extracts] **Ker 298 arts.a, c**
Oxford, St John's College, 154 **Ker 362 art.1**
Worcester, Cathedral, F.174 **Ker 398 art.1**
London, British Museum, Cotton Vitellius C.IX ff.208-13 [16th c transcript] **Ker 405**
See also Oxford, Bodleian, Bodley 730 **Ker 317**

ed Zupitza 1880 [1966], 297-322; T. Wright, *Anglo-Saxon and Old English Vocabularies,* 2nd ed. R.P. Wülcker, London 1884 [Darmstadt 1968], 304-37 [Ker 158]; F. Liebermann, 'Aus Ælfrics Grammatik und Glossar,' *Archiv* 92 [1894] 414-5 [Ker 298 art.a]

1.9.3
Admonitio ad Filium Spiritualem
MS Oxford, Bodleian, Hatton 76   **Ker 328A art.2**
ed H.W. Norman, *The Anglo-Saxon Version of the Hexameron of St. Basil ... and the Anglo-Saxon Remains of St. Basil's Admonitio ad Filium Spiritualem,* London 1848, 2nd ed. 1849
proposed ed. Margaret Locherbie-Cameron [London diss.] , *NM* 66 [1965] 235

1.9.4
De Temporibus Anni
MS Cambridge, University Library, Gg.3.28   **Ker 15 art.93**
Cambridge, Corpus Christi College, 367 pt.II ff.1, 2, 7-10   **Ker 62**
London, British Museum, Cotton Caligula A.XV   **Ker 139B arts.1, 4**
London, British Museum, Cotton Tiberius A.III   **Ker 186 art.13**
London, British Museum, Cotton Tiberius B.V vol.1 ff.2-73   **Ker 193 art.a**
London, British Museum, Cotton Titus D.XXVII   **Ker 202 art.f**
London, British Museum, Cotton Vitellius C.VIII   **Ker 221 art.3**
Vatican City, Reg. Lat. 1283 f.114   **Ker 393**
ed H. Henel, *Ælfric's De Temporibus Anni,* EETS 213, London 1942 [1971] ; E. Steinmeyer, 'Angelsächsisches aus Rom,' *ZfdA* 24 [1880] 192 [Ker 393]

1.9.5
Ely Charter
See B.15.1.38

1.9.6
Admonitions in Lent
MS Cambridge, University Library, Gg.3.28   **Ker 15 art.95**
Cambridge, Corpus Christi College, 198 [adapted]   **Ker 48 art.62**
Cambridge, Corpus Christi College, 320 [extract]   **Ker 58 art.a**
ed Thorpe 1844-6, II, 602-8

1.9.7
Admonitions in Lent
MS Cambridge, University Library, Gg.3.28   **Ker 15 art.96**
Oxford, Bodleian, Hatton 115   **Ker 332 art.13**
ed Thorpe 1844-6, II, 608-9

1.9.8
An Exemplum
See B.3.4.28 and Angus McIntosh, 'Wulfstan's Prose,' *Proceedings of the British Academy* 35 [1949] 129-30

1.9.9
Institutes of Polity
ed Karl Jost, *Die 'Institutes of Polity, Civil and Ecclesiastical, '* Swiss Studies in English 47, Bern 1959, 217-8
See B.13.2

1.9.10
Creeds
See B.12.3.1, 12.3.2

Pater Noster
See B.12.4.1

2
Wulfstan
ed Dorothy Bethurum, *The Homilies of Wulfstan,* Oxford 1957

2.1
Eschatological Homilies

2.1.1
Antichrist
MS Cambridge, Corpus Christi College, 201 **Ker 49B art.32**
    Oxford, Bodleian, Hatton 113 **Ker 331 art.9**
    Oxford, Bodleian, Junius 121 **Ker 338 art.30**
    Oxford, Bodleian, Bodley 343 **Ker 310 art.70**
ed Bethurum 1957, 116-8; A.S. Napier, *Wulfstan,* Sammlung englischer Denkmäler 4,
    Berlin 1883, repr. with app. K. Ostheeren 1967, 78-80

2.1.2
Matthew on the Last Days
MS Cambridge, Corpus Christi College, 201 **Ker 49B art.34**
    Oxford, Bodleian, Hatton 113 **Ker 331 art.12**
ed Bethurum 1957, 119-22; Napier 1883 [1967], 87-90

2.1.3
Luke on the Last Days
MS Cambridge, Corpus Christi College, 421 **Ker 69 art.11**
    Cambridge, Corpus Christi College, 201 **Ker 49B art.35**
    Oxford, Bodleian, Hatton 113, 114 [extracts] **Ker 331 arts.13, 52**
ed Bethurum 1957, 123-7; Napier 1883 [1967], 90-4

2.1.4
The Deeds of Antichrist
MS Cambridge, Corpus Christi College, 201 **Ker 49B art.36**
    Oxford, Bodleian, Hatton 113 **Ker 331 art.14**
    Oxford, Bodleian, Bodley 343 **Ker 310 art.70**
ed Bethurum 1957, 128-33; Napier 1883 [1967], 94-102

2.1.5
The Last Days
MS Cambridge, Corpus Christi College, 201 **Ker 49B art.33**
    Oxford, Bodleian, Hatton 113 **Ker 331 art.11**
    Oxford, Bodleian, Bodley 343 **Ker 310 art.70**
ed Bethurum 1957, 134-41; Napier 1883 [1967], 80-7

2.2
The Christian Faith

2.2.1
An Outline of History
MS Cambridge, University Library, Add. 3206 [extracts]   **Ker 11**
    Cambridge, Corpus Christi College, 419   **Ker 68 art.6**
    Cambridge, Corpus Christi College, 201   **Ker 49B art.3**
    Oxford, Bodleian, Hatton 113, 114 [extracts]   **Ker 331 arts.3, 43**
    Oxford, Bodleian, Bodley 343   **Ker 310 art.72**
    London, British Museum, Cotton Otho B.X   **Ker 177A art.18**
ed Bethurum 1957, 142-56; Napier 1883 [1967], 6-20
    See B.3.4.44

2.2.2
The Creed
MS Cambridge, Corpus Christi College, 419   **Ker 68 art.7**
    Cambridge, Corpus Christi College, 201   **Ker 49B arts.4, 5**
    Oxford, Bodleian, Hatton 113   **Ker 331 arts.4, 5**
ed Bethurum 1957, 157-65; Napier 1883 [1967], 20-9

2.2.3
Translation of the Pater Noster and of the Creed
MS Cambridge, Corpus Christi College, 201 [part]   **Ker 49B art.10**
    Oxford, Bodleian, Junius 121   **Ker 338 art.18**
    London, British Museum, Cotton Tiberius A.III   **Ker 186 art.19j**
ed Bethurum 1957, 166-8; Napier 1883 [1967], 125-7

2.2.4
Baptism
MS Cambridge, Corpus Christi College, 302   **Ker 56 art.5**
ed Bethurum 1957, 172-4
    See B.3.5.3

2.2.5
Baptism
MS Cambridge, Corpus Christi College, 419   **Ker 68 art.5**
    Cambridge, Corpus Christi College, 201   **Ker 49B art.47**
    Oxford, Bodleian, Hatton 113   **Ker 331 art.6**
    Oxford, Bodleian, Bodley 343   **Ker 310 art.66**
    London, British Museum, Cotton Otho B.X [a few lines on f.23]   **Ker 177A art.18**
ed Bethurum 1957, 175-84; Napier 1883 [1967], 32-41

2.2.6
Gifts of the Holy Spirit
MS Oxford, Bodleian, Hatton 113   **Ker 331 art.8**
    Cambridge, Corpus Christi College, 201   **Ker 49B art.31**
    Cambridge, Corpus Christi College, 419   **Ker 68 art.8**

ed Bethurum 1957, 185-91; Napier 1883 [1967], 50-6
   See B.1.6.3

2.2.7
A Rule for Canons [Amalarius, *De Regula Canonicorum* 145]
MS Oxford, Bodleian, Junius 121   **Ker 338 art.12**
ed Bethurum 1957, 192-3; Jost 1959, 248-55

2.2.8
The Christian Life
MS Cambridge, Corpus Christi College, 419   **Ker 68 art.9**
   Cambridge, Corpus Christi College, 201   **Ker 49B arts.25, 29**
   Oxford, Bodleian, Hatton 113   **Ker 331 art.10**
   London, British Museum, Cotton Nero A.I   **Ker 164 art.2**
facs H.R. Loyn, *A Wulfstan Manuscript*, EEMF 17, Copenhagen 1971 [Ker 164 art.2]
ed Bethurum 1957, 200-10; Napier 1883 [1967], 65-76

2.2.9
Isaiah on the Punishment for Sin
MS Cambridge, Corpus Christi College, 201   **Ker 49B art.30**
   Oxford, Bodleian, Hatton 113   **Ker 331 art.7**
ed Bethurum 1957, 214-20; Napier 1883 [1967], 44-50

2.2.10
The False Gods
MS Oxford, Bodleian, Hatton 113   **Ker 331 art.16**
ed Bethurum 1957, 221-4; Napier 1883 [1967], 104-7
   See B.1.4.22

2.3
Archiepiscopal Functions

2.3.1
A Pastoral Letter
MS Cambridge, Corpus Christi College, 419 [parts]   **Ker 68 arts.9, 10**
   Cambridge, Corpus Christi College, 201   **Ker 49B arts. 6-9**
   Oxford, Bodleian, Hatton 113   **Ker 331 arts.17-21**
   London, British Museum, Cotton Tiberius A.III   **Ker 186 art.19a, b**
   London, British Museum, Cotton Otho B.X   **Ker 177A art.17**
ed Bethurum 1957, 225-32; Napier 1883 [1967], 108-15

2.3.2
The First Sunday in Lent
MS Oxford, Bodleian, Hatton 113   **Ker 331 art.15**
ed Bethurum 1957, 233-5; Napier 1883 [1967], 102-4

2.3.3
Cena Domini: The Reconciliation of Penitents

MS Oxford, Bodleian, Hatton 113 **Ker 331 art. 25**
ed Bethurum 1957, 236-8; Napier 1883 [1967], 153-5

2.3.4
Ezekiel on Negligent Priests
MS Cambridge, Corpus Christi College, 201 **Ker 49B art. 38**
ed Bethurum 1957, 240-1; Napier 1883 [1967], 190-1
    See B.3.4.33

2.3.5
The Consecration of a Bishop
MS London, British Museum, Cotton Cleopatra B.XIII **Ker 144 art. 5**
    Oxford, Bodleian, Hatton 113 **Ker 331 arts. 30, 26**
ed Bethurum 1957, 242-5; Napier 1883 [1967], 175-9

2.3.6
The Dedication of a Church
MS London, British Museum, Cotton Cleopatra B.XIII **Ker 144 art. 4**
    Oxford, Bodleian, Hatton 114 f. 246 **Ker 331 art. 78**
ed Bethurum 1957, 246-50; Napier 1883 [1967], 277-82
    proposed ed. R.C. Munn, Harvard [Hatton 114]

2.4
Evil Days

2.4.1
God's Threat to Sinning Israel
MS Cambridge, Corpus Christi College, 201 **Ker 49B art. 13**
    Oxford, Bodleian, Junius 121 **Ker 338 art. 15**
    London, British Museum, Cotton Nero A.I **Ker 164 art. 3**
facs Loyn 1971 [Ker 164 art. 3]
ed Bethurum 1957, 251-4; Napier 1883 [1967], 130-4

2.4.2
Sermo ad Anglos
a
MS Cambridge, Corpus Christi College, 419 **Ker 68 art. 4**
    Oxford, Bodleian, Bodley 343 **Ker 310 art. 71**
ed Bethurum 1957, 255-60
b
MS Cambridge, Corpus Christi College, 201 **Ker 49B art. 40**
ed Bethurum 1957, 261-6
c
MS Oxford, Bodleian, Hatton 113 **Ker 331 art. 27**
    London, British Museum, Cotton Nero A.I **Ker 164 art. 20**
facs Loyn 1971 [Ker 164 art. 20]
ed Bethurum 1957, 267-75; Napier 1883 [1967], 156-67; D. Whitelock, *Sermo Lupi ad Anglos,* MOEL, London 1939, 3rd ed. 1963

2.4.3
Evil Rulers
MS　Oxford, Bodleian, Hatton 113　**Ker 331 art. 28**
　　London, British Museum, Cotton Nero A.I　**Ker 164 art. 21**
　　Cambridge, Corpus Christi College, 201　**Ker 49B arts. 13, 41**
facs　Loyn 1971 [Ker 164 art. 21]
ed　Bethurum 1957, 276-7; Napier 1883 [1967], 167-9

2.5
Other Texts in the Wulfstan Canon
ed　Bethurum 1957, 43-9

2.5.1
Canons of Edgar
See B. 13.1.1

2.5.2
Institutes of Polity
See B. 13.2

2.5.3
Charters
Robertson nos. 74, 83: see **B. 15.4.6, 15.5.20** ›

2.5.4
Laws: Æthelred V-X
See B. 14.23-8

2.5.5
Cnut
See B. 14.30

2.5.6
Edward and Guthrum
See B. 14.6

2.5.7
Grið
See B. 14.51

2.5.8
Geþyncðo
See B. 14.46

2.5.9
Norðleoda laga
See B. 14.47

2.5.10
Mircna laga
See B.14.48

2.5.11
Að
See B.14.49

2.5.12
Hadbot
See B.14.50

2.6
Works attributed to Wulfstan

2.6.1
Northumbrian Priest's Law
See B.14.32

2.6.2
Rectitudines Singularum Personarum
See B.14.44

2.6.3
Gerefa
See B.14.45

2.6.4
Chronicle Poems, Edgar and Edward
See A.10.4

2.6.5
Benedictine Office [prose portions]
See B.12.7

3
Anonymous Homilies

3.1
Collections of Homilies [Individual homilies are listed separately, but only with reference to manuscript and current edition]

3.1.1
The Blickling Homilies
MS   Collection of W.H. Scheide, Titusville [Princeton, N.J.]   **Ker 382**
facs   R. Willard, *The Blickling Homilies*, EEMF 10, Copenhagen 1960
ed   R. Morris, *The Blickling Homilies*, EETS 58, 63, 73, London 1874-80 [1967]
       proposed eds. R.L. Collins, R.M. Dawson, *NM* 66 [1965] 239

3.1.2
The Vercelli Homilies
MS   Vercelli, Biblioteca Capitolare, CXVII   **Ker 394**
facs M. Förster, *Il Codice Vercellese,* Rome 1913
      proposed EEMF facs. C. Sisam
ed   M. Förster, *Die Vercelli-Homilien I-VIII Homilie,* Bib. ags. Prosa 12, Hamburg 1932
      [Darmstadt 1964]; Paul W. Peterson, 'The Unpublished Homilies of the Vercelli Book'
      [New York Univ. diss.] *ADD* 18 [1951] 227
      proposed eds. P.E. Szarmach, *NM* 71 [1970] 499; J. Erickson

3.2
Homilies for Specified Occasions, Temporale

3.2.1
Christmas
MS   Cambridge, Corpus Christi College, 198   **Ker 48 art. 1**
      Oxford, Bodleian, Bodley 340   **Ker 309 art. 1**
      Vercelli, Biblioteca Capitolare, CXVII   **Ker 394 art. 5**
facs Förster 1913
ed   Förster 1932, 107-31

3.2.2
Epiphany
MS   Vercelli, Biblioteca Capitolare, CXVII   **Ker 394 art. 18**
facs Förster 1913
ed   Peterson 1951

3.2.3
First Sunday after Epiphany
MS   Cambridge, Corpus Christi College, 198   **Ker 48 art. 7**
      Oxford, Bodleian, Bodley 340   **Ker 309 art. 7**
      Vercelli, Biblioteca Capitolare, CXVII   **Ker 394 art. 10**
facs Förster 1913
ed   Förster 1932, 149-59

3.2.4
Second Sunday after Epiphany
MS   Oxford, Bodleian, Bodley 340   **Ker 309 art. 8**
      Vercelli, Biblioteca Capitolare, CXVII   **Ker 394 art. 11**
facs Förster 1913
ed   M. Förster, 'Der Vercelli-Codex CXVII nebst Abdruck einiger altenglischer Homilien der
      Handschrift' in F. Holthausen and H. Spies, eds., *Festschrift für Lorenz Morsbach,*
      Studien zur englischen Philologie 50, Halle 1913, 100-61

3.2.5
Third Sunday after Epiphany
MS   Cambridge, Corpus Christi College, 302   **Ker 56 art. 10**
      London, British Museum, Cotton Faustina A.IX   **Ker 153 art. 4**

ed R. Willard, *Two Apocrypha in Old English Homilies,* Beiträge zur englischen Philologie 30, Leipzig 1935 [1967] 38-56 [partial ed.]

3.2.6
Fourth Sunday after Epiphany
MS Cambridge, Corpus Christi College, 302   **Ker 56 art. 11**
London, British Museum, Cotton Faustina A.IX   **Ker 153 art. 5**
ed Assmann 1889, 164-9

3.2.7
Fifth Sunday after Epiphany
MS Cambridge, Corpus Christi College, 302   **Ker 56 art. 12**
London, British Museum, Cotton Faustina A.IX   **Ker 153 art. 6**
proposed ed. T.C. Callison III, Wisconsin
See B.3.2.40

3.2.8
Quinquagesima Sunday
MS Collection of W.H. Scheide, Titusville [Princeton, N.J.]   **Ker 382 art. 2**
ed Morris 1874-80, 15-25

3.2.9
Ash Wednesday
MS Cambridge, Corpus Christi College, 190   **Ker 45B art. 20**
proposed ed. H. Martin

3.2.10
First Sunday in Lent
MS Collection of W.H. Scheide, Titusville [Princeton, N.J.]   **Ker 382 art. 3**
ed Morris 1874-80, 27-39

3.2.11
Second Sunday in Lent
MS Cambridge, Corpus Christi College, 162   **Ker 38 art. 19**
Cambridge, Corpus Christi College, 198   **Ker 48 art. 19**
Oxford, Bodleian, Bodley 340   **Ker 309 art. 19**
Oxford, Bodleian, Bodley 343   **Ker 310 art. 28**
Vercelli, Biblioteca Capitolare, CXVII   **Ker 394 art. 3**
ed Förster 1932, 53-71; Belfour 1909, 40-8 [Ker 310 art. 28]
proposed ed. P.M. Vermeer, *NM* 68 [1967] 205

3.2.12
Second Sunday in Lent
MS Oxford, Bodleian, Hatton 114   **Ker 331 art. 44**
proposed ed. R.C. Munn, Harvard

3.2.13
Third Sunday in Lent

MS   Cambridge, Corpus Christi College, 198   **Ker 48 art. 20**
     Cambridge, Corpus Christi College, 419   **Ker 68 art. 14**
     Oxford, Bodleian, Bodley 340   **Ker 309 art. 20**
ed   Assmann 1889, 138-43

3.2.14
Third Sunday in Lent
MS   Oxford, Bodleian, Junius 85 and 86   **Ker 336 art. 7**
     Collection of W.H. Scheide, Titusville [Princeton, N.J.]   **Ker 382 art. 4**
ed   Morris 1874-80, 39-53, 195; H.C. Snider [Texas diss. 1940] [Ker 336 art. 7] ; R. Willard,
     'The Blickling-Junius Tithing Homily and Caesarius of Arles' in T.A. Kirby and H.B. Woolf,
     eds., *Philologica: The Malone Anniversary Studies,* Baltimore 1949, 72-8 [partial]

3.2.15
Fourth Sunday in Lent
MS   Cambridge, Corpus Christi College, 198   **Ker 48 art. 21**
     Cambridge, Corpus Christi College, 419   **Ker 68 art. 13**
     Oxford, Bodleian, Bodley 340   **Ker 309 art. 21**
     Oxford, Bodleian, Bodley 343   **Ker 310 art. 29**
ed   Belfour 1909, 50-8

3.2.16
Fifth Sunday in Lent
MS   Cambridge, Corpus Christi College, 198   **Ker 48 art. 22**
     Oxford, Bodleian, Bodley 340   **Ker 309 art. 22**
ed   Assmann 1889, 144-50

3.2.17
Fifth Sunday in Lent
MS   Collection of W.H. Scheide, Titusville [Princeton, N.J.]   **Ker 382 art. 5**
ed   Morris 1874-80, 55-65

3.2.18
Palm Sunday
MS   Cambridge, Corpus Christi College, 162   **Ker 38 art. 28**
     Cambridge, Corpus Christi College, 198   **Ker 48 art. 23**
     Oxford, Bodleian, Bodley 340   **Ker 309 art. 23**
     proposed eds. K.G. Schaefer [Columbia diss.] , *NM* 71 [1970] 493; Andrea Lord,
     Manchester

3.2.19
Palm Sunday
MS   Cambridge, Corpus Christi College, 41   **Ker 32 art. 18**
ed   R.J.S. Grant [Cambridge diss. 1970]
     proposed ed. Schaefer [Columbia diss.]

3.2.20
Palm Sunday [Passion Story]

MS Collection of A. Ehrman, no.888   **Ker 112**
    proposed ed. Schaefer [Columbia diss.]
    See B.8.4.4

3.2.21
Palm Sunday
MS London, British Museum, Cotton Faustina A.IX [extract]   **Ker 153 art.23**
    Collection of W.H. Scheide, Titusville [Princeton, N.J.]   **Ker 382 art.6**
ed Morris 1874-80, 65-83

3.2.22
In Cena Domini
MS Cambridge, Corpus Christi College, 162   **Ker 38 art.29**
    Cambridge, Corpus Christi College, 198   **Ker 48 art.24**
    Cambridge, Corpus Christi College, 302   **Ker 56 art.27**
    London, British Museum, Cotton Faustina A.IX   **Ker 153 art.24**
    Oxford, Bodleian, Bodley 340   **Ker 309 art.24**
ed Assmann 1889, 151-63

3.2.23
In Cena Domini
MS Cambridge, Corpus Christi College, 190   **Ker 45B art.21**
ed Bethurum 1957, 366-73 [Appendix I]
    proposed ed. H. Martin

3.2.24
In Parasceve
MS Cambridge, Corpus Christi College, 162   **Ker 38 art.30**
    Cambridge, Corpus Christi College, 198   **Ker 48 art.25**
    Cambridge, Corpus Christi College, 303   **Ker 57 art.15**
    Oxford, Bodleian, Bodley 340   **Ker 309 art.25**
    Vercelli, Biblioteca Capitolare, CXVII   **Ker 394 art.1**
ed Förster 1932, 1-43; J.L. Dillard, '*De Parasceve*: An Old English vernacular Passion'
    [Texas diss.] *ADD* 16 [1956] 142

3.2.25
In Sabbato Sancto
MS Cambridge, Corpus Christi College, 162   **Ker 38 art.31**
    Cambridge, Corpus Christi College, 198   **Ker 48 art.26**
    Oxford, Bodleian, Bodley 340   **Ker 309 art.26**
    proposed ed. Schaefer [Columbia diss.]

3.2.26
Easter Day
MS Collection of W.H. Scheide, Titusville [Princeton, N.J.]   **Ker 382 art.7**
ed Morris 1874-80, 83-97

3.2.27
Easter Day
MS Cambridge, Corpus Christi College, 162 **Ker 38 art.32**
proposed ed. Schaefer [Columbia diss.]
See B.1.2.18

3.2.28
Easter Day
MS Oxford, Bodleian, Junius 121 **Ker 338 art.33**
ed Enid M. Raynes [Edwards], 'Unpublished Old English Homilies' [Oxford D.Phil.]
Index 5 [1954-5] no.136
proposed ed. Schaefer [Columbia diss.]
See B.1.1.15

3.2.29
Easter Day
MS Cambridge, Corpus Christi College, 41 **Ker 32 art.13**
Cambridge, Corpus Christi College, 303 **Ker 57 art.17**
ed W.H. Hulme, 'The Old English Gospel of Nicodemus,' *MP* 1 [1903-4] 610-4
See B.8.5.3

3.2.30
In Letania Maiore
MS Oxford, Bodleian, Hatton 114 **Ker 331 art.52**
ed Willard 1935 [1967], 56 [partial]; Hildegard Tristram [Paul], 'Vier altenglische Predigten
aus der heterodoxen Tradition,' [Freiburg i. Br. diss. 1970], 430-7
proposed ed. J.E. Cross and J. Bazire, *NM* 70 [1969] 525
See also B.1.1.20; B.3.4.44

3.2.31
In Letania Maiore
MS Oxford, Bodleian, Hatton 114 **Ker 331 art.53**
ed Willard 1935 [1967], 38-54
proposed ed. Cross and Bazire

3.2.32
In Letania Maiore
MS Oxford, Bodleian, Hatton 114 **Ker 331 art.54**
ed Raynes 1954-5
proposed eds. Cross and Bazire; R.C. Munn, Harvard

3.2.33
In Letania Maiore
MS Oxford, Bodleian, Hatton 116 **Ker 333 art.26**
ed Förster 1913, 128-37

3.2.34
Monday in Rogationtide

MS Cambridge, Corpus Christi College, 162   **Ker 38 art. 35**
Cambridge, Corpus Christi College, 303   **Ker 57 art. 43**
London, British Museum, Cotton Cleopatra B. XIII   **Ker 144 art. 6**
Vercelli, Biblioteca Capitolare, CXVII   **Ker 394 art. 24**
proposed ed. Cross and Bazire

3.2.35
Monday in Rogationtide
MS Cambridge, Corpus Christi College, 302   **Ker 56 art. 31**
ed Tristram 1970, 173-85
proposed ed. Cross and Bazire

3.2.36
Monday in Rogationtide
MS Vercelli, Biblioteca Capitolare, CXVII   **Ker 394 art. 13**
ed R. Willard, 'Vercelli Homily XI and Its Sources,' *Speculum* 24 [1949] 81-5
proposed ed. Cross and Bazire

3.2.37
Tuesday in Rogationtide
MS Oxford, Bodleian, Hatton 114   **Ker 331 art. 55**
proposed eds. Cross and Bazire; Munn, Harvard

3.2.38
Tuesday in Rogationtide
MS Cambridge, Corpus Christi College, 162   **Ker 38 art. 36**
Cambridge, Corpus Christi College, 303   **Ker 57 art. 44**
Vercelli, Biblioteca Capitolare, CXVII   **Ker 394 art. 25**
proposed ed. Cross and Bazire
See B.9.7

3.2.39
Tuesday in Rogationtide
MS Vercelli, Biblioteca Capitolare, CXVII **Ker 394 art. 14**
proposed ed. Cross and Bazire

3.2.40
Tuesday in Rogationtide
MS Cambridge, Corpus Christi College, 302   **Ker 56 art. 33**
Cambridge, Corpus Christi College, 421   **Ker 69 art. 9**
Oxford, Bodleian, Bodley 343 [extract]   **Ker 310 art. 80**
Oxford, Bodleian, Junius 85 and 86   **Ker 336 art. 1**
Collection of W.H. Scheide, Titusville [Princeton, N.J.]   **Ker 382 art. 9**
Vercelli, Biblioteca Capitolare, CXVII   **Ker 394 art. 12**
ed Napier 1883 [1967], 250-65; Belfour 1909, 124-34 [Ker 310 art. 80]; Morris 1874-80,
105-7 [Ker 382 art. 9]; L.L.R. McCabe, 'An edition and translation of a 10th-century
Anglo-Saxon Homily' [Minnesota diss.] *DA* 29 [1969] 3978A
See B.3.2.7, 3.4.3

3.2.41
Tuesday in Rogationtide
MS   Cambridge, University Library, Ii.4.6   **Ker 21 art. 28**
proposed ed. Cross and Bazire
See **B.1.2.48, 1.3.14**

3.2.42
Wednesday in Rogationtide
MS   Cambridge, Corpus Christi College, 303   **Ker 57 art. 45**
proposed ed. Cross and Bazire

3.2.43
Wednesday in Rogationtide
MS   Vercelli, Biblioteca Capitolare, CXVII   **Ker 394 art. 15**
ed   R.P. Wülcker, 'Ueber das Vercellibuch,' *Anglia* 5 [1882] 464-5
proposed ed. Cross and Bazire

3.2.44
Wednesday in Rogationtide
MS   Cambridge, Corpus Christi College, 162   **Ker 38 art. 37**
proposed ed. Cross and Bazire

3.2.45
Ascension Day
MS   Cambridge, Corpus Christi College, 162   **Ker 38 art. 38**
ed   Tristram 1970, 162-72

3.2.46
Ascension Day
MS   Collection of W.H. Scheide, Titusville [Princeton, N.J.]   **Ker 382 art. 11**
ed   Morris 1874-80, 115-31

3.2.47
Pentecost
MS   Collection of W.H. Scheide, Titusville [Princeton, N.J.]   **Ker 382 art. 12**
ed   Morris 1874-80, 131-7

3.2.48
Virgins ['Evangelium De Virginibus']
MS   Cambridge, Corpus Christi College, 303   **Ker 57 art. 39**
ed   Tristram 1970, 439-45
proposed ed. Keith Brown [Liverpool diss.]

3.2.49
Dedication of a Church
MS   London, Lambeth Palace, 489   **Ker 283 arts. 6, 7**
Paris, Bibliothèque Nationale, Lat. 943   **Ker 364 art. c**
ed   Brotanek 1913, 15-27

3.2.50
Dedication of a Church

MS London, British Museum, Cotton Tiberius C.I ff.43-203 **Ker 197 art.a**
ed N.R. Ker, 'Three Old English Texts in a Salisbury Pontifical, Cotton Tiberius C.I
in P. Clemoes, ed., *The Anglo-Saxons, Studies ... presented to Bruce Dickins,* London
1959, 272-5

3.3
Sanctorale

3.3.1
Saint Andrew

MS Cambridge, Corpus Christi College, 198 **Ker 48 art.64**
   Collection of W.H. Scheide, Titusville [Princeton, N.J.] **Ker 382 art.18**
ed Morris 1874-80, 229-49

3.3.2
Deposition of Saint Augustine in England

MS Cambridge, Corpus Christi College, 162 **Ker 38 art.55**
ed Tristram 1970, 428

3.3.3
Saint Chad

MS Oxford, Bodleian, Hatton 116 **Ker 333 art.1**
ed R. Vleeskruyer, *The Life of Saint Chad,* Amsterdam 1953

3.3.4
Saint Christopher

MS London, British Museum, Cotton Otho B.X **Ker 177A art.11**
   London, British Museum, Cotton Vitellius A.XV **Ker 216 art.1**
ed S. Rypins, *Three Old English Prose Texts,* EETS 161, London 1924, 68-76

3.3.5
Invention of the Cross

MS Cambridge, Corpus Christi College, 557 [fragments] **Ker 73**
   Oxford, Bodleian, Bodley 343 **Ker 310 art.12**
   Kansas, University, Y 103 [fragment]
ed A.S. Napier, *History of the Holy Rood-Tree,* EETS 103, London 1894
   [Ker 310 art.12] ; N.R. Ker, 'An Eleventh-Century Old English Legend of the Cross
   before Christ,' *MÆ* 9 [1940] 84-5 [Ker 73] ; Colgrave and Hyde 1962, 62-4 [Kansas
   fragment]

3.3.6
Invention of the Cross

MS Cambridge, Corpus Christi College, 303 **Ker 57 art.18**
   Oxford, Bodleian, Auct. F.4.32 **Ker 297 art.a**
facs R.W. Hunt, *Saint Dunstan's Classbook from Glastonbury,* Umbrae Codicum
   Occidentalium 4, Amsterdam 1961

ed   R. Morris, *Legends of the Holy Rood,* EETS 46, London 1871, 3-17

3.3.7
Saint Euphrosyne
MS   London, British Museum, Cotton Julius E.VII   **Ker 162 art. 44**
London, British Museum, Cotton Otho B.X   **Ker 177A art. 10**
ed   Skeat 1881-1900 [1966], II, 334-54

3.3.8
Saint Eustace and his Companions
MS   London, British Museum, Cotton Julius E.VII   **Ker 162 art. 41**
London, British Museum, Cotton Vitellius D.XVII   **Ker 222 art. 29**
ed   Skeat 1881-1900 [1966], II, 190-218

3.3.9
Saint Giles
MS   Cambridge, Corpus Christi College, 303   **Ker 57 art. 26**
proposed ed. Keith Brown [Liverpool diss.]

3.3.10
Saint Guthlac
MS   Oxford, Bodleian, Laud Misc. 509 and London, British Museum, Cotton Vespasian
D.XXI ff. 18-40   **Ker 344 art. 5**
Vercelli, Biblioteca Capitolare, CXVII [extract]   **Ker 394 art. 29**
ed   P. Gonser, *Das angelsächsische Prosa-Leben des heiligen Guthlac,* AF 27, Heidelberg 1909;
Jane Crawford [Roberts], '*Guthlac*: An edition of the Old English prose life, together
with the poems in the *Exeter Book*' [Oxford D.Phil.] *Index* 17 [1966-7] no. 331
proposed ed. J.A. Crawford [Roberts], *NM* 70 [1969] 524

3.3.11
James the Greater
MS   London, British Museum, Cotton Vespasian D.XIV   **Ker 209 art. 11**
ed   Warner 1917, 21-5

3.3.12
Nativity of John the Baptist
MS   Collection of W.H. Scheide, Titusville [Princeton, N.J.]   **Ker 382 art. 14**
ed   Morris 1874-80, 161-9

3.3.13
Saint Machutus
MS   London, British Museum, Cotton Otho A.VIII ff. 7-34 and Cotton Otho B.X f. 66   **Ker 168**
proposed ed. Enid M. Edwards [Raynes]

3.3.14
Saint Margaret
MS   Cambridge, Corpus Christi College, 303   **Ker 57 art. 23**
ed   Assmann 1889, 170-80

3.3.15
Saint Margaret

MS London, British Museum, Cotton Otho B.X [burnt] **Ker 177C**
   incipit and explicit from Wanley
ed Ker 1957, 228

3.3.16
Saint Margaret

MS London, British Museum, Cotton Tiberius A.III **Ker 186 art.15**
ed T.O. Cockayne, *Narratiunculae Anglice Conscriptae,* London 1861, 39-49
   proposed ed. Brigitte Rudolph, *NM* 70 [1969] 532

3.3.17
Saint Martin

MS Oxford, Bodleian, Junius 85 and 86 **Ker 336 art.8**
   Collection of W.H. Scheide, Titusville [Princeton, N.J.] **Ker 382 art.17**
   Vercelli, Biblioteca Capitolare, CXVII **Ker 394 art.20**
ed Morris 1874-80, 211-27; A.S. Napier, 'Notes on the Blickling Homilies,' *MP* 1 [1903-4]
   306-7

3.3.18
Nativity of Mary the Virgin

MS Cambridge, Corpus Christi College, 367 pt.II **Ker 63 art.6**
   Oxford, Bodleian, Bodley 343 **Ker 310 art.16**
   Oxford, Bodleian, Hatton 114 **Ker 331 art.72**
ed Assmann 1889, 117-37

3.3.19
Purification of Mary the Virgin

MS Vercelli, Biblioteca Capitolare, CXVII **Ker 394 art.19**
ed Peterson 1951
   proposed eds. Erickson, Szarmach

3.3.20
Assumption of Mary the Virgin

MS Cambridge, Corpus Christi College, 198 **Ker 48 art.54**
   Collection of W.H. Scheide, Titusville [Princeton, N.J.] **Ker 382 art.13**
ed Morris 1874-80, 137-59; R. Willard, 'On Blickling Homily XIII: The Assumption of the
   Virgin,' *Review of English Studies* 12 [1936] 8-10

3.3.21
Assumption of the Virgin

MS Cambridge, Corpus Christi College, 41 **Ker 32 art.11**
ed Tristram 1970, 125-50; Grant 1970

3.3.22
'In Festis Sancte Marie'

MS London, British Museum, Cotton Vespasian D.XIV **Ker 209 art.44**

ed   Warner 1917, 134-9; M. Förster, 'Die spätaltenglische Uebersetzung der Pseudo-
Anselmschen Marienpredigt' in W. Dibelius, H. Hecht, W. Keller, eds., *Anglica, Unter-
suchungen zur englischen Philologie, A. Brandl überreicht,* Palaestra 147, 148, II
Leipzig 1925, 15-39

3.3.23
Mary of Egypt

MS   Gloucester, Cathedral, 35   **Ker 117 art.2**
London, British Museum, Cotton Julius E.VII   **Ker 162 art.31**
London, British Museum, Cotton Otho B.X   **Ker 177A art.12**
ed   Skeat 1881-1900 [1966], II, 2-52

3.3.24
Saint Michael

MS   Cambridge, Corpus Christi College, 41   **Ker 32 art.17**
ed   Tristram 1970, 152-61; Grant 1970

3.3.25
Saint Michael

MS   Collection of W.H. Scheide, Titusville [Princeton, N.J.]   **Ker 382 art.16**
ed   Morris 1874-80, 197-211

3.3.26
Saint Mildred

MS   London, British Museum, Cotton Caligula A.XIV   **Ker 138 art.3**
ed   T.O. Cockayne, *Leechdoms, Wortcunning and Starcraft of Early England,* Rolls Series 35,
3 vols., London 1864-6, III, 422-8
See also B.18.8

3.3.27
Saint Mildred

MS   London, Lambeth Palace, 427 ff.210-1   **Ker 281**
ed   Cockayne 1864-6, III, 428-32; M. Förster, 'Die altenglischen Beigaben des Lambeth-
Psalters,' *Archiv* 132 [1914] 333-5
See also B.17.10

3.3.28
Saint Neot

MS   London, British Museum, Cotton Vespasian D.XIV   **Ker 209 art.43**
ed   Warner 1917, 129-34; Mary Richards, 'An edition of the Old English *Of Seinte Neote*'
[Wisconsin diss.], *DA* 32 [1971] 3266A

3.3.29
Saint Nicholas

MS   Cambridge, Corpus Christi College, 303   **Ker 57 art.34**
proposed ed. Keith Brown [Liverpool diss.]

3.3.30
Saint Pantaleon
MS London, British Museum, Cotton Vitellius D.XVII **Ker 222 art.14**
ed P.M. Matthews, 'The Old English Life of Saint Pantaleon' [University College, London, MA diss.] *Index* 16 [1965-6] no.235
proposed ed. Johannes Söderlind [Uppsala diss.], *NM* 67 [1966] 203

3.3.31
Saint Paulinus
MS Oxford, Bodleian, Bodley 342 **Ker 309 art.75**
ed Sisam 1953, 151-2

3.3.32
Peter and Paul
MS Collection of W.H. Scheide, Titusville [Princeton, N.J.] **Ker 382 art.15**
ed Morris 1874-80, 171-93

3.3.33
Saint Quintin
MS London, British Museum, Cotton Vitellius A.XV ff.4-93 [fragment] **Ker 215 art.4**
ed M. Förster, 'Zur altenglischen Quintinus-Legende,' *Archiv* 106 [1901] 258-9

3.3.34
Seven Sleepers
MS London, British Museum, Cotton Julius E.VII **Ker 162 art.30**
   London, British Museum, Cotton Otho B.X **Ker 177A art.13**
ed Skeat 1881-1900 [1966], 488-540
proposed ed. R.J. Alexander [Wisconsin diss.]

3.3.35
Vitas Patrum
MS London, British Museum, Cotton Otho C.I vol.2 **Ker 182 art.2**
ed Assmann 1889, 195-207

3.4
Homilies for unspecified occasions, published
Listed under the editor's name

3.4.1
Belfour no.10
MS Oxford, Bodleian, Bodley 343 **Ker 310 art.78**
ed Belfour 1909, 96-106

3.4.2
Belfour no.11

MS   Oxford, Bodleian, Bodley 343   **Ker 310 art.79**
ed   Belfour 1909, 106-22

3.4.3
Belfour no.12
MS   Oxford, Bodleian, Bodley 343   **Ker 310 art.80**
ed   Belfour 1909, 124-34
     See B.3.2.40

3.4.4
Belfour no.13: De auaritia
MS   Cambridge, Corpus Christi College, 178   **Ker 41A art.17**
     Oxford, Bodleian, Bodley 343   **Ker 310 art.82**
ed   Belfour 1909, 134
     See B.1.2.33

3.4.5
Buchholz: The Soul to the Body
MS   Worcester, Cathedral, F.174   **Ker 398 art.3**
ed   R. Buchholz, *Die Fragmente der Reden der Seele an den Leichnam,* Erlanger Beiträge
     zur englischen Philologie 2, Erlangen and Leipzig 1890, 1-10; J. Hall, *Selections from
     Early Middle English,* Oxford 1920, 2-4 [partial]

3.4.6
Förster 1913, 116: 'De Die Judicii' [Apocalypse of Thomas]
MS   Vercelli, Biblioteca Capitolare, CXVII   **Ker 394 art.17**
facs   Förster 1913
ed   Förster 1913, 116-28

3.4.7
Förster 1913, 137
MS   Vercelli, Biblioteca Capitolare, CXVII   **Ker 394 art.27**
facs   Förster 1913
ed   Förster 1913, 137-48

3.4.8
Förster 1932, no.2
MS   Vercelli, Biblioteca Capitolare, CXVII   **Ker 394 arts.2, 26**
facs   Förster 1913
ed   Förster 1932, 44-53
     See also B.3.5.13

3.4.9
Förster 1932, no.4
MS   Cambridge, Corpus Christi College, 41   **Ker 32 art.9**
     Cambridge, Corpus Christi College, 367 pt.II   **Ker 63 art.10**
     Vercelli, Biblioteca Capitolare, CXVII   **Ker 394 art.4**
facs   Förster 1913
ed   Förster 1932, 72-107

3.4.10
Förster 1932, no.6: 'Miracula que facta fuerant ...'
MS   Vercelli, Biblioteca Capitolare, CXVII   **Ker 394 art.8**
facs Förster 1913
 ed   Förster 1932, 131-7

3.4.11
Förster 1932, no.7
MS   Vercelli, Biblioteca Capitolare, CXVII   **Ker 394 art.9**
facs Förster 1913
 ed   Förster 1932, 137-49

3.4.12
Förster 1955: Apocalypse of Thomas
MS   Cambridge, Corpus Christi College, 41   **Ker 32 art.12**
 ed   M. Förster, 'A New Version of the Apocalypse of Thomas in Old English,' *Anglia* 73 [1955] 17-27

3.4.13
Hall 1920: 'Sicut oves absque Pastore'
MS   Worcester, Cathedral, F.174   **Ker 398 art.2**
 ed   Hall 1920, 1

3.4.14
Holthausen 1890
MS   Copenhagen, Kongelige Bibliotek, Gl.Kgl.Sam. 1595 [4°]   **Ker 99**
 ed   F. Holthausen, 'Angelsächsisches aus Kopenhagen,' *ZfdA* 34 [1890] 228; corrections: Ker 1957, 140

3.4.15
Kemble 1848
MS   London, British Museum, Cotton Tiberius A.III   **Ker 186 art.18**
       Oxford, Bodleian, Hatton 115   **Ker 332 art.34**
 ed   J.M. Kemble, *The Dialogue of Salomon and Saturnus,* Ælfric Society, London 1848, 84-6; F.C. Robinson, 'The Devil's Account of the Next World,' *NM* 73 [1972] 365-8; Raynes [Edwards] 1954 [Ker 332 art.34]
       See B.3.5.9

3.4.16
Kluge 1885, 472
MS   London, British Museum, Cotton Tiberius A.III   **Ker 186 art.24**
 ed   F. Kluge, 'Zu altenglischen Dichtungen,' *Englische Studien* 8 [1885] 472-4

3.4.17
Kluge 1885, 474: De sancto iohanne
MS   Cambridge, Corpus Christi College, 198   **Ker 48 art.67**
       London, British Museum, Cotton Vespasian D.XIV   **Ker 209 art.51**
 ed   Kluge 1885, 474-9; Warner 1917, 146-8 [Ker 209 art.51]

3.4.18
Morris 1874-80, Blickling Homily no.1
MS Collection of W.H. Scheide, Titusville [Princeton, N.J.]   **Ker 382 art.1**
ed Morris 1874-80, 3-13

3.4.19
Morris 1874-80, Blickling Homily no.8
MS Collection of W.H. Scheide, Titusville [Princeton, N.J.]   **Ker 382 art.8**
ed Morris 1874-80, 97-105

3.4.20
Morris 1874-80, Blickling Homily no.10
MS Cambridge, Corpus Christi College, 198 [extract]   **Ker 48 art.62**
    Collection of W.H. Scheide, Titusville [Princeton, N.J.]   **Ker 382 art.10**
ed Morris 1874-80, 107-15

3.4.21
Napier 1883 [1967] , no.1
MS Cambridge, Corpus Christi College, 201   **Ker 49B art.1**
    London, British Museum, Cotton Tiberius A.XIII   **Ker 190A art.b**
    Oxford, Bodleian, Hatton 113   **Ker 331 art.1**
ed Napier 1883 [1967], 1-5

3.4.22
Napier 1883 [1967], no.23 [parts]: 'To eallum folce'
MS Cambridge, Corpus Christi College, 201   **Ker 49B art.11**
    Cambridge, Corpus Christi College, 419 and 421 pp.1, 2   **Ker 68 art.2**
    London, British Museum, Cotton Tiberius A.III   **Ker 186 art.19f**
ed Napier 1883 [1967], 116-9

3.4.23
Napier 1883 [1967], no.24 [parts]: 'To folce'
MS London, British Museum, Cotton Tiberius A.III   **Ker 186 art.19c, d**
    London, Lambeth Palace, 489   **Ker 283 art.5**
ed Napier 1883 [1967], 122 ll.4-10

3.4.24
Napier 1883 [1967], no.25 [parts]: 'To folce'
MS Cambridge, Corpus Christi College, 201   **Ker 49B art.10**
    London, British Museum, Add. 38651 ff.57-8   **Ker 130**
    London, British Museum, Cotton Tiberius A.III   **Ker 186 art.19i**
    Oxford, Bodleian, Hatton 113   **Ker 331 art.21**
ed Napier 1883 [1967], 122-4
    See B.2.2.3

3.4.25
Napier 1883 [1967], no.27: 'To eallum folce'
MS Cambridge, Corpus Christi College, 201   **Ker 49B art.12**

Cambridge, Corpus Christi College, 421   **Ker 69 art.10**
London, British Museum, Cotton Cleopatra B.XIII   **Ker 144 art.9**
London, British Museum, Cotton Tiberius A.III   **Ker 186 art.19g**
ed   Napier 1883 [1967], 128-30

3.4.26
Napier 1883 [1967], no.29
MS   Oxford, Bodleian, Hatton 113   **Ker 331 art.22**
ed   Napier 1883 [1967], 134-43

3.4.27
Napier 1883 [1967], no.30: 'Be rihtan cristendome'
MS   Cambridge, University Library, Ii.4.6   **Ker 21 art.28**
London, British Museum, Cotton Otho B.X   **Ker 177A art.16**
Oxford, Bodleian, Hatton 113   **Ker 331 art.23**
ed   Napier 1883 [1967], 143-52
proposed ed. M.R. Godden [Ker 21 art.28]

3.4.28
Napier 1883 [1967], no.31
MS   Oxford, Bodleian, Hatton 113   **Ker 331 art.24**
ed   Napier 1883 [1967], 152-3

3.4.29
Napier 1883 [1967], nos.35, 36: 'Be mistlican gelimpan'
MS   Cambridge, Corpus Christi College, 201   **Ker 49B art.14**
London, British Museum, Cotton Tiberius A.III   **Ker 186 art.19e**
Oxford, Bodleian, Hatton 113   **Ker 331 art.29**
ed   Napier 1883 [1967], 169-75

3.4.30
Napier 1883 [1967], no.38
MS   Cambridge, Corpus Christi College, 201   **Ker 49B art.15**
ed   Napier 1883 [1967], 180

3.4.31
Napier 1883 [1967], no.39: 'Ðis man geræde þa se micele here com to lande'
MS   Cambridge, Corpus Christi College, 201   **Ker 49B art.16**
ed   Napier 1883 [1967], 180-1
See B.14.25

3.4.32
Napier 1883 [1967], no.40: 'In die iudicii'
MS   Cambridge, Corpus Christi College, 201   **Ker 49B art.37**
Cambridge, Corpus Christi College, 419   **Ker 68 art.8**
London, British Museum, Cotton Cleopatra B.XIII   **Ker 144 art.1**
London, Lambeth Palace, 489   **Ker 283 art.5**
Oxford, Bodleian, Hatton 114   **Ker 331 art.82**
ed   Napier 1883 [1967], 182-90

3.4.33
Napier 1883 [1967], no.41: 'Verba Ezechiel prophete de pigris aut timidis vel neglegentibus pastoribus'

MS Cambridge, Corpus Christi College, 201 **Ker 49B art.39**
     Oxford, Bodleian, Hatton 115 **Ker 332 art.19**
ed Napier 1883 [1967], 191 ll.20-3
     See B.2.3.4

3.4.34
Napier 1883 [1967], no.42: 'De temporibus anticristi'

MS Cambridge, Corpus Christi College, 419 and 421 pp.1, 2 **Ker 68 art.1**
     Oxford, Bodleian, Hatton 114 **Ker 331 art.56**
ed Napier 1883 [1967], 191-205

3.4.35
Napier 1883 [1967], nos.43, 44: 'Sunnandæges spell'

MS Cambridge, Corpus Christi College, 419 and 421 pp.1, 2 **Ker 68 art.2**
     London, British Museum, Cotton Tiberius A.III **Ker 186 art.17**
ed Napier 1883 [1967], 205-26

3.4.36
Napier 1883 [1967], no.45: 'Sermonem angelorum nomina'

MS Cambridge, Corpus Christi College, 419 **Ker 68 art.3**
ed Napier 1883 [1967], 226-32

3.4.37
Napier 1883 [1967], no.46: 'Larspell'

MS Cambridge, Corpus Christi College, 419 **Ker 68 art.11**
     Oxford, Bodleian, Bodley 343 **Ker 310 art.64**
     Oxford, Bodleian, Junius 121 **Ker 338 art.10**
ed Napier 1883 [1967], 232-42; Jost 1959, 242-7 [Ker 338 art.10]

3.4.38
Napier 1883 [1967], no.47: 'Larspel and scriftboc'

MS Cambridge, Corpus Christi College, 421 **Ker 69 art.7**
     Oxford, Bodleian, Ashmole 328 **Ker 288 art.2**
ed Napier 1883 [1967], 242-5; S.J. Crawford, *Byrhtferth's Manual,* EETS 177, London 1929, 240-2 [Ker 288 art.2]

3.4.39
Napier 1883 [1967], no.48: 'Ammonitio amici'

MS Cambridge, Corpus Christi College, 421 **Ker 69 art.8**
     Oxford, Bodleian, Ashmole 328 **Ker 288 art.3**
ed Napier 1883 [1967], 246-50; Crawford 1929, 247-50 [Ker 288 art.3]

3.4.40
Napier 1883 [1967], no.50: 'Larspell'

MS Cambridge, Corpus Christi College, 421 **Ker 69 art.10**
ed Napier 1883 [1967], 266-74

3.4.41
Napier 1883 [1967], no.51: 'To eallan folke'
MS London, British Museum, Cotton Tiberius A.III **Ker 186 art.19h**
ed Napier 1883 [1967], 274-5

3.4.42
Napier 1883 [1967], no.52: 'To mæssepreostum'
MS London, British Museum, Cotton Tiberius A.III **Ker 186 art.19k**
ed Napier 1883 [1967], 275-6

3.4.43
Napier 1883 [1967], no.53: 'To mæssepreostum'
MS London, British Museum, Cotton Tiberius A.III **Ker 186 art.19l**
ed Napier 1883 [1967], 276-7

3.4.44
Napier 1883 [1967], no.55
MS Oxford, Bodleian, Hatton 114 **Ker 331 arts.43, 52**
ed Napier 1883 [1967], 282-9
   See B.1.2.8, B.2.2.1, B.3.2.30

3.4.45
Napier 1883 [1967], no.56: 'De Confessione'
MS Oxford, Bodleian, Bodley 343 **Ker 310 art.37**
ed Napier 1883 [1967], 289-91
   See B.11.1.5

3.4.46
Napier 1883 [1967], no.57: 'Sermo ad populum dominicis diebus'
MS London, Lambeth Palace, 489 **Ker 283 arts.4, 5**
ed Napier 1883 [1967], 291-9

3.4.47
Napier 1883 [1967], no.58: 'Sermo Bone Praedicatio'
MS London, British Museum, Cotton Otho B.X **Ker 177A art.18**
ed Napier 1883 [1967], 299-306

3.4.48
Napier 1883 [1967], no.59: 'Sermo Lupi'
MS York, Minster **Ker 402 art.b [I]**
ed Napier 1883 [1967], 307-9
   See B.14.24, 14.30

3.4.49
Napier 1883 [1967], no.60: 'Be hæðendome'
MS York, Minster **Ker 402 art.b [II]**
ed Napier 1883 [1967], 309-10

3.4.50
Napier 1883 [1967], no.61: 'Be cristendome'

MS York, Minster **Ker 402 art.b** [III]

ed Napier 1883 [1967], 310-1

3.4.51
Napier 1888, 154: 'De infantibus non baptizandis'

MS Cambridge, Corpus Christi College, 178 **Ker 41A art.15**
Oxford, Bodleian, Hatton 115 **Ker 332 art.14**
Oxford, Bodleian, Hatton 116 **Ker 333 art.24**

ed A.S. Napier, 'Ein altenglisches Leben des heiligen Chad,' *Anglia* 10 [1888] 154-5

3.4.52
Napier 1888, 155: 'De cogitatione'

MS Oxford, Bodleian, Hatton 115 **Ker 332 art.12**
Oxford, Bodleian, Hatton 116 **Ker 333 art.25**

ed Napier 1888, 155

3.4.53
Napier 1901, 356: 'Be þam drihtenlican sunnandæg folces lar'

MS Cambridge, Corpus Christi College, 162 **Ker 38 art.4**

ed A.S. Napier, 'Contributions to Old English Literature 1, An Old English Homily on the Observance of Sunday' in *An English Miscellany presented to Dr. Furnivall,* Oxford 1901, 357-62

3.4.54
Priebsch 1899

MS Cambridge, Corpus Christi College, 140 **Ker 35 art.4**

ed R. Priebsch, 'The Chief Sources of some Anglo-Saxon Homilies,' *Otia Merseiana* 1 [1899] 135-8

3.4.55
Thorpe 1840

MS Cambridge, Corpus Christi College, 201 **Ker 50 art.2**

ed B. Thorpe, *Ancient Laws and Institutes of England,* London 1840, II, 394-400

3.4.56
Warner 1917, 139

MS London, British Museum, Cotton Vespasian D.XIV **Ker 209 art.45**

ed Warner 1917, 139

3.4.57
Warner 1917, 139

MS London, British Museum, Cotton Vespasian D.XIV **Ker 209 art.46**

ed Warner 1917, 139-40; M. Förster, 'Die Weltzeitalter bei den Angelsachsen,' in Fr. Wild, ed., *Neusprachliche Studien, Festgabe Karl Luick zu seinem sechzigsten Geburtstage,* Marburg 1925, 199

3.5
Homilies for unspecified occasions, listed under the opening words

3.5.1
And hit sægð her on ðisum halgum gewrite
MS Oxford, Bodleian, Junius 85 and 86   **Ker 336 art.4**
proposed ed. Hildegard Paul [Tristram] , *NM* 71 [1970] 493; Antonette Healey, Toronto

3.5.2
Forlæte ælc cristen man
MS Oxford, Bodleian, Hatton 115   **Ker 332 art.18**
proposed ed. Enid M. Edwards

3.5.3
Gehadedum mannum is swiðe micclum beboden
MS London, British Museum, Cotton Otho B.X   **Ker 177A art.16**
See B.2.2.4

3.5.4
Geheraðnu men þa leofestan hu se godes lareow wæs sprecende
MS London, British Museum, Cotton Otho C.I   **Ker 182 art.4**
see Sisam 1953, 204

3.5.5
Geheraðnu mæn ða leofestan hu us godes bec
MS Oxford, Bodleian, Junius 85 and 86   **Ker 336 art.6**
ed Willard 1935 [1967] , 39-57 [partial]

3.5.6
Her onginneð þæt gewrit þe com of heofonum to Hierusalem ...
MS London, British Museum, Cotton Otho B.X ff.29, 30   **Ker 178 art.2**
incipit and explicit from Wanley
ed Ker 1957, 229

3.5.7
Ic eow bidde 7 eadmodlice lære. þæt ge þis halige længtenfæsten rihtlice healdan.
mid ælmessum
MS London, British Museum, Cotton Tiberius C.I ff. 43-203   **Ker 197 art.g**
ed Ker 1959, *Dickins Studies,* 278-9

3.5.8
Mage we gyt her gehyran. men þa leofostan. eowre sawle þearfe
MS Cambridge, University Library, Ii.1.33   **Ker 18 art.40**
ed R. Willard, 'The Address of the Soul to the Body,' *PMLA* 50 [1935] 963-5 [partial] ;
Kathleen Murfin [Rice diss.]

3.5.9
De inclusis. Sum deofel gast sæde sumen ancre ... ne mid idelnesse
MS Cambridge, Corpus Christi College, 303   **Ker 57 art.40**
proposed ed. Keith Brown [Liverpool diss.]
See B.3.4.15

3.5.10
Leofa man þe is mycel þearf þæt ðu þas drihtenlican tide georne geþence
MS Oxford, Bodleian, Junius 121   Ker 338 art. 17
    proposed ed. Enid M. Edwards

3.5.11
Larspell to swylcere tide swa man wile. Men ða leofestan þis synt halige dagas 7
gastlice 7 ussum sawlum læcedomlice
MS Vercelli, Biblioteca Capitolare, CXVII   Ker 394 art. 16
ed Peterson 1951

3.5.12
Leofan men understandað þæt hit is swiðe micel riht ...
MS London, British Museum, Cotton Vitellius D. VII [16th c transcript, now lost]   Ker 407

3.5.13
Men ða leofestan us ys mycel þearf þæt we god lufien
MS Vercelli, Biblioteca Capitolare, CXVII   Ker 394 art. 26
ed Peterson 1951
    See B.3.4.8

3.5.14
Men ða leofestan we geleornodon on godcundum gewritum þæt [...] æghwylces
monnes sawul
MS Oxford, Bodleian, Junius 85 and 86   Ker 336 art. 2
ed Willard 1935, 961-3 [partial]
    proposed ed. Antonette Healey, Toronto

3.5.15
Incipits and explicits of thirteen homilies
See Ker 173

4
Prose Romance, Vision Literature

4.1
Apollonius of Tyre
MS Cambridge, Corpus Christi College, 201   Ker 49 art. 53
ed J. Raith, *Die alt- und mittelenglischen Apollonius Bruchstücke,* Studien zur englischen
    Philologie 3, Munich 1956; P. Goolden, *The Old English 'Apollonius of Tyre,'*
    London 1958

4.2
Vision of Leofric
MS Cambridge, Corpus Christi College, 367 pt. II   Ker 64 art. b
ed A.S. Napier, 'An Old English Vision of Leofric, Earl of Mercia,' *TPS* [1907-10], 182-6

5
Prose Dialogues

5.1
Solomon and Saturn
MS   London, British Museum, Cotton Vitellius A.XV   **Ker 215 art.3**
ed   Kemble 1848, 178-93
proposed ed. J.E. Cross and T.D. Hill, *NM* 68 [1967] 194

5.2
Adrian and Ritheus
MS   London, British Museum, Cotton Julius A.II   **Ker 159 art.2**
ed   Kemble 1848, 198-207; M. Förster, 'Zu Adrian und Ritheus,' *Englische Studien* 23
[1897] 431-6
proposed ed. Cross and Hill

6
Letters

6.1
Boniface to Eadburga
MS   London, British Museum, Cotton Otho C.I vol.2   **Ker 182 art.3**
ed   Sisam 1953, 199-224

6.2
Eadwine of New Minster
MS   London, British Museum, Stowe 944   **Ker 274 art.f**
ed   F.E. Harmer, *Anglo-Saxon Writs,* Manchester 1952, 401-3, no.113
See B.15.4.10

6.3
Scribbles
MS   London, British Museum, Royal 2 B.V   **Ker 249 art.j**
ed   Ker 1957, 319-20
See B.27.3.21

7
Proverbs

7.1
Distichs of Cato
MS   Cambridge, Trinity College, R.9.17   **Ker 89 arts.2, 3**
London, British Museum, Cotton Julius A.II   **Ker 159 art.4**
London, British Museum, Cotton Vespasian D.XIV   **Ker 209 art.3**
ed   J. Nehab, *Der altenglische Cato* [Göttingen diss.] , Berlin 1879; M. Förster, 'Zum
altenglische Boethius,' *Archiv* 106 [1901] 342-3; R.S. Cox, 'The Old English Dicts of
Cato,' *Anglia* 90 [1972] 1-42; Ingrid A. Brunner, 'The Anglo-Saxon Translation of the
Distichs of Cato: A critical edition' [Columbia diss.] *DA* 26 [1965] 3296; Warner 1917,
3-7 [Ker 209 art.3]

7.2
MS London, British Museum, Cotton Faustina A.X **Ker 154A arts. 2, 3**
ed J. Zupitza, 'Lateinisch-englische Sprüche,' *Anglia* 1 [1878] 285-6; Dobbie 1942, 109;
Ker 1957, 194
See also A.35

7.3
MS London, British Museum, Royal 2 B.V **Ker 249 art. b**
ed F. Roeder, *Der altenglische Regius-Psalter,* Studien zur englischen Philologie 18, Halle
1904, xii; Dobbie 1942, 109
See A.35

7.4
MS Oxford, Bodleian, Rawlinson C.641 **Ker 348 art. b**
ed M. Förster, 'Frühmittelenglische Sprichwörter,' *Englische Studien* 31 [1902] 16

8
Biblical Translations

8.1
Heptateuch
[See also B.1.7]

8.1.1
MS Cambridge, University Library, Ii.1.33 **Ker 18 art. 1**
ed S.J. Crawford, *The Old English Version of the Heptateuch,* EETS 160, London 1922
[1969], 76-149 [Genesis 1-24:22 partially printed, partially collated]

8.1.2
MS Cambridge, Corpus Christi College, 201 **Ker 49B art. 56**
ed N.R. Ker in Crawford 1922 [1969], 444-56

8.1.3
MS Lincoln, Cathedral, 298, no. 2 **Ker 125**
ed S.J. Crawford, 'The Lincoln Fragment of the Old English Version of the Heptateuch,'
MLR 15 [1920] 2-6

8.1.4
MS London, British Museum, Cotton Claudius B.IV **Ker 142**
EEMF facs. in prep. C.R. Dodwell and P.A.M. Clemoes
ed Crawford 1922 [1969], 78-400

8.1.5
MS London, British Museum, Cotton Otho B.X [burnt] **Ker 177 art. 19**
coll. Crawford 1922 [1969]

8.1.6
MS Oxford, Bodleian, Hatton 115 **Ker 332 art. 30**
coll. Crawford 1922 [1969], 401-17

8.1.7
ɪs   Oxford, Bodleian, Laud Misc. 509   **Ker 344 arts. 1, 2**
      coll. Crawford 1922 [1969]

8.1.8
Fragment of Exodus
Formerly belonging to Edmund Gibson   **Ker 404**
coll. Crawford 1922 [1969] , 236-9, 248-50

8.1.9
ɪs   New York, Pierpont Morgan Library, G.63 [P]
ed   N.R. Ker in Crawford 1922 [1969] , 458-60

8.2
Psalms 1-50
ɪs   Paris, Bibliothèque Nationale, Lat. 8824   **Ker 367**
cs   Bromwich 1958
ed   J.W. Bright and R.L. Ramsay, *The West-Saxon Psalms,* The Belles Lettres Series,
      Boston 1907
      proposed eds. J. Tinkler, *NM* 70 [1969] 530; J.R. Stracke, Vanderbilt

8.3
Scholia on Psalms
ɪs   Vatican City, Pal. Lat. 68   **Ker 388**
ed   A.S. Napier, *Old English Glosses,* Anecdota Oxoniensia, Mediaeval and Modern Series 11,
      Oxford 1900, no.54

8.4
Gospels

8.4.1
ɪs   Collection of Major J.A. Abbey, J.A.3243   **Ker 1**
      Mark I, 27-31, 39-42

8.4.2
ɪs   Cambridge, University Library, Ii.2.11   **Ker 20 art. 1**
ed   M. Grünberg, *The West Saxon Gospels,* Amsterdam 1967
      coll. W.W. Skeat, *The Four Gospels in Anglo-Saxon, Northumbrian and Old Mercian
      Versions,* Cambridge 1871-87 [Darmstadt 1970] , as A

8.4.3
ɪs   Cambridge, Corpus Christi College, 140   **Ker 35 art. 1**
ed   Skeat 1871-87

8.4.4
ɪs   Collection of A. Ehrman, no.888   **Ker 112**
      Matthew 27:45-66
      proposed ed. Schaefer, *NM* 71 [1970] 493
      See B.3.2.20

8.4.5
MS   London, British Museum, Cotton Otho C.I vol. 1   **Ker 181 art.1**
    coll. Skeat 1871-87, as C

8.4.6
MS   London, British Museum, Cotton Vespasian D.XIV   **Ker 209 art.30**
ed   Warner 1917, 77

8.4.7
MS   London, British Museum, Royal 1 A.XIV   **Ker 245**
    coll. Skeat 1871-87, as R

8.4.8
MS   Oxford, Bodleian, Bodley 441   **Ker 312**
    coll. Skeat 1871-87, as B

8.4.9
MS   Oxford, Bodleian, Eng. Bib. C.2   **Ker 322**
ed   A.S. Napier, 'Bruchstücke einer altenglischen Evangelienhandschrift,' *Archiv* 87
    [1891] 257-61

8.4.10
MS   Oxford, Bodleian, Hatton 38   **Ker 325**
ed   Skeat 1871-87

8.5
Apocrypha

8.5.1
Gospel of Pseudo-Matthew
See B.3.3.18, 3.4.10

8.5.2
Gospel of Nicodemus
MS   Cambridge, University Library, Ii.2.11   **Ker 20 art.2**
    London, British Museum, Cotton Vitellius A.XV   **Ker 215 art.2**
ed   W.H. Hulme, 'The Old English Version of the Gospel of Nicodemus,' *PMLA* 13 [1898]
    471-515; T.P. Allen, 'A Critical Edition of the Old English *Gospel of Nicodemus*' [Rice
    diss.], *DA* 29 [1968] 1508A

8.5.3
Gospel of Nicodemus Homilies
MS   Cambridge, Corpus Christi College, 41   **Ker 32 art.13**
    Cambridge, Corpus Christi College, 303   **Ker 57 art.17**
    London, British Museum, Cotton Vespasian D.XIV   **Ker 209 art.31**
ed   Hulme 1903-4, 591-614; Warner 1917, 77-88 [Ker 209 art.31]
    See B.3.2.29

8.5.4
Vindicta Salvatoris
MS Cambridge, University Library, Ii.2.11   **Ker 20 art.3**
Cambridge, Corpus Christi College, 196   **Ker 47 art.2**
London, British Museum, Cotton Vespasian D.XIV   **Ker 209 art.32**
ed Assmann 1889, 181-92; Warner 1917, 88-9 and Assmann 1889, 193-4 [Ker 209 art.32]

8.5.5
Vision of St Paul
See B.3.5.1

8.5.6
Apocalypse of Thomas
See B.3.4.6, 3.4.12

9
Alfredian and Other Translations

9.1
Gregory the Great, The Pastoral Care
MS Cambridge, University Library, Ii.2.4   **Ker 19**
Cambridge, Corpus Christi College, 12   **Ker 30**
Cambridge, Trinity College, R.5.22   **Ker 87**
London, British Museum, Cotton Otho B.II and Cotton Otho B.X   **Ker 175**
London, British Museum, Cotton Tiberius B.XI and Kassel, Landesbibliothek,
Anhang 19   **Ker 195**
Oxford, Bodleian, Junius 53 [transcript]
Oxford, Bodleian, Hatton 20   **Ker 324**
cs N.R. Ker, *The Pastoral Care,* EEMF 6, Copenhagen 1956 [Ker 324 and Ker 195, Kassel
leaf]
ed H. Sweet, *King Alfred's West-Saxon Version of Gregory's Pastoral Care,* EETS 45, 50,
London 1871 [1958] [Ker 195 and 324] ; H. Flasdieck, 'Das Kasseler Bruchstück der
Cura Pastoralis,' Anglia 62 [1938] 193-233 [Ker 195, Kassel leaf]
proposed ed. Ingvar Carlson, *NM* 66 [1965] 237
See A.36, 37

9.2
Orosius, History of the World
MS London, British Museum, Add. 47967   **Ker 133**
London, British Museum, Cotton Tiberius B.I   **Ker 191 art.1**
Oxford, Bodleian, Eng. Hist. e.49   **Ker 323**
Rouen, Bibliothèque Municipale, I.49   **Ker 375**
Vatican City, Reg. Lat. 497   **Ker 391**
cs A. Campbell, *The Tollemache Orosius,* EEMF 3, Copenhagen 1953 [Ker 133]
ed H. Sweet, *King Alfred's Orosius,* EETS 79, London 1883 [1959] [Ker 133] ; J. Bosworth,
King Alfred's Anglo-Saxon version of the compendious history of the world by Orosius,
London 1859 [Ker 191 art.1] ; Sweet 1883 [Ker 191 art.1, printed and coll.] ;

A.S. Napier, 'Two Fragments of Alfred's "Orosius," ' *MLR* 8 [1913] 59-63 [Ker 323];
F. Mossé, 'Another Lost Manuscript of the OE *Orosius?' ES* 36 [1955] 199-203 and Ker
1957, 448 [Ker 375]; J.M. Bately, 'The Vatican Fragment of the Old English Orosius,'
ES 45 [1964] 224-30 [Ker 391]
proposed eds. J.M. Bately, *NM* 70 [1969] 520; Klaus Guddat [Munich diss.] [Ohthere
and Wulfstan passages, Book I], *NM* 71 [1970] 489

9.3
Boethius, The Consolation of Philosophy

MS   London, British Museum, Cotton Otho A.VI   **Ker 167**
     Oxford, Bodleian, Junius 12 [transcript]
     Oxford, Bodleian, Bodley 180   **Ker 305**
     Oxford, Bodleian, Junius 86 end-leaf [now missing]   **Ker 337**
ed   W.J. Sedgefield, *King Alfred's Old English Version of Boethius' De Consolatione
     Philosophiae,* Oxford 1899 [Darmstadt 1968] [Ker 167 and Ker 305, printed and coll.];
     A.S. Napier, 'Bruchstück einer altenglischen Boetiushandschrift,' *ZfdA* 31 [1887] 52-4
     [Ker 337]
     See A.6

9.4
St Augustine, Soliloquies

MS   London, British Museum, Cotton Tiberius A.III   **Ker 186 art.9g**
     London, British Museum, Cotton Vitellius A.XV   **Ker 215 art.1**
     Oxford, Bodleian, Junius 70 [transcript]
ed   H. Logeman, *Anglia* 12 [1889] 511-3 [Ker 186 art.9g]; W. Endter, *König Alfreds des
     Grossen Bearbeitung der Soliloquien des Augustinus,* Bib. ags. Prosa 11, Hamburg 1922
     [Darmstadt 1964]; T.A. Carnicelli, *King Alfred's Version of St. Augustine's Soliloquies,*
     Cambridge, Mass., 1969: see review E.G. Stanley, *N & Q* 215 [1970] 109-12 [Ker 215 art.1]

9.5
Gregory the Great, Dialogues

MS   Cambridge, Corpus Christi College, 322   **Ker 60**
     Canterbury, Cathedral, Add. 25   **Ker 96**
     London, British Museum, Cotton Otho C.I vol.2   **Ker 182 art.1**
     Oxford, Bodleian, Hatton 76   **Ker 328A art.1**
ed   H. Hecht, *Bischof Waerferths von Worcester Uebersetzung der Dialoge Gregors des
     Grossen,* Bib. ags. Prosa 5, Leipzig and Hamburg 1900-7 [Darmstadt 1965] [Ker 60 and
     328A art.1]
     coll. Hecht 1900-7, 307/16-310/13, 313/21-316/16 [Ker 96]; as O [Ker 182 art.1]
     proposed eds. N.C. Hultin, Waterloo; L.H. Malmberg, Durham, *OEN* 4 [1971] 26
     See A.38

9.6
Bede, History of the English Church and Nation

MS   Cambridge, University Library, Kk.3.18   **Ker 23**
     Cambridge, Corpus Christi College, 41   **Ker 32 art.1**
     London, British Museum, Cotton Domitian IX   **Ker 151 art.1**
     London, British Museum, Cotton Otho B.XI   **Ker 180 art.1**

London, British Museum, Add. 43703 [Nowell transcript]
Oxford, Bodleian, Tanner 10   **Ker 351**
Oxford, Corpus Christi College, 279 pt. II   **Ker 354**

ed   T. Miller, *The Old English Version of Bede's Ecclesiastical History of the English People*, EETS 95, 96, 110, 111, London 1890-8 [1959-63] ; J. Schipper, *König Alfreds Uebersetzung von Bedas Kirchengeschichte*, Bib. ags. Prosa 4, Leipzig 1897-9; J. Zupitza, 'Drei alte Excerpte aus Älfreds Beda,' *ZfdA* 30 [1886] 185-6 [Ker 151 art. 1]
proposed ed. R. Schmidt, Göttingen [Nowell transcript]

9.7
Alcuin, De Virtutibus et Vitiis

MS   Cambridge, University Library, Ii. 1.33 chs. 1-13   **Ker 18 art. 41**
London, British Museum, Cotton Tiberius A. III chs. 14, 26   **Ker 186 arts. 26, 27**
London, British Museum, Cotton Vespasian D. XIV chs. 1-16   **Ker 209 art. 35**
Vercelli, Biblioteca Capitolare, CXVII chs. 27-34   **Ker 394 art. 25**

ed   M. Förster, 'Altenglische Predigtquellen II,' *Archiv* 122 [1909] 257-9, 260-1 [Ker 186] arts. 26, 27] ; Warner 1917, 91-105 [Ker 209 art. 35] ; B. Assmann, 'Uebersetzung von Alcuins De virtutibus et vitiis liber ad Widonem comitem,' *Anglia* 11 [1889] 371-91
proposed ed. R. Torkar, Giessen, *NM* 67 [1966] 192-3

9.8
Augustine

MS   London, British Museum, Cotton Vespasian D. XIV   **Ker 209 art. 24**
ed   Warner 1917, 65

9.9
Honorius of Autun, Elucidarium

MS   London, British Museum, Cotton Vespasian D. XIV   **Ker 209 arts. 48, 49**
ed   Warner 1917, 140-5

10
Rules for Monks and Canons

10.1
Amalarius of Metz, De Regula Canonicorum
See B. 2. 2. 7

10.2
Basil, Admonitio ad Filium Spiritualem
See B. 1. 6. 6

10.3
Benedict, Rule

10.3.1
S   Cambridge, Corpus Christi College, 178   **Ker 41B art. 1**
Gloucester, Cathedral, 35   **Ker 117 art. 3**

London, British Museum, Cotton Faustina A.X   **Ker 154B art. 1**
London, British Museum, Cotton Titus A.IV   **Ker 200 art. 1**
Oxford, Corpus Christi College, 197   **Ker 353 art. 1**
ed   A. Schröer, *Die angelsächsischen Prosabearbeitungen der Benediktinerregel,* Bib. ags.
Prosa 2, Kassel 1885-8; reprinted with appendix, H. Gneuss, Darmstadt 1964

10.3.2
MS   Durham, Cathedral, B.IV. 24   **Ker 109**
London, British Museum, Cotton Tiberius A.III   **Ker 186 art. 25**
coll. G. Caro, 'Die Varianten der Durhamer Hs. und des Tiberius-fragments der ae. Prosa-
version der Benedictinerregel,' *Englische Studien* 24 [1898] 161-76 [unreliable]

10.3.3
MS   Wells, Cathedral   **Ker 395**
ed   Schröer 1885-8 [1964] , 78-122

10.3.4
MS   London, British Museum, Cotton Claudius D.III   **Ker p. xix, note 2**
ed   A. Schröer, *Die Winteney-Version der Regula S. Benedicti,* Halle 1888

10.4
Chrodegang of Metz, Regula Canonicorum

10.4.1
MS   Cambridge, Corpus Christi College, 191   **Ker 46**
Canterbury, Cathedral, Box CCC no. XIXa   **Ker 97**
ed   A.S. Napier, *The Old English Version, with the Latin Original, of the Enlarged Rule of
Chrodegang,* EETS 150, London 1916

10.4.2
MS   Cambridge, Corpus Christi College, 190   **Ker 45B art. 7**
ed   R. Spindler, *Das altenglische Bussbuch,* Leipzig 1934, 190 [footnote] ; as Napier 1916, 97

10.4.3
MS   London, British Museum, Add. 34652 f. 3   **Ker 128**
ed   A.S. Napier, 'Two Old English Fragments,' *MLN* 12 [1897] 111-4; Napier 1916, 100-1

10.5
Regularis Concordia

10.5.1
MS   Cambridge, Corpus Christi College, 201   **Ker 49A art. 1**
ed   J. Zupitza, 'Ein weiteres Bruchstück der Regularis Concordia in altenglischer Sprache,'
Archiv 84 [1890] 2-16

10.5.2
MS   London, British Museum, Cotton Tiberius A.III ff. 174-7   **Ker 155**
ed   A. Schröer, 'De Consuetudine Monachorum,' *Englische Studien* 9 [1886] 294-6

10.6
Theodulf of Orleans, Capitula

10.6.1
MS Cambridge, Corpus Christi College, 201 pp. 179-202 **Ker 50 art. 3**
ed B. Thorpe, *Ancient Laws and Institutes of England,* Great Britain Public Records
Commission vol. 28, London 1840, 469-88 [folio edition]

10.6.2
MS Oxford, Bodleian, Bodley 865 **Ker 318**
ed Napier 1916, 102-18

10.7
Rules of Confraternity
MS London, British Museum, Cotton Titus D.XXVI **Ker 202 art. d**
Paris, Bibliothèque Nationale, Lat. 943 **Ker 364 art. b**
ed W. de G. Birch, *Liber Vitae of New Minster and Hyde Abbey,* Hampshire Record Society,
London 1892, 47 [Ker 202 art. d] ; Brotanek 1913, 27-8 [Ker 364 art. b] ; M. Förster,
'Die altenglischen Texte der Pariser Nationalbibliothek,' *Englische Studien* 62 [1927-8]
123-5

11
Confessional and Penitential Texts

11.1
Confessionale Pseudo-Egberti

11.1.1
MS Cambridge, Corpus Christi College, 190 **Ker 45B art. 6**
Oxford, Bodleian, Junius 121 **Ker 338 art. 24**
Oxford, Bodleian, Laud Misc. 482 **Ker 343 art. 11**
ed Spindler 1934, 170-94

11.1.2
MS Cambridge, Corpus Christi College, 320 **Ker 58 art. b**
not edited

11.1.3
MS London, British Museum, Cotton Galba A.XIV **Ker 157 art. III**
not edited

11.1.4
MS London, British Museum, Cotton Tiberius A.III **Ker 186 art. 9** [i]
ed H. Logeman, 'Anglo-Saxonica Minora,' *Anglia* 12 [1889] 515-8

11.1.5
MS Oxford, Bodleian, Bodley 343 **Ker 310 art. 37**
ed Napier 1883 [1967], 289-91
See B.3.4.45

11.2
Additional sections printed by Spindler

11.2.1
Sections a-y

MS Brussels, Bibliothèque Royale, 8558-63 [section x]   **Ker 10C art. 2c**
Cambridge, Corpus Christi College, 190 [sections o-x]   **Ker 45B art. 8**
London, British Museum, Cotton Tiberius A.III [sections a-m, y]   **Ker 186 art. 21h-j**
Oxford, Bodleian, Junius 121 [sections a-l, n-x]   **Ker 338 arts. 16, 22**
Oxford, Bodleian, Laud Misc. 482 [sections x, o-x, y]   **Ker 343 arts. 3, 9, 10**
ed Spindler 1934, 170-4
See also B.11.1.4, 11.1.5

11.2.2
Section z

MS Brussels, Bibliothèque Royale, 8558-63   **Ker 10C art. 2b**
Cambridge, Corpus Christi College, 190   **Ker 45B art. 10**
Oxford, Bodleian, Laud Misc. 482   **Ker 343 art. 2**
ed Spindler 1934, 174-5

11.3
Poenitentiale Pseudo-Egberti

11.3.1

MS Brussels, Bibliothèque Royale, 8558-63 [Book 4]   **Ker 10C art. 2a**
Cambridge, Corpus Christi College, 190 [Books 1-4]   **Ker 45B art. 9**
Oxford, Bodleian, Hatton 114 [Book 3, 15-6]   **Ker 331 arts. 70, 71**
Oxford, Bodleian, Junius 121 [Books 1-4 and extracts]   **Ker 338 arts. 23, 25**
Oxford, Bodleian, Laud Misc. 482 [Books 1-4 and extracts]   **Ker 343 arts. 1, 18**
ed J. Raith, *Die altenglische Version des Halitgar'schen Bussbuches,* Bib. ags. Prosa 13, Hamburg 1933 [Darmstadt 1964]

11.3.2
Sanctus Gregorius

MS Brussels, Bibliothèque Royale 8558-63   **Ker 10C art. 2d**
Oxford, Bodleian, Laud Misc. 482   **Ker 343 art. 4**
ed Raith 1933, 71-3

11.4
Handbook for the Use of a Confessor

MS Brussels, Bibliothèque Royale, 8558-63   **Ker 10C art. 1a-g**
Cambridge, Corpus Christi College, 201   **Ker 49B art. 50a-i**
Cambridge, Corpus Christi College, 265   **Ker 53 art. a**
London, British Museum, Cotton Otho B.X [burnt]   **Ker 177B**
London, British Museum, Cotton Tiberius A.III   **Ker 186 art. 9j-l, 21**
Oxford, Bodleian, Junius 121   **Ker 338 arts. 2, 19-21**
Oxford, Bodleian, Laud Misc. 482   **Ker 343 arts. 8, 12-6**
ed Roger Fowler, 'A Late Old English Handbook for the Use of a Confessor,' *Anglia* 83 [1965] 16-34

11.5
Poenitentiale Theodori and Capitula d'Acheriana
MS   Brussels, Bibliothèque Royale, 8558-63   **Ker 10C art. 2e**
      Cambridge, Corpus Christi College, 190   **Ker 45B art. 12**
      Oxford, Bodleian, Laud Misc. 482   **Ker 343 arts. 5, 7**
ed   F.J. Mone, *Quellen und Forschungen zur Geschichte der teutschen Literatur und Sprache,* Aachen and Leipzig 1830, 515-27; Thorpe 1840, II, 228-30, 236

11.6
Poenitentiale Remense
MS   Oxford, Bodleian, Laud Misc. 482 [sections o-x]   **Ker 343 art. 9**
      coll. Spindler 1934, 172-4
      See B. 11.2.1

11.7
Directions to recite the Penitential Psalms
MS   Cambridge, University Library, Ii. 1.33   **Ker 18 art. 8a**
ed   Ker 1957, 24

11.8
Equivalence of Masses and Fasts
MS   Oxford, Bodleian, Hatton 115   **Ker 332 art. 35g, h**
ed   Cockayne 1864-6, III, 166

11.9
Forms of Confession and Absolution

11.9.1
MS   Cambridge, Corpus Christi College, 190   **Ker 45B art. 13**
ed   M. Förster, 'Zur Liturgik der angelsächsischen Kirche,' *Anglia* 66 [1942] 14-8

11.9.2
MS   London, British Museum, Cotton Galba A. XIV   **Ker 157 art. III**
ed   Ker 1957, 199

11.9.3
MS   London, British Museum, Cotton Tiberius A. III   **Ker 186 art. 9a, e**
      London, British Museum, Royal 2 B. V   **Ker 249 arts. d, g**
ed   Logeman, *Anglia* 12 [1889] 501-3 and *Anglia* 11 [1889] 112-5; L. G. Hallander, 'Two Old English Confessional Prayers,' *Stockholm Studies in Modern Philology,* n.s.3 [1968] 100-2 [Ker 186 art. 9e and 249 art. d]

11.9.4
MS   London, British Museum, Cotton Tiberius C. I   **Ker 197 arts. e, f**
ed   Logeman, *Anglia* 11 [1889] 101-3

11.9.5
MS   Paris, Bibliothèque Nationale, Lat. 10575   **Ker 370 art. a**
ed   Förster 1927-8, 114

11.10
Formulas and Directions for the Use of Confessors

11.10.1
MS Cambridge, Corpus Christi College, 190 **Ker 45B art. 11**
ed Thorpe 1840, II, 224-8

11.10.2
MS Cambridge, Corpus Christi College, 320 **Ker 58 art. a**
    not edited

11.10.3
MS London, British Museum, Cotton Tiberius A.III **Ker 186 art. 9h**
ed Logeman, *Anglia* 12 [1889] 513-5
    See B. 1. 2. 8

11.10.4
MS London, British Museum, Cotton Tiberius C.I **Ker 197 art. h**
ed Ker 1959, 275-7

11.10.5
MS Oxford, Bodleian, Laud Misc. 482 **Ker 343 art. 17**
    not edited
    See B. 3. 4. 26, 11. 1. 5, 11. 10. 2

11.11
Title before a Latin form of confession
MS London, British Museum, Cotton Vespasian D.XV **Ker 211**
ed F. Holthausen, 'Anglo-Saxonica,' *Anglia* 11 [1889] 172; Ker 1957, 277

12
Liturgical Texts, Creeds, Prayers

12.1
Forms of Adjuration

12.1.1
MS   Durham, Cathedral, A.IV. 19 **Ker 106 art. a**
     London, British Museum, Cotton Vitellius A.VII **Ker 213 art. b**
facs T.J. Brown, F. Wormald, A.S.C. Ross, E.G. Stanley, *The Durham Ritual: An English
     Collectar of the Tenth Century*, EEMF 16, Copenhagen 1969 [Ker 106 art. a]
ed   Thompson and Lindelöf 1927, 114 [Ker 106 art. a] ; F. Liebermann, *Die Gesetze der
     Angelsächsen*, Halle 1903-16 [Aalen 1960] 412 [Jud. Dei VI] [Ker 213 art. b]
     See B. 14. 41

12.1.2
MS Cambridge, Corpus Christi College, 146 **Ker 37 arts. a, b**
    London, British Museum, Cotton Vitellius A.VII **Ker 213 arts. c, d**

ed Liebermann 1903-16, 413-4 [Jud. Dei VII, 12.1A, 13A]
See B.14.41

12.1.3
MS Cambridge, Corpus Christi College, 146 **Ker 37 arts.c, d**
ed Liebermann 1903-16, 414 [Jud. Dei VII, 23A, 24A]

12.1.4
MS Cambridge, Corpus Christi College, 422 **Ker 70B art.1**
ed Liebermann 1903-16, 415 [Jud. Dei VIII]

12.2
Forms for use at the Visitation of the Sick
MS London, British Museum, Cotton Titus D.XXIV **Ker 201 arts.a, b**
ed Ker 1957, 264

12.3
Creeds

12.3.1
Se læssa creda
MS Cambridge, University Library, Gg.3.28 **Ker 15 art.94**
London, British Museum, Cotton Cleopatra B.XIII **Ker 144 art.10**
London, British Museum, Cotton Tiberius C.I **Ker 197 art.c**
ed Thorpe 1844-6, II, 596; Logeman 1889, 100-1 [Ker 197 art.c]

12.3.2
Mæsse creda
MS Cambridge, University Library, Gg.3.28 **Ker 15 art.94**
Oxford, Bodleian, Hatton 114 **Ker 331 art.85**
ed Thorpe 1844-6, II, 596; M. Förster, 'Die altenglischen Bekenntnisformeln,' *Englische Studien* 75 [1942-3] 168-9

12.3.3
MS Oxford, Bodleian, Junius 121 **Ker 338 art.41**
ed S.J. Crawford, 'The Worcester Marks and Glosses of the Old English Manuscripts in the Bodleian,' *Anglia* 52 [1928] 5

12.4
Prayers

12.4.1
Pater Noster
MS Cambridge, University Library, Gg.3.28 **Ker 15 art.94**
London, British Museum, Cotton Cleopatra B.XIII **Ker 144 art.10**
London, British Museum, Cotton Tiberius C.II **Ker 197 art.b**
London, British Museum, Cotton Vitellius A.XII **Ker 214**
ed Thorpe 1844-6, II, 596; Logeman, *Anglia* 11 [1889] 100 [Ker 197 art.b] ; Adrian Morey, *Bartholomew of Exeter, Bishop and Canonist,* Cambridge 1937, 300 [Ker 214]
See B.1.9.10

12.4.2
Bidding Prayers
MS York, Minster   **Ker 402 art.e**
ed W.H. Stevenson, 'Yorkshire Surveys and other Eleventh-Century Documents in the York Gospels,' *EHR* 27 [1912] 10

12.4.3
Confessional Prayers

12.4.3.1
MS Cambridge, Corpus Christi College, 391   **Ker 67 art.a**
    London, British Museum, Cotton Tiberius A.III   **Ker 186 art.9d**
    London, British Museum, Royal 2 B.V   **Ker 249 art.c**
ed J. Zupitza, 'Eine weitere Aufzeichnung der Oratio pro peccatis,' *Archiv* 84 [1890] 327-8; Logeman 1889, 499-500

12.4.3.2
MS London, British Museum, Cotton Tiberius A.III   **Ker 186 art.9b**
    London, British Museum, Royal 2 B.V   **Ker 249 art.h**
ed M. Förster, 'Beiträge zur mittelalterlichen Volkskunde III,' *Archiv* 121 [1908] 46

12.4.3.3
MS London, British Museum, Cotton Tiberius A.III   **Ker 186 art.9f**
    London, British Museum, Royal 2 B.V   **Ker 249 art.e**
ed Logeman, *Anglia* 12 [1889] 504-11; Hallander 1968, 102-10

12.4.3.4
MS London, British Museum, Cotton Tiberius C.I   **Ker 197 art.d**
ed Logeman, *Anglia* 11 [1889] 101

12.4.3.5
MS London, British Museum, Cotton Vespasian D.XX   **Ker 212**
ed Logeman, *Anglia* 11 [1889] 97-100

12.4.4
Prayers to the Cross
MS Cambridge, Corpus Christi College, 391   **Ker 69 art.b**
    London, British Museum, Cotton Galba A.XIV   **Ker 157 arts.VI–VIII**
ed J. Zupitza, 'Kreuzandacht,' *Archiv* 88 [1892] 361-4; R.A. Banks, 'Some Anglo-Saxon Prayers from British Museum Ms. Cotton Galba A.XIV,' *N & Q* 210 [1965] 208

12.4.5
Prayers at Tierce
MS London, British Museum, Cotton Galba A.XIV   **Ker 157 arts.IV, V**
ed Banks 1965, 209-13; W. Braekman, 'Some Minor Old English Texts,' *Archiv* 202 [1965] 271-5

12.4.6
Prayer for Victory
MS   London, British Museum, Cotton Galba A.XIV   **Ker 157 art.I**
ed   W. de G. Birch, *Cartularium Saxonicum,* London 1885-99, no.657

12.4.7
Prayer following Boethius translation
MS   Oxford, Bodleian, Bodley 180   **Ker 305**
ed   Sedgefield 1899, 149

12.4.8
Prayer following Homily for the Feast of an Apostle
MS   Cambridge, Corpus Christi College, 303   **Ker 57 art.21**
     Cambridge, Corpus Christi College, 421   **Ker 68 art.16**
ed   Ker 1957, 101 [Ker 57 art.21]; Förster 1942, 49 [Ker 68 art.16]

12.4.9
Directions for private devotion
MS   London, British Museum, Cotton Titus D.XXVI   **Ker 202 art.a**
ed   Birch 1892, 251

12.4.10
Rubrics and Directions for the use of Prayers
MS   London, British Museum, Cotton Galba A.XIV   **Ker 157 arts.II, XI**
     London, British Museum, Cotton Tiberius A.III   **Ker 186 art.10c**
     London, British Museum, Cotton Tiberius C.VI   **Ker 199 art.c**
     London, British Museum, Cotton Titus D.XXVI   **Ker 202 art.b**
     London, British Museum, Royal 2 A.XX   **Ker 248 art.b**
ed   Ker 1957, 199-200 [Ker 157 arts.II, XI], 244 [Ker 186 art.10c], 262 [Ker 199 art.c],
     264 [Ker 202 art.b], 318 [Ker 248 art.b]; J. Zupitza, 'Mercisches aus der Hs. Royal
     2.A.20 im Britischen Museum,' *ZfdA* 33 [1889] 64-6 [Ker 248 art.b]

12.5
Rubrics and Directions for the use of Forms of Service

12.5.1
MS   Cambridge, University Library, Ll.1.10   **Ker 27 art.a**
ed   A.B. Kuypers, *The Book of Cerne,* Cambridge 1902, 3

12.5.2
MS   Cambridge, Corpus Christi College, 41   **Ker 32 art.2**
ed   Ker 1957, 43-4

12.5.3
MS   Cambridge, Corpus Christi College, 422   **Ker 70B arts.k, m, o-q**
ed   B. Fehr, 'Altenglische Ritualtexte für Krankenbesuch, heilige Oelung und Begräbnis,'

in M. Förster and K. Wildhagen, eds., *Texte und Forschungen zur englischen Kultur-geschichte: Festgabe für Felix Liebermann,* Halle 1921, 48-63; Ker 1957, 120 [arts.k, o, p] ; art.m not printed except headings on pp.369, 387, and 400-2

12.5.4
MS Cambridge, Sidney Sussex College, 100 pt.II **Ker 82**
ed Ker 1957, 128

12.5.5
MS Durham, Cathedral, A.IV.19 **Ker 106 arts.b, e, g**
facs Brown et al. 1969
ed Thompson and Lindelöf 1927, 114-9 [art.b] , 160 [art.e] , 213-4 [art.g]

12.5.6
MS London, British Museum, Add. 37517 **Ker 129**
ed Ker 1957, 161

12.5.7
MS London, British Museum, Cotton Vitellius C.VIII **Ker 221 art.1**
ed Ker 1957, 292

12.5.8
MS London, British Museum, Cotton Vitellius E.XVIII **Ker 224 art.q**
ed Ker 1957, 300

12.5.9
MS Oxford, Bodleian, Bodley 572 **Ker 313 arts.a-c**
ed Ker 1957, 376-7

12.5.10
MS Oxford, Bodleian, Hatton 93 **Ker 330**
ed Ker 1957, 390

12.5.11
MS Oxford, Bodleian, Laud Misc. 482 **Ker 343 art.18**
ed Fehr 1921, 46-66

12.5.12
MS Rouen, Bibliothèque Municipale, Y6 **Ker 377 art.a**
ed H.A. Wilson, *The Missal of Robert of Jumièges,* Henry Bradshaw Society 11, London 1896, lxxv, 287-94

12.5.13
MS Worcester, Cathedral, F.173 **Ker 397**
ed Ker 1957, 465-6

12.6
On Allelulia

12.6.1
MS Cambridge, Corpus Christi College, 321 f. 139* **Ker 59**
ed M.R. James, *A Descriptive Catalogue of the Manuscripts in the Library of Corpus Christi College, Cambridge,* Cambridge 1912, II, 138

12.6.2
MS London, British Museum, Harley 3271 **Ker 239 art. 11d**
ed H. Henel, 'Altenglischer Mönchsaberglaube,' *Englische Studien* 69 [1934-5] 349

12.7
Benedictine Office
MS Cambridge, Corpus Christi College, 201 **Ker 49B art. 49**
Oxford, Bodleian, Junius 121 **Ker 338 art. 11**
ed James Ure, *The Benedictine Office,* Edinburgh University Publications in Language and Literature 11, Edinburgh 1957, 81-106

12.8
The Clauses of the Creed
MS London, British Museum, Royal 2 A.XX **Ker 248 art. c**
ed Zupitza 1889, 60

12.9
On the Mass: Celebration on Vigils
MS Cambridge, Corpus Christi College, 190 **Ker 45B arts. 4, 5**
ed Fehr 1914, Anhang I, II, 228-32

12.10
Dialogue between Jerome and Damasus
MS London, British Museum, Cotton Caligula A.XV **Ker 139A art. w**
London, British Museum, Stowe 944 **Ker 274 art. i**
ed A.S. Napier, 'Altenglische Kleinigkeiten,' *Anglia* 11 [1889] 7-8 [Ker 139A art. w] ; Birch 1892, 165 [Ker 274 art. i]

12.11
Admonition on Excommunication
MS London, British Museum, Cotton Tiberius A.XIII **Ker 190B art. c**
ed Ker 1957, 251

13
Laws and Institutes, Ecclesiastical

13.1.1
'Canons of Edgar'
MS Cambridge, University Library, Add. 3206 **Ker 11**
Cambridge, Corpus Christi College, 201 **Ker 49B art. 45**
Oxford, Bodleian, Junius 121 **Ker 338 art. 5**
ed Jost 1959, 178-209; Roger Fowler, *Wulfstan's Canons of Edgar,* EETS 266, London 1972, 1-19; 20 [Ker 11]

13.1.2
Related texts
MS   Cambridge, University Library, Ii.1.33 [Canons of Edgar 14-6]   **Ker 18 art.42**
    not edited

13.2
'Institutes of Polity'
MS   Cambridge, University Library, Add. 3206 [partial]   **Ker 11**
    Cambridge, Corpus Christi College, 201   **Ker 49B arts.18-20, 24, 42, 52**
    Cambridge, Corpus Christi College, 421 [partial]   **Ker 69 art.10**
    London, British Museum, Cotton Nero A.I ff.70-177   **Ker 164 arts.1, 11-3, 15-9, 23-4**
    Oxford, Bodleian, Junius 121   **Ker 338 arts.1-4, 6-7, 13-4**
facs   Loyn 1971 [Ker 164 arts.1, 11-3, 15-9, 23-4]
  ed   Jost 1959, 39-165, 167-77, 210-6

13.3
De ecclesiasticis gradibus
MS   Cambridge, Corpus Christi College, 190   **Ker 45B art.19**
    Cambridge, Corpus Christi College, 201   **Ker 49B art.48**
    Oxford, Bodleian, Junius 121   **Ker 338 art.9**
  ed   Jost 1959, 223-41

13.4
Duties of Bishops
MS   London, British Museum, Cotton Nero A.I ff.70-177   **Ker 164 art.14**
facs   Loyn 1971
  ed   Jost 1959, 262-7

13.5
Duties of Kings
See B.14.19

13.6
Duties of Clergy
MS   Brussels, Bibliothèque Royale, 8558-63   **Ker 10C art.3**
    Cambridge, Corpus Christi College, 201   **Ker 49B art.52**
    Oxford, Bodleian, Junius 121   **Ker 338 art.8**
  ed   Fowler 1972, 21 [Ker 10C art.3]; Jost 1959, 104-5, 256-61 [Ker 49B art.52], 217-22
    [Ker 338 art.8]

14
Laws of England
  ed   F. Liebermann, *Die Gesetze der Angelsächsen,* Halle 1903-16 [Aalen 1960]

14.1
Æthelberht
MS   Rochester, Cathedral, Textus Roffensis   **Ker 373A art.1**
facs   P.H. Sawyer, *Textus Roffensis,* EEMF 7, 11, Copenhagen 1957-62

ed Liebermann 1903-16, 3-8; K.A. Eckhardt, *Leges Anglo-Saxonorum 601-925,* Göttingen 1958, 18-36

14.2
Hlothære and Eadric
MS Rochester, Cathedral, Textus Roffensis   **Ker 373A art.2**
facs Sawyer 1957-62
ed Liebermann 1903-16, 9-11; Eckhardt 1958, 40-4

14.3
Wihtræd
MS Rochester, Cathedral, Textus Roffensis   **Ker 373A art.3**
facs Sawyer 1957-62
ed Liebermann 1903-16, 12-4; Eckhardt 1958, 48-54

14.4
Alfred-Ine
MS Cambridge, Corpus Christi College, 173   **Ker 39 art.2**
Cambridge, Corpus Christi College, 383   **Ker 65 art.1**
London, British Museum, Burney 277 f.42   **Ker 136**
London, British Museum, Cotton Nero A.I ff.3-57   **Ker 163 arts.4, 7**
London, British Museum, Cotton Otho B.XI and Add. 43703   **Ker 180 art.6**
Rochester, Cathedral, Textus Roffensis   **Ker 373A art.6**
facs Flower and Smith 1941 [Ker 39 art.2] ; Loyn 1971 [Ker 163 arts.4, 7] ; Sawyer 1957-62 [Ker 373A art.6]
ed Liebermann 1903-16, 16-123; Eckhardt 1958, 58-172

14.5
Alfred and Guthrum
MS Cambridge, Corpus Christi College, 383   **Ker 65 arts.6, 17**
ed Liebermann 1903-16, 126-8; Eckhardt 1958, 176-8

14.6
Edward and Guthrum
MS Cambridge, Corpus Christi College, 383   **Ker 65 art.7**
Rochester, Cathedral, Textus Roffensis   **Ker 373A art.13**
facs Sawyer 1957-62 [Ker 373A art.13]
ed Liebermann 1903-16, 128-35; Eckhardt 1958, 182-90

14.7
I, II Eadweard
MS Cambridge, Corpus Christi College, 383   **Ker 65 arts.11-3**
Rochester, Cathedral, Textus Roffensis   **Ker 373A arts.15-6**
facs Sawyer 1957-62 [Ker 373A arts.15-6]
ed Liebermann 1903-16, 138-44; Eckhardt 1958, 194-202

14.8
I Æthelstan

MS   Cambridge, Corpus Christi College, 201   **Ker 49B art. 28**
     London, British Museum, Cotton Nero A.I ff. 70-177   **Ker 164 art. 4**
facs   Loyn 1971 [Ker 164 art. 4]
  ed   Liebermann 1903-16, 146-8

14.9
II Æthelstan

MS   Cambridge, Corpus Christi College, 383   **Ker 65 art. 8**
     London, British Museum, Cotton Otho B.XI and Add. 43703   **Ker 180 art. 5**
     Rochester, Cathedral, Textus Roffensis   **Ker 373A art. 9**
facs   Sawyer 1957-62 [Ker 373A art. 9]
  ed   Liebermann 1903-16, 150-64

14.10
V Æthelstan

MS   London, British Museum, Cotton Otho B.XI and Add. 43703   **Ker 180 art. 5**
     Rochester, Cathedral, Textus Roffensis   **Ker 373A art. 10**
facs   Sawyer 1957-62 [Ker 373A art. 10]
  ed   Liebermann 1903-16, 166-8

14.11
IV Æthelstan, 6

MS   Rochester, Cathedral, Textus Roffensis   **Ker 373A art. 10**
facs   Sawyer 1957-62
  ed   Liebermann 1903-16, 171

14.12
VI Æthelstan

MS   Rochester, Cathedral, Textus Roffensis   **Ker 373A art. 27**
facs   Sawyer 1957-62
  ed   Liebermann 1903-16, 173-83

14.13
I Eadmund

MS   Cambridge, Corpus Christi College, 201   **Ker 49B art. 44**
     Cambridge, Corpus Christi College, 383   **Ker 65 art. 14**
     London, British Museum, Cotton Nero A.I ff. 70-177   **Ker 164 art. 5**
     Rochester, Cathedral, Textus Roffensis   **Ker 373A art. 17**
facs   Loyn 1971 [Ker 164 art. 5] ; Sawyer 1957-62 [Ker 373A art. 17]
  ed   Liebermann 1903-16, 184-6

14.14
II Eadmund

MS   Cambridge, Corpus Christi College, 383   **Ker 65 art. 15**
     Rochester, Cathedral, Textus Roffensis   **Ker 373A art. 18**
facs   Sawyer 1957-62
  ed   Liebermann 1903-16, 186-90

14.15
Hundredgemot
MS   Cambridge, Corpus Christi College, 383   **Ker 65 art.4**
ed   Liebermann 1903-16, 192-4

14.16
II Eadgar
MS   Cambridge, Corpus Christi College, 201   **Ker 49B art.22**
London, British Museum, Cotton Nero A.I ff.3-57   **Ker 163 art.3**
London, British Museum, Harley 55 ff.1-4   **Ker 225 art.2**
copy of 1811, belonging to K. Sisam   **Ker 411**
facs   Loyn 1971 [Ker 163 art.3]
ed   Liebermann 1903-16, 194-200

14.17
III Eadgar
MS   Cambridge, Corpus Christi College, 201   **Ker 49B art.23**
London, British Museum, Cotton Nero A.I ff.3-57   **Ker 163 art.3**
London, British Museum, Cotton Nero A.I ff.70-177   **Ker 164 art.6**
London, British Museum, Harley 55 ff.1-4   **Ker 225 art.2**
copy of 1811, belonging to K. Sisam   **Ker 411**
facs   Loyn 1971 [Ker 163 art.3, 164 art.6]
ed   Liebermann 1903-16, 200-6

14.18
IV Eadgar
MS   Cambridge, Corpus Christi College, 265 ff.1-268   **Ker 53 art.b**
London, British Museum, Cotton Nero E.I vol.2 ff.185-6   **Ker 166**
ed   Liebermann 1903-16, 206-14

14.19
Promissio Regis
MS   London, British Museum, Cotton Cleopatra B.XIII ff.1-58   **Ker 144 art.7**
London, British Museum, Cotton Vitellius A.VII ff.1-112   **Ker 213 art.a**
Oxford, Bodleian, Junius 60 [trans.]
ed   Liebermann 1903-16, 214-6; W. Stubbs, *Memorials of St. Dunstan*, Rolls Series 63,
London 1874, 355-7

14.20
I Æthelred
MS   Cambridge, Corpus Christi College, 383   **Ker 65 art.5**
Rochester, Cathedral, Textus Roffensis   **Ker 373A art.19**
facs   Sawyer 1957-62 [Ker 373A art.19]
ed   Liebermann 1903-16, 216-20

14.21
II Æthelred

MS Cambridge, Corpus Christi College, 383 **Ker 65 art. 22**
ed Liebermann 1903-16, 220-6

14.22
III Æthelred
MS Rochester, Cathedral, Textus Roffensis **Ker 373A art. 21**
facs Sawyer 1957-62
ed Liebermann 1903-16, 228-32

14.23
V Æthelred
MS Cambridge, Corpus Christi College, 201 **Ker 49B art. 24**
    London, British Museum, Cotton Nero A.I ff. 70-177 **Ker 164 arts. 7, 22**
facs Loyn 1971 [Ker 164 arts. 7, 22]
ed Liebermann 1903-16, 236-46

14.24
VI Æthelred
MS Cambridge, Corpus Christi College, 201 **Ker 49B art. 51**
    London, British Museum, Cotton Claudius A.III **Ker 141 art. b**
    York, Minster **Ker 402 art. b[I]**
ed Liebermann 1903-16, 246-58
    See B.3.4.48

14.25
VIIa Æthelred
MS Cambridge, Corpus Christi College, 201 **Ker 49B art. 16**
ed Liebermann 1903-16, 262
    See B.3.4.31

14.26
VIII Æthelred
MS Cambridge, Corpus Christi College, 201 **Ker 49B art. 43**
    London, British Museum, Cotton Nero A.I ff. 70-177 **Ker 164 art. 9**
    [cf. Ker 338 art. 13]
facs Loyn 1971 [Ker 164 art. 9]
ed Liebermann 1903-16, 263-8

14.27
IX Æthelred
MS London, British Museum, Cotton Otho A.X [burnt] **Ker 170 art. 3**
ed Liebermann 1903-16, 269 [from Wanley]

14.28
X Æthelred
MS Vatican City, Reg. Lat. 946 ff. 72-6 **Ker 392**
ed Liebermann 1903-16, 269-70

14.29
Cnut, 1020
MS   York, Minster   **Ker 402 art.c**
 ed Liebermann 1903-16, 273-5
     See B.16.24.5

14.30
I, II Cnut
MS   Cambridge, University Library, Add. 3206 [extract]   **Ker 11**
     Cambridge, Corpus Christi College, 201   **Ker 49B arts.51,2**
     Cambridge, Corpus Christi College, 383   **Ker 65 arts.9,10**
     London, British Museum, Cotton Nero A.I ff.3-57   **Ker 163 arts.1, 2**
     London, British Museum, Harley 55 ff.5-13   **Ker 226**
     Oxford, Bodleian, Junius 121 [extract]   **Ker 338 art.1**
     York, Minster [extract]   **Ker 402 art.b[I]**
facs Loyn 1971 [Ker 163 arts.1, 2]
 ed Liebermann 1903-16, 278-370
     See B.3.4.48

14.31
Dunsæte
MS   Cambridge, Corpus Christi College, 383   **Ker 65 art.23**
 ed Liebermann 1903-16, 374-8

14.32
Norðhymbra preosta lagu
MS   Cambridge, Corpus Christi College, 201   **Ker 49B art.21**
 ed Liebermann 1903-16, 380-5
     See B.13.6 [Ker 10C art.3]

14.33
Ordal
MS   Rochester, Cathedral, Textus Roffensis   **Ker 373A art.7**
facs Sawyer 1957-62
 ed Liebermann 1903-16, 386-7

14.34
Blaseras
MS   Cambridge, Corpus Christi College, 383   **Ker 65 art.2**
     Rochester, Cathedral, Textus Roffensis   **Ker 373A art.6**
facs Sawyer 1957-62 [Ker 373A art.6]
 ed Liebermann 1903-16, 388

14.35
Forfang
MS   Cambridge, Corpus Christi College, 383   **Ker 65 arts.2, 3**
     Rochester, Cathedral, Textus Roffensis   **Ker 373A art.6**
facs Sawyer 1957-62 [Ker 373A art.6]
 ed Liebermann 1903-16, 388-90

14.36
Pax
MS   Rochester, Cathedral, Textus Roffensis   **Ker 373A art. 11**
facs   Sawyer 1957-62
ed   Liebermann 1903-16, 390

14.37
Walreaf
MS   Rochester, Cathedral, Textus Roffensis   **Ker 373A art. 8**
facs   Sawyer 1957-62
ed   Liebermann 1903-16, 392

14.38
Wer
MS   Cambridge, Corpus Christi College, 383   **Ker 65 art. 19**
     Rochester, Cathedral, Textus Roffensis   **Ker 373A art. 14**
facs   Sawyer 1957-62 [Ker 373A art. 14]
ed   Liebermann 1903-16, 392-4

14.39
Swerian
MS   Cambridge, Corpus Christi College, 383   **Ker 65 art. 16**
     Rochester, Cathedral, Textus Roffensis   **Ker 373A art. 12**
facs   Sawyer 1957-62 [Ker 373A art. 12]
ed   Liebermann 1903-16, 396-8

14.40
Hit becwæð
MS   Cambridge, Corpus Christi College, 383   **Ker 65 art. 21**
     Rochester, Cathedral, Textus Roffensis   **Ker 373A art. 32**
facs   Sawyer 1957-62 [Ker 373A art. 32]
ed   Liebermann 1903-16, 400

14.41
Judicia Dei IV-VIII
MS   Cambridge, Corpus Christi College, 146   **Ker 37**
     Cambridge, Corpus Christi College, 422   **Ker 70B art.1**
     Durham, Cathedral, A.IV.19   **Ker 106 art.a**
     London, British Museum, Cotton Vitellius A.VII ff. 1-112   **Ker 213 arts.b-d**
facs   Brown et al. 1969 [Ker 106 art.a]
ed   Liebermann 1903-16, 409-15
     See B.12.1

14.42
Excommunicatio VII
MS   Cambridge, Corpus Christi College, 303   **Ker 57 art.69**
ed   Liebermann 1903-16, 438-9

14.43
Wifmannes beweddung

MS Cambridge, Corpus Christi College, 383   **Ker 65 art. 18**
    Rochester, Cathedral, Textus Roffensis   **Ker 373A art. 30**
facs Sawyer 1957-62 [Ker 373A art. 30]
  ed Liebermann 1903-16, 442-4

14.44
Rectitudines

MS Cambridge, Corpus Christi College, 383   **Ker 65 art. 24**
  ed Liebermann 1903-16, 444-53

14.45
Gerefa

MS Cambridge, Corpus Christi College, 383   **Ker 65 art. 25**
  ed Liebermann 1903-16, 453-5

14.46
Geþyncðo

MS Cambridge, Corpus Christi College, 201   **Ker 49B art. 46a**
    Rochester, Cathedral, Textus Roffensis   **Ker 373A art. 28**
facs Sawyer 1957-62 [Ker 373A art. 28]
  ed Liebermann 1903-16, 456-8

14.47
Norðleoda laga

MS Cambridge, Corpus Christi College, 201   **Ker 49B art. 46b**
    Rochester, Cathedral, Textus Roffensis   **Ker 373A art. 29**
facs Sawyer 1957-62 [Ker 373A art. 29]
  ed Liebermann 1903-16, 458-60

14.48
Mircna laga

MS Cambridge, Corpus Christi College, 190   **Ker 45B art. 14**
    Cambridge, Corpus Christi College, 201   **Ker 49B art. 46c**
    Rochester, Cathedral, Textus Roffensis   **Ker 373A art. 12**
facs Sawyer 1957-62 [Ker 373A art. 12]
  ed Liebermann 1903-16, 462-3

14.49
Að

MS Cambridge, Corpus Christi College, 190   **Ker 45B arts. 15, 16**
    Cambridge, Corpus Christi College, 201   **Ker 49B art. 46d, e**
    Rochester, Cathedral, Textus Roffensis   **Ker 373A art. 12**
facs Sawyer 1957-62 [Ker 373A art. 12]
  ed Liebermann 1903-16, 464

14.50
Hadbot
MS Cambridge, Corpus Christi College, 190 **Ker 45B art.16**
Cambridge, Corpus Christi College, 201 **Ker 49B art.46e**
Rochester, Cathedral, Textus Roffensis **Ker 373A art.4**
facs Sawyer 1957-62 [Ker 373A art.4]
ed Liebermann 1903-16, 464-8

14.51
Grið
MS Cambridge, Corpus Christi College, 201 **Ker 49B art.52**
London, British Museum, Cotton Nero A.I ff.70-177 **Ker 164 art.8**
facs Loyn 1971 [Ker 164 art.8]
ed Liebermann 1903-16, 470-3

14.52
Norðhymbra cyricgrið
MS London, British Museum, Cotton Nero A.I ff.70-177 **Ker 164 art.10**
facs Loyn 1971
ed Liebermann 1903-16, 473

14.53
Romscot
MS London, British Museum, Cotton Nero A.I ff.3-57 **Ker 163 art.5**
facs Loyn 1971
ed Liebermann 1903-16, 474

14.54
Judex
MS London, British Museum, Cotton Nero A.I ff.3-57 **Ker 163 art.6**
London, British Museum, Cotton Otho B.XI and Add. 43703 **Ker 180 art.5**
facs Loyn 1971 [Ker 163 art.6]
ed Liebermann 1903-16, 474-6
proposed ed. R. Torkar, Giessen

14.55
Episcopus
MS Oxford, Bodleian, Junius 121 **Ker 338 art.1 [VII]**
ed Liebermann 1903-16, 477-9

14.56
Ymb æbricas
MS London, British Museum, Cotton Otho B.XI and Add. 43703 **Ker 180 art.7**
ed R. Flower, 'The Text of the Burghal Hidage,' *London Mediaeval Studies* 1 [1937] 62

14.57
William I, Lad
MS Rochester, Cathedral, Textus Roffensis **Ker 373A art.20**

facs Sawyer 1957-62
ed Liebermann 1903-16, 483-4

15
Charters in English

15.1
Royal Charters

15.1.1
King Æthelred to St Peter's Minster, Medeshamstede Sawyer 72
MS Oxford, Bodleian, Laud 636 f. 18v-19
facs D. Whitelock, *The Peterborough Chronicle*, EEMF 4, Copenhagen 1954
ed W. de G. Birch, *Cartularium Saxonicum*, London 1885-99 [New York and London 1964], no. 49; C. Plummer, *Two of the Saxon Chronicles Parallel*, Oxford 1892-9, reissued D. Whitelock, Oxford 1952, 35-7

15.1.2
King Æthelred to St Peter's, Gloucester Sawyer 74
MS Cambridge, University Library, Add. 3041 ff. 282v-3
ed H.P.R. Finberg, *The Early Charters of Wessex*, Leicester 1964, 252-3

15.1.3
King Æthelbald to Bishop Milred Sawyer 98
MS London, British Museum, Cotton Tiberius A. XIII f. 20
ed Birch 1885-99, no. 171; A.J. Robertson, *Anglo-Saxon Charters*, Cambridge 1939, 2nd ed. 1956, no. 1

15.1.4
King Offa to Ealdbeorht, Minister Sawyer 125
MS London, British Museum, Stowe Charter 6
London, British Museum, Stowe 853 f. 19rv
London, British Museum, Stowe 1085 f. 109v
facs W.B. Sanders, *Facsimiles of Anglo-Saxon Manuscripts*, Southampton, Ordnance Survey, 1878-84, III, 6 [Stowe Charter 6]
ed Birch 1885-99, no. 248

15.1.5
King Offa to St Mary's Church, Worcester Sawyer 126
MS London, British Museum, Cotton Tiberius A. XIII ff. 147v-8v
ed Birch 1885-99, no. 233; Robertson 1956, no. 2

15.1.6
King Wiglaf to the minster at Hanbury Sawyer 190
MS London, British Museum, Cotton Augustus II.9
Cambridge, Corpus Christi College, 111 pp. 138-7 [sic]
London, British Museum, Cotton Tiberius A. XIII f. 21rv
Oxford, Bodleian, Dodsworth 78 f. 59rv

facs E.A. Bond, *Facsimiles of Ancient Charters in the British Museum,* London 1873-8, II, 24 [Cotton Augustus II.9]
 ed Birch 1885-99, no.416; J. Earle, *A Hand-book to the Land-Charters and other Saxonic Documents,* Oxford 1888, 111-3

15.1.7
King Berhtwulf to Forthred Sawyer 204
 MS Canterbury, Dean and Chapter, Chart. Ant. C.1280
facs Sanders 1878-84, I, 8
 ed Birch 1885-99, no.452; Earle 1888, 122-3

15.1.8
Æthelred, ealdorman, to Berkeley Abbey Sawyer 218
 MS London, British Museum, Cotton Tiberius A.XIII ff.50-1v
      London, British Museum, Cotton Vitellius C.IX f.129
 ed Birch 1885-99, no.551; F.E. Harmer, *Select English Historical Documents of the Ninth and Tenth Centuries,* Cambridge 1914, no.12

15.1.9
Æthelred and Æthelflæd to St Peter's, Worcester Sawyer 223
 MS London, British Museum, Cotton Tiberius A.XIII ff.1v-2
 ed Birch 1885-99, no.579; Harmer 1914, no.13

15.1.10
King Æthelwulf to Ithda Sawyer 287
 MS London, British Museum, Cotton Augustus II.28
facs Bond 1873-8, II, 28
 ed Birch 1885-99, no.426; J.M. Kemble, *Codex Diplomaticus Aevi Saxonici,* English Historical Society, London 1839-48 [1964], no.241

15.1.11
King Æthelwulf to the Church Sawyer 305
 MS London, British Museum, Lansdowne 417 ff.14v-15v
      London, Public Record Office, E 164/24 ff.127-8
      Oxford, Bodleian, Wood empt. 5 ff.29-31
      Oxford, Magdalen College, 172 f.91v
 ed Birch 1885-99, no.470; Kemble 1839-48, no.271

15.1.12
King Æthelwulf to the Church of SS Peter and Paul, Winchester Sawyer 313
 MS Edinburgh, University Library, Laing Charter 18
      London, British Museum, Add. 15350 f.86rv
 ed Birch 1885-99, no.478; Robertson 1956, no.8

15.1.13
King Æthelwulf to Winchester Cathedral Sawyer 325
 MS London, British Museum, Add. 15350 f.117v
 ed Birch 1885-99, no.493; Earle 1888, 349-50

15.1.14
King Æthelberht to Wulflaf   Sawyer 328
MS London, British Museum, Cotton Augustus II.66
acs Bond 1873-8, II, 33
 ed Birch 1885-99, no.496; Robertson 1956, no.10

15.1.15
King Æthelberht to the Church of Sherborne   Sawyer 333
MS London, British Museum, Add. 46487 ff.18v-20v
 ed Birch 1885-99, no.510; Robertson 1956, no.11

15.1.16
King Æthelred to Ælfstan   Sawyer 342
MS London, British Museum, Harley 61 f.20rv
 ed Birch 1885-99, no.526; Robertson 1956, no.12

15.1.17
King Alfred and Archbishop Æthelred to Liaba   Sawyer 344
MS London, British Museum, Stowe Charter 19
acs Sanders 1878-84, III, 19
 ed Birch 1885-99, no.536

15.1.18
King Alfred to Sighelm   Sawyer 350
MS Canterbury, Dean and Chapter, Chart. Ant. F.150
acs Sanders 1878-84, I, 12
 ed Birch 1885-99, no.576; Earle 1888, 157-8

15.1.19
King Alfred to Deormod   Sawyer 355
MS London, British Museum, Cotton Claudius B.VI f.16rv
    London, British Museum, Cotton Claudius C.IX ff.108v-9, 200v
 ed Birch 1885-99, no.581; Kemble 1839-48, no.326 [appendix]

15.1.20
King Alfred to the Church at Shaftesbury   Sawyer 357
MS London, British Museum, Harley 61 ff.21v-2
 ed Birch 1885-99, no.531; Robertson 1956, no.13

15.1.21
King Edward to the familia of Winchester Cathedral   Sawyer 359
MS London, British Museum, Add. 15350 ff.71v-2
 ed Birch 1885-99, no.594; Robertson 1956, no.110

15.1.22
King Edward to Bishop Denewulf   Sawyer 385
MS London, British Museum, Add. 15350 ff.62v-3v
 ed Birch 1885-99, no.622; Robertson 1956, no.20

15.1.23
King Athelstan to Milton Abbey Sawyer 391
MS lost [formerly in K.R. Office]
ed Birch 1885-99, no.738; Robertson 1956, no.23

15.1.24
King Athelstan to Holy Trinity, Winchester Sawyer 427
MS London, British Museum, Add. 15350 f.95rv
ed Birch 1885-99, no.706; Robertson 1956, no.25

15.1.25
King Athelstan to St John's, Beverley Sawyer 451
MS London, British Museum, Cotton Charters IV, 18
London, British Museum, Harley 560 ff.21-2v
London, British Museum, Lansdowne 269 f.97rv
Oxford, Bodleian, Dodsworth 9 f.22
Oxford, Bodleian, Dodsworth 10 ff.43v-4v
Oxford, University College, 82 p.7
ed Birch 1885-99, nos.644-5; Earle 1888, 435-7

15.1.26
Writ of King Athelstan for Church at Ripon Sawyer 457
MS London, P.R.O., DL 41/6/1
Oxford, Bodleian, Dodsworth 160 f.250
facs J.T. Fowler, *Memorials of the Church of SS. Peter and Wilfrid, Ripon,* I, Surtees Society
74, Durham 1881, facing p.90 [P.R.O., DL 41/6/1]
ed Birch 1885-99, no.647; Fowler 1881, 90-3

15.1.27
King Edmund to Æthelgeard Sawyer 463
MS London, British Museum, Add. 15350 ff.106v-7v
ed Birch 1885-99, no.758; Kemble 1839-48, no.1131

15.1.28
King Edmund to Wynflæd Sawyer 485
MS London, British Museum, Harley 61 ff.7-8
Oxford, Bodleian, Dodsworth 38 ff.6v-7v
ed Birch 1885-99, no.775; Kemble 1839-48, no.392 [appendix]

15.1.29
King Edmund to Æthelgeard Sawyer 488
MS London, British Museum, Add. 15350 ff.51-2
ed Birch 1885-99, no.786; Kemble 1839-48, no.1144

15.1.30
King Eadred to Ælfsige Hunlafing Sawyer 566
MS London, Soc. Ant. 60 ff.51-2
ed Birch 1885-99, no.909; Robertson 1956, no.30

15.1.31
King Eadred to Wulfhelm   Sawyer 574
MS   London, British Museum, Add. 15350 ff. 74v-5
ed   Birch 1885-99, no. 987; Kemble 1839-48, no. 1155

15.1.32
King Eadwig to nuns of Wilton   Sawyer 582
MS   London, British Museum, Harley 436 ff. 81v, 83-7v
ed   Birch 1885-99, no. 917; Kemble 1839-48, no. 436 [appendix]

15.1.33
King Eadwig to New Minster, Winchester   Sawyer 660
MS   Shirburn Castle, Earl of Macclesfield, Liber Abbatiae ff. 24v-5
ed   Birch 1885-99, no. 1045

15.1.34
King Edgar to Ælfric   Sawyer 691
MS   London, British Museum, Cotton Claudius B.VI ff. 74v-5
ed   Birch 1885-99, no. 1079; Kemble 1839-48, no. 1234

15.1.35
King Edgar and Bishop Brihthelm to Æthelwulf   Sawyer 693
MS   London, British Museum, Add. 15350 ff. 55v-6
ed   Birch 1885-99, nos. 1077-8; Robertson 1956, no. 33

15.1.36
King Edgar to Abingdon Abbey   Sawyer 700
MS   London, British Museum, Cotton Claudius B.VI ff. 80v-1
     London, British Museum, Cotton Claudius C.IX f. 119v, 197
ed   Birch 1885-99, no. 1095

15.1.37
King Edgar to St Mary's Abbey, Worcester   Sawyer 731
MS   London, British Museum, Harley 7513
     Worcester, Dean and Chapter, Additional MS in safe
     Worcester, Dean and Chapter, A.4
     30 later manuscripts
ed   Birch 1885-99, no. 1135

15.1.38
King Edgar to Ely Abbey   Sawyer 779
MS   London, British Museum, Stowe Charter 31
      11 later manuscripts
facs Sanders 1878-84, III, 32 [Stowe Charter 31]
ed   Birch 1885-99, no. 1267; Robertson 1956, no. 48; John C. Pope, 'Ælfric and the Old
      English version of the Ely Privilege,' in P. Clemoes and K. Hughes, eds., *England before
      the Conquest, Studies ... presented to Dorothy Whitelock,* Cambridge 1971, 85-113

15.1.39
King Edgar to Glastonbury Abbey   Sawyer 783

MS Longleat, Marquess of Bath, 39 ff.60v-1
Cambridge, Trinity College, R.5.33 ff.12v-3
London, British Museum, Cotton Tiberius A.V ff.80-2
London, British Museum, Harley 258 ff.118v-9v
London, British Museum, Royal 13 D.II ff.37v-8
Oxford, Bodleian, Dugdale 21 ff.114v-5v
Oxford, Bodleian, Rawlinson B.252 ff.23-4
Oxford, Bodleian, Wood empt. 1 f.68rv
ed Birch 1885-99, no.1277

15.1.40
King Edgar to Winchester Cathedral   Sawyer 806

MS London, British Museum, Add. 15350 ff.24v-6
ed Birch 1885-99, no.1220; Robertson 1956, no.45

15.1.41
King Edgar to St Mary's, Sherborne   Sawyer 813

MS London, British Museum, Add. 46487 ff.10v-1
ed Birch 1885-99, no.1308; Robertson 1956, no.50

15.1.42
King Edgar to Old Minster, Winchester   Sawyer 817

MS London, British Museum, Add. 15350 f.10
ed Birch 1885-99, no.1148; Robertson 1956, no.38

15.1.43
King Æthelred to Ælfthryth his mother   Sawyer 877

MS Shirburn Castle, Earl of Macclesfield, Liber Abbatiae ff.34v-5v
ed E. Edwards, *Liber Monasterii de Hyda,* Rolls Series 45, London 1866, 242-53; Robertson 1956, no.63

15.1.44
King Æthelred to Wulfric   Sawyer 886

MS Cambridge, Corpus Christi College, 111 pp.175-8
London, British Museum, Cotton Augustus II.48
London, British Museum, Cotton Claudius B.VI ff.94v-5v
London, British Museum, Cotton Vitellius D.VII ff.34v-5
Oxford, Bodleian, James 21 pp.154-6
ed Kemble 1839-48, no.692

15.1.45
King Æthelred to Wherwell Abbey   Sawyer 904

MS London, British Museum, Egerton 2104A ff.15-6
five later manuscripts in the P.R.O
ed Kemble 1839-48, no.707

15.1.46
King Æthelred to Burton Abbey   Sawyer 906
MS   Burton-on-Trent Museum, Burton Muniment 1
London, British Museum, Loan MS 30 ff.8-9
seven later manuscripts
facs   Sanders 1878-84, III, Anglesey 2 [Burton Muniment 1]
ed   Kemble 1839-48, no.710

15.1.47
King Æthelred to Eynsham Abbey   Sawyer 911
MS   Oxford, Christ Church, Eynsham Cart. ff.7-9v
ten later manuscripts
ed   Kemble 1839-48, no.714

15.1.48
King Æthelred to Christ Church, Canterbury   Sawyer 914
MS   London, British Museum, Cotton Claudius A.III ff.4-6
Oxford, Bodleian, Gough Berks. 20 ff.11-2v
ed   Kemble 1839-48, no.715 and last four lines of no.847
See B.16.6.7

15.1.49
King Æthelred confirms the will of Æthelric   Sawyer 939
MS   Canterbury, Dean and Chapter, Chart. Ant. B.1
Canterbury, Dean and Chapter, Reg. A f.142
Canterbury, Dean and Chapter, Reg. E f.43
London, British Museum, Stowe 835 ff.28v-9v
facs   Sanders 1878-84, I, 17 [Chart. Ant. B.1]
ed   Earle 1888, 217-8; Kemble 1839-48, no.704

15.1.50
Writ of King Æthelred, St Paul's, London   Sawyer 945
MS   Oxford, Bodleian, James 23 p.32
ed   Harmer 1952, no.52

15.1.51
Writ of King Æthelred, Winchester   Sawyer 946
MS   London, British Museum, Add. 15350 f.6
ed   Harmer 1952, no.107

15.1.52
King Cnut to Bishop Burhwold   Sawyer 951
MS   Exeter, Dean and Chapter, 2524
London, British Museum, Lansdowne 966 ff.75-6
facs   Sanders 1878-84, II, Exeter 9 [Dean and Chapter, 2524]
ed   J.B. Davidson, 'On some Anglo-Saxon charters at Exeter,' *JBAA* 39 [1883] 287-9

15.1.53
King Cnut to Christ Church, Canterbury   Sawyer 959
MS Canterbury, Dean and Chapter, Chart. Ant. S. 260
    Canterbury, Dean and Chapter, Reg. A f. 144rv
    Canterbury, Dean and Chapter, Reg. E ff. 44v-5
facs Sanders 1878-84, I, 19 [Chart. Ant. S. 260]
ed Kemble 1839-48, no. 737; Robertson 1956, no. 82

15.1.54
King Cnut to Old Minster, Winchester   Sawyer 976
MS London, British Museum, Add. 15350 f. 116rv
ed Kemble 1839-48, no. 753

15.1.55
King Cnut to Bury St Edmunds   Sawyer 980
MS King's Lynn, Borough Archives, Ae. 34
    Cambridge, University Library, Mm. 4. 19 ff. 85-7
    seventeen later manuscripts with English version
ed Kemble 1839-48, no. 735

15.1.56
King Cnut to Christ Church, Canterbury   Sawyer 981
MS London, British Museum, Stowe Charter 40
    London, British Museum, Cotton Vitellius D. VII f. 39
    London, Lambeth Palace, 1212 p. 408
facs Sanders 1878-84, III, 41 [Stowe Charter 40]
ed Kemble 1839-48, no. 1327; Robertson 1956, no. 85

15.1.57
King Cnut to the Abbey of St Benet of Holme   Sawyer 984
MS London, British Museum, Cotton Galba E. II f. 30
ed Kemble 1839-48, no. 740

15.1.58
Writ of King Cnut, Christ Church, Canterbury   Sawyer 985
MS London, British Museum, Royal 1 D. IX f. 44v
ed Harmer 1952, no. 26

15.1.59
Writ of King Cnut, Christ Church, Canterbury   Sawyer 986
MS London, British Museum, Add. 14907 f. 18
    London, Lambeth Palace, 1370 f. 114v
ed Harmer 1952, no. 28
    See B. 16.6.8

15.1.60
Writ of King Cnut, Christ Church, Canterbury   Sawyer 987
MS London, British Museum, Cotton Tiberius B. IV f. 87v

ed Harmer 1952, no. 29
See B.16.6.8

15.1.61
Writ of King Cnut, Christ Church, Canterbury   Sawyer 988
MS London, British Museum, Cotton Tiberius B.IV f. 87
ed Harmer 1952, no. 30
See B.16.6.8

15.1.62
Writ of King Cnut, St Paul's, London   Sawyer 992
MS London, St Paul's, Dean and Chapter, Liber B f. 20v [lost]
ed Harmer 1952, no. 53

15.1.63
King Edward to Horton Abbey   Sawyer 1032
MS London, British Museum, Add. 46487 f. 31rv
ed Kemble 1839-48, no. 1341; Robertson 1956, no. 120

15.1.64
King Edward to St Edmund's Abbey   Sawyer 1045
MS Cambridge, University Library, Ff. 2. 33 f. 22
seventeen other manuscripts of English version
ed Kemble 1839-48, no. 895

15.1.65
King Edward to St Edmund's Abbey   Sawyer 1046
MS Cambridge, University Library, Ff. 2. 33 f. 23
London, British Museum, Add. 14847 f. 31rv
ed Kemble 1839-48, no. 1346

15.1.66
King Edward to Christ Church, Canterbury   Sawyer 1047
MS London, British Museum, Cotton Claudius A.III f. 6v
Oxford, Bodleian, Gough Berks. 20 f. 13rv
ed Kemble 1839-48, no. 896; Robertson 1956, no. 95
See B.16.6.2

15.1.67
King Edward to Fécamp Abbey   Sawyer 1054
MS London, P.R.O., Cart. Ant. R. 29 no. 1
ed Kemble 1839-48, no. 890

15.1.68
King Edward to the church of St Benet of Holme   Sawyer 1055
MS London, British Museum, Cotton Galba E.II f. 30rv
eight other manuscripts
ed Kemble 1839-48, no. 785; J. Conway Davies, *The Cartae Antiquae Rolls 11-20,* Pipe Roll
Society n.s. 33, London 1960, 82-3

15.1.69
King Edward to Osferth   Sawyer 1058

MS London, British Museum, Cotton Vespasian B.XXIV f.38
ed Kemble 1839-48, no.797

15.1.70
King Edward to Old Minster, Winchester   Sawyer 1062

MS London, British Museum, Cotton Charter X.17
facs Bond 1873-8, IV, 37
ed Robertson 1956, no.118

15.1.71
Writ of King Edward, Abbotsbury   Sawyer 1063

MS London, P.R.O., Ch.R.8 Edw.II no.5
London, P.R.O., Conf.R.23 no.1
ed Harmer 1952, no.1

15.1.72
Writ of King Edward, Abbotsbury   Sawyer 1064

MS London, P.R.O., Ch.R.8 Edw.II no.5
London, P.R.O., Conf.R.23 no.1
ed Harmer 1952, no.2

15.1.73
Writ of King Edward, Abingdon   Sawyer 1065

MS London, British Museum, Cotton Claudius B.VI f.113
London, British Museum, Cotton Claudius C.IX f.132
ed Harmer 1952, no.4

15.1.74
Writ of King Edward, Abingdon   Sawyer 1066

MS London, British Museum, Cotton Claudius B.VI f.113
London, British Museum, Cotton Claudius C.IX f.132
ed Harmer 1952, no.5

15.1.75
Writ of King Edward, Beverley   Sawyer 1067

MS London, P.R.O., Ch.R.4 Edw.II m.20
seven later manuscripts
ed Harmer 1952, no.7

15.1.76
Writ of King Edward, Bury St Edmunds   Sawyer 1068

MS Cambridge, University Library, Add. 4220 f.61
Cambridge, University Library, Ff.2.33 f.22v
London, British Museum, Add. 14847 f.30v
ed Harmer 1952, no.8

15.1.77
Writ of King Edward, Bury St Edmunds Sawyer 1069
MS Cambridge, University Library, Ff.2.33 f.22
London, British Museum, Harley 638 f.26
sixteen later manuscripts
ed Harmer 1952, no.9

15.1.78
Writ of King Edward, Bury St Edmunds Sawyer 1070
MS London, British Museum, Add. 14847 f.30
ed Harmer 1952, no.10

15.1.79
Writ of King Edward, Bury St Edmunds Sawyer 1071
MS London, British Museum, Cotton Augustus II.80
Cambridge, University Library, Ff.2.33 f.22v
London, British Museum, Add. 14847 f.30v
acs Bond 1873-8, IV, 29; T.A.M. Bishop and P. Chaplais, *Facsimiles of English Royal Writs to AD 1100 presented to V.H. Galbraith,* Oxford 1957, plate 1 [Cotton Augustus II.80]
ed Harmer 1952, no.11

15.1.80
Writ of King Edward, Bury St Edmunds Sawyer 1072
MS Cambridge, University Library, Ff.2.33 f.22v
Cambridge, University Library, Mm.4.19 f.105v
London, British Museum, Add. 14847 f.30v
ed Harmer 1952, no.12

15.1.81
Writ of King Edward, Bury St Edmunds Sawyer 1073
MS Cambridge, University Library, Ff.2.33 f.23
London, British Museum, Add.14847 f.31
ed Harmer 1952, no.13

15.1.82
Writ of King Edward, Bury St Edmunds Sawyer 1074
MS Cambridge, University Library, Ff.2.33 f.23
London, British Museum, Add. 14847 f.31v
ed Harmer 1952, no.14

15.1.83
Writ of King Edward, Bury St Edmunds Sawyer 1075
MS Cambridge, University Library, Ff.2.33 f.23
London, British Museum, Harley 638 f.26
sixteen later manuscripts
ed Harmer 1952, no.15

15.1.84
Writ of King Edward, Bury St Edmunds   Sawyer 1076

MS Cambridge, University Library, Ff.2.33 f.23v
London, British Museum, Add. 14847 f.31v

ed Harmer 1952, no.16

15.1.85
Writ of King Edward, Bury St Edmunds   Sawyer 1077

MS Cambridge, University Library, Ff.2.33 f.23
London, British Museum, Add. 14847 f.31

ed Harmer 1952, no.17

15.1.86
Writ of King Edward, Bury St Edmunds   Sawyer 1078

MS Cambridge, University Library, Ff.2.33 f.22rv
Cambridge, University Library, Ff.4.35 f.23v
London, British Museum, Add. 14847 f.30

ed Harmer 1952, no.18

15.1.87
Writ of King Edward, Bury St Edmunds   Sawyer 1079

MS Cambridge, University Library, Ff.2.33 f.22v
Cambridge, University Library, Ff.4.35 f.23v
London, British Museum, Add. 14847 f.30v
London, British Museum, Harley 743 f.59v

ed Harmer 1952, no.19

15.1.88
Writ of King Edward, Bury St Edmunds   Sawyer 1080

MS Cambridge, University Library, Ff.2.33 f.23
London, British Museum, Add. 14847 f.31v

ed Harmer 1952, no.20

15.1.89
Writ of King Edward, Bury St Edmunds   Sawyer 1081

MS Cambridge, University Library, Ff.2.33 f.23
London, British Museum, Add. 14847 f.31v

ed Harmer 1952, no.21

15.1.90
Writ of King Edward, Bury St Edmunds   Sawyer 1082

MS Cambridge, University Library, Ff.2.33 ff.22v-3
London, British Museum, Add. 14847 f.31

ed Harmer 1952, no.22

15.1.91
Writ of King Edward, Bury St Edmunds   Sawyer 1083

MS Cambridge, University Library, Ff.2.33 f.22v

Cambridge, University Library, Ff.4.35 f.23v
London, British Museum, Add. 14847 ff.30v-1
ed   Harmer 1952, no.23

15.1.92
Writ of King Edward, Bury St Edmunds   Sawyer 1084
MS   London, British Museum, Cotton Augustus II.49
     nineteen later manuscripts
cs   Bond 1873-8, IV, 39; Bishop and Chaplais 1957, plate 2 [Cotton Augustus II.49]
ed   Harmer 1952, no.24

15.1.93
Writ of King Edward, Bury St Edmunds   Sawyer 1085
MS   London, P.R.O., Chart. Ant. R.15 no.4
     seventeen later manuscripts
ed   Harmer 1952, no.25

15.1.94
Writ of King Edward, Christ Church, Canterbury   Sawyer 1088
MS   London, British Museum, Campbell Charter XXI.5
     six later manuscripts
cs   Bond 1873-8, IV, plate after 37; Harmer 1952, plate 1; Bishop and Chaplais 1957,
     plate 3 [Campbell Charter XXI.5]
ed   Harmer 1952, no.33

15.1.95
Writ of King Edward, Christ Church, Canterbury   Sawyer 1089
MS   Canterbury, Dean and Chapter, Chart. Ant. C.3
     eight later manuscripts
ed   Harmer 1952, no.34

15.1.96
Writ of King Edward, Christ Church, Canterbury   Sawyer 1090
MS   London, British Museum, Cotton Claudius A.III f.5v
     Oxford, Bodleian, Gough Berks. 20 f.12v
ed   Harmer 1952, no.35
     See B.16.6.9

15.1.97
Writ of King Edward, St Augustine's, Canterbury   Sawyer 1091
MS   London, P.R.O., Chart. Ant. R.9 no.12
     five later manuscripts
ed   Harmer 1952, no.38

15.1.98
Writ of King Edward, St Augustine's, Canterbury   Sawyer 1092
MS   London, British Museum, Cotton Claudius D.X ff.63v, 175
     ten later manuscripts
ed   Harmer 1952, no.39

15.1.99
Writ of King Edward, Chertsey   Sawyer 1093

MS   London, British Museum, Cotton Vitellius A.XIII f.50v
ed   Harmer 1952, no.40

15.1.100
Writ of King Edward, Chertsey   Sawyer 1094

MS   London, British Museum, Cotton Vitellius A.XIII f.50rv
     London, P.R.O., Chart. Ant. R.4 no.7
ed   Harmer 1952, no.41

15.1.101
Writ of King Edward, Chertsey   Sawyer 1095

MS   London, British Museum, Cotton Vitellius A.XIII f.50
     London, P.R.O., Chart. Ant. R.4 no.8
ed   Harmer 1952, no.42

15.1.102
Writ of King Edward, Chertsey   Sawyer 1096

MS   London, British Museum, Cotton Vitellius A.XIII ff.50v-1
     London, P.R.O., Chart. Ant. R.4 no.9
     Oxford, Bodleian, James 24 p.33
ed   Harmer 1952, no.43

15.1.103
Writ of King Edward, Cirencester   Sawyer 1097

MS   Northleach, Lady Vestey, Stowell Park, Registrum A p.26
ed   Harmer 1952, no.44

15.1.104
Writ of King Edward, Coventry   Sawyer 1098

MS   London, British Museum, Add. Ch. 28657
     London, British Museum, Cotton Claudius A.VIII f.81rv
     Oxford, Bodleian, Dugdale 13 pp.440-1
ed   Harmer 1952, no.45

15.1.105
Writ of King Edward, Coventry   Sawyer 1099

MS   Stratford-upon-Avon, Shakespeare Birthplace Library, Gregory Leiger-Book pp.23-4
ed   F. Harmer, 'A Bromfield and a Coventry Writ of King Edward the Confessor' in
     P. Clemoes, ed., *The Anglo-Saxons,* London 1959, 103

15.1.106
Writ of King Edward, Ely   Sawyer 1100

MS   Cambridge, Trinity College, O.2.1 f.79
     five later manuscripts
ed   Harmer 1952, no.47
     See B.16.9.5

15.1.107
Writ of King Edward, Hereford   Sawyer 1101
MS   Oxford, Bodleian, Rawlinson B.329 f.104
ed   Harmer 1952, no.49

15.1.108
Writ of King Edward, The English Cnihtengild, London   Sawyer 1103
MS   Glasgow, University Library, Hunter U.2.6 f.149
     London, Corporation of London Records Office, Letter Book C f.134v
     London, Corporation of London Records Office, Liber Dunthorne f.79
ed   Harmer 1952, no.51

15.1.109
Writ of King Edward, St Paul's, London   Sawyer 1104
MS   London, St Paul's, Dean and Chapter, A Box 69 dorse
     eighteen later manuscripts
ed   Harmer 1952, no.54

15.1.110
Writ of King Edward, St Denis   Sawyer 1105
MS   Paris, Archives Nationales, K.19 no.6
     Paris, Archives Nationales, LL 1156 ff.83-4
cs   Harmer 1952, plate 2; Bishop and Chaplais 1957, 18 [K.19 no.6]
ed   Harmer 1952, no.55

15.1.111
Writ of King Edward, Ramsey   Sawyer 1109
MS   London, P.R.O., Ch.R.8 Edw. III no.29
     eight later manuscripts
ed   Harmer 1952, no.61

15.1.112
Writ of King Edward, Ramsey   Sawyer 1110
MS   London, P.R.O., Ch.R.8 Edw. III no.29
     eight later manuscripts
ed   Harmer 1952, no.62

15.1.113
Writ of King Edward, Wells   Sawyer 1111
MS   Wells, Dean and Chapter, Liber Albus I f.14
ed   Harmer 1952, no.64

15.1.114
Writ of King Edward, Wells   Sawyer 1112
MS   Wells, Dean and Chapter, Liber Albus I f.14
ed   Harmer 1952, no.65

15.1.115
Writ of King Edward, Wells   Sawyer 1113

MS   Wells, Dean and Chapter, Liber Albus I f. 17v
ed   Harmer 1952, no. 66

15.1.116
Writ of King Edward, Wells   Sawyer 1114

MS   Wells, Dean and Chapter, Liber Albus II ff. 21v-2
      Wells, Dean and Chapter, Liber Fuscus f. 14
ed   Harmer 1952, no. 67

15.1.117
Writ of King Edward, Wells   Sawyer 1115

MS   Wells, Dean and Chapter, Liber Albus I f. 17v
ed   Harmer 1952, no. 68

15.1.118
Writ of King Edward, Wells   Sawyer 1116

MS   Wells, Dean and Chapter, Liber Albus I f. 14
ed   Harmer 1952, no. 69

15.1.119
Writ of King Edward, Westminster   Sawyer 1117

MS   London, British Museum, Cotton Faustina A. III f. 108
ed   Harmer 1952, no. 73

15.1.120
Writ of King Edward, Westminster   Sawyer 1118

MS   London, British Museum, Cotton Faustina A. III f. 107rv
      London, Westminster Abbey, Muniment Book 11 f. 269
ed   Harmer 1952, no. 74

15.1.121
Writ of King Edward, Westminster   Sawyer 1119

MS   London, British Museum, Cotton Faustina A. III f. 111rv
      London, Westminster Abbey, Muniment Book 11 f. 506rv
ed   Harmer 1952, no. 75

15.1.122
Writ of King Edward, Westminster   Sawyer 1120

MS   London, Westminster Abbey, W. A. M. XI
      London, British Museum, Add. 4558 f. 138
      London, British Museum, Cotton Faustina A. III ff. 105v-6
      London, Westminster Abbey, Muniment Book 11 f. 647
facs Sanders 1878-84, II, Westminster 9 [W. A. M. XI]
  ed   Harmer 1952, no. 76

15.1.123
Writ of King Edward, Westminster   Sawyer 1121

MS   London, British Museum, Cotton Charter VII. 6

London, British Museum, Cotton Faustina A.III ff.108v-9
London, Westminster Abbey, Muniment Book 11 f.114v
facs   Bond 1873-8, IV, 34 [Cotton Charter VII.6]
  ed   Harmer 1952, no.77

15.1.124
Writ of King Edward, Westminster   Sawyer 1122
MS   London, British Museum, Cotton Faustina A.III f.106rv
London, Westminster Abbey, Muniment Book 11 ff.185v-6
  ed   Harmer 1952, no.78

15.1.125
Writ of King Edward, Westminster   Sawyer 1123
MS   London, British Museum, Cotton Faustina A.III f.107
London, Westminster Abbey, Muniment Book 11 f.227
  ed   Harmer 1952, no.79

15.1.126
Writ of King Edward, Westminster   Sawyer 1124
MS   London, British Museum, Sloane Charter XXXIV.1
London, British Museum, Cotton Faustina A.III f.109
London, Westminster Abbey, Muniment Book 11 f.648
facs   Bond 1873-8, IV, 35 [Sloane Charter XXXIV.1]
  ed   Harmer 1952, no.80

15.1.127
Writ of King Edward, Westminster   Sawyer 1125
MS   London, Westminster Abbey, W.A.M. XVIII
London, Westminster Abbey, Muniment Book 11 f.46
facs   Sanders 1878-84, II, Westminster 17; Bishop and Chaplais 1957, plate 23a [W.A.M. XVIII]
  ed   Harmer 1952, no.81

15.1.128
Writ of King Edward, Westminster   Sawyer 1126
MS   London, Westminster Abbey, W.A.M. XIX
London, British Museum, Cotton Faustina A.III f.110rv
London, Westminster Abbey, Muniment Book 11 f.46
facs   Sanders 1878-84, II, Westminster 16 [W.A.M. XIX]
  ed   Harmer 1952, no.82

15.1.129
Writ of King Edward, Westminster   Sawyer 1127
MS   London, British Museum, Cotton Faustina A.III f.111v
London, Westminster Abbey, Muniment Book 11 f.46
  ed   Harmer 1952, no.83

15.1.130
Writ of King Edward, Westminster   Sawyer 1128

MS London, British Museum, Cotton Faustina A.III ff.107v-8
ed Harmer 1952, no.84

15.1.131
Writ of King Edward, Westminster   Sawyer 1129

MS London, British Museum, Cotton Faustina A.III f.105rv
London, Westminster Abbey, Muniment Book 11 f.647v
ed Harmer 1952, no.85

15.1.132
Writ of King Edward, Westminster   Sawyer 1130

MS London, British Museum, Cotton Faustina A.III f.108rv
London, Westminster Abbey, Muniment Book 11 f.154v
ed Harmer 1952, no.86

15.1.133
Writ of King Edward, Westminster   Sawyer 1131

MS London, Westminster Abbey, Muniment Book 11 f.154v
ed Harmer 1952, no.87

15.1.134
Writ of King Edward, Westminster   Sawyer 1132

MS London, British Museum, Cotton Faustina A.III f.105
ed Harmer 1952, no.88

15.1.135
Writ of King Edward, Westminster   Sawyer 1133

MS London, Westminster Abbey, Muniment Book 11 f.129v
ed Harmer 1952, no.89

15.1.136
Writ of King Edward, Westminster   Sawyer 1134

MS London, British Museum, Cotton Augustus II.81
London, British Museum, Cotton Faustina A.III f.107
London, Westminster Abbey, Muniment Book 11 f.647
facs Bond 1873-8, IV, 40 [Cotton Augustus II.81]
ed Harmer 1952, no.90

15.1.137
Writ of King Edward, Westminster   Sawyer 1135

MS London, British Museum, Cotton Faustina A.III ff.106v-7
London, Westminster Abbey, Muniment Book 11 f.226v
ed Harmer 1952, no.91

15.1.138
Writ of King Edward, Westminster   Sawyer 1136

MS London, British Museum, Cotton Faustina A.III f.105

London, Westminster Abbey, Muniment Book 11 f.505
ed   Harmer 1952, no.92

15.1.139
Writ of King Edward, Westminster   Sawyer 1137
MS   London, Westminster Abbey, W.A.M. XVII
London, Westminster Abbey, Muniment Book 11 f.465rv
facs   Sanders 1878-84, II, Westminster 15 [W.A.M. XVII]
ed   Harmer 1952, no.93

15.1.140
Writ of King Edward, Westminster   Sawyer 1138
MS   London, Westminster Abbey, W.A.M. XIV
London, British Museum, Cotton Faustina A.III f.109rv
London, Westminster Abbey, Muniment Book 11 f.594
facs   Sanders 1878-84, II, Westminster 13 [W.A.M. XIV]
ed   Harmer 1952, no.94

15.1.141
Writ of King Edward, Westminster   Sawyer 1139
MS   London, British Museum, Cotton Faustina A.III ff.103v-4
London, Westminster Abbey, Muniment Book 11 f.275
ed   Harmer 1952, no.95

15.1.142
Writ of King Edward, Westminster   Sawyer 1140
MS   London, Westminster Abbey, W.A.M. XII
London, Westminster Abbey, W.A.M. XIII
London, British Museum, Cotton Faustina A.III f.109v
London, Westminster Abbey, Muniment Book 11 f.648
facs   Sanders 1878-84, II, Westminster 11-2; Bishop and Chaplais 1957, plate 23b [W.A.M. XII, W.A.M. XIII]
ed   Harmer 1952, no.96

15.1.143
Writ of King Edward, Westminster   Sawyer 1141
MS   London, British Museum, Cotton Charters VII.13
four later manuscripts
facs   Bond 1873-8, IV, 36 [Cotton Charters VII.13]
ed   Harmer 1952, no.97

15.1.144
Writ of King Edward, Westminster   Sawyer 1142
MS   London, Westminster Abbey, W.A.M. XVI
five later manuscripts
facs   Sanders 1878-84, II, Westminster 10 [W.A.M. XVI]
ed   Harmer 1952, no.98

15.1.145
Writ of King Edward, Westminster   Sawyer 1143

MS   London, Westminster Abbey, Muniment Book 11 f.316
ed   Harmer 1952, no.99

15.1.146
Writ of King Edward, Westminster   Sawyer 1144

MS   London, British Museum, Cotton Faustina A.III f.112
London, Westminster Abbey, Muniment Book 11 f.278
London, Westminster Abbey, W.A.M. 12752
ed   Harmer 1952, no.100

15.1.147
Writ of King Edward, Westminster   Sawyer 1145

MS   London, Westminster Abbey, W.A.M. XV
London, British Museum, Add. 4558 f.139
London, Westminster Abbey, Muniment Book 11 f.278
facs   Sanders 1878-84, II, Westminster 14 [W.A.M. XV]
ed   Harmer 1952, no.101

15.1.148
Writ of King Edward, Westminster   Sawyer 1146

MS   London, British Museum, Cotton Faustina A.III ff.109v-10
London, Westminster Abbey, Muniment Book 11 f.278
ed   Harmer 1952, no.102

15.1.149
Writ of King Edward, Westminster   Sawyer 1147

MS   London, Westminster Abbey, Muniment Book 11 f.270
ed   Harmer 1952, no.103

15.1.150
Writ of King Edward, Westminster   Sawyer 1148

MS   London, British Museum, Cotton Faustina A.III f.103rv
London, Westminster Abbey, Muniment Book 11 f.270
Oxford, Bodleian, James 24 p.54
ed   Harmer 1952, no.104

15.1.151
Writ of King Edward, Westminster   Sawyer 1149

MS   London, British Museum, Cotton Faustina A.III ff.110v-1
London, Westminster Abbey, Muniment Book 11 f.96
ed   Harmer 1952, no.105

15.1.152
Writ of King Edward, Westminster   Sawyer 1150

MS   London, British Museum, Cotton Faustina A.III ff.111v-2
London, Westminster Abbey, Muniment Book 11 f.96
ed   Harmer 1952, no.106

15.1.153
Writ of King Edward, Winchester Sawyer 1151
MS London, British Museum, Add. 29436 f. 10
ed Harmer 1952, no. 109

15.1.154
Writ of King Edward, Winchester Sawyer 1152
MS London, British Museum, Add. 29436 f. 10rv
   fourteen later manuscripts
ed Harmer 1952, no. 110

15.1.155
Writ of King Edward, Winchester Sawyer 1153
MS London, British Museum, Add. 29436 f. 10v
   fifteen later manuscripts
ed Harmer 1952, no. 111

15.1.156
Writ of King Edward, Winchester Sawyer 1154
MS London, British Museum, Add. 15350 f. 7
ed Harmer 1952, no. 112

15.1.157
Writ of King Edward, Wolverhampton Sawyer 1155
MS London, British Museum, Harley Ch. 43 D29
   four later manuscripts
ed Harmer 1952, no. 114

15.1.158
Writ of King Edward, Worcester Sawyer 1156
MS London, British Museum, Add. Ch. 19802
acs Bond 1873-8, IV, 41; Bishop and Chaplais 1957, plate 26
ed Harmer 1952, no. 115

15.1.159
Writ of King Edward, Worcester Sawyer 1157
MS London, P.R.O., Ch. R. 6 Edw. II, no. 27
   thirteen later manuscripts
ed Harmer 1952, no. 116

15.1.160
Writ of King Edward, Worcester Sawyer 1158
MS Worcester, Worcestershire R.O. BA 3814 [ref. 821] f.38v
ed Harmer 1952, no. 117

15.1.161
Writ of King Edward, York Sawyer 1159
MS York, Dean and Chapter, Mag. Reg. Alb. pt. 1 ff.61v, 62v
ed Harmer 1952, no. 118

15.1.162
Writ of King Edward, York   Sawyer 1160
MS   London, British Museum, Harley 560 f.23
ed   Harmer 1952, no. 119

15.1.163
Writ of King Edward, York   Sawyer 1161
MS   York, Dean and Chapter, Mag. Reg. Alb. pt. 1 f.61v
ed   Harmer 1952, no. 120

15.1.164
Writ of King Edward, Bromfield   Sawyer 1162
MS   Hereford, Dioc. Reg., Registrum Ricardi de Swinfield f. 152
ed   Harmer 1959, 101-2

15.1.165
Writ of King Harold, Wells   Sawyer 1163
MS   Wells, Dean and Chapter, Liber Albus I f. 14
ed   Harmer 1952, no. 71

15.2
Lay Charters

15.2.1
Oswulf and Beornthryth to Christ Church, Canterbury   Sawyer 1188
MS   London, British Museum, Cotton Augustus II.79
      London, Lambeth Palace, 1212 pp.406-7
facs   Bond 1873-8, I, 15 [Cotton Augustus II.79]
ed   Birch 1885-99, no. 330; Earle 1888, 79-81

15.2.2
Ealhburg and Eadweald to Christ Church, Canterbury   Sawyer 1195
MS   London, British Museum, Cotton Augustus II.52
facs   Bond 1873-8, II, 21
ed   Birch 1885-99, no. 403; Earle 1888, 104-5

15.2.3
Æthelmod to Plegred   Sawyer 1196
MS   London, British Museum, Cotton Augustus II.16
      Oxford, Bodleian, James 24 pp.95-6
facs   Bond 1873-8, II, 34 [Cotton Augustus II.16]
ed   Birch 1885-99, no. 497; Earle 1888, 130-1

15.2.4
Lufu to Christ Church, Canterbury   Sawyer 1197
MS   London, British Museum, Cotton Augustus II.92
facs   Bond 1873-8, II, 22
ed   Birch 1885-99, no. 405; Earle 1888, 105-7

15.2.5
Ealhburg to St Augustine's Abbey   Sawyer 1198
MS   Cambridge, Corpus Christi College, 286 f.74v
ed   Birch 1885-99, no.501; Harmer 1914, no.6
See B.16.7.2

15.2.6
Eadweald and Cynethryth   Sawyer 1200
MS   London, British Museum, Cotton Augustus II.19
facs   Bond 1873-8, II, 19
ed   Birch 1885-99, no.404; Earle 1888, 102-4

15.2.7
Alfred, dux, and Archbishop Æthelred   Sawyer 1202
MS   Canterbury, Dean and Chapter, Reg.C f.148v
London, British Museum, Stowe 853 f.27rv
London, Lambeth Palace, 1212 p.407
ed   Birch 1885-99, no.529; Harmer 1914, no.8

15.2.8
Athelstan, senator, to St Mary's, Abingdon   Sawyer 1208
MS   London, British Museum, Cotton Claudius B.VI f.21
London, British Museum, Cotton Claudius C.IX f.196v
ed   Birch 1885-99, no.688; Robertson 1956, no.22

15.2.9
Queen Eadgifu to Christ Church, Canterbury   Sawyer 1211
MS   London, British Museum, Stowe Charter 28
facs   Sanders 1878-84, III, 29
ed   Birch 1885-99, no.1064; Harmer 1914, no.23

15.2.10
Æthelflæd to Ælfwold   Sawyer 1215
MS   London, British Museum, Stowe Charter 30
facs   Sanders 1878-84, III, 31
ed   Birch 1885-99, no.1212

15.2.11
Ælfhere, ealdorman, to Abbot Osgar   Sawyer 1216
MS   London, British Museum, Cotton Claudius C.IX f.202
ed   Birch 1885-99, no.1262; Robertson 1956, no.51

15.2.12
Ulfketel to Bury St Edmunds   Sawyer 1219
MS   Cambridge, University Library, Ff.2.33 f.49v
London, British Museum, Add. 14847 f.19v
London, British Museum, Add. 14850 f.85
ed   Birch 1885-99, no.1013; Robertson 1956, no.73

15.2.13
Godwine to Leofwine the Red Sawyer 1220
MS Biddenden, Kent, Mrs M. Sturges
ed Kemble 1839-48, no. 1315; Robertson 1956, no. 75

15.2.14
Thored to Christ Church Sawyer 1222
MS London, British Museum, Cotton Claudius A.III f. 6
Oxford, Bodleian, Gough Berks. 20 f. 13
ed Robertson 1956, no. 88
See B. 16.6.2

15.2.15
Stigand to Bury St Edmunds Sawyer 1224
MS Cambridge, University Library, Ff. 2.33 f. 50
ed Kemble 1839-48, no. 978; Robertson 1956, no. 92

15.2.16
Thurketel to Bury St Edmunds Sawyer 1225
MS London, British Museum, Cotton Augustus II. 84
Cambridge, University Library, Ff. 2.33 f. 50
London, British Museum, Add. 14847 f. 19v
London, British Museum, Add. 42055 f. 1
Oxford, Bodleian, James 24 p. 72
facs Bond 1873-8, IV, 44 [Cotton Augustus II. 84]
ed Birch 1885-99, nos. 1018-9; Robertson 1956, no. 93

15.2.17
Lady Ælfgifu to Christ Church Sawyer 1229
MS London, British Museum, Cotton Claudius A.III f. 6
Oxford, Bodleian, Gough Berks 20 f. 13
Oxford, Bodleian, James 10 p. 91
ed Kemble 1839-48, no. 965; Robertson 1956, no. 96
See B. 16.6.2

15.2.18
Leofric and Godgifu to St Mary's, Worcester Sawyer 1232
MS London, British Museum, Cotton Tiberius A.XIII f. 183rv
Oxford, Bodleian, Ballard 67 f. 45v
ed Kemble 1839-48, no. 766; Robertson 1956, no. 113

15.2.19
Brihtmær to Christ Church, Canterbury Sawyer 1234
MS Canterbury, Dean and Chapter, Reg. A ff. 143v-4
Canterbury, Dean and Chapter, Reg. E ff. 44v
London, British Museum, Stowe 835 ff. 32v-3
ed Kemble 1839-48, no. 799; Robertson 1956, no. 116

15.2.20
Lulla to St Augustine's, Canterbury   Sawyer 1239
MS   London, British Museum, Cotton Claudius D.X f.104
ed   W. Dugdale, *Monasticon Anglicanum,* ed. J. Caley, H. Ellis, B. Bandinel, London 1846, I, 140, no.44

15.2.21
Writ of Queen Edith, Wells   Sawyer 1240
MS   Wells, Dean and Chapter, Liber Albus I f.18
ed   Harmer 1952, no.70

15.2.22
Writ of Queen Edith, Wells   Sawyer 1241
MS   Wells, Dean and Chapter, Liber Albus I f.17v
ed   Harmer 1952, no.72

15.2.23
Writ of Ælfthryth, Winchester   Sawyer 1242
MS   London, British Museum, Add. 15350 f.26rv
ed   Harmer 1952, no.108

15.2.24
Writ of Gospatric   Sawyer 1243
MS   Lowther Castle, Earl of Lonsdale
ed   Harmer 1952, no.121

15.3
Bishops' Charters

15.3.1
Bishop Ealhferth to Cuthred   Sawyer 1275
MS   London, British Museum, Add. 15350 f.75rv
ed   Birch 1885-99, no.543; Robertson 1956, no.14

15.3.2
Bishop Swithwulf to Beorhtwulf   Sawyer 1276
MS   Canterbury, Dean and Chapter, Chart. Ant. H.130
facs   Sanders 1878-84, I, 11
ed   Birch 1885-99, no.562; Earle 1888, 152-3

15.3.3
Bishop Wærferth to Æthelred and Æthelflæd   Sawyer 1280
MS   London, British Museum, Cotton Nero E.I pt.2 f.182
     London, British Museum, Cotton Tiberius A.XIII ff.6v-7v
ed   Birch 1885-99, no.608; Robertson 1956, no.19

15.3.4
Bishop Wærferth to Wulfsige   Sawyer 1281

MS London, British Museum, Add. Ch. 19791
facs Bond 1873-8, III, 2
  ed Birch 1885-99, no.609; Robertson 1956, no.18

15.3.5
Bishop Wærferth to Cyneswith Sawyer 1283
MS London, British Museum, Cotton Vespasian A.V f.161
  ed Birch 1885-99, no.560; Robertson 1956, no.16

15.3.6
Bishop Denewulf to Beornwulf Sawyer 1285
MS London, British Museum, Add. 15350 ff.61v-2
  ed Birch 1885-99, no.599; Harmer 1914, no.17

15.3.7
Bishop Denewulf to Alfred Sawyer 1287
MS London, British Museum, Add. 15350 f.61rv
  ed Birch 1885-99, no.617; Robertson 1956, no.15

15.3.8
Bishop Wilfrid to the community at Worcester Sawyer 1289
MS London, British Museum, Harley 4660 f.8
  ed Birch 1885-99, no.636; Robertson 1956, no.21

15.3.9
Bishop Brihthelm and Abbot Æthelwold Sawyer 1292
MS London, British Museum, Cotton Claudius B.VI f.54
  ed Birch 1885-99, no.972; Robertson 1956, no.31

15.3.10
Archbishop Dunstan to King Æthelred Sawyer 1296
MS Oxford, Bodleian, Eng. hist. a.2 no.xiv
  ed A.S. Napier and W.H. Stevenson, *The Crawford Collection of Early Charters and Documents,* Oxford 1895, no.7

15.3.11
Bishop Oswald to Æthelm Sawyer 1299
MS London, British Museum, Cotton Tiberius A.XIII f.59
  ed Birch 1885-99, no.1086

15.3.12
Bishop Oswald to Ælfric Sawyer 1303
MS London, British Museum, Cotton Tiberius A.XIII ff.63rv, 158v-9
  ed Birch 1885-99, nos.1106-7; Robertson 1956, no.35

15.3.13
Bishop Oswald to Athelstan Sawyer 1305
MS London, British Museum, Cotton Tiberius A.XIII ff.88-9
  ed Birch 1885-99, no.1110; Robertson 1956, no.36

15.3.14
Bishop Oswald to Ælfhild Sawyer 1309
MS London, British Museum, Cotton Tiberius A.XIII f.80rv
ed Birch 1885-99, no.1180; Robertson 1956, no.42

15.3.15
Bishop Oswald to Eadric Sawyer 1310
MS London, British Museum, Cotton Tiberius A.XIII ff.96v-7
ed Birch 1885-99, no.1182; Robertson 1956, no.43

15.3.16
Bishop Oswald to Æthelweard Sawyer 1312
MS London, British Museum, Cotton Tiberius A.XIII ff.59v-60
ed Birch 1885-99, no.1206; Kemble 1839-48, no.541

15.3.17
Bishop Oswald to Eadmær Sawyer 1313
MS London, British Museum, Cotton Nero E.I pt.2 f.184
    London, British Museum, Cotton Tiberius A.XIII f.111v
ed Birch 1885-99, nos.1202-3; Kemble 1839-48, no.539

15.3.18
Bishop Oswald to Osulf Sawyer 1315
MS Somers Charter 14 [lost]
ed Birch 1885-99, no.1204

15.3.19
Bishop Oswald to Wulfgar Sawyer 1316
MS London, British Museum, Cotton Tiberius A.XIII f.60rv
    London, British Museum, Cotton Vitellius C.IX f.129v
ed Birch 1885-99, no.1207; Kemble 1839-48, no.540

15.3.20
Bishop Oswald to Æthelweard Sawyer 1317
MS London, British Museum, Cotton Tiberius A.XIII f.58rv
ed Birch 1885-99, no.1236; Kemble 1839-48, no.550

15.3.21
Bishop Oswald to Æthelweard Sawyer 1318
MS London, British Museum, Cotton Tiberius A.XIII ff.94v-5
ed Birch 1885-99, no.1232; Kemble 1839-48, no.552

15.3.22
Bishop Oswald to Brihtmær Sawyer 1320
MS London, British Museum, Cotton Tiberius A.XIII ff.80v-1, 160v
ed Birch 1885-99, no.1241; Kemble 1839-48, no.560

15.3.23
Bishop Oswald to Osulf Sawyer 1326

MS   London, British Museum, Add. Ch. 19792
　　　London, British Museum, Cotton Tiberius A.XIII ff.83v-4
facs Bond 1873-8, III, 28 [Add. Ch. 19792]
 ed   Birch 1885-99, no. 1233; Robertson 1956, no.46

15.3.24
Bishop Oswald to Wulfgar   Sawyer 1327
MS   London, British Museum, Cotton Tiberius A.XIII ff.64v-5, 162
 ed   Birch 1885-99, no.1240; Kemble 1839-48, no.559

15.3.25
Archbishop Oswald to Æthelwold   Sawyer 1332
MS   London, British Museum, Cotton Tiberius A.XIII f.77v
 ed   Kemble 1839-48, no.612; Robertson 1956, no.55

15.3.26
Archbishop Oswald to Eadric   Sawyer 1334
MS   London, British Museum, Cotton Tiberius A.XIII f.96rv
 ed   Kemble 1839-48, no.617

15.3.27
Archbishop Oswald to Wynsige   Sawyer 1336
MS   London, British Museum, Cotton Tiberius A.XIII f.82v
 ed   Kemble 1839-48, no.616

15.3.28
Archbishop Oswald to Ælfnoth   Sawyer 1337
MS   London, British Museum, Cotton Tiberius A.XIII f.90rv
 ed   Kemble 1839-48, no.620

15.3.29
Archbishop Oswald to Æthelmund   Sawyer 1338
MS   London, British Museum, Cotton Tiberius A.XIII ff.83rv, 159
 ed   Kemble 1839-48, no.619

15.3.30
Archbishop Oswald to Æthelnoth   Sawyer 1339
MS   London, British Museum, Cotton Tiberius A.XIII ff.71-2, 160v
 ed   Kemble 1839-48, no.618

15.3.31
Archbishop Oswald to Wulfgar   Sawyer 1342
MS   London, British Museum, Cotton Tiberius A.XIII ff.67v-8v, 160rv
 ed   Kemble 1839-48, no.627

15.3.32
Archbishop Oswald to Eadric   Sawyer 1350
MS   London, British Museum, Cotton Tiberius A.XIII ff.95-6
 ed   Kemble 1839-48, no.651

15.3.33
Bishop Oswald to Ælfwine Sawyer 1355
MS London, British Museum, Cotton Tiberius A.XIII f.82
ed Birch 1885-99, no.1205; Kemble 1839-48, no.542

15.3.34
Archbishop Oswald to Eadric Sawyer 1358
MS London, British Museum, Cotton Tiberius A.XIII ff.93v-4
ed Kemble 1839-48, no.666

15.3.35
Archbishop Oswald to Æthelmær Sawyer 1362
MS London, British Museum, Add. 46204
London, British Museum, Cotton Tiberius A.XIII ff.60v-1v
ed Kemble 1839-48, no.675; Robertson 1956, no.65

15.3.36
Archbishop Oswald to Beornheah and Byrhstan Sawyer 1363
MS London, British Museum, Cotton Tiberius A.XIII ff.84v-5
London, British Museum, Cotton Vitellius C.IX f.129v
London, British Museum, Harley 4660 f.9
ed Kemble 1839-48, no.674; Robertson 1956, no.64

15.3.37
Archbishop Oswald to Eadric Sawyer 1366
MS London, British Museum, Cotton Tiberius A.XIII f.91
ed Kemble 1839-48, no.676; Robertson 1956, no.67

15.3.38
Archbishop Oswald to Ælfsige Sawyer 1367
MS London, British Museum, Cotton Tiberius A.XIII ff.74v-5
ed Kemble 1839-48, no.679

15.3.39
Archbishop Oswald to Goding Sawyer 1369
MS London, British Museum, Cotton Tiberius A.XIII ff.66-7, 161v-2
ed Kemble 1839-48, no.683; Robertson 1956, no.61

15.3.40
Archbishop Oswald to Wulfgar Sawyer 1372
MS London, British Museum, Cotton Tiberius A.XIII ff.65v-6, 159v
ed Kemble 1839-48, no.682; Robertson 1956, no.58

15.3.41
Archbishop Oswald to Wulfgeat Sawyer 1373
MS London, British Museum, Cotton Tiberius A.XIII ff.72rv, 161
ed Kemble 1839-48, no.680; Robertson 1956, no.56

15.3.42
Archbishop Oswald to Wulfheah   Sawyer 1374
MS   London, British Museum, Cotton Tiberius A.XIII f.67rv
ed   Kemble 1839-48, no.681; Robertson 1956, no.57

15.3.43
Bishop Æthelwold to Ælfwine   Sawyer 1376
MS   London, British Museum, Add. 15350 f.8
ed   Kemble 1839-48, no.1347; Robertson 1956, no.53

15.3.44
Bishop Æthelwold and Wulfstan Uccea   Sawyer 1377
MS   London, Society of Antiquaries, 60 ff.54v-5
ed   Birch 1885-99, no.1131; Robertson 1956, no.37

15.3.45
Archbishop Ealdwulf to Leofenath   Sawyer 1381
MS   London, British Museum, Cotton Tiberius A.XIII f.89rv
ed   Kemble 1839-48, no.695

15.3.46
Writ of Bishop Æthelric, Sherborne   Sawyer 1383
MS   Paris, Bibliothèque Nationale, Lat. 943 f.170v
ed   Harmer 1952, no.63
     See B.16.18

15.3.47
Writ of Archbishop Wulfstan, Christ Church, Canterbury   Sawyer 1386
MS   London, British Museum, Add. 14907 ff.16v-7
     London, Lambeth Palace, 1370 f.69v
ed   Harmer 1952, no.27
     See B.16.6.11

15.3.48
Bishop Eadnoth to Beorhtnoth   Sawyer 1387
MS   Oxford, Bodleian, Eng. hist. a.2 no.iii
     London, British Museum, Cotton R.II.11
ed   Earle 1888, 422; Napier and Stevenson 1895, no.4

15.3.49
Bishop Leofsige to Godric   Sawyer 1388
MS   Somers Charter 19 [lost]
ed   Kemble 1839-48, no.724

15.3.50
Archbishop Æthelnoth to Christ Church   Sawyer 1389
MS   London, British Museum, Cotton Claudius A.III f.6
     Oxford, Bodleian, Gough Berks. 20 f.13

ed Kemble 1839-48, no.974; Robertson 1956, no.89
See B.16.6.2

15.3.51
Bishop Ælfwine to Osgod   Sawyer 1391
MS London, British Museum, Add. 15350 f.43v
ed Kemble 1839-48, no.768; Robertson 1956, no.98

15.3.52
Bishop Lyfing to Æthelric   Sawyer 1394
MS London, British Museum, Add. Ch. 19799
facs Bond 1873-8, IV, 23
ed Earle 1888, 242-3; Robertson 1956, no.94

15.3.53
Bishop Brihtheah to Wulfmær   Sawyer 1399
MS London, British Museum, Add. Ch. 19797
facs Bond 1873-8, IV, 19
ed Earle 1888, 238; Robertson 1956, no.87

15.3.54
Archbishop Eadsige to St Augustine's, Canterbury   Sawyer 1400
MS London, British Museum, Stowe Charter 42
facs Sanders 1878-84, III, 43
ed Robertson 1956, no.108

15.3.55
Bishop Stigand to Æthelmær   Sawyer 1402
MS London, British Museum, Add. 15350 f.96
ed Kemble 1839-48, no.820; Robertson 1956, no.106

15.3.56
Bishop Stigand to Wulfric   Sawyer 1403
MS London, British Museum, Add. 15350 f.74v
ed Kemble 1839-48, no.949; Robertson 1956, no.107

15.3.57
Bishop Ealdred to Athelstan   Sawyer 1406
MS London, British Museum, Harley 4660 f.10
ed Kemble 1839-48, no.923; Robertson 1956, no.112

15.3.58
Bishop Ealdred to Wulfgeat   Sawyer 1409
MS Somers Charter 24 [lost]
ed Kemble 1839-48, no.804; Robertson 1956, no.111

15.4
Other Ecclesiastical Grants

15.4.1
The familia at Worcester to Bishop Wærferth   Sawyer 1416
MS London, British Museum, Harley 4660 f.4v
ed Birch 1885-99, no.570; Kemble 1839-48, no.1071

15.4.2
Æthelnoth, priest, to New Minster, Winchester   Sawyer 1418
MS Shirburn Castle, Earl of Macclesfield, Liber Abbatiae f.21
ed Edwards 1866, 146-7; Birch 1885-99, no.804; Robertson 1956, no.28

15.4.3
Eadwulf to New Minster and Nuns' Minster, Winchester   Sawyer 1419
MS Shirburn Castle, Earl of Macclesfield, Liber Abbatiae f.23v
ed Edwards 1866, 165-6; Birch 1885-99, no.825; Robertson 1956, no.29

15.4.4
Ælfsige, abbot, to Wulfmær   Sawyer 1420
MS Shirburn Castle, Earl of Macclesfield, Liber Abbatiae f.36v
ed Edwards 1866, 258-60; Robertson 1956, no.70

15.4.5
The familia at Worcester to Fulder   Sawyer 1421
MS London, British Museum, Harley Charter 83 A3
facs Bond 1873-8, IV, 43
ed Birch 1885-99, no.1318; Robertson 1956, no.79

15.4.6
The community at Sherborne to Edmund Ætheling   Sawyer 1422
MS London, British Museum, Add. 46487 f.16v
ed Kemble 1839-48, no.1302; Robertson 1956, no.74

15.4.7
Ælfweard, abbot of Evesham, to Æthelmær   Sawyer 1423
MS London, British Museum, Add. Ch. 19796
facs Bond 1873-8, IV, 15
ed Earle 1888, 235-6; Robertson 1956, no.81

15.4.8
Abbot Ælfwig to Archbishop Stigand   Sawyer 1426
MS Cambridge, Corpus Christi College, 111 pp.74-5
ed Birch 1885-99, no.929; Robertson 1956, no.117

15.4.9
Writ of Abbot Wulfwold, Bath   Sawyer 1427
MS Cambridge, Corpus Christi College, 111 p.92
ed Harmer 1952, no.6

15.4.10
Writ of the monk Edwin   Sawyer 1428

MS London, British Museum, Add. 15350 ff.116-7
    London, British Museum, Stowe 944 f.40rv
ed Harmer 1952, no.113
    See B.6.2

15.5
Miscellaneous Texts

15.5.1
Memorandum on land at Bromsgrove, Worcs. Sawyer 1432
MS London, British Museum, Add. 46204 r
    London, British Museum, Cotton Nero E.I pt.2 f.182v
    London, British Museum, Cotton Tiberius A.XIII f.9
    London, British Museum, Harley 4660 f.6v
    London, Lambeth Palace, 585 p.540
ed Birch 1885-99, no.308; Robertson 1956, no.4

15.5.2
Record of the settlement of a dispute at Sinton in Leigh, Worcs. Sawyer 1437
MS Somers Charter 6 [lost]
ed Birch 1885-99, no.386; Robertson 1956, no.5

15.5.3
Agreement between Abbot Ceolred and Wulfred Sawyer 1440
MS London, Society of Antiquaries, 60 f.46rv
ed Birch 1885-99, no.464; Robertson 1956, no.7

15.5.4
Agreement between Bishop Wærferth and Æthelwold Sawyer 1441
MS London, British Museum, Cotton Tiberius A.XIII ff.43-4
ed Birch 1885-99, no.574; Harmer 1914, no.14

15.5.5
Aquisition of land by King Edward Sawyer 1443
MS London, British Museum, Add. 15350 f.8
    London, British Museum, Stowe 944 f.57rv
ed Birch 1885-99, nos.605, 1338; Harmer 1914, no.16
    See B.16.21.1

15.5.6
Letter of Bishop Denewulf Sawyer 1444
MS London, British Museum, Add. 15350 ff.96v-7
ed Birch 1885-99, no.619

15.5.7
Letter to King Edward Sawyer 1445
MS   Canterbury, Dean and Chapter, Chart. Ant. C.1282
facs Sanders 1878-84, I, 13
ed   Birch 1885-99, no.591; Harmer 1914, no.18

15.5.8
Settlement of a dispute, Bishop Wærferth and Eadnoth   Sawyer 1446
MS London, British Museum, Cotton Tiberius A.XIII ff.56-7
ed Birch 1885-99, no.582; Harmer 1914, no.15

15.5.9
Record of a dispute over lands purchased by Archbishop Dunstan   Sawyer 1447
MS London, Westminster Abbey, W.A.M. VIII
London, British Museum, Add. 4558 ff.143-6
facs Sanders 1878-84, II, Westminster 7 [W.A.M. VIII]
ed Birch 1885-99, no.1063; Robertson 1956, no.44

15.5.10
Record of Gifts of Bishop Æthelwold   Sawyer 1448
MS London, Society of Antiquaries, 60 ff.39v-40v
ed Birch 1885-99, no.1128; Robertson 1956, no.39

15.5.11
Boundaries of monasteries, Winchester   Sawyer 1449
MS London, British Museum, Add. 15350 f.8v
ed Birch 1885-99, no.1163; Robertson 1956, no.49

15.5.12
Sureties between Abbess Eadgifu and Abbot Leofric   Sawyer 1452
MS Oxford, Bodleian, Bodley 579 f.11v
ed Birch 1885-99, no.1244; Robertson 1956, no.47
See B.16.10.9

15.5.13
Archbishop Oswald's memoranda on the estates of the see of York   Sawyer 1453
MS London, British Museum, Harley 55 f.4v
London, British Museum, Harley 6841 f.129rv
ed Birch 1885-99, nos.1278-9; Robertson 1956, no.54
See B.16.24.2

15.5.14
Dispute between Wynflæd and Leofwine   Sawyer 1454
MS London, British Museum, Cotton Augustus II.15
Oxford, Bodleian, James 24 pp.99-100
Oxford, Bodleian, Junius 62 ff.1-2
facs Bond 1873-8, III, 37 [Cotton Augustus II.15]
ed Kemble 1839-48, no.693; Robertson 1956, no.66

15.5.15
Agreement between Abbot Wulfric and Ealdred   Sawyer 1455
MS Cambridge, Corpus Christi College, 286 f.77v
ed Kemble 1839-48, no.429; Robertson 1956, no.62
See B.16.7.2

15.5.16
Dispute between Bishop Godwine and Leofwine   Sawyer 1456
MS Rochester, Dean and Chapter, Textus Roffensis ff. 155-6v
    Rochester, Diocesan Registry, Liber Temporalium f. 10v
facs Sawyer 1957-62 [Textus Roffensis]
ed Robertson 1956, no. 69

15.5.17
Land disputes in Kent   Sawyer 1457
MS Rochester, Dean and Chapter, Textus Roffensis ff. 162v-3v
facs Sawyer 1957-62
ed Birch 1885-99, no. 1296; Robertson 1956, no. 59

15.5.18
History of estates in Kent   Sawyer 1458
MS London, British Museum, Cotton Charters VIII. 20
    Rochester, Dean and Chapter, Textus Roffensis ff. 147-8
facs Bond 1873-8, III, 34 [Cotton Charters VIII. 20] ; Sawyer 1957-62 [Textus Roffensis]
ed Birch 1885-99, no. 1097; Robertson 1956, no. 41

15.5.19
Marriage agreement of Wulfric   Sawyer 1459
MS Somers Charter 18 [lost]
    Oxford, Bodleian, Ballard 67 f. 44
ed Kemble 1839-48, no. 738; Robertson 1956, no. 76

15.5.20
Dispute between Bishop Athelstan and Wulfstan   Sawyer 1460
MS London, British Museum, Cotton Charters VIII. 37
facs Bond 1873-8, IV, 14
ed Kemble 1839-48, no. 898; Robertson 1956, no. 83

15.5.21
Marriage agreement between Godwine and Brihtric   Sawyer 1461
MS lost
ed Earle 1888, 228-9; Robertson 1956, no. 77

15.5.22
Dispute between Edwin and his mother   Sawyer 1462
MS Hereford, Dean and Chapter, P. i. 2 f. 134rv
ed Kemble 1839-48, no. 755; Robertson 1956, no. 78
    See B. 16.11.2

15.5.23
Agreement between Archbishop Æthelnoth and Toki   Sawyer 1464
MS London, British Museum, Add. 14907 ff. 18v-9
    London, Lambeth Palace, 1370 f. 115
ed Kemble 1839-48, no. 1321; Robertson 1956, no. 80
    See B. 16.6.1

15.5.24
Arrangements between Eadsige and Christ Church   Sawyer 1465
MS Canterbury, Dean and Chapter, Reg. A f. 143
    Canterbury, Dean and Chapter, Reg. E ff. 43v-4
    London, British Museum, Stowe 835 ff. 29v-30v
ed Kemble 1839-48, no. 745; Robertson 1956, no. 86

15.5.25
Agreement between Eadsige and Toki   Sawyer 1466
MS London, British Museum, Add. 14907 ff. 21v-2
    London, Lambeth Palace, 1370 f. 114
ed Kemble 1839-48, no. 1336; Robertson 1956; no. 90
    See B. 16.6.1

15.5.26
Restoration of Sandwich to Christ Church   Sawyer 1467
MS London, British Museum, Cotton Augustus II. 90
facs Bond 1873-8, IV, 20
ed Kemble 1839-48, no. 758; Robertson 1956, no. 91

15.5.27
Agreement between Æthelmær and Abbot Ufi   Sawyer 1468
MS Cambridge, University Library, Ff. 2.33 f. 49
ed Robertson 1956, no. 97

15.5.28
Memorandum of Leofwine's land purchase   Sawyer 1469
MS Hereford, Dean and Chapter, P. i. 2 f. 135
ed Kemble 1839-48, no. 802; Robertson 1956, no. 99
    See B. 16.11.3

15.5.29
Agreement between Abbot of Bury St Edmunds and Wulfgeat   Sawyer 1470
MS Cambridge, University Library, Ff. 2.33 f. 49v
    London, British Museum, Add. 14847 f. 19rv
ed Kemble 1839-48, no. 1340; Robertson 1956, no. 100

15.5.30
Agreement between Archbishop Eadsige and Æthelric   Sawyer 1471
MS London, British Museum, Cotton Augustus II. 70
    London, British Museum, Stowe 853 ff. 30v-1v
facs Bond 1873-8, IV, 27 [Cotton Augustus II. 70]
ed Kemble 1839-48, no. 773; Robertson 1956, no. 101

15.5.31
Agreement between Abbot Ælfstan and Leofwine   Sawyer 1472
MS Canterbury, Dean and Chapter, Chart. Ant. A. 207
facs Sanders 1878-84, I, 23
ed Kemble 1839-48, no. 790; Robertson 1956, no. 102

15.5.32
Purchase of Land, Godric of Bourne   Sawyer 1473
MS London, British Museum, Cotton Augustus II.35
facs Bond 1873-8, IV, 28
 ed Kemble 1839-48, no.789; Robertson 1956, no.103

15.5.33
Agreement between Bishop Ælfwold and Care   Sawyer 1474
MS London, British Museum, Add. 46487 f.23rv
 ed Kemble 1839-48, no.1334; Robertson 1956, no.105

15.5.34
Agreement between Bishop Stigand and Wulfweard   Sawyer 1476
MS London, British Museum, Add. 15350 ff.100v-1
 ed Birch 1885-99, no.980; Robertson 1956, no.114

15.5.35
Notification by King Edward   Sawyer 1477
MS London, British Museum, Cotton Vitellius A.XIII f.51rv
 ed Kemble 1839-48, no.844

15.5.36
Agreement between Bishop Wulfwig and Earl Leofric   Sawyer 1478
MS Oxford, Christ Church, Eynsham Cartulary ff.9v-10v
   four later manuscripts
 ed Kemble 1839-48, no.956; Robertson 1956, no.115

15.6
Wills

15.6.1
Will of Abba   Sawyer 1482
MS London, British Museum, Cotton Augustus II.64
acs Bond 1873-8, II, 23
 ed Birch 1885-99, no.412; Harmer 1914, no.2

15.6.2
Will of Ælfgar   Sawyer 1483
MS Cambridge, University Library, Ff.2.33 f.46
   London, British Museum, Add. 14847 ff.16v-7
 ed Dorothy Whitelock, *Anglo-Saxon Wills,* Cambridge 1930, no.2

15.6.3
Will of Ælfgifu   Sawyer 1484
MS London, British Museum, Add. 15350 f.96rv
 ed Whitelock 1930, no.8

15.6.4
Will of Ælfheah   Sawyer 1485

MS London, British Museum, Add. 15350 ff.95v-6
ed Whitelock 1930, no.9

15.6.5
Will of Ælfflæd   Sawyer 1486
MS London, British Museum, Harley Charter 43 C.4
    Cambridge, University Library, Ff.2.33 f.47
facs Bond 1873-8, III, 35 [Harley Charter 43 C.4]
ed Whitelock 1930, no.15

15.6.6
Will of Ælfhelm   Sawyer 1487
MS London, British Museum, Stowe Charter 36
    Oxford, Bodleian, Eng. hist. a.2 no.xviii
facs Sanders 1878-84, III, 37 [Stowe Charter 36]
ed Whitelock 1930, no.13

15.6.7
Will of Archbishop Ælfric   Sawyer 1488
MS London, British Museum, Cotton Claudius B.VI f.102
ed Whitelock 1930, no.18

15.6.8
Will of Bishop Ælfric   Sawyer 1489
MS London, British Museum, Cotton Augustus II.85
    four later manuscripts
facs Bond 1873-8, IV, 21
ed Whitelock 1930, no.26

15.6.9
Will of Ælfric Modercope   Sawyer 1490
MS Cambridge, University Library, Ff.2.33 f.45
    London, British Museum, Add. 14847 f.15
ed Whitelock 1930, no.28

15.6.10
Will of Bishop Ælfsige   Sawyer 1491
MS Shirburn Castle, Earl of Macclesfield, Liber Abbatiae f.19v
ed Whitelock 1930, no.4

15.6.11
Will of Bishop Ælfwold   Sawyer 1492
MS Oxford, Bodleian, Eng. hist. a.2 no.xiii
ed Napier and Stevenson 1895, no.10

15.6.12
Will of Æthelflæd   Sawyer 1494
MS London, British Museum, Harley Charter 43 C.4

Cambridge, University Library, Ff.2.33 ff.46v-7
facs Bond 1873-8, III, 35 [Harley Charter 43 C.4]
  ed Whitelock 1930, no.14

15.6.13
Æthelflæd to St Paul's, London   Sawyer 1495
MS London, St Paul's, Dean and Chapter, Liber B f.20v [lost]
  ed Whitelock 1930, no.22

15.6.14
Æthelgeard to New Minster, Winchester   Sawyer 1496
MS Shirburn Castle, Earl of Macclesfield, Liber Abbatiae f.24v
  ed Whitelock 1930, no.6

15.6.15
Will of Æthelgifu   Sawyer 1497
MS Morgan, Grenfell & Co. [auctioned 1970]
  ed D. Whitelock and N.R. Ker, *The Will of Æthelgifu*, Roxburghe Club, Oxford 1968

15.6.16
Will of Æthelmær   Sawyer 1498
MS Shirburn Castle, Earl of Macclesfield, Liber Abbatiae ff.35v-6v
  ed Whitelock 1930, no.10

15.6.17
Bishop Æthelmær to St Edmunds   Sawyer 1499
MS Cambridge, University Library, Ff.2.33 f.49
  ed Whitelock 1930, no.35

15.6.18
Will of Æthelnoth   Sawyer 1500
MS London, British Museum, Stowe Charter 8
    London, British Museum, Stowe 853 ff.12v-3
facs Sanders 1878-84, III, 8 [Stowe Charter 8]
  ed Birch 1885-99, no.318; Robertson 1956, no.3

15.6.19
Will of Æthelric   Sawyer 1501
MS Canterbury, Dean and Chapter, Chart. Ant. B.2
    five later manuscripts
facs Sanders 1878-84, I, 16 [Chart. Ant. B.2]
  ed Whitelock 1930, no.16[1]

15.6.20
Will of the Ætheling Athelstan   Sawyer 1503
MS London, British Museum, Stowe Charter 37
    Canterbury, Dean and Chapter, Chart. Ant. H.68
    four later manuscripts

facs Sanders 1878-84, III, 38 [Stowe Charter 37], I, 18 [Chart. Ant. H.68]
  ed Whitelock 1930, no.20

15.6.21
Will of Ealdorman Æthelwold   Sawyer 1504

MS London, British Museum, Add. 15350 f.87rv
  ed Birch 1885-99, no.819; Harmer 1914, no.20

15.6.22
Will of Æthelwold   Sawyer 1505

MS Shirburn Castle, Earl of Macclesfield, Liber Abbatiae ff.33v-4
  ed Whitelock 1930, no.12

15.6.23
Will of Æthelwyrd   Sawyer 1506

MS London, British Museum, Stowe Charter 27
   Canterbury, Dean and Chapter, Reg.A f.141v
   Canterbury, Dean and Chapter, Reg.E ff.42v-3
facs Sanders 1878-84, III, 28 [Stowe Charter 27]
  ed Birch 1885-99, no.1010; Robertson 1956, no.32

15.6.24
Will of King Alfred   Sawyer 1507

MS London, British Museum, Stowe 944 ff.29v-33
   London, British Museum, Stowe 945 ff.2v-8v
   Shirburn Castle, Earl of Macclesfield, Liber Abbatiae ff.8v-9
facs Sanders 1878-84, III, 22 [Stowe 944 ff.29v-33]
  ed Birch 1885-99, no.553; Harmer 1914, no.11

15.6.25
Will of Alfred Ealdorman   Sawyer 1508

MS London, British Museum, Stowe Charter 20
   London, British Museum, Stowe 945 ff.19-23
facs Sanders 1878-84, III, 20 [Stowe Charter 20]
  ed Birch 1885-99, no.558; Harmer 1914, no.10

15.6.26
Bequest of Alfred, thegn   Sawyer 1509

MS Shirburn Castle, Earl of Macclesfield, Liber Abbatiae f.19v
  ed Birch 1885-99, no.649; Robertson 1956, no.27

15.6.27
Will of Badanoth Beotting   Sawyer 1510

MS London, British Museum, Cotton Augustus II.42
facs Bond 1873-8, II, 25
  ed Birch 1885-99, no.417; Robertson 1956, no.6

15.6.28
Will of Brihtric and Ælfswith   Sawyer 1511

MS   Rochester, Dean and Chapter, Textus Roffensis ff. 144-5
facs Sawyer 1957-62
ed   Whitelock 1930, no. 11

15.6.29
Brihtric Grim to Old Minster, Winchester   Sawyer 1512
MS   London, British Museum, Add. 15350 f. 52v
ed   Whitelock 1930, no. 7

15.6.30
Ceolwynn to the community at Winchester   Sawyer 1513
MS   London, British Museum, Add. 15350 ff. 76v-7
ed   Birch 1885-99, no. 566; Robertson 1956, no. 17

15.6.31
Will of Dunn   Sawyer 1514
MS   Rochester, Dean and Chapter, Textus Roffensis f. 140rv
facs Sawyer 1957-62
ed   Birch 1885-99, no. 486[2]; Robertson 1956, no. 9

15.6.32
Will of King Eadred   Sawyer 1515
MS   Shirburn Castle, Earl of Macclesfield, Liber Abbatiae f. 22
ed   Birch 1885-99, no. 912; Harmer 1914, no. 21

15.6.33
Will of Eadwine   Sawyer 1516
MS   Cambridge, University Library, Ff. 2.33 f. 45rv
      London, British Museum, Add. 14847 f. 15v
ed   Whitelock 1930, no. 33

15.6.34
Will of Ketel   Sawyer 1519
MS   Cambridge, University Library, Ff. 2.33 ff. 45v-6
      London, British Museum, Add. 14847 f. 16
ed   Whitelock 1930, no. 34

15.6.35
Will of Leofgifu   Sawyer 1521
MS   Cambridge, University Library, Ff. 2.33 f. 45
      London, British Museum, Add. 14847 f. 15rv
ed   Whitelock 1930, no. 29

15.6.36
Will of Leofwine   Sawyer 1522
MS   Oxford, Bodleian, Eng. hist. a. 2 no. xii
      Oxford, Bodleian, Eng. hist. a. 2 nos. xvi, xvii
facs W. Keller, *Angelsächsische Palaeographie*, Palaestra 43 pt. 2, Berlin 1906, no. 6 [no. xii]
ed   Napier and Stevenson 1895, no. 9

15.6.37
Will of Mantat   Sawyer 1523
MS Cambridge, University Library, Add. 3020 f. 18
ed Whitelock 1930, no. 23

15.6.38
Ordnoth and his wife to Old Minster, Winchester   Sawyer 1524
MS London, British Museum, Add. 15350 f.61v
ed Whitelock 1930, no.5

15.6.39
Wills of Siflæd   Sawyer 1525
MS Cambridge, University Library, Ff.2.33 ff.49v-50
London, British Museum, Add. 14847 f. 19v
ed Whitelock 1930, nos. 37-8

15.6.40
Will of Bishop Theodred   Sawyer 1526
MS Cambridge, University Library, Ff.2.33 f.48
London, British Museum, Add. 14847 ff. 17v-8
ed Whitelock 1930, no. 1

15.6.41
Will of Thurketel   Sawyer 1527
MS Cambridge, University Library, Ff.2.33 f.48v
London, British Museum, Add. 14847 ff. 18v-9
London, British Museum, Add. 45951 f. 1
ed Whitelock 1930, no. 24

15.6.42
Will of Thurketel Heyng   Sawyer 1528
MS Cambridge, University Library, Ff.2.33 f.45
London, British Museum, Add. 14847 f. 15
ed Whitelock 1930, no. 25

15.6.43
Thurkil and Æthelgyth to St Edmunds   Sawyer 1529
MS Cambridge, University Library, Ff.2.33 f.50
ed Whitelock 1930, no. 36

15.6.44
Bequest by Thurstan   Sawyer 1530
MS Canterbury, Dean and Chapter, Chart. Ant. C.70
London, British Museum, Cotton Augustus II.34
London, British Museum, Add. 4548 ff.22-4
facs Sanders 1878-84, I, 25 [Chart. Ant. C.70] ; Bond 1873-8, IV, 33 [Cotton Augustus II.34]
ed Whitelock 1930, no.30

15.6.45
Will of Thurstan   Sawyer 1531
MS   Cambridge, University Library, Ff.2.33 f.49rv
London, British Museum, Add. 14847 f.19
ed   Whitelock 1930, no.31

15.6.46
Will of Wulfgar   Sawyer 1533
MS   London, British Museum, Cotton Charter VIII.16
London, British Museum, Add. 15350 f.83
facs   Bond 1873-8, III, 3 [Cotton Charter VIII.16]
ed   Birch 1885-99, no.678; Robertson 1956, no.26

15.6.47
Will of Wulfgeat   Sawyer 1534
MS   London, British Museum, Harley Charter 83 A.2
facs   Bond 1873-8, IV, 42
ed   Whitelock 1930, no.19

15.6.48
Will of Wulfgyth   Sawyer 1535
MS   Canterbury, Dean and Chapter, Reg.A f.143v
Canterbury, Dean and Chapter, Reg.E f.44rv
London, British Museum, Stowe 853 ff.31v-2v
ed   Whitelock 1930, no.32

15.6.49
Will of Wulfric   Sawyer 1536
MS   Burton-on-Trent Museum, Burton Muniments 1
five later manuscripts
facs   Sanders 1878-84, III, Anglesey 2 [Burton Muniments 1]
ed   Whitelock 1930, no.17

15.6.50
Will of Wulfsige   Sawyer 1537
MS   Cambridge, University Library, Ff.2.33 f.50
ed   Whitelock 1930, no.27

15.6.51
Will of Wulfwaru   Sawyer 1538
MS   Cambridge, Corpus Christi College, 111 pp.88-90
ed   Whitelock 1930, no.21

15.6.52
Will of Wynflæd   Sawyer 1539
MS   London, British Museum, Cotton Charter VIII.38
facs   Bond 1873-8, III, 38
ed   Whitelock 1930, no.3

15.7
Incomplete Texts

15.7.1
Osulf and Leofrun to St Edmunds Abbey   Sawyer 1608
MS London, British Museum, Harley 1005 f.195
 ed C. Hart, *The Early Charters of Eastern England,* Leicester 1966, 86

15.7.2
Extract from a charter of Archbishop Wulfred   Sawyer 1622
MS unknown
 ed W. Somner, *A Treatise of Gavelkind,* 2nd ed. London 1726, 88

15.7.3
King Æthelred to Christ Church, Canterbury   Sawyer 1636
MS Oxford, Bodleian, Ballard 67 f.47v
    Oxford, St John's College, 194 f.2v
 ed Dugdale 1846, I, 111 no.38

15.7.4
Godweald to St Augustine's, Canterbury   Sawyer 1656
source London, P.R.O., E164/27 f.6

15.7.5
Abbot Æthelsige to Blæcmann and Æthelred   Sawyer 1658
source London, P.R.O., E164/27 f.6v

15.7.6
Eorl Northman to St Cuthbert's   Sawyer 1659
 MS London, British Museum, Cotton Domitian VII f.47v
facs *Liber Vitae Ecclesiae Dunelmensis,* Surtees Society 136, Durham 1923
 ed Birch 1885-99, no.1256; Robertson 1956, no.68
    See B.16.8.2

15.7.7
Eorl Thored to St Cuthbert's   Sawyer 1660
 MS London, British Museum, Cotton Domitian VII f.47v
facs Durham 1923
 ed Birch 1885-99, no.1255; Robertson 1956, no.60
    See B.16.8.2

15.7.8
Ulfketel to St Cuthbert's   Sawyer 1661
 MS London, British Museum, Cotton Domitian VII f.47v
facs Durham 1923
 ed Birch 1885-99, no.1256; Robertson 1956, no.68
    See B.16.8.2

15.7.9
Bishop Ceolbeorht to Sigeric Sawyer 1791
MS Oxford, Bodleian, James 23
ed M. Gibbs, *Early Charters of the Cathedral Church of St. Paul, London,* Camden Society
Third Series 58, London 1939, 7-8, no.J16

15.7.10
King Alfred to the church of Winchester Sawyer 1812
rce W.R.W. Stephens and F.T. Madge, *Documents relating to the History of the Cathedral
Church of Winchester AD 1636-83,* Hampshire Record Society, 1897, p.61, no.5

15.7.11
Grants of Land in Somerset Sawyer 1819
MS London, British Museum, Add. 15350 f.27v
ed A.G.C. Turner, 'Some Old English passages relating to the episcopal manor of Taunton,'
Proceedings, Somersetshire Archaeological and Natural History Society 98 [1953] 119

15.7.12
List of Lands, Chilcomb, Hants. Sawyer 1820
MS London, British Museum, Add. 15350 f.6
ed Birch 1885-99, no.1160; Harmer 1952, no.107 note

15.7.13
List of Lands belonging to Winchester Cathedral Sawyer 1821
MS London, British Museum, Add. 15350 f.6
ed Birch 1885-99, no.1161

15.7.14
Bishop Ealhhun to the church of Worcester Sawyer 1833
ce London, British Museum, Cotton Vitellius C.IX f.130
Oxford, Bodleian, Dugdale 12 p.503 no.18

15.7.15
Bishop Wærferth to –   Sawyer 1838
ce Oxford, Bodleian, Dugdale 12 p.505 no.62

15.7.16
Bishop Wilfrid to –   Sawyer 1840
ce Oxford, Bodleian, Dugdale 12 p.506 no.92

15.7.17
King Athelstan to Æthelnoth Sawyer 1841
ce Oxford, Bodleian, Dugdale 12 p.505 no.72
London, British Museum, Cotton Vitellius C.IX f.131

15.7.18
Bishop Oswald to –   Sawyer 1843
ce Oxford, Bodleian, Dugdale 12 p.503 no.20

15.7.19
King Edgar to Ely Abbey   Sawyer 1844
source London, British Museum, Cotton Vitellius C.IX f. 131
Oxford, Bodleian, Dugdale 12 p. 504 no. 55

15.7.20
Archbishop Wulfstan to —   Sawyer 1846
source Oxford, Bodleian, Dugdale 12 p. 503 no. 23

15.7.21
Archbishop Wulfstan to—   Sawyer 1847
source Oxford, Bodleian, Dugdale 12 p. 502 no. 8

15.7.22
Bishop Leofsige to —   Sawyer 1848
source Oxford, Bodleian, Dugdale 12 p. 502 no. 7

15.7.23
Bishop Lyfing to —   Sawyer 1849
source Oxford, Bodleian, Dugdale 12 p. 503 no. 31

15.7.24
Bishop Lyfing to —   Sawyer 1851
source Oxford, Bodleian, Dugdale 12 p. 504 no. 37

15.7.25
Bishop Lyfing to — ·   Sawyer 1852
source Oxford, Bodleian, Dugdale 12 p. 504 no. 36

15.7.26
Bishop Lyfing to—   Sawyer 1853
source Oxford, Bodleian, Dugdale 12 p. 503 no. 28

15.7.27
Bishop Lyfing to—   Sawyer 1854
source Oxford, Bodleian, Dugdale 12 p. 505 no. 57

15.7.28
Bishop Ealdred to —   Sawyer 1857
source Oxford, Bodleian, Dugdale 12 p. 504 no. 38

15.7.29
Alhun to—   Sawyer 1858
source Oxford, Bodleian, Dugdale 12 p. 502 no. 5

15.7.30
Note of descent of lease   Sawyer 1859
MS London, British Museum, Cotton Tiberius A.XIII f. 118v

ed   N.R. Ker, 'Hemming's Cartulary: a description of the two Worcester Cartularies in
Cotton Tiberius A.XIII,' in R.W. Hunt, W.A. Pantin, and R.W. Southern, eds., *Studies
in Medieval History presented to F.M. Powicke*, Oxford 1948, 74
See B.16.23.4

15.8
Bounds in English
Sawyer nos. 1 35 43 50 54 55 60 64 67 78 79 80 84 99 104 108 115 124 140
141 142 145 168 174 175 179 201 202 203 211 212 214 216 217 219 222 229
236 242 244 247 249 251 254 255 258 265 266 270a 272 273 274 275 276 277
282 283 284 286 290 292 298 300 304 308 309 310 312 317 321 326 327 329
331 334 335 336 339 340 341 343 345 347 348 349 351 352 354 360 361 362
364 365 366 367 368 369 371 374 376 377 378 379 380 381 382 383 386 387
388 389 390 393 396 399 400 401 402 403 404 405 411 412 413 414 416 417
418 419 422 423 424 425 429 430 431 432 433 437 438 440 441 442 443 444
445 446 447 448 449 452 455 459 461 462 464 465 466 467 468 469 470 471
472 473 474 475 476 478 480 481 482 486 487 489 490 491 492 493 494 495
496 497 498 500 501 502 503 504 507 508 509 510 511 512 513 514 516 517
518 519 522 523 524 525 526 527 528 529 531 532 533 534 535 536 540 541
542 543 544 545 546 547 550 552 553 555 556 557 558 559 560 561 562 563
564 565 567 568 570 571 573 575 577 578 579 583 584 585 586 587 588 589
590 591 592 593 594 595 596 597 598 600 601 602 603 604 605 606 607 608
609 610 611 612 613 614 615 617 618 619 620 621 622 623 624 626 627 630
631 632 633 635 636 638 639 640 641 642 643 645 647 648 649 650 651 653
654 655 656 657 659 661 663 664 666 668 669 670 671 672 673 675 676 677
678 679 680 681 682 683 684 685 688 689 690 692 694 695 696 697 698 699
702 703 704 705 706 708 709 710 711 712 713 714 715 716 717 718 721 722
723 724 725 726 727 734 735 736 737 738 740 743 744 747 748 751 753 754
755 756 757 758 759 760 761 762 763 764 765 766 767 770 771 772 773 777
780 781 782 784 785 786 789 790 791 793 794 795 800 801 802 803 804 805
811 812 820 828 829 830 831 832 833 834 835 836 837 840 842 843 845 846
847 848 849 850 852 854 855 856 857 858 860 861 862 864 865 867 868 869
870 872 873 874 878 881 883 885 887 889 890 891 892 893 896 898 899 901
902 903 905 907 909 910 915 916 918 920 925 927 930 931 933 934 935 938
942 943 944 950 955 956 960 961 962 963 964 967 968 969 970 971 972 974
975 977 993 994 998 999 1001 1003 1004 1005 1006 1007 1008 1009 1010
1012 1013 1014 1020 1022 1023 1025 1026 1027 1028 1031 1033 1034 1036
1044 1165 1174 1185 1227 1238 1248 1254 1272 1276 1277 1291 1297 1300
1301 1304 1306 1307 1311 1314 1319 1321 1322 1323 1325 1329 1330 1335
1340 1346 1347 1348 1351 1352 1353 1356 1361 1370 1379 1380 1384 1385
1393 1395 1396 1405 1434 1450 1451 1540 1541 1542 1543 1544 1545 1546
1547 1549 1550 1551 1552 1553 1554 1555 1556 1557 1558 1559 1560 1561
1562 1564 1565 1566 1567 1568 1569 1570 1571 1572 1573 1574 1577 1578
1581 1585 1588 1589 1590 1591 1592 1593 1594 1595 1596 1597 1598 1599
1600 1601 1602 1604 1662 1663 1664 1811 1862 1863

16
Records

16.1
Barking, List of Lands
MS Oxford, Bodleian, Bodley 155 **Ker 303**
ed Hickes 1705, Dissertatio Epistolaris 10

16.2
Bath

16.2.1
Agreement of Prior
MS Cambridge, Corpus Christi College, 140 **Ker 35 art.3**
ed Earle 1888, 270

16.2.2
Confraternity with other houses
MS Cambridge, Corpus Christi College, 140 **Ker 35 art.9**
ed W. Hunt, *Two Chartularies of the Priory of St. Peter at Bath,* Somerset Record Society
7, London 1893, 3-4

16.2.3
Manumissions
MS Cambridge, Corpus Christi College, 140 **Ker 35 arts.2, 8**
ed Earle 1888, 268-71

16.2.4
Relics
MS Cambridge, Corpus Christi College, 140 **Ker 35 art.7**
ed Hunt 1893, lxxv-lxxvi

16.3
Bedwyn, Guild regulations, manumissions, tithe records
MS Bern, Stadtbibliothek, 671 **Ker 6 arts. a, b, c**
ed M. Förster, *Der Flussname Themse und seine Sippe,* Sitzungsberichte der Bayerischen
Akademie der Wissenschaften, Phil.-Hist. Abt., Jahrgang 1941, Band 1, Munich 1941,
791-5; H.D. Meritt, 'Old English Entries in a Manuscript at Bern,' *JEGP* 33 [1934] 343-
51

16.4
Bodmin, Manumissions
MS London, British Museum, Add. 9381 **Ker 126**
ed M. Förster, 'Die Freilassungsurkunden des Bodmin-Evangeliars,' in N. Bøgholm,
A. Brusendorff, C.A. Bodelsen, eds., *A Grammatical Miscellany offered to Otto
Jespersen,* London and Copenhagen 1930, 77-99

16.5
Bury St Edmunds

16.5.1
Boundaries of land
MS Oxford, Bodleian, Bodley 297   **Ker 306 art.b**
ed T. Arnold, *Memorials of St Edmund's Abbey,* Rolls Series 96, London 1890, I, 340-1

16.5.2
List of Farm Goods
MS Cambridge, Pembroke College, 88   **Ker 77 art.a**
ed Robertson 1956, App.II, no.3

16.5.3
Payments at a Burial
MS Cambridge, Pembroke College, 83   **Ker 76**
ed Robertson 1956, App.II, no.8

16.5.4
Possessions, Rents and Grants
MS Oxford, Corpus Christi College, 197   **Ker 353 arts.3-8**
ed Robertson 1956, no.104

16.5.5
Service Books
MS Oxford, Bodleian, Auct. D.2.14 f.173   **Ker 290**
ed Robertson 1956, App.II, no.7

16.6
Christ Church, Canterbury

16.6.1
Agreements
MS London, Lambeth Palace 1370 [771]   **Ker 284 arts.c, e**
ed Robertson 1956, no.90 [art.c], no.80 [art.e]
See B.15.5.23, 15.5.25

16.6.2
Benefactions
MS London, British Museum, Cotton Claudius A.III   **Ker 185 arts.c-f**
ed Robertson 1956, no.96 [art.c], no.89 [art.d], no.88 [art.e], no.95 [art.f]
See B.15.1.66, 15.2.14, 15.2.17, 15.3.50

16.6.3
Boundaries
MS London, Lambeth Palace, 1370 [771]   **Ker 284 art.b**
ed Kemble 1839-48, no.1363

16.6.4
Confraternity notice
MS London, British Museum, Royal 1 D.IX   **Ker 247 art.a**
ed Ker 1957, 317

16.6.5
Codex Aureus Inscription
MS Stockholm, Kungl. Biblioteket **Ker 385**
ed D. Whitelock, *Sweet's Anglo-Saxon Reader,* 15th ed. Oxford 1967, 205

16.6.6
Manumission
MS London, British Museum, Royal 1 B.VII **Ker 246**
ed Harmer 1914, no. 19; Birch 1885-99, no. 639

16.6.7
Privilege
MS London, British Museum, Cotton Claudius A.III **Ker 185 art. a**
ed Kemble 1839-48, no. 715
See B.15.1.48

16.6.8
Writs of Cnut
MS London, British Museum, Royal 1 D.IX **Ker 247 art. b**
London, Lambeth Palace, 1370 [771] and British Museum, Cotton Tiberius
B.IV f.87 **Ker 284 arts. d, f, g**
ed Harmer 1952, no. 26 [Ker 247 art. b], nos. 28-30 [Ker 284 arts. d, f, g]
See B.15.1.59, 15.1.60, 15.1.61

16.6.9
Writ of King Edward
MS London, British Museum, Cotton Claudius A.III **Ker 185 art. b**
ed Harmer 1952, no. 35
See B.15.1.96

16.6.10
Writ of William I
MS Cambridge, Corpus Christi College, 173
London, British Museum, Cotton Vitellius D.VII f.40 [Joscelyn's transcript] **Ker 408**
not edited

16.6.11
Writ of Archbishop Wulfstan
MS London, Lambeth Palace, 1370 [771] **Ker 284 art. a**
ed Harmer 1952, no. 27
See B.15.3.47

16.7
St Augustine's, Canterbury

16.7.1
Booklist

MS London, British Museum, Cotton Domitian I **Ker 146 art.e**
ed Robertson 1956, App. II, no.6

16.7.2
Grants

MS Cambridge, Corpus Christi College, 286 **Ker 55 arts.a, b**
ed Harmer 1914, no.6 [art.a] ; Robertson 1956, no.62 [art.b]
See B.15.2.5, 15.5.15

16.8
Congregation of St Cuthbert

16.8.1
Gifts of King Æthelstan

MS London, British Museum, Cotton Otho B.IX **Ker 176 arts.a, b**
ed Robertson 1956, no.24

16.8.2
Grants

MS Cambridge, Corpus Christi College, 183 **Ker 42 art.c**
London, British Museum, Cotton Domitian VII **Ker 147 arts.b, c**
facs Durham 1923
ed Robertson 1956, App. I, no.2 [Ker 42 art.c] ; no.60 [Ker 147 art.b] , no.68 [Ker
147 art.c]
See B.15.7.6, 15.7.7, 15.7.8

16.8.3
Manumissions

MS London, British Museum, Cotton Domitian VII **Ker 147 art.a**
London, British Museum, Cotton Otho B.IX **Ker 176 arts.c-f**
[Oxford, Bodleian, James 18 transcript]
ed Birch 1885-99, no.1254 [Ker 147 art.a] ; H.H.E. Craster, 'Some Anglo-Saxon Records
of the See of Durham,' *Archaeologia Aeliana,* 4th series 1 [1925] 190-1 [Ker 176
arts.c-f]

16.8.4
List of Plate

MS Cambridge, Corpus Christi College, 183 **Ker 42 art.b**
ed Robertson 1956, App. II, no.4

16.9
Ely

16.9.1
Farm accounts

MS Cambridge, Queens' College, [Horne] 74 **Ker 80**
ed Robertson 1956, App. II, no.9

16.9.2
List of Freeholders
MS   London, British Museum, Cotton Tiberius B.V f.76v   **Ker 22 art.a**
ed   Earle 1888, 275-7

16.9.3
Grant of Land
MS   London, British Museum, Cotton Tiberius B.V f.74v   **Ker 22 art.b**
ed   Robertson 1956, no.71

16.9.4
Guild Regulations
MS   London, British Museum, Cotton Tiberius B.V f.74   **Ker 22 art.c**
ed   B. Thorpe, *Diplomatarium Anglicum Ævi Saxonici,* London 1865, 610

16.9.5
Writ of King Edward
MS   Cambridge, Trinity College, O.2.1   **Ker 93 art.b**
     Ely Cathedral   **Ker 113 art.b**
ed   Harmer 1952, no.47
     See B.15.1.106

16.10
Exeter

16.10.1
List of Books given by Bishop Leofric
MS   Exeter, Cathedral, 3501 ff.1-2v   **Ker 20 art.6**
     Oxford, Bodleian, Auct. D.2.16   **Ker 291 art.a**
facs Chambers et al. 1933 [Ker 20 art.6]
ed   Chambers 1933, 18-30 [Ker 20 art.6] ; Robertson 1956, App.I, no.1 [Ker 291 art.a]

16.10.2
List of Guild Members
MS   Exeter, Cathedral, 3501 f.7rv   **Ker 20 art.4**
facs Chambers et al. 1933
ed   Hickes 1705, Dissert. Epist. 18-9

16.10.3
Notice of Guild Assembly
MS   London, British Museum, Cotton Tiberius B.V vol.1 f.75   **Ker 194 art.b**
ed   Thorpe 1865, 613

16.10.4
Inscription of Donation
MS   Oxford, Bodleian, Bodley 311   **Ker 307 art.a**
ed   Ker 1957, 360

16.10.5
Leofric Inscriptions
MS Cambridge, University Library, Ii.2.11 **Ker 20 art.10**
    Cambridge, Corpus Christi College, 41 **Ker 32 art.19**
    Cambridge, Trinity College, B.11.2 **Ker 84 art.b**
    London, British Museum, Harley 2961 [missing] **Ker 236**
    Oxford, Bodleian, Auct. D.2.16 **Ker 291 art.b**
    Oxford, Bodleian, Auct. F.1.15 **Ker 294 art.b**
    Oxford, Bodleian, Auct. F.3.6 **Ker 296 art.c**
    Oxford, Bodleian, Bodley 579 **Ker 315 art.b**
    Oxford, Bodleian, Bodley 708 **Ker 316**
ed Chambers 1933, 11

16.10.6
Manumissions
MS Exeter, Cathedral, 3501 f.7 **Ker 20 art.5**
    Cambridge, University Library, Ii.2.11 f.202v and Exeter, Cathedral, 3501 ff.4rv,
    6rv **Ker 20 art.13**
    London, British Museum, Cotton Tiberius B.V f.75 **Ker 194 arts.a, c**
    Oxford, Bodleian, Bodley 579 **Ker 315 arts.c, d**
acs F. Rose-Troup, 'Exeter Manumissions and Quittances of the Eleventh and Twelfth
    Centuries,' *Transactions of the Devonshire Association* 69 [1937] pls.57-9 [Ker 315 arts.c, d]
ed Thorpe 1865, 634 [Ker 20 art.5] ; Earle 1888, 257-64 and B. Dickins, 'The Beheaded
    Manumission in the Exeter Book' in Cyril Fox and Bruce Dickins, eds., *The Early*
    Cultures of North-West Europe, H.M. Chadwick Memorial Studies, Cambridge 1950,
    363-7 [Ker 20 art.13] ; Kemble 1839-48, no.1353 [Ker 194 art.a] ; Thorpe 1865, 623
    [Ker 194 art.c] ; Earle 1888, 253-4 [Ker 315 art.c] , 256-7 [art.d]

16.10.7
Permission to Ring Bells
MS Exeter, Cathedral, 3501 f.5 **Ker 20 art.12**
acs Chambers et al. 1933
ed Earle 1888, 260

16.10.8
List of Relics
MS Oxford, Bodleian, Auct. D.2.16 **Ker 291 art.c**
ed M. Förster, *Zur Geschichte des Reliquienkultus in Altengland,* Sitzungsberichte der
    Bayerischen Akademie der Wissenschaften, Phil.-Hist. Abt., Jahrgang 1943, Heft 8,
    Munich 1943, 63-80

16.10.9
List of Sureties
MS Oxford, Bodleian, Bodley 579 **Ker 315 art.a**
ed Robertson 1956, no.47
    See B.15.5.12

16.10.10
Sales of Land
MS   Exeter, Cathedral, 3501 f.6v   **Ker 20 art. 14**
facs   Chambers et al. 1933
not edited

16.11
Hereford

16.11.1
Boundaries of See
MS   Cambridge, Pembroke College, 302   **Ker 78**
ed   Förster 1941, 769

16.11.2
Record of a Shiremoot
MS   Hereford, Cathedral, P.I.2   **Ker 119 art.a**
ed   Robertson 1956, no.78; C.B. Judge, 'Anglo-Saxonica in Hereford Cathedral Library,'
Harvard Studies and Notes in Philology and Literature 16 [1934] 94
See B.15.5.22

16.11.3
Sale of Land
MS   Hereford, Cathedral, P.I.2   **Ker 119 art.b**
ed   Robertson 1956, no.99; Judge 1934, 95
See B.15.5.28

16.12
Horton, Inscription recording gift
MS   El Escorial, Real Biblioteca, E.11.1   **Ker 115**
ed   Ker 1957, 152

16.13
Lichfield, Record of Lawsuit
MS   Lichfield, Cathedral, Gospels of St Chad   **Ker 123**
facs   E.H. Zimmermann, *Vorkarolingische Miniaturen*, Berlin 1916, pl.245
ed   Earle 1888, 236-7

16.14
London, St Paul's Cathedral, List of 'scipmen'
MS   Cambridge, Corpus Christi College, 383   **Ker 65 art. 26**
ed   Robertson 1956, no.72

16.15
Malmesbury, Bull of Pope Sergius
MS   London, British Museum, Cotton Otho C.I vol.1   **Ker 181 art. 2**
ed   Birch 1885-99, no.106

16.16
Rochester

16.16.1
List of Estates
MS Rochester, Cathedral, Textus Roffensis f. 166v-7 **Ker 373B**
facs Sawyer 1957-62
ed Robertson 1956, no.52

16.16.2
List of Serfs
MS Rochester, Cathedral, Textus Roffensis f. 162 **Ker 373B**
facs Sawyer 1957-62
not edited   .

16.17
Sens, Cathédral, label inscription
MS Sens, Trésor de la Cathédrale, Authentique **Ker 383**
facs and ed. M. Prou and E. Chartraire, 'Authentiques de Reliques conservées au trésor de la cathédrale de Sens,' *Mémoires de la société nationale des antiquaires de France* 59 [6 série IX] [1900] 166, no.158

16.18
Sherborne, Writ of Bishop Æthelric
MS Paris, Bibliothèque Nationale, Lat. 943 **Ker 364 art.d**
ed Harmer 1952, no.63
See B.15.3.46

16.19
Tavistock, Manumissions
MS Oxford, Bodleian, Bodley 579 **Ker 315 art.e**
ed Earle 1888, 254-6

16.20
Thorney

16.20.1
Inscription recording gift
MS London, British Museum, Add. 40000 **Ker 131 art.c**
ed Ker 1957, 163

16.20.2
Names in Liber Vitae
MS London, British Museum, Add. 40000 **Ker 131 art.d**
ed E. Jørgensen, 'Bidrag til ældre nordisk Kirke- og Litteraturhistorie,' *Nordisk Tidskrift för Bok- och Biblioteksväsen* 20 [1933] 187

16.21
New Minster, Winchester

16.21.1
Boundaries of an Estate
MS   London, British Museum, Stowe 944   **Ker 274 art.g**
ed   Birch 1885-99, no. 1338
See B.15.5.5

16.21.2
Names in Liber Vitae
MS   London, British Museum, Stowe 944   **Ker 274 art.a**
ed   Birch 1892, 64-72

16.21.3
List of Relics
MS   London, British Museum, Stowe 944   **Ker 274 art.h**
ed   Birch 1892, 159-63; Förster 1943, 116-20

16.22
Nunnaminster, Winchester, Estate Boundaries
MS   London, British Museum, Harley 2965   **Ker 237**
ed   Birch 1885-99, no. 630

16.23
Worcester

16.23.1
List of Books
MS   Cambridge, Corpus Christi College, 367 pt. II   **Ker 64 art.a**
ed   Robertson 1956, App. II, no. 5

16.23.2
Inscription on Pastoral Care
MS   Oxford, Bodleian, Hatton 20 f. 1   **Ker 324**
facs   Ker 1956
ed   Ker 1957, 385

16.23.3
Payment to William I
MS   London, British Museum, Cotton Tiberius A.XIII   **Ker 190B art.a**
ed   Robertson 1956, App. I, no. 6; Ker 1957, 251

16.23.4
Dues
MS   London, British Museum, Cotton Tiberius A.XIII   **Ker 190A art.a**
ed   Ker 1948, 74
See B.15.7.30

16.24
York

16.24.1
Survey of Lands
MS York, Minster **Ker 402 art.a**
ed Robertson 1956, no.84

16.24.2
List of Lands
MS London, British Museum, Harley 55 **Ker 225 art.3**
ed Robertson 1956, no.54
    See B.15.5.13

16.24.3
List of Service Books
MS York, Minster **Ker 402 art.d**
ed Robertson 1956, App.II, no.2

16.24.4
List of Sureties
MS York, Minster **Ker 402 art.f**
ed Stevenson 1912, 12-3

16.24.5
Writ of Cnut
MS York, Minster **Ker 402 art.c**
ed Liebermann 1903-16, 273-5
    See B.14.29

16.25
Boundary
MS Paris, Bibliothèque Nationale, Lat. 10575 **Ker 370 art.c**
ed Ker 1957, 441-2

16.26.1
Burghal Hidage
MS London, British Museum, Cotton Otho B.XI and Add. 43703 **Ker 180 art.8**
ed Robertson 1956, App.II, no.1; Flower 1937, 63-4. See David Hill, 'The Burghal Hidage:
    The Establishment of a Text,' *Medieval Archaeology* 13 [1969] 84-92

16.26.2
Tribal Hidage
MS London, British Museum, Harley 3271 **Ker 239 art.3**
ed Birch 1885-99, no.297

16.26.3
Hidage for Defence

MS London, British Museum, Cotton Otho B.XI and Add. 43703 **Ker 180 art.9**
ed Robertson 1956, App.II, no. 1

17
Chronicles and Historical Texts

17.1
The Parker Chronicle

MS Cambridge, Corpus Christi College, 173 **Ker 39 art.1**
facs R. Flower and A.H. Smith, *The Parker Chronicle and Laws,* EETS 208, London 1941
ed C. Plummer, *Two of the Saxon Chronicles Parallel,* Oxford 1892-9; reissued D. Whitelock, Oxford 1952 as A

17.2

MS London, British Museum, Cotton Caligula A.XV **Ker 139A art.r**
ed F. Liebermann, *Ungedruckte anglonormannische Geschichtsquellen,* Strassburg 1879 [1966] 3-8

17.3

MS London, British Museum, Cotton Domitian VIII **Ker 148**
ed B. Thorpe, *The Anglo-Saxon Chronicle,* Rolls Series 23, London 1861, as F
coll. F.P. Magoun, Jr, 'The Domitian Bilingual of the *Old-English Annals*: Notes on the F-Text,' *MLQ* 6 [1945] 371-80

17.4

MS London, British Museum, Cotton Domitian IX f.9 **Ker 150**
ed Plummer 1892-9, 243-5, as H

17.5

MS London, British Museum, Cotton Otho B.XI **Ker 180 art.3**
ed Thorpe 1861, 110-41, as G; K. Horst, 'Die Reste der Handschrift G der altenglischen Annalen,' *Englische Studien* 22 [1896] 447-50

17.6

MS London, British Museum, Cotton Tiberius A.VI **Ker 188 art.1**
ed Thorpe 1861, as B

17.7

MS London, British Museum, Cotton Tiberius B.I **Ker 191 art.4**
ed H.A. Rositzke, *The C-Text of the Old English Chronicles,* Beiträge zur englischen Philologie 34, Bochum-Langendreer 1940 [1967]

17.8

MS London, British Museum, Cotton Tiberius B.IV **Ker 192**
ed E. Classen and F.E. Harmer, *An Anglo-Saxon Chronicle,* Manchester 1926

17.9

MS Oxford, Bodleian, Laud Misc. 636 **Ker 346**

facs D. Whitelock, *The Peterborough Chronicle,* EEMF 4, Copenhagen 1954
  ed Plummer 1892-9, as E; C. Clark, *The Peterborough Chronicle 1070-1154,* Oxford 1958,
      2nd ed. 1970

17.10
Kentish Royal Saints
MS London, Lambeth Palace, 427 ff. 210-1   **Ker 281**
 ed M. Förster, 'Die altenglischen Beigaben des Lambeth-Psalters,' *Archiv* 132 [1914] 333-5
      See also B.3.3.27

17.11
Revival of Monasticism
MS London, British Museum, Cotton Faustina A.X   **Ker 154B art.4**
 ed Cockayne 1864-6, III, 432-44

17.12
Wulfstan II of Worcester
MS London, British Museum, Cotton Tiberius A.XIII   **Ker 190B art.b**
 ed Thorpe 1865, 445

18
Lists of Kings, Saints, and Bishops

18.1
MS Cambridge, Corpus Christi College, 383   **Ker 65 art.27**
 ed B. Dickins, *The Genealogical Preface to the Anglo-Saxon Chronicle,* Occasional Papers:
      Number II printed for the Department of Anglo-Saxon, Cambridge 1952, 2-4

18.2
MS London, British Museum, Add. 23211   **Ker 127 art.1**
 ed Henry Sweet, *The Oldest English Texts,* EETS 83, London 1885, 179

18.3
MS London, British Museum, Add. 34652 f.2   **Ker 180 art.2**
 ed Napier 1897, 105-11

18.4
MS London, British Museum, Cotton Tiberius A.III f.178   **Ker 188 art.2**
 ed Dickins 1952, 3-5

18.5
MS London, British Museum, Cotton Tiberius B.V vol.1   **Ker 193 art.c**
 ed T. Wright and J.O. Halliwell, *Reliquiae Antiquae,* London 1841-3, II, 171-3 [partial]

18.6
MS London, British Museum, Stowe 944   **Ker 274 art.e**
 ed Birch 1892, 94-6

18.7
MS Rochester, Cathedral, Textus Roffensis   **Ker 373A arts.5, 36, 37**
facs Sawyer 1957-62
ed J. Ingram, *The Saxon Chronicle,* Oxford 1823, 375-6 [art.5] ; T. Hearne, *Textus Roffensis,* Oxford 1720, 59-62 [arts.36-7, art.37 partially printed]
See also B.9.6 [Ker 23] , B.17.1

18.8
MS Cambridge, Corpus Christi College, 201   **Ker 49A arts.54-5**
ed F. Liebermann, *Die Heiligen Englands,* Hannover 1889, 1-19
See B.3.3.26

18.9
MS London, British Museum, Cotton Vitellius D.XVII [burnt]   **Ker 222 art.55**
as Liebermann 1889, 9-19

18.10
MS London, British Museum, Stowe 944   **Ker 274 art.d**
ed Birch 1892, 83-94
See B.3.3.26, 3.3.27

18.11
Bishops of Winchester
MS London, British Museum, Arundel 60   **Ker 134 art.4**
ed Logeman 1889, 106

19
Martyrology

19.1
MS Cambridge, Corpus Christi College, 41   **Ker 32 art.3**
ed G. Herzfeld, *An Old English Martyrology,* EETS 116, London 1900, 2-10 [inaccurate]
proposed ed. Günter Kotzor, Munich diss. [all MSS]

19.2
MS Cambridge, Corpus Christi College, 196   **Ker 47 art.1**
ed Herzfeld 1900, 40-222 [inaccurate]

19.3
MS London, British Museum, Add. 23211   **Ker 127 art.2**
ed Sweet 1885, 177-8

19.4
MS London, British Museum, Add. 40165A   **Ker 132**
ed C. Sisam, 'An Early Fragment of the Old English Martyrology,' *RES* n.s. 4 [1953] 217-20

19.5
MS London, British Museum, Cotton Julius A.X   **Ker 161**

ed   Herzfeld 1900 [inaccurate] ; corrections by Gustav Binz, *Beiblatt zur Anglia* 12
      [1901] 363-8

19.6
MS   London, British Museum, Harley 3271   **Ker 239 art.11[i]**
ed   Henel 1934-5, 347; as Herzfeld 1900, 80 ll.10-2, 202 ll.8-10

20
Computus

20.1
Rules for Finding Movable Feasts

20.1.1
MS   Cambridge, Corpus Christi College, 422   **Ker 70B arts.d, e**
      coll. H. Henel, *Studien zum altenglischen Computus,* Beiträge zur englischen Philologie
      26, Leipzig 1934 [1967] , 40-1 [art.d]
ed   Henel 1934, 42-3, 45-7 [art.e]

20.1.2
MS   London, British Museum, Cotton Caligula A.XV   **Ker 139A arts.f, g, j, l**
ed   Henel 1934, 47 [art.f] , 46 [art.g] , 44 [art.l] ; Cockayne 1864-6, III, 226 [art.j]

20.1.3
MS   London, British Museum, Cotton Titus D.XXVII   **Ker 202 art.g**
      coll. Henel 1934, 40-1

20.1.4
MS   London, British Museum, Cotton Vitellius C.VIII   **Ker 221 art.4**
      as Henel 1934, 40-1

20.1.5
MS   London, British Museum, Cotton Vitellius E.XVIII   **Ker 224 arts.b, f**
ed   Henel 1934, 44 [art.b]
      coll. Henel 1934, 40-1 [art.f]

20.1.6
MS   London, British Museum, Harley 3271   **Ker 239 arts.11b, 12**
ed   Henel 1934, 40-1 [art.11b]
      coll. Henel 1934, 40-1 [art.12]

20.2
On Epacts

20.2.1
MS   Cambridge, Corpus Christi College, 422   **Ker 70B arts.b, e**
      coll. Henel 1934, 48-9 [art.b]
ed   Henel 1934, 49 [art.e]

20.2.2

MS London, British Museum, Cotton Caligula A.XV   **Ker 139A arts.k, m**
ed Cockayne 1864-6, III, 226 [art.k]
   coll. Henel 1934, 51 [art.k] , 48-9 [art.m] ; Cockayne 1864-6, III, 228 [art.m]

20.2.3

MS London, British Museum, Cotton Caligula A.XV   **Ker 139B art.3**
ed Crawford 1929 [1966] , 36-7

20.2.4

MS London, British Museum, Cotton Titus D.XXVII   **Ker 202 art.h**
ed Henel 1934, 51

20.2.5

MS London, British Museum, Cotton Vitellius C.VIII   **Ker 221 art.5**
   as Henel 1934, 51

20.2.6

MS London, British Museum, Cotton Vitellius E.XVIII   **Ker 224 art.e**
   coll. Henel 1934, 51

20.2.7

MS London, British Museum, Harley 3271   **Ker 239 art.11a**
ed Henel 1934, 48-9

20.3
On Concurrents

20.3.1

MS London, British Museum, Cotton Caligula A.XV   **Ker 139B art.2**
ed Henel 1934, 53-4

20.3.2

MS London, British Museum, Harley 3271   **Ker 239 art.11c**
ed Henel 1934, 49

20.4
On Ferial Regulars
See **20.3.1**

20.5
De Bissexto

MS London, British Museum, Cotton Caligula A.XV   **Ker 139A art.c**
 ed M. Förster, 'Die altenglischen Traumlunare,' *Englische Studien* 60 [1925-6] 75

20.6
Rules for Finding the Age of the Moon

MS Cambridge, Corpus Christi College, 422   **Ker 70B art.e**

London, British Museum, Cotton Caligula A.XV **Ker 139A art.n**
London, British Museum, Cotton Vitellius E.XVIII **Ker 224 art.c**
ed Henel 1934, 55

20.7
On Moonrise
MS London, British Museum, Royal 2 A.XX **Ker 248 art.d**
ed Henel 1934, 56

20.8
On Moon and Tide
MS London, British Museum, Cotton Titus D.XXVII **Ker 202 art.j**
ed Napier 1889, 6

20.9
Table of Duration of Moonshine
MS London, British Museum, Cotton Caligula A.XV **Ker 139A art.b**
ed Cockayne 1864-6, III, 222-4

20.10
On the Four Ember-fasts
MS Brussels, Bibliothèque Royale, 8558-63 **Ker 10C art.2f**
Cambridge, Corpus Christi College, 422 **Ker 70B art.e**
Oxford, Bodleian, Laud Misc. 482 **Ker 343 art.6**
ed Henel 1934, 61

20.11
On the Three Fridays for Fasting

20.11.1
MS Cambridge, Corpus Christi College, 422 **Ker 70B art.f**
London, British Museum, Cotton Tiberius A.III **Ker 186 art.8c**
ed Henel 1934, 64

20.11.2
MS London, British Museum, Cotton Caligula A.XV **Ker 139A art.o**
ed Cockayne 1864-6, III, 228

20.11.3
MS London, British Museum, Royal 2 B.V **Ker 249 art.f**
ed Roeder 1904, xii

20.12
On the Length of Shadow

20.12.1
MS Cambridge, Corpus Christi College, 422 **Ker 70B art.c**
London, British Museum, Harley 3271 **Ker 239 art.11g**
ed Henel 1934, 59-60

20.12.2
MS   London, British Museum, Cotton Tiberius A.III f. 179   **Ker 187 art. 1**
ed   Cockayne 1864-6, III, 218-22

20.13
On the Number of Weeks, etc., in the Year

20.13.1
MS   Cambridge, Corpus Christi College, 422   **Ker 70B art. h**
     London, British Museum, Harley 3271   **Ker 239 art. 11f, h**
ed   Henel 1934, 67

20.13.2
MS   London, British Museum, Cotton Titus D. XXVII   **Ker 202 art. e**
ed   Henel 1934, 65

20.14
On the Number of Days in the Month
MS   Cambridge, Corpus Christi College, 422   **Ker 70B art. c**
ed   F. Wormald, *English Kalendars before A.D. 1100,* Henry Bradshaw Society 72, London
     1934, no. 14

20.15
On the Number and Names of the Seasons
MS   London, British Museum, Harley 3271   **Ker 239 art. 11e**
ed   Henel 1934, 67

20.16
On the Length of Summer and Winter
See B. 19.6

20.17
On the Length of Day and Night
See B. 20. 14

20.18
De diebus festis
MS   Cambridge, Corpus Christi College, 422   **Ker 70B art. g**
     London, British Museum, Harley 3271   **Ker 239 art. 10**
ed   Henel 1934, 71-3

20.19
Quaedam de computo ecclesiastico
MS   London, British Museum, Cotton Galba A.II or III [burnt]   **Ker 156**

20.20
Byrhtferth's Manual

20.20.1
MS   Oxford, Bodleian, Ashmole 328   **Ker 288 art.1**
ed   S.J. Crawford, *Byrhtferth's Manual,* EETS 177, London 1929 [1966]

20.20.2
MS   Cambridge, University Library, Kk.5.32   **Ker 26**
ed   H. Henel, 'Ein Bruchstück aus Byrhtferþs *Handbuch*,' *Anglia* 61 [1937] 123-4
See also B.20.2.3

20.21
Ælfric: De Temporibus Anni
See B.1.9.4

21
Medical Texts

21.1.1
Pseudo-Apuleius: Herbarius, Medicina de Quadrupedibus
MS   London, British Museum, Cotton Vitellius C.III ff.11-85   **Ker 219 art.1**
London, British Museum, Harley 585   **Ker 231 art.1**
Oxford, Bodleian, Hatton 76   **Ker 328B art.1**
EEMF facs. in prep. L.R.H. Smith [Ker 219]
ed   Cockayne 1864-6, I, 2-373; A.J.G. Hilbelink, *Cotton Ms Vitellius C.III of the Herbarium Apuleii,* Amsterdam 1930
proposed eds. Wilma Fraser, Ottawa, *NM* 71 [1970] 493 [*Herbarius*] ; H.J. de Vriend, Groningen, *NM* 70 [1969] 528 [*Medicina de Quadrupedibus*]

21.1.2
Plant Names
MS   Oxford, Bodleian, Bodley 130   **Ker 302**
facs   R.T. Gunther, *The Herbal of Apuleius Barbarus,* Roxburghe Club, Oxford 1925
ed   Ker 1957, 357

21.2.1
Bald's Leechbook
MS   London, British Museum, Royal 12 D.XVII   **Ker 264**
facs   C.E. Wright, *Bald's Leechbook,* EEMF 5, Copenhagen 1955
ed   Cockayne 1864-6, II; G. Leonhardi, *Kleinere angelsächsische Denkmäler,* Bib. ags. Prosa 6, Hamburg 1905

21.2.2
MS   London, British Museum, Cotton Galba A.XIV   **Ker 157 art.IX**
as Cockayne 1864-6, II, 294-6

21.2.3
MS   London, British Museum, Cotton Otho B.XI   **Ker 180 art.11**
London, British Museum, Add. 43703 ff.261-4 [Nowell transcript]
as Cockayne 1864-6, II; Braekman 1965, 275-6

21.2.4

MS   London, British Museum, Harley 55   **Ker 225 art. 1**
ed   Cockayne 1864-6, II, 280-8; Leonhardi 1905, 84

21.3
Lacnunga

MS   London, British Museum, Harley 585   **Ker 231 art. 2**
ed   Cockayne 1864-6, III, 2-80; H.G. Grattan and C. Singer, *Anglo-Saxon Magic and Medicine,* Publications of the Wellcome Historical Medical Museum n.s.3, London 1952, 96-204

21.4
On the Human Foetus

MS   London, British Museum, Cotton Tiberius A.III   **Ker 186 art. 7n**
ed   Cockayne 1864-6, III, 146

21.5
Recipes

21.5.1
Wið eah wærce

MS   Cambridge, Corpus Christi College, 41   **Ker 32 art. 8**
ed   Cockayne 1864-6, I, 382

21.5.2

MS   London, Wellcome Historical Medical Library, 75.46   **Ker 98**
ed   A.S. Napier, 'Altenglische Miscellen,' *Archiv* 84 [1890] 325-6

21.5.3

MS   London, British Museum, Cotton Domitian I   **Ker 146 art. d**
ed   Cockayne 1864-6, I, 382

21.5.4

MS   London, British Museum, Cotton Faustina A.X   **Ker 154B arts. 2, 3**
ed   Cockayne 1864-6, III, 292

21.5.5

MS   London, British Museum, Cotton Galba A.II and III [burnt]   **Ker 156**

21.5.6

MS   London, British Museum, Cotton Galba A.XIV   **Ker 157 art. XII**
not edited

21.5.7

MS   London, British Museum, Cotton Titus D.XXVI   **Ker 202 art. c**
ed   Cockayne 1864-6, I, 380

21.5.8

MS   London, British Museum, Cotton Vitellius C.III   **Ker 219 arts. 2, 3**
ed   Cockayne 1864-6, I, 374-8

21.5.9
MS   London, British Museum, Cotton Vitellius E.XVIII   **Ker 224 arts.n, o**
ed   Cockayne 1864-6, I, 388

22
Other Scientific Texts

22.1
Alexander's Letter to Aristotle
MS   London, British Museum, Cotton Vitellius A.XV   **Ker 216 art.3**
facs   K. Malone, *The Nowell Codex,* EEMF 12, Copenhagen 1963
ed   S. Rypins, *Three Old English Prose Texts,* EETS 161, London 1924, 1-50

22.2
The Marvels of the East
MS   London, British Museum, Cotton Tiberius B.V vol. 1   **Ker 193 art.b**
     London, British Museum, Cotton Vitellius A.XV   **Ker 216 art.2**
facs   M.R. James, *Marvels of the East,* Roxburghe Club, Oxford 1929 [Ker 193 art.b] ;
     Malone 1963 [Ker 216 art.2]
     EEMF facs. in prep. P. McGurk, R.I. Page and P. Clemoes [Ker 193 art.b]
     coll. Rypins 1924, 51-67 [Ker 193 art.b]
ed   Rypins 1924, 51-67 [Ker 216 art.2]

22.3
Lapidary
MS   London, British Museum, Cotton Tiberius A.III   **Ker 186 art.23**
ed   J. Evans and M.S. Serjeantson, *English Mediaeval Lapidaries,* EETS 190, London 1933,
     13-4

23
Folklore

23.1
Prose charms and charm headings
[For verse charms, see A.43.1-12]

23.1.1
MS   Cambridge, Corpus Christi College, 41   **Ker 32 art.7**
ed   Storms 1948, no.12

23.1.2
MS   Cambridge, Corpus Christi College, 41   **Ker 32 art.10**
ed   Storms 1948, no.48

23.1.3
MS   Cambridge, Corpus Christi College, 41   **Ker 32 art.14**
ed   Storms 1948, App. nos.4-6

23.1.4
MS Cambridge, Corpus Christi College, 190 **Ker 45A art.b**
ed Storms 1948, no.11A

23.1.5
MS London, British Museum, Cotton Tiberius A.III **Ker 186 art.28**
ed Cockayne 1864-6, III, 286

23.1.6
MS Cambridge, Corpus Christi College, 383 **Ker 65 art.20**
   Rochester, Cathedral, Textus Roffensis **Ker 373A art.31**
facs Sawyer 1957-62 [Textus Roffensis]
ed Storms 1948, no.11B

23.1.7
MS Cambridge, Corpus Christi College, 391 **Ker 67 art.c**
   London, British Museum, Cotton Tiberius A.III **Ker 186 art.10d**
ed J. Zupitza, 'Kreuzzauber,' *Archiv* 88 [1892] 364-5

23.1.8
MS London, British Museum, Add. 37517 f.139 **Ker 129**
ed Ker 1957, 161

23.1.9
MS London, British Museum, Cotton Caligula A.XV **Ker 139A arts.d, u, v**
ed Cockayne 1864-6, III, 295 and Storms 1948, no.68 [art.d] ; Storms 1948, no.34 [art.u] ,
   no.69 [art.v]

23.1.10
MS London, British Museum, Cotton Faustina A.X **Ker 154B arts.2, 3**
ed Cockayne 1864-6, III, 292-4; Storms 1948, nos.39, 40, 82

23.1.11
MS London, British Museum, Cotton Galba A.XIV **Ker 157 art.X**
ed Logeman 1889, 111; Ker 1957, 200

23.1.12
MS London, British Museum, Cotton Vitellius E.XVIII **Ker 224 arts.k-m, p, q**
ed Cockayne 1864-6, I, 397 [art.k] , 395 and Storms 1948, no.85 [art.l] ; Storms 1948,
   no.86 [art.m] , no.50 [art.p] , no.50 and Ker 1957, 300 [art.q]

23.1.13
MS Oxford, Bodleian, Auct. F.3.6 **Ker 296 art.b**
ed Storms 1948, nos.77-8

23.1.14
MS Oxford, Bodleian, Barlow 35 **Ker 298 art.b**
ed Ker 1957, 356

23.1.15
MS   Oxford, Bodleian, Junius 85 and 86   **Ker 336 art.3**
ed   Storms 1948, nos. 45, 49, 41; Ker 1957, 410

23.1.16
MS   Oxford, St John's College, 17   **Ker 360 art.f**
ed   Ker 1957, 435

23.1.17
MS   Vatican City, Reg. Lat. 338   **Ker 390 arts. a, b**
ed   W. Stokes, 'Glosses from Turin and Rome,' *Beiträge zur Kunde der indogermanischen Sprachen* 17 [1891] 144-5; Ker 1957, 458

23.1.18
MS   Worcester, Cathedral, Q.5   **Ker 399 art.b**
ed   Napier 1890, 324

23.2
Tables of Lucky and Unlucky Days

23.2.1
MS   Cambridge, Corpus Christi College, 391   **Ker 67 arts.d [vi, vii], e**
ed   M. Förster, 'Die altenglischen Verzeichnisse von Glücks- und Unglückstagen' in K. Malone and M.B. Ruud, eds., *Studies in English Philology: A Miscellany in Honor of Frederick Klaeber,* Minneapolis, Minn., 1929, 258-77, 260 [art.d[vi]], 273 [art.d[vii]]; Förster 1925-6, 77 [art.e]

23.2.2
MS   Cambridge, Corpus Christi College, 422   **Ker 70B art.a**
ed   Henel 1934-5, 334-5

23.2.3
MS   London, British Museum, Cotton Caligula A.XV   **Ker 139A arts.e, h, i**
ed   Förster 1929, 262 [art.e], 266 [art.h], 260 [art.i]

23.2.4
MS   London, British Museum, Cotton Vitellius C.VIII   **Ker 221 art.2**
ed   Förster 1929, 271-3

23.2.5
MS   London, British Museum, Cotton Vitellius E.XVIII   **Ker 224 arts.d, h, i, j**
ed   Förster 1929, 262 [art.d], 273 [art.i], 266 [art.j]; Henel 1934-5, 346-7 [art.h]

23.2.6
MS   London, British Museum, Harley 3271   **Ker 239 arts.8, 9**
ed   Henel 1934-5, 336-7

23.3
Prognostics
[For interlinear glosses of Prognostics, see C.16]

23.3.1
MS Cambridge, Corpus Christi College, 391 **Ker 67 art.d**
ed M. Förster, 'Beiträge zur mittelalterlichen Volkskunde VI,' *Archiv* 128 [1912] 65
    [art.d[i]] ; M. Förster, 'Beiträge zur mittelalterlichen Volkskunde I,' *Archiv* 120 [1908]
    46-8 [art.d[ii]] ; M. Förster, 'Beiträge zur mittelalterlichen Volkskunde VII,' *Archiv* 128
    [1912] 297-300 [art.d[iii]] ; M. Förster, 'Beiträge zur mittelalterlichen Volkskunde VIII,'
    Archiv 129 [1912] 21 [art.d[iv]], 34-6 and Ker 1957, 114 [art.d[v]] ; Förster 1925-6,
    79-86 [art.d[viii]]

23.3.2
MS London, British Museum, Cotton Caligula A.XV **Ker 139A arts.a, p, q**
ed Förster 1912, 2-34 [art.a], 21-6 [art.q] ; Förster 1925-6, 79-86 [art.p]

23.3.3
MS London, British Museum, Cotton Tiberius A.III **Ker 186 art.7h-m, o-r**
ed Förster 1925-6, 79-86 [art.7h] ; M. Förster, 'Beiträge zur mittelalterlichen Volkskunde
    IX,' *Archiv* 134 [1916] 270-93 [art.7i] ; Förster 1912, 43 [art.7j], 34 [art.7k], 21-6
    [art.7o] ; Cockayne 1864-6, III, 180 [art.7l], 180-2 [art.7m], 144 [art.7r] ; M. Förster,
    'Beiträge zur mittelalterlichen Volkskunde II,' *Archiv* 120 [1908] 297-8 [art.7p], 302-5
    and *Archiv* 121 [1908] 37 [art.7q]

23.3.4
MS London, British Museum, Cotton Titus D.XXVII **Ker 202 art.i**
ed E. Sievers, 'Bedeutung der Buchstaben,' *ZfdA* 21 [1877] 189-90
    See A.27

23.3.5
MS London, British Museum, Cotton Vespasian D.XIV **Ker 209 arts.26, 34**
ed Warner 1917, 66, 91; B. Assmann, 'Prophezeiung aus dem 1.Januar für das Jahr,' *Anglia*
    11 [1889] 369 [art.26] ; B. Assmann, 'Eine Regel über den Donner,' *Anglia* 10 [1888]
    185

23.3.6
MS Oxford, Bodleian, Hatton 115 **Ker 332 art.35a-f, i-k**
ed Cockayne 1864-6, III, 158-68

23.4
Prohibition against Blood-letting
MS London, British Museum, Cotton Vitellius E.XVIII **Ker 224 art.g**
ed Henel 1934-5, 331

24
Notes and Commonplaces

24.1
Historical Notes
MS London, British Museum, Royal 10 C.V **Ker 262**
ed Ker 1957, 331

24.2
Monasteriales indicia
MS London, British Museum, Cotton Tiberius A.III **Ker 186 art. 22**
ed F. Kluge, 'Zur Geschichte der Zeichensprache. Angelsächsische Indicia Monasterialia,'
    Techmers internationale Zeitschrift für Sprachwissenschaft 2 [1885] 118-29
    proposed ed. Eduard Kolb, *OEN* 5 [1972] 21

24.3
Names of Week Days
MS Oxford, St John's College, 17 **Ker 360 art. d**
ed C.W. Jones, *Bedae Opera de Temporibus,* Mediaeval Academy of America Publ. 41,
    Cambridge, Mass., 1943, 340

24.4
Names of Months
MS Cambridge, Corpus Christi College, 422 **Ker 70B art. c**
    Cambridge, Trinity College, R.15.32 **Ker 90 art. a**
    London, British Museum, Cotton Vitellius E.XVIII **Ker 224 art. a**
    Oxford, St John's College, 17 **Ker 360 art. c**
    Rouen, Bibliothèque Municipale, Y.6 **Ker 377 art. b**
    Oxford, Bodleian, Douce 296
    London, British Museum, Cotton Appendix 56
ed Wormald 1934, no. 14 [Ker 70B art. c], 10 [Ker 90 art. a], 12 [Ker 224 art. a], 20
    [Douce 296]; Wilson 1896, 9-20 [Ker 377 art. b]

24.5
Names of the Winds
MS Cambridge, University Library, Kk.3.21 **Ker 24 art. c**
    London, British Museum, Cotton Galba A.II and III [burnt] **Ker 156**
    London, British Museum, Cotton Tiberius C.I ff. 2-42 and Harley 3667 **Ker 196**
    London, British Museum, Harley 1005 **Ker 233**
    London, British Museum, Royal 10 A.VIII **Ker 261**
ed Logeman 1889, 103-5 [Ker 196]; other MSS not edited

24.6
Names of Letters
MS London, British Museum, Stowe 57 **Ker 272 art. a**
ed Ker 1957, 337

24.7
Names of Numbers

MS Oxford, Corpus Christi College, 197 **Ker 353 art.3**
ed Ker 1957, 430-1

24.8
Names of Relationship
MS Oxford, Jesus College, 26 **Ker 355**
ed Ker 1957, 433
See also C.95

24.9
Significance of Church Bells
MS Cambridge, Corpus Christi College, 44 **Ker 33 art.b**
proposed ed. J.B. Trahern, Illinois

24.10
Note on Adam

24.10.1
MS   London, British Museum, Add. 47967 **Ker 133 art.2**
facs Campbell 1953
ed   Ker 1957, 165

24.10.2
MS London, British Museum, Cotton Tiberius A.III **Ker 186 art.8**
ed Napier 1889, 1-3

24.10.3
MS Oxford, Bodleian, Hatton 115 **Ker 332 art.37**
ed Ker 1957, 402

24.11
Note on Noah, etc.
MS London, British Museum, Cotton Caligula A.XV **Ker 139A art.t**
ed Napier 1889, 6-7
Also in B.24.10.1, 24.10.2

24.12
Note on Noah's Ark, etc.

24.12.1
MS London, British Museum, Cotton Julius A.II **Ker 159 art.3**
ed Napier 1889, 5-6

24.12.2
MS London, British Museum, Cotton Tiberius A.III **Ker 186 art.14**
ed Napier 1889, 4

24.12.3
MS London, British Museum, Harley 3271 **Ker 239 art.7**
[extracts from *Interrogationes Sigewulfi*]
as MacLean 1884, 34-6
Also in B.24.10.1

24.13
Shem and his Descendants
In B.24.10.1

24.14
The Temple of Solomon
In B.24.12.1, 24.12.2

24.15
Note on the Gold Brought to Solomon
MS London, British Museum, Harley 3271 **Ker 239 art.13**
ed Napier 1889, 8

24.16
Note on the Age of the Virgin

24.16.1
MS London, British Museum, Cotton Titus D.XXVII **Ker 202 art.k**
as Birch 1892, 83

24.16.2
MS London, British Museum, Stowe 944 **Ker 274 art.c**
ed Birch 1892, 83

24.16.3
MS Oxford, Bodleian, Bodley 343 **Ker 310 art.76**
ed Napier 1889, 6 footnote
Also in B.24.10.2, 24.11

24.17
The Age of Christ
In B.24.11, 24.16.3

24.18
The Two Thieves
In B.24.12.1, 24.12.2

24.19
The Thirty Pieces of Silver
MS London, British Museum, Harley 3271 **Ker 239 art.6**
ed Napier 1889, 8

24.20
The Church of St Peter
In B. 24.12.1, 24.12.2

24.21
The Coming of Antichrist
MS   London, British Museum, Cotton Vespasian D.XIV   **Ker 209 art. 27**
ed   Warner 1917, 66-7; M. Förster, 'Kleinere mittelenglische Texte,' *Anglia* 42 [1918] 222-3

24.22
The Fifteen Days before Judgement
MS   London, British Museum, Cotton Vespasian D.XIV   **Ker 209 art. 33**
ed   Warner 1917, 89-91

24.23
The Dimensions of the World
In B. 24.12.1

24.24
The Number of Bones and Veins in the Human Body
In B. 24.12.1

24.25
The Six Ages of the World

24.25.1
MS   Cambridge, Corpus Christi College, 178   **Ker 41B art. 2**
ed   Schröer 1885-8 [1964], xxi

24.25.2
MS   Cambridge, Corpus Christi College, 201   **Ker 49B art. 2**
     Oxford, Bodleian, Hatton 113   **Ker 331 art. 2**
ed   Napier 1883, no. 62, 311-3

24.25.3
MS   London, British Museum, Arundel 60   **Ker 134 art. 3**
     London, British Museum, Cotton Caligula A.XV   **Ker 139A art.s**
ed   M. Förster, 'Die Weltzeitalter bei den Angelsachsen' in Fr. Wild, ed., *Neusprachliche Studien, Festgabe Karl Luick zu seinem sechzigsten Geburtstage,* Marburg 1925, 192-3

24.25.4
MS   London, British Museum, Stowe 944   **Ker 274 art.c**
ed   Birch 1892, 81-3; Förster 1925, 191-2

24.26
The Age of the World

24.26.1
MS London, British Museum, Cotton Vespasian D.VI   **Ker 207 art.d**
ed Förster 1925, 195-7

24.26.2
MS London, British Museum, Cotton Vespasian D.XIV   **Ker 209 art.47**
ed Warner 1917, 140-1; Förster 1925, 199

24.26.3
MS London, British Museum, Harley 3271   **Ker 239 art.23**
ed Napier 1889, 9-10; Förster 1925, 197-8

25
Runic Texts
For Runic Inscriptions, see Section E
For the Rune Poem, see A.12
For other poems with occasional runes, see The Fates of the Apostles [A.2.2], Elene
[A.2.6], Christ [A.3.1], Juliana [A.3.5], Riddles [A.3.22, 3.34], Beowulf [A.4.1]
Solomon and Saturn [A.13]

25.1
English Runic Futhorcs

25.1.1
MS London, British Museum, Cotton Domitian IX   **Ker 151 art.2**
ed Hickes 1705, Gramm. 136; G. Hempl, 'Hickes's Additions to the Runic Poem,' *MP* 1
    [1903-4] 135-41; R. Derolez, *Runica Manuscripta, The English Tradition*, Bruges 1954,
    3-16

25.1.2
MS London, British Museum, Cotton Otho B.X   **Ker 179**
ed Hickes 1705, Gramm. 135; Derolez 1954, 16-26

25.1.3
MS Oxford, St John's College, 17   **Ker 360 art.a**
ed C.L. Wrenn, 'Late Old English Rune Names,' *MÆ* 1 [1932] 24-34; C.E. Wright, 'A Post-
    script to "Late Old English Rune Names," ' *MÆ* 5 [1936] 149-51; Derolez 1954, 26-34

25.1.4
MS London, British Museum, Cotton Galba A.II and III [burnt]   **Ker 156 art.IV**
ed see Hickes 1705, Gramm. Island. Tabella VI; Derolez 1954, 34-52

25.2
English Runic Futhorcs in Continental Copies

25.2.1
MS Vienna, Osterreichische Nationalbibliothek, 795
ed Derolez 1954, 52-63

25.2.2
MS   Brussels, Bibliothèque Royale, 9311-9319
ed   Derolez 1954, 63-73

25.2.3
MS   St Gall, Stiftsbibliothek, 878
ed   Derolez 1954, 73-83

25.2.4
MS   Ghent, Universiteitsbibliothek, 306
ed   Derolez 1954, 83-6

25.2.5
MS   St Gall, Stiftsbibliothek, 270
ed   Derolez 1954, 90-4

25.2.6
MS   Brussels, Bibliothèque Royale, 9565-9566[B]
ed   Derolez 1954, 95-102

25.2.7
MS   Trier, Priesterseminar, R.III.13
ed   Derolez 1954, 102-6

25.2.8
MS   Vatican City, Codex Urbinas Latinas 290
ed   Derolez 1954, 106-13

25.2.9
MS   Salzburg, Stift St Peter, a.IX.32
ed   Derolez 1954, 113-9

25.3
Runic Alphabets
For a listing of manuscripts and discussion, see Derolez 1954, 171-383

25.4
Occasional Runes

25.4.1
MS   Cambridge, Corpus Christi College, 41 pp.436, 448   **Ker 32**
ed   Derolez 1954, 421

25.4.2
MS   London, British Museum, Add. 47967 p.iii
facs   Campbell 1953
        proposed ed. A. Campbell; see Campbell 1953, 19

25.4.3
MS   London, British Museum, Royal 12 D.XVII   **Ker 264**
ed   Storms 1948, no.33; Derolez 1954, 417

25.4.4
MS   Leningrad, Public Library, F.v.I.8
See R.I. Page, 'The Inscriptions,' Appendix A in D.M. Wilson, *Anglo-Saxon Ornamental Metalwork, 700-1100 in the British Museum,* London 1964, 70 f.8, and E.A. Lowe, *Codices Latini Antiquiores XI,* London 1966, no.1605

26
Cryptograms

26.1
MS   London, British Museum, Cotton Vitellius E.XVIII   **Ker 224 arts.s, t**
ed   M. Förster, 'Ein altenglisches Prosa-Rätsel,' *Archiv* 115 [1905] 392-3 [art.s]; M. Förster, 'Ae. *fregen* "die Frage," ' *Englische Studien* 36 [1906] 325-8 [art.t]; see also, M. Förster, 'Die Lösung des ae. Prosarätsels,' *Archiv* 116 [1906] 367-71; M. Förster, 'Nochmals ae. *fregen* "Frage," ' *Archiv* 135 [1916] 399-401

26.2
MS   Oxford, Bodleian, Bodley 572   **Ker 313 arts.d, e**
ed   Förster 1916, 400; Ker 1957, 377

27
Directions to Readers; Scribbles

27.1
MS   **Coleman   Ker 23; 41A arts.8, 27; 53 p.41; 331**
See N.R. Ker, 'Old English Notes signed "Coleman",' *MÆ* 18 [1949] 29-31

27.2
Directions to Readers

27.2.1
MS   Cambridge, University Library, Ii.4.6 ff.145, 229v   **Ker 21**
ed   Ker 1957, 31

27.2.2
MS   Cambridge, Corpus Christi College, 9 and London, British Museum, Cotton Nero E.I vol.1   **Ker 29 art.b**
ed   Napier 1900, xx; Ker 1957, 41

27.2.3
MS   Cambridge, Corpus Christi College, 162 pp.293-4   **Ker 38**
ed   Ker 1957, 51

27.2.4
MS   Cambridge, Corpus Christi College, 178   **Ker 41A art. 19**
ed   Ker 1957, 62

27.2.5
MS   Cambridge, Trinity College, B. 10.5 ff. 62v, 66v   **Ker 83 art. b**
ed   Ker 1957, 129

27.2.6
MS   Cambridge, Trinity College, R. 15.32   **Ker 90 art. b**
ed   Henel 1934, 9; Ker 1957, 135

27.2.7
MS   London, British Museum, Cotton Vitellius A.XIX   **Ker 217 art. c**
ed   Ker 1957, 283

27.2.8
MS   London, British Museum, Royal 7 C.XII f. 124v   **Ker 257**
ed   Ker 1957, 325

27.2.9
MS   Oxford, Bodleian, Junius 11 pp. 98, 100   **Ker 334**
ed   Ker 1957, 407

27.3
Scribbles

27.3.1
MS   Arras, Bibliothèque Municipale, 764   **Ker 4**
ed   Ker 1957, 4

27.3.2
MS   Cambridge, University Library, Kk. 3.21   **Ker 24 art. b**
ed   Ker 1957, 38

27.3.3
MS   Cambridge, Corpus Christi College, 188 p. 408   **Ker 43**
ed   Ker 1957, 66

27.3.4
MS   Cambridge, Corpus Christi College, 198   **Ker 48 art. 63a**
ed   Ker 1957, 81

27.3.5
MS   Cambridge, Corpus Christi College, 326   **Ker 61 art. c**
ed   Ker 1957, 107

27.3.6
MS   Cambridge, Corpus Christi College, 473   **Ker 72**
ed   Ker 1957, 122

27.3.7
MS   Cambridge, Pembroke College, 88   **Ker 77 art.b**
ed   Ker 1957, 125

27.3.8
MS   Cambridge, Trinity College, R. 17. 1 f. 10   **Ker 91**
acs   James 1935
ed   Ker 1957, 136

27.3.9
MS   Dublin, Trinity College, 174   **Ker 103**
ed   Ker 1957, 143

27.3.10
MS   Durham, Cathedral, A. II. 17   **Ker 105**
ed   Ker 1957, 144

27.3.11
MS   Durham, Cathedral, A. IV. 19   **Ker 106 art.h**
acs   Brown et al. 1969
ed   Ker 1957, 145

27.3.12
MS   Lincoln, Cathedral, 182   **Ker 124**
ed   Ker 1957, 158

27.3.13
MS   London, British Museum, Add. 38651   **Ker 130**
ed   Ker 1957, 162

27.3.14
MS   London, British Museum, Add. 47967   **Ker 133 art.3**
acs   Campbell 1953
ed   Ker 1957, 165

27.3.15
MS   London, British Museum, Cotton Julius A. X f. 160v   **Ker 161**
ed   Ker 1957, 206

27.3.16
MS   London, British Museum, Cotton Tiberius B. V   **Ker 193 art.d**
ed   Ker 1957, 255

27.3.17

MS London, British Museum, Cotton Tiberius C.II **Ker 198 arts.b, d**
ed Ker 1957, 261

27.3.18
Ælfmær pattafox

MS London, British Museum, Harley 55 **Ker 225 art.2**
ed Ker 1957, 301

27.3.19

MS London, British Museum, Harley 208 **Ker 229**
ed Ker 1957, 304
     cf. *Beowulf* 869

27.3.20

MS London, British Museum, Royal 2 A.XX **Ker 248 art.e**
ed Zupitza 1889, 59, 63 note 10, 64-6

27.3.21

MS London, British Museum, Royal 2 B.V **Ker 249 art.j**
ed Ker 1957, 319-20
     See B.6.3

27.3.22

MS London, British Museum, Royal 5 F.III **Ker 253 art.b**
ed Napier 1900, xvi

27.3.23

MS London, British Museum, Royal 7 C.IV **Ker 256 art.3**
ed Ker 1957, 323

27.3.24

MS London, British Museum, Royal 10 C.V **Ker 262**
facs Ker 1957, plate VIII
ed Ker 1957, 331

27.3.25

MS London, Lambeth Palace, 149 **Ker 275**
ed Ker 1957, 340

27.3.26

MS London, Lambeth Palace, 204 **Ker 277 art.c**
ed M. Förster, 'König Eadgars Tod,' *Englische Studien* 62 [1937-8] 10

27.3.27

MS London, Lambeth Palace, 237 **Ker 278**
ed Ker 1957, 341

27.3.28
MS   London, Lambeth Palace, 377   **Ker 279**
ed   Ker 1957, 342

27.3.29
MS   Oxford, Bodleian, Auct. F.3.6   **Ker 296 art.b**
ed   Napier 1900, no.46; Ker 1957, 354

27.3.30
MS   Oxford, Bodleian, Auct. F.4.32   **Ker 297 art.b**
acs   R.W. Hunt, *Saint Dunstan's Classbook from Glastonbury,* [UCO 4] Amsterdam 1961
ed   Ker 1957, 355

27.3.31
MS   Oxford, Bodleian, Barlow 35   **Ker 298 art.d**
ed   Ker 1957, 356

27.3.32
MS   Oxford, Bodleian, Digby 63   **Ker 319 arts.a, b, c**
ed   Ker 1957, 381

27.3.33
MS   Oxford, Bodleian, Hatton 20 f.53v, 55   **Ker 324**
acs   Ker 1956
ed   Ker 1957, 385

27.3.34
MS   Oxford, Bodleian, Hatton 48 f.18v, 42v   **Ker 327**
acs   D.H. Farmer, *The Rule of St. Benedict,* EEMF 15, Copenhagen 1968
ed   Ker 1957, 388

27.3.35
MS   Oxford, Bodleian, Hatton 93   **Ker 329**
ed   Ker 1957, 390

27.3.36
MS   Oxford, Bodleian, Hatton 114 f.4v   **Ker 331 art.83**
ed   Ker 1957, 398

27.3.37
MS   Oxford, St John's College, 154 ff.97, 114   **Ker 362**
ed   Ker 1957, 436

27.3.38
MS   Rouen, Bibliothèque Municipale, A.27   **Ker 374 art.c**
ed   G.H. Doble, *Pontificale Lanaletense,* Henry Bradshaw Society 74, London 1937, 2, 143; Ker 1957, 448

27.3.39
MS Rouen, Bibliothèque Municipale, U. 107 **Ker 376**
ed Ker 1957, 448

27.3.40
MS Salisbury, Cathedral, 150 f. iv^v **Ker 379**
ed Ker 1957, 450

27.3.41
MS Salisbury, Cathedral, 173 **Ker 381**
ed Ker 1957, 451

28
Colophons, Inscriptions, Names

28.1
Aldred

28.1.1
MS Durham, Cathedral, A. IV. 19 **Ker 106 art. f**
facs Brown et al. 1969
ed Thompson and Lindelöf 1927, 185

28.1.2
MS London, British Museum, Cotton Nero D. IV **Ker 165 arts. a, b**
facs Kendrick et al. 1956-60
see N.R. Ker, 'Aldred the Scribe,' *Essays and Studies* 28 [1943] 7-12; Kendrick et al. 1956-60, introduction

28.2
Bald and Cild
MS London, British Museum, Royal 12 D. XVII **Ker 264 art. 2**
facs Wright 1955
ed Ker 1957, 332

28.3
Cuthswith
MS Würzburg, Universitätsbibliothek, M. p. th. q. 2 **Ker 401**
ed Ker 1957, 467

28.4
Farmon and Owun
MS Oxford, Bodleian, Auct. D. 2. 19 ff. 50v, 168v-9 **Ker 292**
ed Ker 1957, 352

28.5
Lyfing, Bishop of Crediton

MS Rouen, Bibliothèque Municipale, A.27 **Ker 374 art.a**
ed Doble 1937, 143

28.6
Siferð and Tate
MS Cambridge, Corpus Christi College, 286 **Ker 55**
ed Ker 1957, 95

28.7
Wulfwi
MS London, British Museum, Cotton Otho C.I vol. 1 **Ker 181**
ed Ker 1957, 235

C GLOSSES

Continuous interlinear glosses

1
Abbo of St Germain, Bella Parisiacae Urbis

1.1
MS London, British Museum, Harley 3271 **Ker 239 art. 17**
ed J. Zupitza, 'Altenglische Glossen zu Abbos Clericorum Decus,' *ZfdA* 31 [1887] 1-27

1.2
MS Oxford, St John's College, 154 **Ker 362 art. 5**
ed W.H. Stevenson and W.M. Lindsay, *Early Scholastic Colloquies,* Anecdota Oxoniensia, Mediaeval and Modern Series 15, Oxford 1929, no. 7, 103-12

2
Abbreviations list
MS Durham, Cathedral, A.IV. 19 pp. 169-71 **Ker 106 art. d**
facs Brown et al. 1969
ed A.H. Thompson and U. Lindelöf, *Rituale Ecclesiae Dunelmensis,* Surtees Society 140, Durham 1927

3
Ælfric, Colloquy
MS London, British Museum, Cotton Tiberius A.III **Ker 186 art. 11**
ed G.N. Garmonsway, *Ælfric's Colloquy,* MOEL, London 1939, 2nd ed. 1947 [1965]

4
Benedictine Rule
MS London, British Museum, Cotton Tiberius A.III **Ker 186 art. 1**
ed H. Logeman, *The Rule of St. Benet,* EETS 90, London 1888

5
Benedict of Aniane, Memoriale
MS London, British Museum, Cotton Tiberius A.III **Ker 186 art. 3**
ed A.S. Napier, *The Old English Version, with the Latin Original, of the Enlarged Rule of Chrodegang,* EETS 150, London 1916, 119-28

6
Bible, Ecclesiasticus extracts
MS London, British Museum, Royal 7 C.IV **Ker 256 art. 2**
ed E.W. Rhodes, *Defensor's Liber Scintillarum,* EETS 93, London 1889, 223-36

7
Psalms

7.1
MS Cambridge, University Library, Ff. 1. 23 **Ker 13**

ed   K. Wildhagen, *Der Cambridger Psalter,* Bib. ags. Prosa 7, Hamburg 1910 [Darmstadt 1964]

7.2

MS   Cambridge, Pembroke College, 312C nos. 1, 2   **Ker 79**
ed   K. Dietz, 'Die æ. Psalterglossen der Hs. Cambridge, Pembroke College 312,' *Anglia* 86 [1968] 273-9
proposed ed. R. Derolez in *Neophilologus* [2nd fragment]

7.3

MS   Cambridge, Trinity College, R. 17. 1   **Ker 91**
facs   James 1935
ed   Harsley 1889; B.L. Liles, '*The Canterbury Psalter*: An edition with notes and glossary' [Stanford diss.] *DA* 28 [1967] 1053A
proposed ed. F.-G. Berghaus, 'Kommentierte Ausgabe der altenglischen Interlinearversion des Eadwine-Psalters,' Göttingen, *NM* 70 [1969] 523

7.4

MS   London, British Museum, Add. 37517   **Ker 129**
ed   U. Lindelöf, 'Die altenglischen Glossen im Bosworth-Psalter,' *Mémoires de la société néophilologique de Helsingfors* 5 [1909] 137-230
proposed ed. A.P. Campbell, Ottawa, *NM* 70 [1969] 521

7.5

MS   London, British Museum, Arundel 60   **Ker 134 art. 1**
ed   G. Oess, *Der altenglische Arundel-Psalter,* AF 30, Heidelberg 1910

7.6

MS   London, British Museum, Cotton Tiberius C. VI   **Ker 199 art. a**
proposed ed. A.P. Campbell, Ottawa, *NM* 67 [1966] 203

7.7

MS   London, British Museum, Cotton Vespasian A. I   **Ker 203**
facs   D.H. Wright and A. Campbell, *The Vespasian Psalter,* EEMF 14, Copenhagen 1967
ed   S.M. Kuhn, *The Vespasian Psalter,* Ann Arbor 1965

7.8

MS   London, British Museum, Cotton Vitellius E. XVIII   **Ker 224 art. a**
ed   J.L. Rosier, *The Vitellius Psalter,* Cornell Studies in English 42, Ithaca 1962; see review: C. Sisam, *RES* 15 [1964] 59-61

7.9

MS   London, British Museum, Royal 2 B. V   **Ker 249 art. a**
ed   F. Roeder, *Der altenglische Regius-Psalter,* Studien zur englischen Philologie 18, Halle 1904

7.10

MS   London, British Museum, Stowe 2   **Ker 271**

ed A.C. Kimmens, 'An edition of the British Museum Ms Stowe 2: *The Stowe Psalter*' [Princeton diss.] *DA* 30 [1969] 1139A

7.11

MS London, Lambeth Palace, 427 **Ker 280 art. 1**
ed U. Lindelöf, *Der Lambeth-Psalter,* Acta Societatis Scientiarum Fennicae 35, i and 43, iii, Helsinki 1909-14

7.12

MS Oxford, Bodleian, Junius 27 **Ker 335**
ed E. Brenner, *Der altenglische Junius-Psalter,* AF 23, Heidelberg 1908

7.13

MS Salisbury, Cathedral, 150 **Ker 379**
ed C. and K. Sisam, *The Salisbury Psalter,* EETS 242, London 1959

8
Bible, Gospels

8.1
The Lindisfarne Gospels

MS London, British Museum, Cotton Nero D.IV **Ker 165**
facs T.D. Kendrick et al., *Codex Lindisfarnensis,* Olten-Lausanne 1956-60
ed W.W. Skeat, *The Four Gospels in Anglo-Saxon, Northumbrian and Old Mercian Versions,* Cambridge 1871-87 [Darmstadt 1970]
proposed ed. J.M. Penhalluriack, Flinders, *NM* 70 [1969] 527 [St John's Gospel]

8.2
The Rushworth Gospels

MS Oxford, Bodleian, Auct. D.2.19 **Ker 292**
ed Skeat 1871-87 [1970]; D.H. McAllister, 'An Edition of the Mercian Portions of the Rushworth Manuscript' [Oxford B.Litt.] *Index* 3 [1952-3] no. 129
proposed ed. P. Bibire, Oxford, *NM* 71 [1970] 498 [Northumbrian portion of the gloss to the *Rushworth Gospels*]

9
Boethius, De Consolatione Philosophiae

MS Cambridge, Corpus Christi College, 214 **Ker 51**
ed J.W. Bright, 'Anglo-Saxon Glosses to Boethius,' *American Journal of Philology* 5 [1884] 488-92; J.L. Rosier, 'Contributions to OE Lexicography: Some Boethius Glosses,' *Archiv* 200 [1963-4] 197-8

10
Boniface IV, Letter

MS London, British Museum, Cotton Tiberius A.VI?
London, British Museum, Cotton Vitellius E.XIV [Joscelyn's trans.] **Ker 409**
ed J.L. Rosier, 'Old English Glosses to an epistle of Boniface,' *JEGP* 59 [1960] 710-3

11

Canticles of the Psalter
[For fuller listing, see Bible, Psalms]

11.1
MS Cambridge, University Library, Ff.1.23   **Ker 13**
ed Wildhagen 1910, 371-407

11.2
MS Cambridge, Trinity College, R.17.1   **Ker 91**
ed Harsley 1889; Liles 1967, 245-69

11.3
MS London, British Museum, Add. 37517   **Ker 129**
ed Lindelöf 1909, 190-200

11.4
MS London, British Museum, Arundel 60   **Ker 134**
ed Oess 1910, 231-54

11.5
MS London, British Museum, Cotton Tiberius C.VI   **Ker 199**
    proposed ed. A.P. Campbell

11.6
MS London, British Museum, Cotton Vespasian A.I   **Ker 203**
ed Kuhn 1965, 146-58, 312-5

11.7
MS London, British Museum, Cotton Vitellius E.XVIII   **Ker 224 art.a**
ed Rosier 1962, 365-96

11.8
MS London, British Museum, Harley 863   **Ker 232**
ed F. Holthausen, 'Eine altenglische Interlinearversion des athanasianischen Glaubens-
    bekenntnisses,' *Englische Studien* 75 [1942-3] 6-8

11.9
MS London, British Museum, Royal 2 B.V   **Ker 249 art.a**
ed Roeder 1904, 275-302

11.10
MS London, British Museum, Stowe 2   **Ker 271**
ed J.L. Rosier, 'The Stowe Canticles,' *Anglia* 82 [1964] 397-432

11.11
MS London, Lambeth Palace, 427   **Ker 280**
ed Lindelöf 1909-14, 235-57

11.12

MS Salisbury, Cathedral, 150   **Ker 379**
ed Sisam 1959, 285-308

12
Monastic Canticles

MS Durham, Cathedral, B.III.32   **Ker 107A art.2**
London, British Museum, Cotton Julius A.VI   **Ker 160 art.c**
London, British Museum, Cotton Vespasian D.XII   **Ker 208 art.c**
proposed ed. Michael Korhammer, 'An edition of the Latin Monastic Canticles and
their OE Interlinear Glosses in Mss Cot. Jul. A VI, Cot. Vesp. D XII, Durham Chap.
B.III.32' [Munich diss.] *NM* 70 [1969] 522

13
Commonplaces

MS Durham, Cathedral, A.IV.19 pp.171-6   **Ker 106 art.d**
facs Brown et al. 1969
ed Thompson and Lindelöf 1927

14
Form of Confession

MS London, Lambeth Palace, 427   **Ker 280 art.2**
ed M. Förster, 'Die altenglischen Beigaben des Lambeth-Psalters,' *Archiv* 132 [1914]
329-31
See B.11.9

15
Defensor, Liber Scintillarum

MS London, British Museum, Royal 7 C.IV   **Ker 256 art.1**
ed E.W. Rhodes, *Defensor's Liber Scintillarum*, EETS 93, London 1889; Sarah S. Getty, 'An
Edition, with Commentary, of the Latin/Anglo-Saxon *Liber Scintillarum*' [Pennsylvania
diss.] *DA* 31 [1970] 1250A

16
Prognostics

MS London, British Museum, Cotton Tiberius A.III   **Ker 186 art.7a-g**
ed M. Förster, 'Beiträge zur mittelalterlichen Volkskunde IV,' *Archiv* 125 [1910] 47-70
[art.a] ; M. Förster, 'Vom Fortleben antiker Sammellunare im Englischen und in anderen
Volkssprachen,' *Anglia* 67 [1944] 79-129 [art.b] ; M. Förster, 'Die altenglischen
Traumlunare,' *Englische Studien* 60 [1925-6] 67-74 [art.c] ; M. Förster, 'Beiträge zur
mittelalterlichen Volkskunde I, II,' *Archiv* 120 [1908] 50, 296-7 [arts.d, g] ; M. Förster,
'Beiträge zur mittelalterlichen Volkskunde VIII,' *Archiv* 129 [1912] 18-21, 32-4 [e, f]
See B.23.3

17
Fulgentius, Injunction

MS London, British Museum, Cotton Tiberius A.III   **Ker 186 art.2**
ed Logeman 1888, xxiv [Latin only]

18
Hymns

18.1
MS   Durham, Cathedral, A.IV.19   **Ker 106 art.c**
facs Brown et al. 1969
ed   Thompson and Lindelöf 1927

18.2
MS   Durham, Cathedral, B.III.32   **Ker 107A art.1**
ed   J. Stevenson, *The Latin Hymns of the Anglo-Saxon Church,* Surtees Society 23,
     Durham 1851
     proposed ed. H. Gneuss, Munich, *NM* 70 [1969] 523

18.3
MS   London, British Museum, Cotton Julius A.VI   **Ker 160 arts.a, b**
     London, British Museum, Cotton Vespasian D.XII   **Ker 208 arts.a, b**
ed   H. Gneuss, *Hymnar und Hymnen im englischen Mittelalter,* Buchreihe der Anglia 12,
     Tübingen 1968, 265-413

18.4
MS   London, British Museum, Cotton Vespasian A.I ff.152-4   **Ker 203**
facs Wright and Campbell 1967
ed   Kuhn 1965, 158-60

19
Isidore, De Miraculis Christi
MS   Oxford, Bodleian, Bodley 319   **Ker 308**
ed   A.S. Napier, *Old English Glosses,* Anecdota Oxoniensia, Mediaeval and Modern Series 11,
     Oxford 1900, no.40

20
Isidore, Sententiae
MS   London, British Museum, Royal 7 C.IV   **Ker 256 art.2**
ed   Rhodes 1889, 223-6

21
Liturgical texts
MS   Durham, Cathedral, A.IV.19   **Ker 106 arts.c, d**
facs Brown et al. 1969
ed   Thompson and Lindelöf 1927

22
Lorica of Gildas
MS   London, British Museum, Harley 585   **Ker 231 art.2**
ed   Grattan and Singer 1952, 130-46

23
Prayers

23.1
MS London, British Museum, Arundel 155   **Ker 135**
ed F. Holthausen, 'Altenglische Interlinearversionen lateinischer Gebete und Beichten,'
   Anglia 65 [1941] 230-54; J.J. Campbell, 'Prayers from Ms Arundel 155,' *Anglia* 81
   [1963] 82-117; Logeman 1889, 115-20 [no. 12]

23.2
MS London, British Museum, Cotton Otho A.VIII ff. 88-90 [burnt]   **Ker 169**
   incipit and explicit from Wanley, Ker 1957, 220

23.3
MS Salisbury, Cathedral, 150 f. 138   **Ker 379**
ed Sisam 1959, 284-5

24
Prosper, Epigrammata and Versus ad coniugem
MS London, British Museum, Cotton Tiberius A.VII ff. 165-6   **Ker 189**
ed T. Wright, *Anglo-Saxon and Old English Vocabularies,* 2nd ed. R.P. Wülcker, London
   1884 [Darmstadt 1968] no. 7, pp. 248-57

25
Proverbs
MS Durham, Cathedral, B.III.32   **Ker 107A art. 3**
ed O. Arngart, *The Durham Proverbs,* Lunds Universitets Årsskrift. N.F. Avd. 1, Bd. 52, Nr. 2,
   Lund 1956
   See B. 7

26
Prudentius, Psychomachia titles
MS Cambridge, Corpus Christi College, 23   **Ker 31 art. b**
   London, British Museum, Cotton Cleopatra C.VIII   **Ker 145 art. a**
ed J. Zupitza, 'Englisches aus Prudentiushandschriften,' *ZfdA* 20 [1876] 36-45

27
Regularis Concordia
MS London, British Museum, Cotton Tiberius A.III   **Ker 186 art. 6**
ed W. Logeman, 'De consuetudine monachorum,' *Anglia* 13 [1891] 365-448; *Anglia* 15
   [1893] 20-40

Occasional glosses

28
Ælfric Bata, Colloquies
MS Oxford, St John's College, 154   **Ker 362 arts. 2-4**
ed Napier 1900, no. 56; Stevenson and Lindsay 1929, nos. 4, 5

29
Alcuin, De virtutibus et vitiis
MS London, British Museum, Cotton Vespasian D. VI **Ker 207 art.b**
ed J. Zupitza, ' Kentische Glossen des neunten Jahrhunderts,' *ZfdA* 21 [1877] 44;
J. Zupitza, 'Zu den kentischen Glossen, ZS.21,1 ff.,' *ZfdA* 22 [1878] 225

30
Alcuin, Libellus ... beati Columbani
MS Copenhagen, Kongelige Bibliotek, Gl.Kgl.Sam. 2034 [4°] **Ker 100 art.b**
ed Ker 1957, 141

31
Aldhelm, De laude virginitatis [prose] and Epistola ad Ehfridum

31.1
MS Brussels, Bibliothèque Royale, 1650 **Ker 8**
facs G. van Langenhove, *Aldhelm's De Laudibus Virginitatis,* Rijksuniversiteit te Gent. Werken
uitgegeven door de Faculteit van de Wijsbegeerte en Letteren. Extra serie: Facsimiles, 2,
Bruges 1941
ed C.W. Bouterwek, 'Angelsächsische Glossen,' *ZfdA* 9 [1853] 401-530; E. Hausknecht,
'Die altenglischen Glossen des Codex ms 1650 der kgl. Bibliothek zu Brüssel,' *Anglia* 6
[1883] 96-103; O.B. Schlutter, 'Zu den Brüsseler Aldhelmglossen,' *Anglia* 33 [1910]
232-8; R. Derolez, 'Zu den Brüsseler Aldhelmglossen,' *Anglia* 74 [1956] 153-80
proposed ed. Louis Goossens, *NM* 68 [1967] 202

31.2
Fragments
MS Cambridge, University Library, Add. 3330 **Ker 12**
Oxford, Bodleian, Lat. Th. d. 24 ff.1, 2
W. Merton Collection, 41
Yale University, 401
Oxford, Bodleian, Don. F. 482
London, British Museum, Add. 50453K
Philadelphia, Free Library, Lewis, European MSS, Text leaves 121
ed Napier 1900, no.12 [Cambridge, University Library, Add. 3330], no.11 and xxxiii,
and H.D. Meritt, 'Old English Glosses, Mostly Dry Point,' *JEGP* 60 [1961] 441 [Yale
University, 401]; H.D. Meritt, 'Old English Aldhelm Glosses,' *MLN* 67 [1952] 553-4
[W. Merton Collection, 41]

31.3
MS Cambridge, Corpus Christi College, 326 **Ker 61 art.b**
ed Napier 1900, xxxiii and no.4; H.D. Meritt, *Old English Glosses: A Collection,* MLA
General Series 16, New York 1945, no.1

31.4
MS Hereford, Cathedral, P.I.17 **Ker 120**
ed Napier 1900, no.3

31.5
MS   London, British Museum, Cotton Domitian IX ff. 2-7   **Ker 149**
ed   Napier 1900, no. 13

31.6
MS   London, British Museum, Harley 3013   **Ker 238**
ed   Napier 1900, no. 10

31.7
MS   London, British Museum, Royal 5 E.XI   **Ker 252**
ed   Napier 1900, xxxiii and nos. 8, 8b; Meritt 1945, no. 2; F.C. Robinson, 'Old English Lexicographical Notes,' *Philologica Pragensia* 8 [1965] 305 footnote 16

31.8
MS   London, British Museum, Royal 5 F.III   **Ker 253 art.a**
ed   Napier 1900, no. 9

31.9
MS   London, British Museum, Royal 6 A.VI   **Ker 254**
ed   Napier 1900, nos. 7, 13

31.10
MS   London, British Museum, Royal 6 B.VII   **Ker 255**
ed   Napier 1900, no. 2

31.11
MS   London, British Museum, Royal 7 D.XXIV   **Ker 259**
ed   Napier 1900, no. 5

31.12
MS   Oxford, Bodleian, Bodley 97   **Ker 300**
ed   Napier 1900, no. 6

31.13
MS   Oxford, Bodleian, Digby 146   **Ker 320**
ed   Napier 1900, nos. 1, 13

31.14
MS   Salisbury, Cathedral, 38   **Ker 378**
ed   H. Logeman, 'New Aldhelm Glosses,' *Anglia* 13 [1891] 26-41; A.S. Napier, 'Collation der altenglischen Aldhelmglossen des Codex 38 der Kathedralbibliothek zu Salisbury,' *Anglia* 15 [1893] 204-9

32
Aldhelm, De laude virginum [verse]

32.1
MS   Cambridge, University Library, Gg. 5.35   **Ker 16**
ed   Napier 1900, no. 16

32.2
MS Cambridge, Corpus Christi College, 285   **Ker 54**
ed Napier 1900, nos. 18, 22

32.3
MS Oxford, Bodleian, Bodley 49   **Ker 299**
ed Napier 1900, nos. 15, 20

32.4
MS Oxford, Bodleian, Bodley 577   **Ker 314**
ed Napier 1900, nos. 14, 19

32.5
MS Oxford, Bodleian, Rawlinson C.697   **Ker 349**
ed Napier 1900, nos. 17, 21

32.6
MS Einsiedeln, Stiftsbibliothek, 32   **Ker A.9**
ed Meritt 1945, no. 3

33
Aldhelm, Ænigmata

33.1
MS Cambridge, University Library, Gg. 5.35   **Ker 16**
ed Napier 1900, no. 23

33.2
MS London, British Museum, Royal 12 C.XXIII   **Ker 263 art.a**
ed Napier 1900, no. 26

33.3
MS London, British Museum, Royal 15 A.XVI   **Ker 267**
ed Napier 1900, no. 25

33.4
MS Oxford, Bodleian, Rawlinson C.697   **Ker 349**
ed Napier 1900, no. 24

33.5
MS St Gallen, Stiftsbibliothek, 1394
ed Meritt 1961, 441

34
Amalarius, Liber Officialis
MS Cambridge, Trinity College, B. 11.2   **Ker 84 art.a**
ed Ker 1957, 129

35
Ambrose, De patriarchis
MS   Boulogne-sur-Mer, Bibliothèque Municipale, 32   **Ker 6***
ed   H.D. Meritt, 'Old English Glosses to Gregory, Ambrose and Prudentius,' *JEGP* 56 [1957] 66

36
Pseudo-Apuleius, Herbarius
MS   Oxford, Bodleian, Ashmole 1431   **Ker 289**
proposed ed. J. Gough, Leicester

37
Apuleii Sphera, Text
MS   London, British Museum, Cotton Vitellius E.XVIII   **Ker 224 art.r**
ed   M. Förster, 'Beiträge zur mittelalterlichen Volkskunde VIII,' *Archiv* 129 [1912] 45-7

38
Arator, De actibus apostolorum
MS   Cambridge, Trinity College, B.14.3 f.23   **Ker 85**
ed   Ker 1957, 129

39
Augustine, Enchiridion

39.1
MS   Cambridge, Trinity College, O.1.18   **Ker 92**
ed   Napier 1900, no.27

39.2
MS   Salisbury, Cathedral, 172   **Ker 380**
ed   Ker 1957, 451

40
Avianus, Fables
MS   Oxford, Bodleian, Rawlinson G.III   **Ker 350**
ed   Napier 1900, no.28

41
Bede, Comment. in Epistolas Catholicas
MS   Oxford, Oriel College, 34 f.153v   **Ker 359**
ed   Ker 1957, 434

42
Bede, De Arte Metrica
MS   Worcester, Cathedral, Q.5   **Ker 399 art.a**
ed   Napier 1900, no.30

43
Bede, De Die Iudicii

MS London, British Museum, Cotton Domitian I **Ker 146 art.b**
ed Napier 1900, no.33

44
Bede, De Temporum Ratione

44.1
MS London, British Museum, Cotton Vespasian B. VI **Ker 205**
ed Napier 1900, no.31

44.2
MS Oxford, St John's College, 17 **Ker 360 art.d**
ed Jones 1943, 340
See B.24.3

45
Bede, Historia Ecclesiastica Gentis Anglorum

45.1
MS London, British Museum, Cotton Tiberius C.II **Ker 198 arts.c, e**
ed Ker 1957, 261 [art.c] ; H.D. Meritt, 'Old English Scratched Glosses in Cotton Ms
    Tiberius C.II,' *American Journal of Philology* 54 [1933] 305-22 and Meritt 1945, no.4
    [art.e]

45.2
MS London, Lambeth Palace, 173 **Ker 276**
ed Meritt 1945, no.5

45.3
MS Oxford, Bodleian, Bodley 163 **Ker 304 art.c**
ed Napier 1900, no.29

46
Bede, Vita S. Cuthberhti [prose]
MS London, British Museum, Cotton Vitellius A.XIX **Ker 217 art.a**
ed Meritt 1945, no.6 glosses 1, 2

47
Bede, Vita S. Cuthberhti [verse]

47.1
MS Copenhagen, Kongelige Bibliotek, Gl.Kgl.Sam. 2034 [4°] **Ker 100 art.a**
ed Meritt 1945, no.9

47.2
MS London, British Museum, Cotton Vitellius A.XIX **Ker 217 art.b**
ed Meritt 1945, no.6 glosses 3-14

47.3

MS London, British Museum, Harley 526 **Ker 230**
ed Meritt 1945, no. 11

47.4

MS London, British Museum, Harley 1117 **Ker 234**
ed Meritt 1945, no. 7

47.5

MS Oxford, Bodleian, Bodley 109 **Ker 301**
ed Ker 1957, 357

47.6

MS Paris, Bibliothèque Nationale, Lat. 2825 **Ker 365**
ed Meritt 1945, no. 10

47.7

MS Vatican City, Reg. Lat. 204 **Ker 389**
ed Napier 1900, no. 32; Ker 1957, 458

48
Benedictine Rule

48.1

MS Cambridge, Corpus Christi College, 57 **Ker 34**
ed Napier 1900, no. 57

48.2

MS Cambridge, Trinity College, O. 2.30 **Ker 94**
ed Napier 1900, no. 58

48.3

MS Oxford, Corpus Christi College, 197 f. 80rv **Ker 353**
ed Ker 1957, 430

49
Bible, Proverbs

MS London, British Museum, Cotton Vespasian D. VI **Ker 207 art. a**
ed Zupitza 1877, 18-44; Zupitza 1878, 223-6
    proposed ed. Aimé Noël, Liège, *NM* 67 [1966] 200

50
Bible, Psalms

50.1

MS New York, Pierpont Morgan Library, 776 **Ker 287**
ed E. Brock, 'The Blickling Glosses' in R. Morris, *The Blickling Homilies*, EETS 58, 63, 73,
    London 1874-80 [1967] 253-63; R.L. Collins, 'A Reexamination of the Old English
    Glosses in the *Blickling Psalter*,' *Anglia* 81 [1963] 124-8

50.2
MS   Paris, Bibliothèque Nationale, Lat. 8846
ed   H. Hargreaves and C. Clark, 'An unpublished Old English Psalter-gloss fragment,' *N & Q* 210 [1965] 443-6

51
Bible, Gospels

51.1
MS   Ripon, Bradfer-Laurence Collection   **Ker 7***
ed   Napier 1900, xxxiii and no.61; Meritt 1961, 443

51.2
MS   London, British Museum, Add. 40000   **Ker 131 arts.a, b**
ed   Meritt 1961, 442

51.3
MS   Oettingen-Wallerstein Collection, Schloss Harburg Schwaben   **Ker 287***
ed   Meritt 1961, 442; J. Hofmann, 'Altenglische und althochdeutsche Glossen aus Würzburg und dem weiteren angelsächsischen Missionsgebiet,' *BGDSL* [Halle] 85 [1963] 39

51.4
MS   Oxford, Bodleian, Auct. D.5.3   **Ker 293**
ed   Meritt 1945, nos.60-2

52
Bible, Pauline Epistles
MS   Cambridge, Trinity College, B.10.5   **Ker 83 art.a**
ed   Napier 1900, no.62

53
Boethius, De consolatione philosophiae

53.1
MS   Antwerp, Plantin-Moretus Museum, 190   **Ker 3**
ed   Ker 1957, 3

53.2
MS   Cambridge, University Library, Kk.3.21   **Ker 24 art.a**
ed   Meritt 1961, 443-5

53.3
MS   Cambridge, Trinity College, O.3.7   **Ker 95***
ed   Meritt 1945, no.12

53.4
MS   Oxford, Bodleian, Auct. F.1.15   **Ker 294 art.a**
ed   Napier 1900, no.34

54
Canticles of the Psalter, Creed, Epistola Salvatoris
MS London, British Museum, Royal 2 A.XX **Ker 248 art.a**
ed J. Zupitza, 'Mercisches aus der Hs. Royal 2 A 20 im Britischen Museum,' *ZfdA* 33 [1889] 47-66

55
Catonis Disticha

55.1
MS Cambridge, Trinity College, O.2.31 **Ker 95**
ed Meritt 1945, no. 13

55.2
MS Oxford, Bodleian, Rawlinson G.57 ff. 1-5v **Ker 350**
ed M. Förster and A.S. Napier, 'Englische Cato- und Ilias-Glossen des 12. Jahrhunderts,' *Archiv* 117 [1906] 17-28

56
Council of Chelsea, Decisions
MS London, British Museum, Cotton Vespasian A.XIV **Ker 204**
ed A.W. Haddan and W. Stubbs, *Councils and Ecclesiastical Documents relating to Great Britain and Ireland,* Oxford 1869-71, III, 584

57
Rule of Chrodegang of Metz
MS Brussels, Bibliothèque Royale, 8558-63 **Ker 10A**
ed Meritt 1945, no. 14

58
Chronicle fragment
MS Oxford, Bodleian, Lat. Misc. d. 13 f. 23v **Ker 339**
ed Ker 1957, 418

59
Instituta Cnuti
MS Oxford, Bodleian, Rawlinson C.641 **Ker 348 art.a**
      Rochester, Cathedral, Textus Roffensis **Ker 373 art.24**
facs Sawyer 1957-62
ed Liebermann 1903-16, 295 notes 5, 14; 315 col.2 note 11; 317 col.2 note 15; 325 col.2 note 23; 81 col.2 notes 18, 22, 34; 83 col.2 note 24 [Ker 373 art.24]

60
Defensor, Liber Scintillarum
MS Cambridge, Corpus Christi College, 190 **Ker 45A art.d**
ed Ker 1957, 70

61
Dialogue Lesson

MS   Oxford, Bodleian, Bodley 572   **Ker 313 art.f**
ed   Meritt 1945, no. 65

62
Ecgberht, Poenitentiale
MS   Cambridge, Corpus Christi College, 265   **Ker 53 art.c i, ii, iii**
ed   Ker 1957, 93

63
Egesippus, Historiae Libri
MS   Berlin, Deutsche Staatsbibliothek, Theol. F.65   **Ker 121***
ed   Meritt 1961, 448; Hofmann 1963, 51

64
Ephraem Syrus, De compunctione cordis
MS   London, Lambeth Palace, 204   **Ker 277 art.b**
ed   Ker 1957, 341

65
Ethicus, Cosmographia
MS   London, British Museum, Cotton Vespasian B.X   **Ker 206**
ed   Meritt 1961, 445

66
Felix, Vita S. Guthlaci

66.1
MS   London, British Museum, Cotton Nero E.I vol. 1   **Ker 29 art.a**
ed   Napier 1900, no. 37

66.2
MS   Cambridge, Corpus Christi College, 389   **Ker 66**
ed   Meritt 1945, no. 15

66.3
MS   London, British Museum, Royal 4 A.XIV ff. 107-8   **Ker 251**
ed   Napier 1900, v

66.4
MS   London, British Museum, Royal 13 A.XV   **Ker 266**
ed   Napier 1900, no. 36; Meritt 1945, no. 16; Ker 1957, 334
   For C.66, see also B. Colgrave, *Felix's Life of St Guthlac*, Cambridge 1956, 52-4

67
Folklore, Dies Egyptiaci
MS   London, British Museum, Harley 3271   **Ker 239 art. 19**
ed   Henel 1934-5, 340 footnote 1; Ker 1957, 311

68
Frithegod, Vita S. Wilfredi
MS London, British Museum, Cotton Claudius A.I **Ker 140**
ed A. Campbell, *Frithegodi Monachi Breviloquium Vitae Beati Wilfredi et Wulfstani Cantoris Narratio Metrica de Sancto Swithuno,* Thesaurus Mundi, Zurich 1950, footnotes 226, 338, 376, 1143; Napier 1900, 38

69
Gregory the Great, Dialogi

69.1
MS Canterbury, Cathedral, Add. 32 **Ker 97***
ed Ker 1957, lxiii

69.2
MS London, Lambeth Palace, 204 **Ker 277 art.a**
ed Meritt 1945, no. 17

70
Gregory the Great, Regula Pastoralis

70.1
MS Oxford, St John's College, 28 **Ker 361**
ed Napier 1900, no. 39

70.2
MS Paris, Bibliothèque Nationale, Lat. 9561 **Ker 369**
ed Meritt 1957, 65

71
Names of Herbs, Medical Texts

71.1
MS Cambridge, Corpus Christi College, 223 **Ker 52 art.b**
ed Meritt 1945, no. 66

71.2
MS Dresden, Sächsische Landesbibliothek, Dc. 187 + 160 + 186 + 185 **Ker 102**
ed Meritt 1945, no. 73 [arts. a-d] ; M. Manitius, 'Angelsächsische Glossen in Dresdner Handschriften,' *Anglia* 24 [1901] 428-35 [art.e] ; corrections H. Varnhagen, *De Glossis Nonnullis Anglicis,* Erlangen 1902

71.3
MS Oxford, Bodleian, Bodley 130 **Ker 302 art.a**
facs R.T. Gunther, *The Herbal of Apuleius Barbarus,* Roxburghe Club, Oxford 1925
ed Ker 1957, 357

72
Liber Omeri

MS Oxford, Bodleian, Rawlinson G.57   **Ker 350**
ed Forster and Napier 1906, 27-8

73.1
Hymns
MS Ripon, Cathedral   **Ker 372**
ed Ker 1957, 443

73.2
MS Cambridge, Corpus Christi College, 391 p.656   **Ker 67 corrigenda**
ed Gneuss 1968, 103

74
Isidore, De naturis rerum

74.1
MS Exeter, Cathedral, 3507   **Ker 116***
ed Ker 1957, 153-4

74.2
MS London, British Museum, Cotton Domitian I   **Ker 146 art.a**
ed Napier 1900, no.41

75
Isidore, De ortu et obitu patrum
MS Arras, Bibliothèque Municipale, 764   **Ker 5**
ed Ker 1957, 4

76
Isidore, De summo bono
MS London, Lambeth Palace, 377   **Ker 279**
ed Meritt 1945, no.20

77
Isidore, Etymologiae

77.1
MS Paris, Bibliothèque Nationale, Lat. 7585   **Ker 366 art.b**
ed Meritt 1961, 448

77.2
MS Paris, Bibliothèque Nationale, Lat. 1750
ed W. Riehle, 'Ueber einige neuentdeckte altenglische Glossen,' *Anglia* 84 [1966] 150-5

78
Isidore, Synonyma

78.1
MS London, British Museum, Cotton Vespasian D.XIV   **Ker 210 art.a**
ed Meritt 1961, 449

78.2
MS London, British Museum, Harley 110 **Ker 228 art. b**
ed Meritt 1945, no. 21

78.3
MS Würzburg, Universitätsbibliothek, M.p.th. f. 79 **Ker 400**
ed Hofmann 1963, 60-1

78.4
MS Fulda, Domschatz, Cod. Bonif. 2
ed Hofmann 1963, 56

79
Julian of Toledo, Prognosticon
MS London, British Museum, Royal 12 C. XXIII **Ker 263 art. b**
ed Napier 1900, no. 42

80
Juvencus, Evangeliorum Libri Quattuor
MS Cambridge, University Library, Gg. 5. 35 **Ker 16**
ed Napier 1900, no. 43

81
Libellus de nominibus naturalium rerum
MS London, British Museum, Stowe 57 **Ker 272 art. b**
ed R.M. Garrett, 'Middle English and French Glosses from Ms Stowe 57,' *Archiv* 121 [1908] 411-2

82
Liturgical Pieces

82.1
MS Cambridge, Corpus Christi College, 44 **Ker 33 art. c**
ed Ker 1957, 46

82.2
MS Cambridge, Corpus Christi College, 190 **Ker 45A art. c**
ed B. Fehr, *Die Hirtenbriefe Ælfrics,* Bib. ags. Prosa 9, Hamburg 1914 [reprinted with supplement P. Clemoes, Darmstadt 1966] 247

82.3
MS Cambridge, Corpus Christi College, 422 **Ker 70B arts. i, j, n**
ed Ker 1957, 120 [arts. i, j] ; B. Fehr, 'Altenglische Ritualtexte für Krankenbesuch, heilige Oelung und Begräbnis' in M. Förster and K. Wildhagen, eds., *Texte und Forschungen zur englischen Kulturgeschichte: Festgabe für Felix Liebermann,* Halle 1921, 65-7

82.4
MS Rouen, Bibliothèque Municipale, A. 27 **Ker 374 art. b**
ed Doble 1937, 121

82.5
MS   London, British Museum, Add. 57337
See Sotheby and Co., *Catalogue of Western Manuscripts and Miniatures,* 12 July 1971, lot 35

83
Lorica of Gildas
MS   Cambridge, University Library, Ll. 1. 10   **Ker 27 art. b**
ed   A.B. Kuypers, *The Book of Cerne,* Cambridge 1902, 85-8

84
Macer, De viribus herbarum
MS   London, British Museum, Cotton Vitellius C.III f. 10v   **Ker 218**
proposed ed. J. Gough, Leicester

85
Medical Texts
MS   London, British Museum, Cotton Vitellius C.III   **Ker 219 art. 4**
ed   Cockayne 1864-6, I, 376

86
Medicina de quadrupedibus
MS   Oxford, Bodleian, Bodley 130   **Ker 302 art. b**
ed   Ker 1957, 357

87
Milo, De sobrietate
MS   Cambridge, University Library, Gg. 5. 35   **Ker 16**
ed   Napier 1900, no. 44

88
Month and Season Names
MS   Cambridge, Corpus Christi College, 422   **Ker 70B art. c**
ed   Wormald 1934, no. 14; Meritt 1945, no. 63

89
Penitentials and Rules

89.1
Pseudo-Theodore
MS   Brussels, Bibliothèque Royale, 8558-63   **Ker 10B**
ed   O.B. Schlutter, 'Anglo-Saxonica,' *Anglia* 32 [1909] 513

89.2
MS   Cambridge, Corpus Christi College, 190   **Ker 45A art. a**
ed   Ker 1957, 70

89.3
Theodore, Egbert, Theodulf of Orleans

MS Cambridge, Corpus Christi College, 265 **Ker 53 art.c**
ed Ker 1957, 93-4

89.4
Collectio canonum
MS Cologne, Dombibliothek, 213 **Ker 98***
ed Hofmann 1963, 43

89.5
MS Oxford, Bodleian, Bodley 311 **Ker 307 arts.a, b**
ed Ker 1957, 360

90
Phocas, Ars grammatici
MS Oxford, Bodleian, Auct. F.2.14 **Ker 295 art.c**
ed Napier 1900, no.45

91
Prayers

91.1
MS Cambridge, University Library, Ll.1.10 **Ker 27 art.c**
ed Kuypers 1902, 113; Ker 1957, 40

91.2
MS London, British Museum, Cotton Galba A.XIV ff.27, 34? **Ker 157**
ed Ker 1957, 200

91.3
MS London, British Museum, Harley 7653 **Ker 244**
ed Ker 1957, 315

91.4
MS London, Lambeth Palace, 427 **Ker 280 art.3**
ed Förster 1914, 328-9

92
Excerptiones de Prisciano

92.1
MS Antwerp, Plantin-Moretus Museum, 47 **Ker 2 art.a**
ed Meritt 1945, no.22

92.2
MS Paris, Bibliothèque Nationale, Nouv. Acq. Lat. 586 **Ker 371**
ed Ker 1957, 442-3

93
Prosper, Epigrammata

93.1

MS Cambridge, Trinity College, O.2.31 **Ker 95**
ed Meritt 1945, no.24

93.2

MS London, British Museum, Harley 110 **Ker 228 art.a**
ed Meritt 1945, no.23

94
Prudentius, Psychomachia

94.1

MS Boulogne-sur-Mer, Bibliothèque Municipale, 189 **Ker 7**
ed H.D. Meritt, *The Old English Prudentius Glosses at Boulogne-sur-Mer,* Stanford Studies in Language and Literature 16, Stanford 1959 [New York 1967]

94.2

MS Cambridge, University Library, Gg.5.35 **Ker 16**
ed Napier 1900, no.49

94.3

MS Cambridge, Corpus Christi College, 23 **Ker 31 art.a**
ed Meritt 1945, no.25

94.4

MS Cambridge, Corpus Christi College, 223 **Ker 52 art.a**
ed Meritt 1945, no.27

94.5

MS Durham, Cathedral, B.IV.9 **Ker 108**
ed Napier 1900, no.47

94.6

MS London, British Museum, Cotton Cleopatra C.VIII **Ker 145 art.b**
ed Napier 1900, no.50 and xxxiii; Ker 1957, 185

94.7

MS Munich, Bayerische Staatsbibliothek, CLM 29031b **Ker 286**
ed Meritt 1945, no.26

94.8

MS Oxford, Bodleian, Auct. F.3.6 **Ker 296 art.a**
ed Napier 1900, no.46

94.9

MS Oxford, Oriel College, 3 **Ker 358**
ed Napier 1900, no.48

95
Names of Relationship

95
Names of Relationship

95.1
MS Cambridge, Corpus Christi College, 265   **Ker 53 art.c** [viii]
ed Ker 1957, 94

95.2
MS Oxford, St John's College, 17   **Ker 360 art.b**
proposed ed. J. Gough, Leicester

96
Saints' Lives

96.1
St Egwin
MS London, British Museum, Cotton Nero E.I vol. 1   **Ker 29 art.a**
ed Napier 1900, no.35

96.2
St Salvius
MS Cambridge, Corpus Christi College, 9   **Ker 29 art.a**
ed Ker 1957, 41

97
Sedulius, Carmen Paschale

97.1
MS Cambridge, University Library, Gg.5.35   **Ker 16**
ed Napier 1900, no.51

97.2
MS Cambridge, Corpus Christi College, 173 ff.57-83   **Ker 40**
ed Meritt 1945, nos.28, 31

97.3
MS Edinburgh, National Library of Scotland, Advocates' 18.7.7   **Ker 111**
ed Meritt 1945, no.30

97.4
MS London, British Museum, Royal 15 B.XIX   **Ker 268**
ed Meritt 1945, no.29

97.5
MS Oxford, Bodleian, Lat. Th. C.4   **Ker 340**
ed Ker 1957, 418

98
Wulfstan of Winchester, Miracula S. Swithuni

98.1
MS London, British Museum, Royal 15 C.VII **Ker 270**
ed Meritt 1945, no. 32; Campbell 1950, 154, 158

98.2
MS Oxford, Bodleian, Auct. F. 2. 14 **Ker 295 art. b**
ed Napier 1900, no. 52

D LATIN–OLD ENGLISH GLOSSARIES

1

MS Antwerp, Plantin-Moretus Museum, 47 + London, British Museum, Add. 32246 **Ker 2**
ed M. Förster, 'Die altenglische Glossenhandschrift Plantinus 32 [Antwerpen] und
Additional 32246 [London],' *Anglia* 41 [1917] 94-161 [arts.b, c, d, e Antwerp MS] ;
T. Wright, *Anglo-Saxon and Old English Vocabularies,* 2nd ed. R.P. Wülcker, London
1884 [Darmstadt 1968] , nos.4, 5 [from Junius transcript, Oxford, Bodleian, Junius 71] ;
L. Kindschi, 'The Latin-Old English Glossaries in Plantin-Moretus 32 and British Museum
Ms Additional 32246' [Stanford diss.] *DA* 16 [1956] 117
see also C.A. Ladd, 'The "Reubens" Manuscript and Archbishop Ælfric's Vocabulary,'
RES 11 [1960] 353-64

2

MS Brussels, Bibliothèque Royale, 1828-30 **Ker 9**
ed Wright and Wülcker 1884, no.9; corrections H. Logeman, 'Zu Wright-Wülcker I, 204-303,'
Archiv 85 [1890] 316-8
proposed ed. Paula Simmonds, University College, Dublin, *NM* 68 [1967] 202

3

MS Cambridge, University Library, Kk.5. 16 f. 128v **Ker 25**
facs P. Hunter Blair, *The Moore Bede,* EEMF 9, Copenhagen 1959
ed E.V.K. Dobbie, *The Manuscripts of Caedmon's Hymn and Bede's Death Song,* Columbia
University Studies in English and Comparative Literature 128, New York 1937, 11

4

MS Cambridge, Corpus Christi College, 144 **Ker 36**
ed J.H. Hessels, *An Eighth-Century Latin-Anglo-Saxon Glossary,* Cambridge 1890;
W.M. Lindsay, *The Corpus Glossary,* Cambridge 1921; J.B. Wynn, 'An edition of the
Anglo-Saxon Corpus glosses' [Oxford, D.Phil.] *Index* 12 [1961-2] no.149

5

MS Cambridge, Corpus Christi College, 183 **Ker 42 art.a**
ed Meritt 1945, no.8

6

MS Durham, Cathedral, Hunter 100 **Ker 110**
ed B. von Lindheim, *Das Durhamer Pflanzenglossar,* Beiträge zur englischen Philologie 35,
Bochum-Langendreer 1941

7

MS Epinal, Bibliothèque Municipale, 72 **Ker 114**
facs O.B. Schlutter, *Faksimile und Transliteration des Epinaler Glossars,* Bib. ags. Prosa 8,
Hamburg 1912
ed H. Sweet, *The Oldest English Texts,* EETS 83, London 1885, 36-106 [OE entries] ;
J.J.M.D. Pheifer, 'A new edition of the Epinal Glossary' [Oxford B.Litt.] *Index* 13
[1962-3] no.151; A.K. Brown, 'The Epinal Glossary' [Stanford diss.] *DA* 30 [1970]
5428A

8

MS   London, British Museum, Cotton Cleopatra A.III   **Ker 143**
ed   Wright and Wülcker 1884, art. 1 no. 11, art. 2 no. 8, art. 3 no. 12; William G. Stryker, 'The Latin-Old English glossary in Ms Cotton Cleopatra A III' [Stanford diss.] *ADD* 19 [1952] 230; John Joseph Quinn, 'The Minor Latin-Old English Glossaries in Ms Cotton Cleopatra A III' [Stanford diss.] *DA* 16 [1956] 1902

9

MS   London, British Museum, Cotton Domitian I   **Ker 146 art. c**
ed   Napier 1900, no. 55

10

Additional glosses to the glossary in Ælfric's Grammar
MS   London, British Museum, Cotton Faustina A.X ff. 93, 101   **Ker 154A art. 1**
     not edited

11

MS   London, British Museum, Cotton Otho E.I   **Ker 184**
ed   Meritt 1961, 445-6 [partial]

12

MS   London, British Museum, Cotton Tiberius C.II   **Ker 198 art. a**
ed   F. Holthausen, 'Die altenglischen Beda-Glossen,' *Archiv* 136 [1917] 290-2

13

MS   London, British Museum, Cotton Vespasian D.VI   **Ker 207 art. f**
ed   J. Zupitza, 'Kentische Glossen des neunten Jahrhunderts,' *ZfdA* 21 [1877] 44; corrections 'Zu den kentischen Glossen ZS. 21, 1ff.,' *ZfdA* 22 [1878] 225

14

MS   London, British Museum, Cotton Vespasian D.XIV   **Ker 210 art. b**
ed   Ker 1957, 277

15

MS   London, British Museum, Harley 107   **Ker 227 art. 3**
ed   J. Zupitza, 'Altenglische Glossen,' *ZfdA* 33 [1889] 239-42

16.1

MS   London, British Museum, Harley 3376   **Ker 240**
ed   Wright and Wülcker 1884, no. 6; R.T. Oliphant, *The Harley Latin-Old English Glossary,* Janua Linguarum, Series Practica 20, The Hague 1966
     see review H. Schabram, *Anglia* 86 [1968] 495-500

16.2

MS   Oxford, Bodleian, Lat. Misc. A.3 f. 49   **Ker 240**
ed   Meritt 1961, 447

16.3
MS   Lawrence, Kansas, University of Kansas Library
ed   Napier 1900, no.60 [from Libri Sale Catalogue]
     proposed ed. R.L. Collins, 'MS Harley 3376 and the Kansas Glossary Fragment,' *NM* 68
     [1967] 202

17
MS   London, British Museum, Harley 3826   **Ker 241**
ed   Meritt 1961, 447-8

18
MS   London, British Museum, Royal 2 B.V   **Ker 249 art.i**
ed   Meritt 1945, no.64

19
MS   London, British Museum, Royal 7 C.IV   **Ker 256 art.3**
ed   Meritt 1961, 445, 449

20
MS   London, British Museum, Royal 7 D.II   **Ker 258**
ed   Meritt 1945, no.69

21
MS   Oxford, Bodleian, Auct. F.2.14   **Ker 295 art.a**
ed   A.S. Napier, 'Altenglische Glossen,' *Englische Studien* 11 [1888] 62-7; Napier 1900,
     no.18B

22
MS   Oxford, Bodleian, Barlow 35   **Ker 298 arts.a, c**
ed   F. Liebermann, 'Aus Ælfrics Grammatik und Glossar,' *Archiv* 92 [1894] 414-5 [art.a];
     Ker 1957, 356 [art.c]

23
MS   Oxford, Bodleian, Bodley 163   **Ker 304 art.b**
ed   Zupitza 1889, 238-9
     proposed ed. A.K. Brown

24
MS   Oxford, Bodleian, Bodley 381   **Ker 311**
ed   Napier 1900, no.59

25
MS   Oxford, Bodleian, Bodley 730   **Ker 317**
     not edited

26
MS   Oxford, Bodleian, Laud Misc. 567   **Ker 345**
ed   see G. Goetz, *Corpus Glossariorum Latinorum,* Leipzig and Berlin 1882-1923, III

xxxiii-iv; Cockayne 1864-6, I, lxxxvii
proposed ed. J.R. Stracke, Vanderbilt University

27
MS   Oxford, Bodleian, Norfolk Rolls 81   **Ker 347**
not edited

28
MS   Oxford, St John's College, 17   **Ker 360 art.e**
ed   A.S. Napier, 'Contributions to Old English Lexicography,' *TPS* [1903-6] 278, s.v. *culling*

29
MS   Paris, Bibliothèque Nationale, Nouv. Acq. Lat. 586   **Ker 371 art.b**
ed   Ker 1957, 442-3

30
MS   London, British Museum, Cotton Vitellius C.IX ff.213-5 [16 c. transcript]   **Ker 406**
ed   as Ælfric's Glossary: J. Zupitza 1880, 315/16-322/2 [art.a] ; Ker 1957, 470-1 [arts.b-d]

31
MS   Berlin, Öffentliche Wissenschaftliche Bibliothek, Lat. 4° 676 ff.2-3   **Ker A.4**
ed   E. Steinmeyer and E. Sievers, *Die althochdeutschen Glossen,* Berlin 1879-1922,
no. DCLXIII

32
MS   Bern, Stadtbibliothek, 258   **Ker A.5**
ed   Meritt 1945, nos.44, 52, 54

33
MS   Brussels, Bibliothèque Royale, 8654-72   **Ker A.6**
ed   Ker 1957, 476

34
MS   Cologne, Dombibliothek, 211   **Ker A.7**
ed   Steinmeyer and Sievers 1879-1922, nos. XIX, CXLI

35
MS   Einsiedeln, Stiftsbibliothek, 32   **Ker A.9**
ed   Steinmeyer and Sievers 1879-1922, nos. DXIV, DCLXXXIV, DCXCIII

36
MS   Erfurt, Wissenschaftliche Allgemeinbibliothek, Amplonianus F.42   **Ker A.10**
ed   Sweet 1885, 36-110; Goetz 1882-1923, V, 337-401 and A.K. Brown [Stanford diss.]
DA 30 [1970] 5428A [Erf.[1]] ; Goetz 1882-1923, V, 259-337, II, 563-74/46, 581/57-
586/26 [Erf.[2], Erf.[3]]
also in Paris, Bibliothèque Nationale, Lat. 7690
proposed ed. A.K. Brown
See also D.59

37

MS Fulda, Landesbibliothek, Aa 2 **Ker A.11**
ed Steinmeyer and Sievers 1879-1922, nos. DCLX, DC

38

MS Karlsruhe, Landesbibliothek, Aug. 99 [86] **Ker A.14**
ed Steinmeyer and Sievers 1879-1922, V, 135-225 and nos. CXLIV, CLXVI, CLXXXI, CXCI,
    CC, CCIX, CCLXV, CCLXXVI, CCXCVIII, CCCXV, CCCXXXVII, CCCLXVII, CCCLXXXVII,
    DCXCIII, DCCXI, DCCXII; cf. IV, 399

39

MS Karlsruhe, Landesbibliothek, Aug. 135 [54] **Ker A.15**
ed Steinmeyer and Sievers 1879-1922, nos. LXXV, LXXXV, CXXXI, CLXVI, CLVI, CLXXXI,
    CXCI, CC, CCIX, CCLXXVI, CCXCVIII, CCCX, CCCL; Meritt 1945, nos. 38, 39, 43, 46, 49, 50,
    57-9

40

MS Leiden, Rijksuniversiteit, Vossianus Lat. Fol. 24 **Ker A.17**
ed Steinmeyer and Sievers 1879-1922, nos. XLI, CCLXV, CCXCVIII, CCCXV, CCCXXXVII,
    DCXCIII, DCCXI, DCCXII; O.B. Schlutter, 'Anglo-Saxonica,' *Anglia* 33 [1910] 246-51;
    Meritt 1945, no. 70

41

MS Leiden, Rijksuniversiteit, Vossianus Lat. 4° 69 **Ker A.18**
ed J.H. Hessels, *A Latin-Anglo-Saxon Glossary,* Cambridge 1906; P. Glogger, *Das Leidener
    Glossar,* Augsburg 1901-8; F. Holthausen, 'Die Leidener Glossen,' *Englische Studien* 50
    [1916-7] 327-40

42

MS Leiden, Rijksuniversiteit, Vossianus Lat. 4° 106 **Ker A.19**
ed Meritt 1945, no. 71

43

MS Leiden, BPL 191
ed W. Stüben, 'Nachträge zu den althochdeutschen Glossen,' *BGDSL* 63 [1939] 454-6;
    Schlutter 1910, 251

44

MS Milan, Ambrosiana, M. 79 sup. **Ker A.20**
ed F.C. Robinson, 'Old English Lexicographical Notes,' *Philologica Pragensia* 8 [1965]
    305-6

45

MS Munich, Bayerische Staatsbibliothek, Clm 6408 **Ker A.21**
ed Steinmeyer and Sievers 1879-1922, no. DCXCIII

46
MS Oxford, Bodleian, Add. C.144   **Ker A.22**
ed Napier 1900, no.53

47
MS Paris, Bibliothèque Nationale, Lat. 2685   **Ker A.23**
ed Steinmeyer and Sievers 1879-1922, nos. XX, XXXIII, XXXIX, LXVI, LXXV, LXXXV, CXI,
   CXV, CXXIX, CXLV, CXCI, CCIX, CCLV, CCLXV, CCLXXVI, CCXCVIII, DCXCIII; Meritt 1945,
   nos.33-5, 40-2, 45, 48, 53

48.1
MS St Gallen, Stiftsbibliothek, 9   **Ker A.24**

48.2
MS St Gallen, Stiftsbibliothek, 295   **Ker A.27**

48.3
MS Vienna, Nationalbibliothek, Lat. 1761 [Theol. 863]   **Ker A.38**
ed Steinmeyer and Sievers 1879-1922, I, 342, no.XLI

49
MS Karlsruhe, Landesbibliothek, Aug. 231   **Ker A.16**
   St Gallen, Stiftsbibliothek, 283   **Ker A.26**
ed Steinmeyer and Sievers 1879-1922, no. XL

50
MS St Gallen, Stiftsbibliothek, 299   **Ker A.28**
ed Steinmeyer and Sievers 1879-1922, no.DCCCXXIIIa; Meritt 1945, nos.18, 51, 55-6

51
MS St Gallen, Stiftsbibliothek, 913   **Ker A.29**
ed Meritt 1945, nos.36, 47

52
MS St Omer, Bibliothèque Municipale, 150   **Ker A.30**
ed Steinmeyer and Sievers 1879-1922, nos.DCLX, DC

53
MS St Paul im Lavanttal, Carinthia, Stiftsbibliothek, XXV d.82   **Ker A.31**
ed Steinmeyer and Sievers 1879-1922, nos.XLI, CCLXXVI, CCXCVIII, DCXCIII

54
MS Salzburg, Carolino-Augusteum Musaeum [lost]   **Ker A.32**
ed Meritt 1945, no.72

55
MS Sélestat, Bibliothèque Municipale, 100   **Ker A.33**
ed Steinmeyer and Sievers 1879-1922, nos.DCLXIb, DCCCXXIIIb

56
MS Stuttgart, Württembergische Landesbibliothek, Theol. et Phil. Fol. 218   **Ker A.34**
ed Steinmeyer and Sievers 1879-1922, nos. CXCI, CC

57
MS Trier, Stadtbibliothek, 40   **Ker A.35**
ed O.B. Schlutter, 'Altenglisch-Althochdeutsches aus dem Codex Trevirensis No. 40,'
     Anglia 35 [1912] 145-54
     Principal glossary also appears in the following MSS:
     Bern, Stadtbibliothek, 688
     Cambridge, Peterhouse College, 2.4.6
     Admont, Stiftsbibliothek, 508
     Oxford, Bodleian, Digby 151
     Paris, Bibliothèque Nationale, Lat. 8048

58
MS Trier, Bibliothek des Priesterseminars, 61 [R. iii. 13]   **Ker A.36**
ed Steinmeyer and Sievers 1879-1922, no. DCXLIII

59
MS Werden, Pfarrhof + Münster, Universitätsbibliothek, Paulinianus 271 [719] + Munich,
     Bayerische Staatsbibliothek, Cgm 187 [e. 4] + missing leaves   **Ker A.39**
     For detailed description, see Ker 1957, 483-4

For Ælfric's glossary, see **B.1.9.2**

For further work on Old English materials in Old High German glossaries, see
C. Leydecker, 'Angelsächsisches in althochdeutschen Glossen' [Bonn diss., 1910] ;
H. Michiels, 'Altenglisches in altdeutschen Glossen' [Bonn diss., 1911]

E RUNIC INSCRIPTIONS

1
Alnmouth shaft
Bruce Dickins and Alan S.C. Ross, 'The Alnmouth Cross,' *JEGP* 39 [1940] 169-78;
R.I. Page, 'Runes and Non-Runes' in D.A. Pearsall and R.A. Waldron, eds., *Medieval Literature and Civilization, Studies in Memory of G.N. Garmonsway,* London 1969, 34
See F.2

2
Auzon casket [Franks casket]
A.S. Napier, 'Contributions to Old English Literature 2. The Franks Casket' in *An English Miscellany presented to Dr. Furnivall,* Oxford 1901, 362-81; R.W.V. Elliott, *Runes, an Introduction,* Manchester 1959, 96-109, figs. 19-23; L. Musset, *Introduction à la Runologie,* Bibliothèque de philologie germanique 20, Paris 1965, 372-4, no. 39; C.J.E. Ball, 'The Franks Casket: Right Side,' *ES* 47 [1966] 119-26
See A.42

3
Bakewell stone
George Stephens, *The Old-Northern Runic Monuments of Scandinavia and England,* 4 vols., London and Copenhagen 1866-1901, I, 373-4; J.R. Allen, in *Victoria History of the Counties of England: Derbyshire,* London 1905, I, 280-1

4
Bewcastle cross
A.S. Cook, *Some Accounts of the Bewcastle Cross between the years 1607 and 1861,* Yale Studies in English 50, New York 1914; R.I. Page, 'The Bewcastle Cross,' *Nottingham Medieval Studies* 4 [1960] 36-57

5
Bingley font
Stephens 1866-1901, I, 486; III, 194-9; H.M. Chadwick, 'Early Inscriptions in the North of England,' *Transactions of the Yorkshire Dialect Society* 1 [1901] 82

6
Bramham Moor ring
Stephens 1866-1901, I, 499; Bruce Dickins, 'Runic Rings and Old English Charms,' *Archiv* 167 [1935] 252

7
Brunswick casket [Gandersheim casket]
Hermann Harder, 'Das Braunschweiger Runenkästchen,' *Archiv* 162 [1932] 227-9; A. Fink, 'Zum Gandersheimer Runenkästchen' in *Karolingische und Ottonische Kunst,* Forschungen zur Kunstgeschichte und christlichen Archäologie 3, Wiesbaden 1957, 277-81

8
Caistor-by-Norwich astragalus
C.L. Wrenn, 'Magic in an Anglo-Saxon Cemetery' in N. Davis and C.L. Wrenn, eds.,
English and Medieval Studies presented to J. R. R. Tolkien, London 1962, 306-20;
C.L. Wrenn, 'Some Earliest Anglo-Saxon Cult Symbols' in J.B. Bessinger, Jr, and
R.P. Creed, eds., *Medieval and Linguistic Studies in honor of F. P. Magoun,* London and
New York 1965, 40-55; R.I. Page, 'The Old English Rune *Eoh*, *Ih* "Yew tree," ' *MÆ* 37
[1968] 125-36

9
Chessell Down scabbard plate
George Hempl, 'The Runic Inscription on the Isle of Wight Sword,' *PMLA* 18 [1903]
95-8; Hermann Harder, 'Die Runen der ags. Schwertinschrift im Britischen Museum,'
Archiv 161 [1932] 86-7; Elliott 1959, 79, pl. 10; S.C. Hawkes and R.I. Page, 'Swords
and Runes in south-east England,' *AJ* 47 [1967] 1-26; K. Schneider, 'Six OE Runic
Inscriptions Reconsidered ' in A.H. Orrick, ed., *Nordica et Anglica: Studies in Honor of
Stefan Einarsson,* The Hague 1968, 40-3

10
Chester-le-Street stone
Stephens 1866-1901, III, 461-3; R.I. Page, 'Language and Dating in OE Inscriptions,'
Anglia 77 [1959] 386
See F.10

11
Collingham cross
Stephens 1866-1901, I, 390-1, III, 183; Henry Sweet, *The Oldest English Texts,* EETS 83,
London 1885, 128

12
Coquet Island ring [lost]
Stephens 1866-1901, I, 480-1; Sweet 1885, 128; Schneider 1968, 48-9

13
Cramond ring
Stephens 1866-1901, III, 215-6

14
Crowle cross
Stephens 1866-1901, III, 185-8

15
Derbyshire bone piece
Stephens 1866-1901, IV, 47-9; Elliott 1959, 73 and fig. 25; J.M. Bately and V.I. Evison,
'The Derby bone piece,' *Medieval Archaeology* 5 [1961] 301-5; Musset 1965, 377,
no. 45; Schneider 1968, 45-8

16
Dover brooch
V.I. Evison, 'The Dover Rune Brooch,' *AJ* 44 [1964] 242-5

17
Dover stone
Stephens 1866-1901, I, 465-6; Sweet 1885, 129

18
England A coin [skanomodu]
P. Berghaus and K. Schneider, *Anglo-friesische Runensolidi im Lichte des Neufundes von Schweindorf [Ostfriesland]*, Arbeitsgemeinschaft für Forschung des Landes Nordrhein-Westfalen 134, Köln and Opladen 1967; R.I. Page, 'The Runic Solidus of Schweindorf, Ostfriesland, and Related Runic Solidi,' *Medieval Archaeology* 12 [1968] 12-25; Schneider 1968, 37-40

19
England C agate amulet ring
Stephens 1866-1901, I, 499-500; III, 217; Hermann Harder, 'Eine angelsächsische Runen-inschrift,' *Archiv* 160 [1931] 87-9; Dickins 1935, 252; Hermann Harder, 'Die Inschriften angelsächsischer Runenringe,' *Archiv* 169 [1936] 224-8

20
Falstone stone
Stephens 1866-1901, I, 456-60; Sweet 1885, 127; Chadwick 1901, 83-4
See F.14

21
Gilton pommel
R.W.V. Elliott, 'Two neglected English Runic Inscriptions: Gilton and Overchurch,' *Mélanges de Linguistique et de Philologie: Fernand Mossé in memoriam,* Paris 1959, 140-7; Hawkes and Page 1967, 3-6; J.M. Bately, 'Interpretation of the Runes on the Gilton Pommel' in V.I. Evison, 'The Dover ring-sword and other sword rings and beads,' *Archaeologia* 101 [1967] 97-102; Schneider 1968, 43-5

22
Hackness stone
Stephens 1866-1901, I, 467-8; III, 215; Chadwick 1901, 82; G. Baldwin Brown, *The Arts in Early England,* 6 vols., London 1930, I, 52-75; Elliott 1959, 83-6 and fig.33

23
Hartlepool stones [2x]
Stephens 1866-1901, I, 392-7; Sweet 1885, 128; Chadwick 1901, 83; F.S. Scott, 'The Hildithryth Stone and the other Hartlepool Name-Stones,' *Archaeologia Aeliana,* 4th series 34 [1956] 196-212; Elliott 1959, 81-2 and fig.30

24
Isle of Man, Maughold stones [2x]

P.M.C. Kermode, 'Inscription in Anglian Runes from Kirk Maughold, Isle of Man,' *Reliquary,* n.s. 13 [1907] 265-7; P.M.C. Kermode, 'Some Early Christian Monuments recently discovered at Kirk Maughold, Isle of Man,' *Reliquary,* n.s. 14 [1908] 182-93

25
Kingmoor ring [Greymoor Hill ring]
Stephens 1866-1901, I, 496-7; Harder 1931, 87-9; Dickins 1935, 252; Harder 1936, 224-8; R.I. Page, 'The Inscriptions,' Appendix A in D.M. Wilson, *Anglo-Saxon Ornamental Metalwork 700-1100 in the British Museum,* London 1964, 73-5

26
Kirkheaton stone
Stephens 1866-1901, IV, 51-2; Chadwick 1901, 81; Elliott 1959, 87

27
Lancashire ring
Stephens 1866-1901, I, 463; Sweet 1885, 130; Hermann Harder, 'Eine angelsächsische Ring-Inschrift,' *Archiv* 161 [1932] 37-9; Page in Wilson 1964, 75-7; Schneider 1968, 49-52
See F.24

28
Lancaster cross
Stephens 1866-1901, I, 375-7; III, 184; Sweet 1885, 128; Chadwick 1901, 83; Elliott 1959, 86-7 and fig.34; Musset 1965, 376, no.43

29
Leeds stone [lost]
Stephens 1866-1901, I, 487-8; III, 215; Page 1969, 35-7

30
Leek stone
R.W.V. Elliott, 'A Runic Fragment at Leek,' *Medieval Archaeology* 8 [1964] 213-4

31
Lindisfarne, St Cuthbert's Coffin
Bruce Dickins, 'The Inscriptions upon the Coffin' in F.C. Battiscombe, ed., *The Relics of St. Cuthbert: Studies by various authors,* Oxford 1956, 305-7

32
Lindisfarne stones
C.R. Peers, 'The Inscribed and Sculptured Stones of Lindisfarne,' *Archaeologia* 74 [1925] 255-70; A.S.C. Ross, 'Notes on the Runic Stones at Holy Island,' *Englische Studien* 70 [1935-6] 36-9; Hawkes and Page 1967, 25 n.5

33
Llysfaen ring
Page in Wilson 1964, 75-6
See F.30

34
Loveden Hill urns
Wrenn 1965, 51-2; Hawkes and Page 1967, 22-3; Page 1968, 125-36

35
Monkwearmouth stones [2x]
Stephens 1866-1901, I, 477-9; Sweet 1885, 128; Chadwick 1901, 83; R.J. Cramp, 'A
Name-stone from Monkwearmouth,' *Archaeologia Aeliana*, 4th series 42 [1964] 294-8;
B. Colgrave and R. Cramp, *St Peter's Church*, [Monkwearmouth] Gloucester n.d.

36
Mortain casket
Maurice Cahen and Magnus Olsen, 'L'inscription runique du coffret de Mortain,'
Collection linguistique publiée par la société de linguistique de Paris 32, Paris 1930;
Musset 1965, 374-5, no.40

37
Orpington stone
R.I. Page, 'Note on the Inscription' in M. Bowen, 'Saxon Sundial in the Parish Church of
All Saints, Orpington,' in 'Researches and Discoveries in Kent,' *Archaeologia Cantiana*
82 [1967] 289-91
See F.35

38
Overchurch stone
Elliott 1959 [Mossé volume] , 144-7; Musset 1965, 375, no.41

39
Ruthwell cross
G. Baldwin Brown, *The Arts in Early England*, V, London 1921; Bruce Dickins and
A.S.C. Ross, eds., *The Dream of the Rood*, MOEL, London 1934, 4th ed. 1954; Elliott
1959, 90-6 and figs.38-40
See A.40

40
St Ninian's Cave cross
Stephens 1866-1901, IV, 36-8; J.R. Allen, *The Early Christian Monuments of Scotland*,
Edinburgh 1903, pt.3, 487; C.A.R. Radford and G. Donaldson, *Whithorn and Kirk-
madrine, Wigtownshire*, Ministry of Works Guide, Edinburgh 1953, 42-3

41
Sandwich stone
Stephens 1866-1901, I, 363-7; Sweet 1885, 129; Bruce Dickins, 'The Sandwich Runic
Inscription RAEHAEBUL' in K.H. Schlottig, ed., *Beiträge zur Runenkunde und nordischer
Sprachwissenschaft* [Neckel Festschrift] Leipzig 1938, 83-5; Elliott 1959, 81 and figs.
26-7; V.I. Evison, Review of R.W.V. Elliott, *Runes: An Introduction, AJ* 40 [1960]
242-4

42
Sarre pommel
Hawkes and Page 1967, 1-3

43
Selsey gold fragments
Stephens 1866-1901, III, 463; Hawkes and Page 1967, 26 n. 1

44
Southampton [Hamwih] bone
Page 1969, 47; R.I. Page in P.V. Addyman and D.H. Hill, 'Saxon Southampton: A Review of the Evidence' Pt. II, 86-8 in *Proceedings of the Hampshire Field Club and Archaeological Society* 26 [1969] 61-96

45
Thames silver mount
Stephens 1866-1901, II, 891-2; III, 204-9; Page in Wilson 1964, 77-9

46
Thames scramasax
Stephens 1866-1901, I, 361-2; Sweet 1885, 129; Elliott 1959, 79 and fig. 7; Page in Wilson 1964, 69-73; V.I. Evison, Review of D.M. Wilson, *Catalogue of Antiquities of the later Saxon period, AJ* 45 [1965] 288-90

47
Thornhill stones [3x]
Stephens 1866-1901, III, 209-11, 414-20; Chadwick 1901, 81-2; L. Whitbread, 'The Thornhill Cross Inscription,' *N & Q* 193 [1948] 156; Elliott 1959, 87-90, figs. 35-7; Musset 1965, 375-6, no. 42

48
Urswick cross
Magnus Olsen, 'Notes on the Urswick Inscription,' *Norsk Tidsskrift for Sprogvidenskap* 4 [1930] 282-6; Musset 1965, 376-7, no. 44

49
Welbeck Hill bracteate
Hawkes and Page 1967, 21-2; H. Vierck, 'Der C-Brakteat von Longbridge in der ost-englischen Gruppe' in K. Hauck, *Goldbrakteaten aus Sievern,* Münstersche Mittelalter-Schriften 1, Munich 1970, Anhang VIII, 37-9 and fig. 47.7

50
Whitby comb
Stephens 1866-1901, III, 180-2; R.I. Page, 'The Whitby Runic Comb,' *Whitby Literary and Philosophical Society Annual Report* 1966, 11-5

51
Whitby disc
C.R. Peers and C.A.R. Radford, 'The Saxon Monastery of Whitby,' *Archaeologia* 89 [1943] 74, fig. 18, no. 5

52
Whithorn stone
Allen 1903, pt. 3, 488-90; Radford and Donaldson 1953, 40

53
York spoon
D.M. Waterman, 'Late Saxon, Viking, and Early Medieval Finds from York,' *Archaeologia* 97 [1959] 85-6; Page 1969, 47

F VERNACULAR INSCRIPTIONS IN THE LATIN ALPHABET

1
Aldbrough sun-dial   Okasha 1
J. Taylor and H.M. Taylor, 'Architectural sculpture in pre-Norman England,' *JBAA*, 3rd
series 29 [1966] 18-9; Elisabeth Okasha, *Hand-list of Anglo-Saxon Non-runic Inscriptions,*
Cambridge 1971, 47

2
Alnmouth shaft   Okasha 2
Dickins and Ross 1940, 169-78; Okasha 1971, 47-8
See E.1

3
Ardwall shaft   Okasha 3
A.C. Thomas, 'An Early Christian Cemetery and Chapel on Ardwall Isle, Kirkcudbright,'
Medieval Archaeology 11 [1967] 153-5; Okasha 1971, 48

4
Athelney, Alfred Jewel   Okasha 4
J.R. Clarke and D.A. Hinton, *The Alfred and Minster Lovell Jewels,* Oxford 1971;
Okasha 1971, 48-9

5
Bishopstone sun-dial   Okasha 12
Taylor and Taylor 1966, 19, 49; Okasha 1971, 54

6
Bodsham gold ring   Okasha 13
E. Okasha and L. Webster, 'An Anglo-Saxon Ring from Bodsham, Kent,' *AJ* 50 [1970]
102-4; Okasha 1971, 55

7
Breamore archway   Okasha 15
Okasha 1971, 56

8
Brussels Cross reliquary   Okasha 17
S.T.R.O. d'Ardenne, 'The Old English Inscription on the Brussels Cross,' *ES* 21 [1939]
145-64, 271-2; Okasha 1971, 57-8
See A.41

9
Carlisle cross head   Okasha 23
W.G. Collingwood, *Northumbrian Crosses of the Pre-Norman Age,* London 1927, 58;
Okasha 1971, 61

10
Chester-le-Street stone   Okasha 25
Stephens 1866-1901, III, 461-3; Page 1959, 386; Okasha 1971, 62
See E.10

11
Cuxton brooch   Okasha 27
Page in Wilson 1964, 84; Okasha 1971, 63

12
Dewsbury shaft   Okasha 30
Collingwood 1927, 58-9; Okasha 1971, 65-6

13
Essex ring   Okasha 36
R.C. Neville, Baron Braybrooke, *A Catalogue of Rings in the Collection of the Right Hon. Lord Braybrooke, Audley End,* Saffron Walden 1860, 46, no.158; Okasha 1971, 70-1

14
Falstone stone   Okasha 39
Stephens 1866-1901, I, 456-60; Sweet 1885, 127; Chadwick 1901, 83-4; Okasha 1971, 71-2
See E.20

15
Gainford stone   Okasha 40
R.J. Cramp, *Durham Cathedral: A Short Guide to the Pre-Conquest Sculptured Stones in the Dormitory,* Durham 1965, 7, no.46; Okasha 1971, 72

16
Great Edstone sundial   Okasha 41
Taylor and Taylor 1966, 21-2; Okasha 1971, 73

17
Hartlepool stone III   Okasha 45
R.A. Smith, *British Museum: A Guide to the Anglo-Saxon and Foreign Teutonic Antiquities in the Department of British and Mediaeval Antiquities,* London 1923, 121-2; Okasha 1971, 77

18
Hartlepool stone VII   Okasha 49
Smith 1923, 121-2; Okasha 1971, 78-9

19
Hartlepool stone VIII   Okasha 50
Smith 1923, 121-2; Okasha 1971, 79

20
Hexham stone   Okasha 52
H.M. Taylor and J. Taylor, 'The seventh-century church at Hexham: A new appreciation,'
Archaeologia Aeliana, 4th series 39 [1961] 123; Okasha 1971, 80

21
Ipswich stone   Okasha 58
K.J. Galbraith, 'Early Sculpture at St. Nicholas' Church, Ipswich,' *Proceedings of the
Suffolk Institute of Archaeology* 31 [1968] 172-84; Okasha 1971, 82-3

22
Kirkdale sun-dial   Okasha 64
Taylor and Taylor 1966, 22; Okasha 1971, 87-8

23
Knells stone   Okasha 65
W.G. Collingwood et al., 'Proceedings' in *Transactions of the Cumberland and Westmore-
land Antiquarian and Archaeological Society,* n.s. 11 [1911] 481-3; Okasha 1971, 88-9

24
Lancashire ring   Okasha 66
Page in Wilson 1964, 75-7; Okasha 1971, 89
See E.27

25
Lanteglos shaft   Okasha 69
R.A.S. Macalister, 'The Ancient Inscriptions of the south of England,' *Archaeologia
Cambrensis* 84 [1929] 184; Okasha 1971, 90-1

26
Laverstock ring   Okasha 70
Page in Wilson 1964, 82; Okasha 1971, 91-2

27
Lincoln stone   Okasha 73
Bruce Dickins, 'The Dedication Stone of St. Mary-le-Wigford, Lincoln,' *The
Archaeological Journal* 103 [1946] 163-5; Okasha 1971, 92-3

28
Lindisfarne stone I   Okasha 75
Peers 1925, 259 and fig. 1; Okasha 1971, 94

29
Lindisfarne stone II   Okasha 76
Peers 1925, 259-60 and fig. 2; Okasha 1971, 94-5
See E.32
Stones IV, VII, VIII, and X probably have Old English personal names on them

30
Llysfaen ring   Okasha 86
Page in Wilson 1964, 75-6; Okasha 1971, 98-9
See E.33

31
London, All Hallows, Barking cross   Okasha 87
E. Okasha, 'An Anglo-Saxon inscription from All Hallows, Barking-by-the-Tower,'
Medieval Archaeology 11 [1967] 249-51; Okasha 1971, 99

32
London, All Hallows, Barking cross-shaft   Okasha 88
Okasha 1967, 249-50; Okasha 1971, 99-100

33
Monkwearmouth stone   Okasha 91
Cramp 1964, 294-8; Okasha 1971, 101
See E.35

34
Newent stone   Okasha 94
G. Zarnecki, 'The Newent Funerary Tablet,' *Transactions of the Bristol and Gloucester-shire Archaeological Society* 72 [1953] 49-55; Okasha 1971, 102-3

35
Orpington sun-dial   Okasha 99
Taylor and Taylor 1966, 23-5; Page in Bowen 1967, 289-91; Okasha 1971, 105
See E.37

36
Pershore censer cover   Okasha 100
Page in Wilson 1964, 84; Okasha 1971, 106

37
Plymstock stone   Okasha 101
E.N.M. Phillips, 'Supplementary Notes on the Ancient Stone Crosses of Devon [4th paper],' *Transactions of the Devonshire Association for the Advancement of Science, Literature and Art* 86 [1954] 184-5; Okasha 1971, 106

38
Ripon cross   Okasha 102
Collingwood 1927, 94; Okasha 1971, 107

39
Rome ring   Okasha 103
C.C. Oman, *Victoria and Albert Museum, Department of Metalwork, Catalogue of Rings,* London 1930, 64, no.228; Okasha 1971, 107-8

40
Rome brooch   Okasha 104
Wilson 1964, no.64; Okasha 1971, 108

41
Sherburn ring   Okasha 107
Page in Wilson 1964, 82-3; Okasha 1971, 112-3

42
Sittingbourne knife   Okasha 109
Page in Wilson 1964, 86; Okasha 1971, 113-4

43
Sutton disc-brooch   Okasha 114
Page in Wilson 1964, 86-9; Okasha 1971, 116-7

44
Swindon ring   Okasha 115
Page in Wilson 1964, 83-4; Okasha 1971, 117

45
Thornhill stone   Okasha 116
Collingwood 1927, 17; Okasha 1971, 118

46
Wallingford weaver's sword   Okasha 118
Okasha 1971, 119; N.P. Brooks [forthcoming]

47
Wensley stone I   Okasha 120
Collingwood 1927, 12 and fig.17b; Okasha 1971, 120

48
Wensley stone II   Okasha 121
Collingwood 1927, 12 and fig.17c; Okasha 1971, 120-1

49
Whitby stone IV   Okasha 125
Peers and Radford 1943, 45 and fig.7; Okasha 1971, 122

50
Whitby stone VII   Okasha 128
Peers and Radford 1943, 45-6 and fig.8; Okasha 1971, 123

51
Whitby stone XIV   Okasha 132
Peers and Radford 1943, 42-4 and fig.5; Okasha 1971, 124

52
Winchester stone   Okasha 138
M. Biddle, 'Excavations at Winchester, 1965,' *AJ* 46 [1966] 325; Okasha 1971, 126-7

53
Winchester brooch   Okasha 141
Okasha 1971, 128

54
Workington shaft [lost]   Okasha 143
J.R. Mason and H. Valentine, 'Find of pre-Norman Stones at St. Michael's Church, Workington,' *Transactions of the Cumberland and Westmoreland Antiquarian and Archaeological Society,* n.s. 28 [1928] 59-60; Okasha 1971, 129

55
Wycliffe shaft   Okasha 144
J.D. Cowen and E. Barty [Okasha] , 'A lost Anglo-Saxon inscription recovered,' *Archaeologia Aeliana,* 4th series 44 [1966] 61-70; Okasha 1971, 129-30

56
Yarm shaft   Okasha 145
Collingwood 1927, 61-2; Okasha 1971, 130

57
York stone   Okasha 146
Okasha 1971, 131

58
'eawen' ring   Okasha 155
Page in Wilson 1964, 89-90; Okasha 1971, 136

59
'sigerie' ring   Okasha 156
C.C. Oman, 'Anglo-Saxon Finger Rings,' *Apollo* 14 [1931] 107 and fig. A. 11; Okasha 1971, 136-7

60
'ðancas' ring [lost]   Okasha 157
T. Beevor, *Memoirs illustrative of the History and Antiquities of Norfolk ...,* London 1851, xxx; Okasha 1971, 137

INDEX OF PRINTED EDITIONS

Algeo 1961
J.T..Algeo, 'Ælfric's *The Forty Soldiers*: An Edition' [Florida diss.] *DA* 20 [1961] 4656
B.1.3.12
Allen 1903
J.R. Allen, *The Early Christian Monuments of Scotland,* Edinburgh 1903, part 3
E.40, 52
Allen 1905
J.R. Allen in *Victoria History of the Counties of England: Derbyshire,* vol. 1, London 1905
E.3
Allen 1968
T.P. Allen, 'A Critical Edition of the Old English *Gospel of Nicodemus*' [Rice diss.]
DA 29 [1968] 1508A
B.8.5.2
d'Ardenne 1939
S.T.R.O. d'Ardenne, 'The Old English Inscription on the Brussels Cross,' *ES* 21 [1939]
145-64, 271-2
F.8
Arngart 1952
O. Arngart, *The Leningrad Bede,* EEMF 2, Copenhagen 1952
A.32.1
Arngart 1956
O. Arngart, *The Durham Proverbs,* Lunds Universitets Årsskrift, N.F. Avd. 1, Bd. 52, Nr. 2,
Lund 1956
C.25
Arnold 1890
T. Arnold, *Memorials of St. Edmund's Abbey,* Rolls Series 96, London 1890
B.16.5.1
Assmann 1888
B. Assmann, 'Eine Regel über den Donner,' *Anglia* 10 [1888] 185
B.23.3.5
Assmann 1889
B. Assmann, 'Prophezeiung aus dem 1. Januar für das Jahr,' *Anglia* 11 [1889] 369
B.23.3.5
Assmann 1889 [1964]
B. Assmann, *Angelsächsische Homilien und Heiligenleben,* Bib. ags. Prosa 3, Kassel 1889;
reprint with int. P. Clemoes, Darmstadt 1964
B.1.5.4-5, 1.5.8, 1.5.11, 1.5.14-5, 1.8.4-6, 3.2.6, 3.2.13, 3.2.16, 3.2.22, 3.3.14, 3.3.18,
3.3.35, 8.5.4
Assmann 1889
B. Assmann, 'Uebersetzung von Alcuins De virtutibus et vitiis liber ad Widonem comitem,'
Anglia 11 [1889] 371-91
B.9.7
Ball 1966
C.J.E. Ball, 'The Franks Casket: Right Side,' *ES* 47 [1966] 119-26
E.2

Banks 1965

R.A. Banks, 'Some Anglo-Saxon Prayers from British Museum Ms Cotton Galba A.XIV,'
N & Q 210 [1965] 207-13
B.12.4.4-5

Bately 1964

J.M. Bately, 'The Vatican Fragment of the Old English Orosius,' *ES* 45 [1964] 224-30
B.9.2

Bately in Evison 1967

J.M. Bately, 'Interpretation of the Runes on the Gilton Pommel' in V.I. Evison, 'The
Dover ring-sword and other sword-rings and beads,' *Archaeologia* 101 [1967] 97-102
E.21

Bately and Evison 1961

J.M. Bately and V.I. Evison, 'The Derby bone piece,' *Medieval Archaeology* 5 [1961]
301-5
E.15

Beevor 1851

T. Beevor, *Memoirs illustrative of the History and Antiquities of Norfolk ...*, London
1851
F.60

Belfour 1909

A.O. Belfour, *Twelfth-century Homilies in Ms. Bodley 343*, EETS 137, London 1909
[1962]
B.1.3.2, 1.4.6, 1.4.8, 1.4.13, 1.5.1-3, 1.5.6-7, 1.5.9, 3.2.11, 3.2.15, 3.2.40, 3.4.1-4

Berghaus and Schneider 1967

P. Berghaus and K. Schneider, *Anglo-friesisische Runensolidi im Lichte des Neufundes
von Schweindorf [Ostfriesland]*, Arbeitsgemeinschaft für Forschung des Landes
Nordrhein-Westfalen 134, Köln and Opladen 1967
E.18

Bethurum 1957

Dorothy Bethurum, *The Homilies of Wulfstan*, Oxford 1957
B.2, 3.2.23

Biddle 1966

M. Biddle, 'Excavations at Winchester, 1965,' *AJ* 46 [1966] 308-32
F.52

Birch 1885-99

W. de G. Birch, *Cartularium Saxonicum*, 3 vols., London 1885-99 [New York and
London 1964]
B.12.4.6, 15, 16

Birch 1892

W. de G. Birch, *Liber Vitae of New Minster and Hyde Abbey*, Hampshire Record Society,
London 1892
B10.7, 12.4.9, 12.10, 16.21.1-3, 18.6, 18.10, 24.16, 24.25.4

Bishop and Chaplais 1957

T.A.M. Bishop and P. Chaplais, *Facsimiles of English Royal Writs to AD 1100 presented
to V.H. Galbraith*, Oxford 1957
B.15

Blackburn 1907

F.A. Blackburn, *Exodus and Daniel, Two Old English Poems,* Belles Lettres Series, Boston 1907

A.1.2, 1.3

Hunter Blair 1959

P. Hunter Blair, *The Moore Bede,* EEMF 9, Copenhagen 1959

A.32.1, D.3

Blake 1962

E.O. Blake, *Liber Eliensis,* Royal Historical Society, Camden Society 3rd series 92, London 1962

A.45

Blake 1964

N.F. Blake, *The Phoenix,* Manchester 1964

A.3.4

Bliss 1971

A.J. Bliss, 'Some unnoticed lines of Old English verse,' *N & Q* 216 [1971] 404

A.1.1.1

Bond 1873-8

E.A. Bond, *Facsimiles of Ancient Charters in the British Museum,* London 1873-8

B.15

Bosworth 1859

J. Bosworth, *King Alfred's Anglo-Saxon Version of the compendious history of the world by Orosius,* London 1859

B.9.2

Bouterwek 1853

C.W. Bouterwek, 'Angelsächsische Glossen,' *ZfdA* 9 [1853] 401-530

C.31.1

Braekman 1963

W. Braekman, 'Ælfric's Old English Homily *De Doctrina Apostolica:* An Edition,' *SGG* 5 [1963] 141-73

B.1.4.20

Braekman 1965

W. Braekman, 'Some Minor Old English Texts,' *Archiv* 202 [1965] 271-6

B.12.4.5, 21.2.3

Braekman 1966

W. Braekman, '*Wyrdwriteras*: An Unpublished Ælfrician Text in Manuscript Hatton 115,' *RBPH* 44 [1966] 959-70

B.1.4.23

Braybrooke 1860

R.C. Neville, Baron Braybrooke, *A Catalogue of Rings in the Collection of the Right Hon. Lord Braybrooke, Audley End,* Saffron Walden 1860

F.13

Brennan 1967

F.C. Brennan, 'The Old English *Daniel*' [North Carolina diss.] *DA* 27 [1967] 3421A

A.1.3

Brenner 1908

E. Brenner, *Der altenglische Junius-Psalter,* AF 23, Heidelberg 1908

C.7.12

Bright 1884

J.W. Bright, 'Anglo-Saxon Glosses to Boethius,' *American Journal of Philology* 5 [1884] 488-92

C.9

Bright and Ramsay 1907

J.W. Bright and R.L. Ramsay, *The West-Saxon Psalms,* The Belles Lettres Series, Boston 1907

B.8.2

Brock in Morris 1874-80

E. Brock, 'The Blickling Glosses' in R. Morris, *The Blickling Homilies,* EETS 58, 63, 73, London 1874-80 [1967] 253-63

C.50.1

Bromwich 1958

J. Bromwich et al., *The Paris Psalter,* EEMF 8, Copenhagen 1958

A.5, B.8.2

Brooks 1961

K.R. Brooks, *Andreas and The Fates of the Apostles,* Oxford 1961

A.2.1, 2.2

Brotanek 1913

R. Brotanek, *Texte und Untersuchungen zur altenglischen Literatur und Kirchengeschichte,* Halle 1913

B.1.5.12, 3.2.49, 10.7

Brown 1970

A.K. Brown, 'The Epinal Glossary' [Stanford diss.] *DA* 30 [1970] 5428A

D.7, 36

Brown 1969

T.J. Brown, F. Wormald, A.S.C. Ross, E.G. Stanley, *The Durham Ritual: An English Collectar of the Tenth Century,* EEMF 16, Copenhagen 1969

B.12.1.1, 12.5.5, 14.41, 27.3.11, 28.1.1, C.2, 13, 18.1, 21

Baldwin Brown 1921

G. Baldwin Brown, *The Arts in Early England,* vol.5, London 1921

E.39

Baldwin Brown 1930

G. Baldwin Brown, *The Arts in Early England,* vol.6, London 1930

E.22

Brunner 1965

I.A. Brunner, 'The Anglo-Saxon Translation of the Distichs of Cato: A critical edition' [Columbia diss.] *DA* 26 [1965] 3296

B.7.1

Buchholz 1890

R. Buchholz, *Die Fragmente der Reden der Seele an den Leichnam,* Erlanger Beiträge zur englischen Philologie 2, Erlangen and Leipzig 1890

A.47, B.3.4.5

Cahen and Olsen 1930

Maurice Cahen and Magnus Olsen, 'L'inscription runique du coffret de Mortain,' Collection linguistique publiée par la société de linguistique de Paris 32, Paris 1930

E.36

Campbell 1938

A. Campbell, *The Battle of Brunanburh,* London 1938

A.10.1

Campbell 1950

A. Campbell, *Frithegodi Monachi Breviloquium Vitae Beati Wilfredi et Wulfstani Cantoris Narratio Metrica de Sancto Swithuno,* Thesaurus Mundi, Zurich 1950

C.68, 98.1

Campbell 1953

A. Campbell, *The Tollemache Orosius,* EEMF 3, Copenhagen 1953

B.9.2, 25.4.2, 27.3.14

Campbell 1959

J.J. Campbell, *The Advent Lyrics of the Exeter Book,* Princeton 1959

A.3.1

Campbell 1963

J.J. Campbell, 'Prayers from Ms Arundel 155,' *Anglia* 81 [1963] 82-117

C.23.1

Carnicelli 1969

T.A. Carnicelli, *King Alfred's Version of St. Augustine's Soliloquies,* Cambridge, Mass., 1969

B.9.4

Caro 1898

G. Caro, 'Die Varianten der Durhamer Hs. und des Tiberius-fragments der ae. Prosa-version der Benedictinerregel,' *Englische Studien* 24 [1898] 161-76

B.10.3.2

Chadwick 1901

H.M. Chadwick, 'Early Inscriptions in the North of England,' *Transactions of the York-shire Dialect Society* 1 [1901] 79-85

E.5, 20, 22, 23, 26, 28, 35, 47, F.14

Chambers [et al.] 1933

R.W. Chambers, M. Förster, R. Flower, *The Exeter Book of Old English Poetry,* London 1933

A.3, B.16.10.1-2, 16.10.5, 16.10.10

Chapman 1968

H.M. Chapman, 'An edition of the Old English poem *Judgement Day* [Ms CCCC 201]' [University of Wales, Aberystwyth, M.A.] *Index* 18 [1967-8] no.320

A.17

Clark 1958

C. Clark, *The Peterborough Chronicle 1070-1154,* Oxford 1958, 2nd ed. 1970

B.17.9

Clarke and Hinton 1971

J.R. Clarke and D.A. Hinton, *The Alfred and Minster Lovell Jewels,* Oxford 1971

F.4

Classen and Harmer 1926

E. Classen and F.E. Harmer, *An Anglo-Saxon Chronicle,* Manchester 1926

B.17.8

Clubb 1925

M.D. Clubb, *Christ and Satan, An Old English Poem,* Yale Studies in English 70, New Haven 1925

A.1.4

Cockayne 1861

T.O. Cockayne, *Narratiunculae Anglice Conscriptae,* London 1861

B.3.3.16

Cockayne 1864-6

T.O. Cockayne, *Leechdoms, Wortcunning and Starcraft of Early England,* Rolls Series 35,
3 vols., London 1864-6 [New York 1965]

B.3.3.26-7, 11.8, 17.11, 20.1.2, 20.2.2, 20.9, 20.11.2, 20.12.2, 21, 23.1.5, 23.1.9-10,
23.1.12, 23.3.3, 23.3.6, C.85, D.26

Colgrave 1956

B. Colgrave, *Felix's Life of St. Guthlac,* Cambridge 1956

C.66

Colgrave and Cramp n.d.

B. Colgrave and R. Cramp, *St. Peter's Church,* [Monkwearmouth] Gloucester n.d.

E.35

Colgrave and Hyde 1962

B. Colgrave and A. Hyde, 'Two Recently Discovered Leaves from Old English Manuscripts,' *Speculum* 37 [1962] 60-78

B.1.5.11, 3.3.5

Collingwood 1911

W.G. Collingwood et al., 'Proceedings' in *Transactions of the Cumberland and Westmoreland Antiquarian and Archaeological Society* n.s. 11 [1911] 481-3

F.23

Collingwood 1927

W.G. Collingwood, *Northumbrian Crosses of the Pre-Norman Age,* London 1927

F.9, 12, 38, 45, 47, 48, 56

Collins 1963

R.L. Collins, 'A Reexamination of the Old English Glosses in the *Blickling Psalter,'*
Anglia 81 [1963] 124-8

C.50.1

Cook 1900 [1964]

A.S. Cook, *The Christ of Cynewulf: A Poem in Three Parts,* Boston 1900, reprinted with
pref. by J.C. Pope, 1964

A.3.1

Cook 1914

A.S. Cook, *Some Accounts of the Bewcastle Cross between the years 1607 and 1861,*
Yale Studies in English 50, New York 1914

E.4

Cook 1921

A.S. Cook, *The Old English Physiologus,* Yale Studies in English 63, New Haven 1921

A.3.16-8

Cowen and Barty 1966

J.D. Cowen and E. Barty [Okasha], 'A lost Anglo-Saxon inscription recovered,'
Archaeologia Aeliana, 4th series, 44 [1966] 61-70

F.55

Cox 1972

R.S. Cox, 'The Old English Dicts of Cato,' *Anglia* 90 [1972] 1-42

B.7.1

Cramp 1964
R.J. Cramp, 'A Name-stone from Monkwearmouth,' *Archaeologia Aeliana,* 4th series, 42 [1964] 294-8
E.35, F.33

Cramp 1965
R.J. Cramp, *Durham Cathedral: A Short Guide to the Pre-Conquest Sculptured Stones in the Dormitory,* Durham 1965
F.15

Craster 1925
H.H.E. Craster, 'Some Anglo-Saxon Records of the See of Durham,' *Archaeologia Aeliana,* 4th series, 1 [1925] 189-98
B.16.8.3

Crawford [Roberts] 1967
Jane Crawford, '*Guthlac:* an edition of the Old English prose life, together with the poems in the *Exeter Book*' [Oxford D.Phil.] *Index* 17 [1966-7] no.331
A.3.2, B.3.3.10

Crawford 1920
S.J. Crawford, 'The Lincoln Fragment of the Old English Version of the Heptateuch,' *MLR* 15 [1920] 1-6
B.8.1.3

Crawford 1921 [1968]
S.J. Crawford, *Exameron Anglice or The Old English Hexameron,* Bib. ags. Prosa 10, Hamburg 1921 [Darmstadt 1968]
B.1.5.13

Crawford 1922 [1969]
S.J. Crawford, *The Old English Version of the Heptateuch,* EETS 160, London 1922, reprinted with additions by N.R. Ker 1969
B.1.8.4, 8.1

Crawford 1928
S.J. Crawford, 'The Worcester Marks and Glosses of the Old English Manuscripts in the Bodleian,' *Anglia* 52 [1928] 1-25
B.12.3.3

Crawford 1929 [1966]
S.J. Crawford, *Byrhtferth's Manual,* EETS 177, London 1929 [1966]
B.3.4.38-9, 20.2.3, 20.20.1

Davidson 1883
J.B. Davidson, 'On some Anglo-Saxon charters at Exeter,' *JBAA* 39 [1883] 259-303
B.15.1.52

Conway Davies 1957
J. Conway Davies, *The Cartae Antiquae Rolls 11-20,* Pipe Roll Society n.s. 33, London 1960 [for 1957]
B.15.1.68

Dawson 1953
R. MacG. Dawson, 'An edition of the Gnomic Poems' [Oxford B.Litt. 1953] *Index* 3 [1952-3] no.128
A.3.13, 15

Derolez 1954
R. Derolez, *Runica Manuscripta, The English Tradition,* Bruges 1954
B.25

Derolez 1956
R. Derolez, 'Zu den Brusseler Aldhelmglossen,' *Anglia* 74 [1956] 153-80
C.31.1
Dickins 1935
Bruce Dickins, 'Runic Rings and Old English Charms,' *Archiv* 167 [1935] 252
E6, 19, 25
Dickins 1938
Bruce Dickins, 'The Sandwich Runic Inscription RAEHAEBUL' in K.H. Schlottig, ed.,
Beiträge zur Runenkunde und nordischer Sprachwissenschaft, [Neckel Festschrift]
Leipzig 1938, 83-5
E.41
Dickins 1946
Bruce Dickins, 'The Dedication Stone of St. Mary-le-Wigford, Lincoln,' *The Archae-
ological Journal* 103 [1946] 163-5
F.27
Dickins 1950
Bruce Dickins, 'The Beheaded Manumission in the Exeter Book' in Cyril Fox and Bruce
Dickins, eds., *The Early Cultures of North-West Europe,* H.M. Chadwick Memorial
Studies, Cambridge 1950, 363-7
B.16.10.6
Dickins 1952
Bruce Dickins, *The Genealogical Preface to the Anglo-Saxon Chronicle,* Occasional
Papers: Number II printed for the Department of Anglo-Saxon, Cambridge 1952
B.18.1, 18.4
Dickins 1956
Bruce Dickins, 'The Inscriptions upon the Coffin' in F.C. Battiscombe, ed., *The Relics of
St. Cuthbert: Studies by various authors,* Oxford 1956, 305-7
E.31
Dickins and Ross 1934
Bruce Dickins and A.S.C. Ross, *The Dream of the Rood,* MOEL, London 1934, 4th ed.
1954
A.2.5, 40-1, E.39
Dickins and Ross 1940
Bruce Dickins and A.S.C. Ross, 'The Alnmouth Cross,' *JEGP* 39 [1940] 169-78
E.1, F.2
Dietz 1968
K. Dietz, 'Die ae. Psalterglossen der Hs. Cambridge, Pembroke College 312,' *Anglia* 86
[1968] 273-9
C.7.2
Dillard 1956
J.L. Dillard, *'De Parasceve:* An Old English vernacular Passion' [Texas diss.] *ADD* 16
[1956] 142
B.3.2.24
Dobbie 1937
E.V.K. Dobbie, *The Manuscripts of Cædmon's Hymn and Bede's Death Song,* Columbia
University Studies in English and Comparative Literature 128, New York 1937
A.32-3, D.3

Dobbie 1942
E.V.K. Dobbie, *The Anglo-Saxon Minor Poems,* ASPR 6, New York 1942
A.7-43
Dobbie 1953
E.V.K. Dobbie, *Beowulf and Judith,* ASPR 4, New York 1953
A.4
Doble 1937
G.H. Doble, *Pontificale Lanaletense,* Henry Bradshaw Society 74, London 1937
B.27.3.38, 28.5, C.82.4
Dugdale 1846
W. Dugdale, *Monasticon Anglicanum,* ed. J. Caley, H. Ellis, B. Bandinel, London 1846
B.15.2.20, 15.7.3
Dunning and Bliss 1969
T.P. Dunning and A.J. Bliss, *The Wanderer,* MOEL, London 1969
A.3.6
Earle 1888
J. Earle, *A Hand-book to the Land-Charters and other Saxonic Documents,* Oxford 1888
B.15-6
Eckhardt 1958
K.A. Eckhardt, *Leges Anglo-Saxonorum 601-925,* Göttingen 1958
B.14.1-7
Edwards 1866
E. Edwards, *Liber Monasterii de Hyda,* Rolls Series 45, London 1866
B.15.1.43, 15.4.2-4
Eliason and Clemoes 1966
N. Eliason and P. Clemoes, *Ælfric's First Series of Catholic Homilies,* EEMF 13, Copenhagen 1966
B.1.1
Elliott 1959
R.W.V. Elliott, *Runes, an Introduction,* Manchester 1959
E.2, 9, 15, 22-3, 26, 28, 39, 41, 46-7
Elliott 1959
R.W.V. Elliott, 'Two neglected English Runic Inscriptions: Gilton and Overchurch' in *Mélanges de Linguistique et de Philologie: Fernand Mossé in memoriam,* Paris 1959, 140-7
E.21, 38
Elliott 1964
R.W.V. Elliott, 'A Runic Fragment at Leek,' *Medieval Archaeology* 8 [1964] 213-4
E.30
Endter 1922 [1964]
W. Endter, *König Alfreds des Grossen Bearbeitung der Soliloquien des Augustinus,* Bib. ags. Prosa 11, Hamburg 1922 [Darmstadt 1964]
B.9.4
Evans and Serjeantson 1933
J. Evans and M.S. Serjeantson, *English Mediaeval Lapidaries,* EETS 190, London 1933
B.22.3
Evison 1960
V.I. Evison, Review of R.W.V. Elliott, *Runes, an Introduction,* AJ 40 [1960] 242-4
E.41

Evison 1964

V.I. Evison, 'The Dover Rune Brooch,' *AJ* 44 [1964] 242-5

E.16

Evison 1965

V.I. Evison, Review of D.M. Wilson, *Catalogue of Antiquities of the later Saxon period,* *AJ* 45 [1965] 288-90

E.46

Farmer 1968

D.H. Farmer, *The Rule of St. Benedict,* EEMF 15, Copenhagen 1968

B.27.3.34

Fehr 1914 [1966]

B. Fehr, *Die Hirtenbriefe Ælfrics,* Bib. ags. Prosa 9, Hamburg 1914, reprinted with supplement by P. Clemoes, Darmstadt 1966

B.1.8.1-3, 12.9, C.82.2

Fehr 1921

B. Fehr, 'Altenglische Ritualtexte für Krankenbesuch, heilige Oelung und Begräbnis' in M. Förster and K. Wildhagen, eds., *Texte und Forschungen zur englischen Kultur-geschichte: Festgabe für Felix Liebermann,* Halle 1921, 20-67

B.12.5.3, 12.5.11, C.82.3

Finberg 1964

H.P.R. Finberg, *The Early Charters of Wessex,* Leicester 1964

B.15.1.2

Fink 1957

A. Fink,' Zum Gandersheimer Runenkästchen' in *Karolingische und Ottonische Kunst,* Forschungen zur Kunstgeschichte und christlichen Archäologie 3, Wiesbaden 1957, 277-81

E.7

Flasdieck 1938

H. Flasdieck, 'Das Kasseler Bruchstück der *Cura Pastoralis,*' *Anglia* 62 [1938] 193-233

B.9.1

Flower 1937

R. Flower, 'The Text of the Burghal Hidage,' *London Mediaeval Studies* 1 [1937] 60-4

B.14.56, 16.26.1

Flower and Smith 1941

R. Flower and A.H. Smith, *The Parker Chronicle and Laws,* EETS 208, London 1941

A.10, B.14.4, 17.1

Förster 1897

M. Förster, 'Zu Adrian und Ritheus,' *Englische Studien* 23 [1897] 431-6

B.5.2

Förster 1901

M. Förster, 'Zur altenglischen Quintinus-Legende,' *Archiv* 106 [1901] 258-61

B.3.3.33

Förster 1901

M. Förster, 'Zum altenglische Boethius,' *Archiv* 106 [1901] 342-3

B.7.1

Förster 1902

M. Förster, 'Frühmittelenglische Sprichwörter,' *Englische Studien* 31 [1902] 1-20

B.7.4

Förster 1905

M. Förster, 'Ein altenglisches Prosa-Rätsel,' *Archiv* 115 [1905] 392-3

B.26

Förster 1906

M. Förster, 'Die Lösung des ae. Prosarätsels,' *Archiv* 116 [1906] 367-71

B.26

Förster 1906

M. Förster, 'Ae. *fregen* "die Frage," ' *Englische Studien* 36 [1906] 325-8

B.26

Förster 1908

M. Förster, 'Beiträge zur mittelalterlichen Volkskunde I,' *Archiv* 120 [1908] 43-52

B.23.3.1, C.16

Förster 1908

M. Förster, 'Beiträge zur mittelalterlichen Volkskunde II,' *Archiv* 120 [1908] 296-305

B.23.3.3, C.16

Förster 1908

M. Förster, 'Beiträge zur mittelalterlichen Volkskunde III,' *Archiv* 121 [1908] 30-46

B.12.4.3.2, 23.3.3

Förster 1909

M. Förster, 'Altenglische Predigtquellen II,' *Archiv* 122 [1909] 246-62

B.9.7

Förster 1910

M. Förster, 'Beiträge zur mittelalterlichen Volkskunde IV,' *Archiv* 125 [1910] 39-70

C.16

Förster 1912

M. Förster, 'Beiträge zur mittelalterlichen Volkskunde VI,' *Archiv* 128 [1912] 55-71

B.23.3.1

Förster 1912

M. Förster, 'Beiträge zur mittelalterlichen Volkskunde VII,' *Archiv* 128 [1912] 285-308

B.23.3.1

Förster 1912

M. Förster, 'Beiträge zur mittelalterlichen Volkskunde VIII,' *Archiv* 129 [1912] 16-49

B.23.3.1-3, C.16, 37

Förster 1913

M. Förster, *Il Codice Vercellese,* Rome 1913

A.2, B.3.1.2

Förster 1913

M. Förster, 'Der Vercelli-Codex CXVII nebst Abdruck einiger altenglischer Homilien der Handschrift' in F. Holthausen and H. Spies, eds., *Festschrift für Lorenz Morsbach,* Studien zur englischen Philologie 50, Halle 1913, 20-179

B.3.2.4, 3.2.33, 3.4.6-7

Förster 1914

M. Förster, 'Die altenglischen Beigaben des Lambeth-Psalters,' *Archiv* 132 [1914] 328-35

B.3.3.27, 17.10, C.14, 91.4

Förster 1916

M. Förster, 'Beiträge zur mittelalterlichen Volkskunde IX,' *Archiv* 134 [1916] 264-93

B.23.3.3

Förster 1916

M. Förster, 'Nochmals ae. *fregen* "Frage," ' *Archiv* 135 [1916] 399-401
B.26

Förster 1917

M. Förster, 'Die altenglische Glossenhandschrift Plantinus 32 [Antwerpen] und
Additional 32246 [London],' *Anglia* 41 [1917] 94-161
D.1

Förster 1918

M. Förster, 'Kleinere mittelenglische Texte,' *Anglia* 42 [1918] 145-223
B.24.21

Förster 1925

M. Förster, 'Die spätaltenglische Uebersetzung der Pseudo-Anselmschen Marienpredigt' in W. Dibelius, H. Hecht and W. Keller, eds., *Anglica, Untersuchungen zur
englischen Philologie, A. Brandl überreicht,* Palaestra 147, 148, II Leipzig 1925, 8-69
B.3.3.22

Förster 1925

M. Förster, 'Die Weltzeitalter bei den Angelsachsen' in Fr. Wild, ed., *Neusprachliche
Studien, Festgabe Karl Luick zu seinem sechzigsten Geburtstage,* Marburg 1925, 183-203
B.3.4.57, 24.25.3-4, 24.26

Förster 1925-6

M. Förster, 'Die altenglischen Traumlunare,' *Englische Studien* 60 [1925-6] 58-93
B.20.5, 23.2.1, 23.3.1-3, C.16

Förster 1927-8

M. Förster, 'Die altenglischen Texte der Pariser Nationalbibliothek,' *Englische Studien*
62 [1927-8] 113-31
B.10.7, 11.9.5

Förster 1929

M. Förster, 'Die altenglischen Verzeichnisse von Glücks- und Unglückstagen' in
K. Malone and M.B. Ruud, eds., *Studies in English Philology: A Miscellany in Honor of
Frederick Klaeber,* Minneapolis, Minn., 1929, 258-77
B.23.2.1, 23.2.3-5

Förster 1930

M. Förster, 'Die Freilassungsurkunden des Bodmin-Evangeliars' in N. Bøgholm,
A. Brusendorff and C.A. Bodelsen, eds., *A Grammatical Miscellany offered to Otto
Jespersen,* London and Copenhagen 1930, 77-99
B.16.4

Förster 1932 [1964]

M. Förster, *Die Vercelli-Homilien I-VIII Homilie,* Bib. ags. Prosa 12, Hamburg 1932
[Darmstadt 1964]
B.3.1.2

Förster 1937-8

M. Förster, 'König Eadgars Tod,' *Englische Studien* 62 [1937-8] 10-3
B.27.3.26

Förster 1941

M. Förster, *Der Flussname Themse und seine Sippe,* Sitzungsberichte der Bayerischen
Akademie der Wissenschaften, Phil.-Hist. Abt., Jahrgang 1941, Band 1, Munich 1941
B.16.3, 16.11.1

Förster 1942

M. Förster, 'Zur Liturgik der angelsächsischen Kirche,' *Anglia* 66 [1942] 1-51
B.11.9.1, 12.4.8

Förster 1942-3

M. Förster, 'Die altenglischen Bekenntnisformeln,' *Englische Studien* 75 [1942-3] 159-69
B. 12.3.2

Förster 1943

M. Förster, *Zur Geschichte des Reliquienkultus in Altengland,* Sitzungsberichte der Bayerischen Akademie der Wissenschaften, Phil.-Hist. Abt., Jahrgang 1943, Heft 8, Munich 1943
B.16.10.8, 16.21.3

Förster 1944

M. Förster, 'Vom Fortleben antiker Sammellunare im Englischen und in anderen Volkssprachen,' *Anglia* 67 [1944] 1-171
C.16

Förster 1955

M. Förster, 'A New Version of the Apocalypse of Thomas in Old English,' *Anglia* 73 [1955] 6-36
B.3.4.12

Förster and Napier 1906

M. Förster and A.S. Napier, 'Englische Cato- und Ilias-Glossen des 12. Jahrhunderts,' *Archiv* 117 [1906] 17-28
C.55.2, 72

Fowler 1881

J.T. Fowler, *Memorials of the Church of SS. Peter and Wilfrid, Ripon,* I, Surtees Society 74, Durham 1881
B.15.1.26

Fowler 1965

Roger Fowler, 'A Late Old English Handbook for the Use of a Confessor,' *Anglia* 83 [1965] 1-34
B.11.4

Fowler 1972

Roger Fowler, *Wulfstan's Canons of Edgar,* EETS 266, London 1972
B.13.1.1, 13.6

Galbraith 1968

K.J. Galbraith, 'Early Sculpture at St. Nicholas' Church, Ipswich,' *Proceedings of the Suffolk Institute of Archaeology* 31 [1968] 172-84
F.21

Garmonsway 1939

G.N. Garmonsway, *Ælfric's Colloquy,* MOEL, London 1939, 2nd ed. 1947 [1965]
C.3

Garrett 1908

R.M. Garrett, 'Middle English and French Glosses from Ms Stowe 57,' *Archiv* 121 [1908] 411-2
C.81

Geoghegan 1969
P.M. Geoghegan, *'Judgment Day II*: An edition' [Illinois diss.] *DA* 30 [1969] 280A
A.17
Gerritsen 1969
J. Gerritsen, 'The Text of the Leiden Riddle,' *ES* 50 [1969] 529-44
A.34
Getty 1970
S.S. Getty, 'An Edition with Commentary of the Latin/Anglo-Saxon *Liber Scintillarum*'
[Pennsylvania diss.] *DA* 31 [1970] 1250A
C.15
Gibbs 1939
M. Gibbs, *Early Charters of the Cathedral Church of St. Paul, London,* Camden Society
Third Series 58, London 1939
B.15.7.9
Glogger 1901-8
P. Glogger, *Das Leidener Glossar,* Augsburg 1901-8
D.41
Gneuss 1968
H. Gneuss, *Hymnar und Hymnen im englischen Mittelalter,* Buchreihe der Anglia 12,
Tübingen 1968
C.18.3, 73.2
Goetz 1882-1923
G. Goetz, *Corpus Glossariorum Latinorum,* 5 vols., Leipzig and Berlin 1882-1923
D.26, 36
Gollancz 1927
I. Gollancz, *The Caedmon Manuscript of Anglo-Saxon Biblical Poetry,* Oxford 1927
A.1
Gonser 1909
P. Gonser, *Das angelsächsische Prosa-leben des heiligen Guthlac,* AF 27, Heidelberg 1909
B.3.3.10
Goolden 1958
P. Goolden, *The Old English 'Apollonius of Tyre,'* London 1958
B.4.1
Gordon 1937
E.V. Gordon, *The Battle of Maldon,* MOEL, London 1937, 2nd ed. 1957
A.9
Gordon 1960
I.L. Gordon, *The Seafarer,* MOEL London 1960
A.3.9
Gradon 1958
P.O.E. Gradon, *Cynewulf's Elene,* MOEL, London 1958
A.2.6
Grattan and Singer 1952
J.H.G. Grattan and C. Singer, *Anglo-Saxon Magic and Medicine,* Publications of the
Wellcome Historical Medical Museum n.s. 3, London 1952
A.43.2-6, B.21.3, C.22

Greeson 1971
H.S. Greeson, Jr, 'Two Old English Observance Poems: *Seasons for Fasting* and *The Menologium*: An Edition' [Oregon diss.] *DA* 31 [1971] 3503A
A.14, 31

Grünberg 1967
M. Grünberg, *The West Saxon Gospels,* Amsterdam 1967
B.8.4.2

Gunther 1925
R.T. Gunther, *The Herbal of Apuleius Barbarus,* Roxburghe Club, Oxford 1925
B.21.1.2, C.71.3

Guntner 1970
J.C. Guntner, 'An Edition of Three Old English Poems' [Wisconsin diss.] *DA* 31 [1970] 2877A
A.3.10, 3.14, 3.25

Haddan and Stubbs 1869-71
A.W. Haddan and W. Stubbs, *Councils and Ecclesiastical Documents relating to Great Britain and Ireland,* 3 vols., Oxford 1869-71
C.56

Hall 1920
J. Hall, *Selections from Early Middle English,* Oxford 1920
A.46, B.3.4.5, 3.4.13

Hallander 1968
L.-G. Hallander, 'Two Old English Confessional Prayers,' *Stockholm Studies in Modern Philology,* n.s.3 [1968] 87-110
B.11.9.3, 12.4.3.3

Harder 1931
Hermann Harder, 'Eine angelsächsische Runeninschrift,' *Archiv* 160 [1931] 87-9
E.19, 25

Harder 1932
Hermann Harder, 'Eine angelsächsische Ring-Inschrift,' *Archiv* 161 [1932] 37-9
E.27

Harder 1932
Hermann Harder, 'Die Runen der ags. Schwertinschrift im Britischen Museum,' *Archiv* 161 [1932] 86-7
E.9

Harder 1932
Hermann Harder, 'Das Braunschweiger Runenkästchen,' *Archiv* 162 [1932] 227-9
E.7

Harder 1936
Hermann Harder, 'Die Inschriften angelsächsischer Runenringe,' *Archiv* 169 [1936] 224-8
E.19, 25

Hargreaves and Clark 1965
H. Hargreaves and C. Clark, 'An unpublished Old English Psalter-gloss fragment,' *N & Q* 210 [1965] 443-6
C.50.2

Harmer 1914
F.E. Harmer, *Select English Historical Documents of the Ninth and Tenth Centuries,*

Cambridge 1914

B.15, 16.6.6

Harmer 1952

F.E. Harmer, *Anglo-Saxon Writs,* Manchester 1952

B.6.2, 15-6

Harmer 1959

F.E. Harmer, 'A Bromfield and a Coventry Writ of King Edward the Confessor' in
P. Clemoes, ed., *The Anglo-Saxons, Studies … presented to Bruce Dickins,* London 1959,
89-103

B.15.1.105, 15.1.164

Harsley 1889

F. Harsley, *Eadwine's Canterbury Psalter,* EETS 92, London 1889

A.51, C.7.3, 11.2

Hart 1966

C. Hart, *The Early Charters of Eastern England,* Leicester 1966

B.15.7.1

Hausknecht 1883

E. Hausknecht, 'Die altenglischen Glossen des Codex ms 1650 der kgl. Bibliothek zu
Brüssel,' *Anglia* 6 [1883] 96-103

C.31.1

Hawkes and Page 1967

S.C. Hawkes and R.I. Page, 'Swords and Runes in south-east England,' *AJ* 47 [1967]
1-26

E.9, 21, 32, 34, 42-3, 49

Hearne 1720

T. Hearne, *Textus Roffensis,* Oxford 1720

B.18.7

Hecht 1900-7 [1965]

H. Hecht, *Bischof Waerferths von Worcester Uebersetzung der Dialoge Gregors des
Grossen,* Bib. ags. Prosa 5, Leipzig and Hamburg 1900-7 [Darmstadt 1965]

A.38, B.9.5

Hempl 1903

George Hempl, 'The Runic Inscription on the Isle of Wight Sword,' *PMLA* 18 [1903]
95-8

E.9

Hempl 1903-4

George Hempl, 'Hickes's Additions to the Runic Poem,' *MP* 1 [1903-4] 135-41

B.25.1.1

Henel 1934

H. Henel, *Studien zum altenglischen Computus,* Beiträge zur englischen Philologie 26,
Leipzig 1934 [1967]

B.20, 27.2.6

Henel 1934-5

H. Henel, 'Altenglischer Mönchsaberglaube,' *Englische Studien* 69 [1934-5] 329-49

B.12.6.2, 19.6, 23.2.2, 23.2.5-6, 23.4, C.67

Henel 1937

H. Henel, 'Ein Bruchstück aus Byrhtferþs *Handbuch,*' *Anglia* 61 [1937] 122-5

B.20.20.2

Henel 1942 [1971]
H. Henel, *Ælfric's De Temporibus Anni*, EETS 213, London 1942 [1971]
B.1.9.4

Herzfeld 1900
G. Herzfeld, *An Old English Martyrology*, EETS 116, London 1900
B.19.1-2, 19.5-6

Hessels 1890
J.H. Hessels, *An Eighth-Century Latin-Anglo-Saxon Glossary*, Cambridge 1890
D.4

Hessels 1906
J.H. Hessels, *A Latin-Anglo-Saxon Glossary*, Cambridge 1906
D.41

Hickes 1705 [1970]
G. Hickes, *Linguarum Vett. Septentrionalium Thesaurus*, Oxford 1705 [Hildesheim and New York 1970]
A.7, 11-2, B.16.1, 16.10.2, 25.1

Hilbelink 1930
A.J.G. Hilbelink, *Cotton Ms Vitellius C.III of the Herbarium Apuleii*, Amsterdam 1930
B.21.1.1

Hill 1969
David Hill, 'The Burghal Hidage: The Establishment of a Text,' *Medieval Archaeology* 13 [1969] 84-92
B.16.26.1

Hofmann 1963
J. Hofmann, 'Altenglische und althochdeutsche Glossen aus Würzburg und dem weiteren angelsächsischen Missionsgebiet,' *BGDSL* [Halle] 85 [1963] 27-131
C.51.3, 63, 78.3-4, 89.4

Holthausen 1889
F. Holthausen, 'Anglo-Saxonica,' *Anglia* 11 [1889] 170-4
B.11.11

Holthausen 1890
F. Holthausen, 'Angelsächsisches aus Kopenhagen,' *ZfdA* 34 [1890] 228
B.3.4.14

Holthausen 1913
F. Holthausen, 'Das altenglische Reimlied' in F. Holthausen and H. Spies, eds., *Festschrift für Lorenz Morsbach*, Studien zur englischen Philologie 50, Halle 1913, 190-200
A.3.15

Holthausen 1914
F. Holthausen, *Die ältere Genesis*, Heidelberg 1914
A.1.1

Holthausen 1916-7
F. Holthausen, 'Die Leidener Glossen,' *Englische Studien* 50 [1916-7] 327-40
D.41

Holthausen 1917
F. Holthausen, 'Die altenglischen Beda-Glossen,' *Archiv* 136 [1917] 290-2
D.12

Holthausen 1941
F. Holthausen, 'Altenglische Interlinearversionen lateinischer Gebete und Beichten,'

Anglia 65 [1941] 230-54
C.23.1
Holthausen 1942-3
F. Holthausen, 'Eine altenglische Interlinearversion des athanasianischen Glaubens-
bekenntnisses,' *Englische Studien* 75 [1942-3] 6-8
C.11.8
Horst 1896
K. Horst, 'Die Reste der Handschrift G der altenglischen Annalen,' *Englische Studien*
22 [1896] 447-50
B.17.5
Hulme 1898
W.H. Hulme, 'The Old English Version of the Gospel of Nicodemus,' *PMLA* 13 [1898]
457-542
B.8.5.2
Hulme 1903-4
W.H. Hulme, 'The Old English Gospel of Nicodemus,' *MP* 1 [1903-4] 579-614
B.3.2.29, 8.5.3
Hunt 1961
R.W. Hunt, *Saint Dunstan's Classbook from Glastonbury,* Umbrae Codicum
Occidentalium 4, Amsterdam 1961
B.3.3.6, 27.3.30
Hunt 1893
W. Hunt, *Two Chartularies of the Priory of St. Peter at Bath,* Somerset Record Society
7, London 1893
B.16.2.2, 16.2.4
Ingram 1823
J. Ingram, *The Saxon Chronicle,* Oxford 1823
A.52, B.18.7
Irving 1953
Edward B. Irving, Jr, *The Old English Exodus,* Yale Studies in English 122, New Haven
1953
A.1.2
James 1912
M.R. James, *A Descriptive Catalogue of the Manuscripts in the Library of Corpus Christi
College, Cambridge,* 2 vols. Cambridge 1912
B.12.6.1
James 1929
M.R. James, *Marvels of the East,* Roxburghe Club, Oxford 1929
B.22.2
James 1935
M.R. James, *The Canterbury Psalter,* London 1935
A.51, B.27.3.8, C.7.3
Jørgensen 1933
E. Jørgensen, 'Bidrag til ældre nordisk Kirke- og Litteraturhistorie,' *Nordisk Tidskrift
för Bok- och Biblioteksväsen* 20 [1933] 186-98
B.16.20.2
Jones 1943
C.W. Jones, *Bedae Opera de Temporibus,* Mediaeval Academy of America Publ. 41,

Cambridge, Mass., 1943
B.24.3, C.44.2

Jones 1968
F.G. Jones, Jr, 'The Old English *Rune Poem*: An Edition' [Florida diss.] *DA* 29
[1968] 231A
A.12

Jost 1959
K. Jost, *Die 'Institutes of Polity, Civil and Ecclesiastical,'* Swiss Studies in English 47,
Bern 1959
B.1.9.9, 2.2.7, 3.4.37, 13.1.1, 13.2-4, 13.6

Judge 1934
C.B. Judge, 'Anglo-Saxonica in Hereford Cathedral Library,' *Harvard Studies and Notes
in Philology and Literature* 16 [1934] 89-96
B.16.11.2-3

Keller 1906
W. Keller, *Angelsächsische Palaeographie*, Palaestra 43, Berlin 1906
B.15.6.36

Kemble 1839-48 [1964]
J.M. Kemble, *Codex Diplomaticus Aevi Saxonici*, English Historical Society, London
1839-48 [1964]
B.15-6

Kemble 1848
J.M. Kemble, *The Dialogue of Salomon and Saturnus*, Ælfric Society, London 1848
A.13, B.3.4.15, 5.1-2

Kendrick 1956-60
T.D. Kendrick et al., *Codex Lindisfarnensis*, Olten-Lausanne 1956-60
B.28.1.2, C.8.1

Ker 1939
N.R. Ker, 'The Hague Manuscript of the Epistola Cuthberti de obitu Bedae with Bede's
Death Song,' *MÆ* 8 [1939] 40-4
A.33.2

Ker 1940
N.R. Ker, 'An Eleventh-Century Old English Legend of the Cross before Christ,' *MÆ* 9
[1940] 84-5
B.3.3.5

Ker 1943
N.R. Ker, 'Aldred the Scribe,' *Essays and Studies* 28 [1943] 7-12
B.28.1.2

Ker 1948
N.R. Ker, 'Hemming's Cartulary: a description of the two Worcester Cartularies in
Cotton Tiberius A.XIII' in R.W. Hunt, W.A. Pantin and R.W. Southern, eds., *Studies in
Medieval History presented to F.M. Powicke*, Oxford 1948, 49-75
B.15.7.30, 16.23.4

Ker 1949
N.R. Ker, 'Old English Notes signed "Coleman," ' *MÆ* 18 [1949] 29-31
B.27.1

Ker 1956
N.R. Ker, *The Pastoral Care*, EEMF 6, Copenhagen 1956
A.36-7, B.9.1, 16.23.2, 27.3.33

Ker 1957
N.R. Ker, *Catalogue of Manuscripts containing Anglo-Saxon,* Oxford 1957
Ker 1959
N.R. Ker, 'Three Old English Texts in a Salisbury Pontifical, Cotton Tiberius C.I' in
P. Clemoes, ed., *The Anglo-Saxons, Studies ... presented to Bruce Dickins,* London
1959, 262-79
B.3.2.50, 3.5.7, 11.10.4
Ker 1962
N.R. Ker, 'The Bodmer Fragment of Ælfric's Homily for Septuagesima Sunday' in
N. Davis and C.L. Wrenn, eds., *English and Medieval Studies Presented to J.R.R. Tolkien,*
London 1962, 77-83
B.1.2.6
Kermode 1907
P.M.C. Kermode, 'Inscription in Anglian Runes from Kirk Maughold, Isle of Man,'
Reliquary, n.s. 13 [1907] 265-7
E.24
Kermode 1908
P.M.C. Kermode, 'Some Early Christian Monuments recently discovered at Kirk
Maughold, Isle of Man,' *Reliquary,* n.s. 14 [1908] 182-93
E.24
Kimmens 1969
A.C. Kimmens, 'An edition of the British Museum Ms Stowe 2: *The Stowe Psalter'*
[Princeton diss.] *DA* 30 [1969] 1139A
C.7.10
Kindschi 1956
L. Kindschi, 'The Latin-Old English Glossaries in Plantin-Moretus 32 and British Museum
Ms Additional 32246' [Stanford diss.] *DA* 16 [1956] 117
D.1
Klaeber 1950
F. Klaeber, *Beowulf and The Fight at Finnsburg,* 3rd ed. with 1st and 2nd supplements,
Boston 1950
A.4.1, 7
Kluge 1885
F. Kluge, 'Fragment eines angelsächsischen Briefes,' *Englische Studien* 8 [1885] 62-3
B.1.8.7
Kluge 1885
F. Kluge, 'Zur Geschichte der Zeichensprache. Angelsächsische Indicia Monasterialia,'
Techmers internationale Zeitschrift für Sprachwissenschaft 2 [1885] 116-37
B.24.2
Kluge 1885
F. Kluge, 'Zu altenglischen Dichtungen,' *Englische Studien* 8 [1885] 472-9
B.3.4.16-7
Krämer 1902
Ernst Krämer, *Die altenglischen Metra des Boetius,* Bonner Beiträge zur Anglistik 8,
Bonn 1902
A.6
Krapp 1931
G.P. Krapp, *The Junius Manuscript,* ASPR 1, New York 1931
A.1

Krapp 1932

G.P. Krapp, *The Vercelli Book,* ASPR 2, New York 1932

A.2

Krapp 1932

G.P. Krapp, *The Paris Psalter and the Meters of Boethius,* ASPR 5, New York 1932

A.5-6

Krapp and Dobbie 1936

G.P. Krapp and E.V.K. Dobbie, *The Exeter Book,* ASPR 3, New York 1936

A.3

Kuhn 1965

S.M. Kuhn, *The Vespasian Psalter,* Ann Arbor 1965

C.7.7, 11.6, 18.4

Kuypers 1902

A.B. Kuypers, *The Book of Cerne,* Cambridge 1902

B.12.5.1, C.83, 91.1

van Langenhove 1941

G. van Langenhove, *Aldhelm's De Laudibus Virginitatis,* Rijksuniversiteit te Gent. Werken uitgegeven door de Faculteit van de Wijsbegeerte en Letteren. Extra Serie: Facsimiles, 2, Bruges 1941

C.31.1

Leonhardi 1905

G. Leonhardi, *Kleinere angelsächsische Denkmäler,* Bib. ags. Prosa 6, Hamburg 1905

B.21.2.1, 21.2.4

Leslie 1961

R.F. Leslie, *Three Old English Elegies,* Manchester 1961 [1966]

A.3.23, 3.32-3

Leslie 1966

R.F. Leslie, *The Wanderer,* Manchester 1966

A.3.6

Liber Vitae 1923

Liber Vitae Ecclesiae Dunelmensis, Surtees Society 136, Durham 1923

B.15.7.6-8, 16.8.2

Liebermann 1879

F. Liebermann, *Ungedruckte anglonormannische Geschichtsquellen,* Strassburg 1879 [1966]

B.17.2

Liebermann 1889

F. Liebermann, *Die Heiligen Englands,* Hannover 1889

B.18.8-9

Liebermann 1894

F. Liebermann, 'Aus Ælfrics Grammatik und Glossar,' *Archiv* 92 [1894] 413-5

B.1.9.2, D.22

Liebermann 1903-16 [1960]

F. Liebermann, *Die Gesetze der Angelsachsen,* Halle 1903-16 [Aalen 1960]

B.12.1, 14, 16.24.5, C.59

Liles 1967

B.L. Liles, '*The Canterbury Psalter*: An edition with notes and glossary' [Stanford diss.] *DA* 28 [1967] 1053A

C.7.3, 11.2

Lindelöf 1909

U. Lindelöf, 'Die altenglischen Glossen im Bosworth-Psalter,' *Mémoires de la société néophilologique de Helsingfors* 5 [1909] 137-230

C.7.4, 11.3

Lindelöf 1909-14

U. Lindelöf, *Der Lambeth-Psalter,* Acta Societatis Scientiarum Fennicae 35, i and 43, iii, Helsinki 1909-14

C.7.11, 11.11

von Lindheim 1941

B. von Lindheim, *Das Durhamer Pflanzenglossar,* Beiträge zur englischen Philologie 35, Bochum-Langendreer 1941

D.6

Lindsay 1921

W.M. Lindsay, *The Corpus Glossary,* Cambridge 1921

D.4

Löhe 1907

H. Löhe, *Be Domes Dæge,* Bonner Beiträge zur Anglistik 22, Bonn 1907

A.17

Logeman 1888

H. Logeman, *The Rule of St. Benet,* EETS 90, London 1888

C.4, 17

Logeman 1889

H. Logeman, 'Anglo-Saxonica Minora,' *Anglia* 11 [1889] 97-120

B.1.6.3, 11.9.3-4, 12.3.1, 12.4.1, 12.4.3.4-5, 18.11, 23.1.11, 24.5, C.23.1

Logeman 1889

H. Logeman, 'Anglo-Saxonica Minora,' *Anglia* 12 [1889] 497-518

B.1.2.8, 9.4, 11.1.4, 11.9.3, 11.10.3, 12.4.3.1, 12.4.3.3

Logeman 1890

H. Logeman, 'Zu Wright-Wülcker I, 204-303,' *Archiv* 85 [1890] 316-8

D.2

Logeman 1891

H. Logeman, 'New Aldhelm Glosses,' *Anglia* 13 [1891] 26-41

C.31.14

Logeman 1891-3

W. Logeman, 'De consuetudine monachorum,' *Anglia* 13 [1891] 365-448; *Anglia* 15 [1893] 20-40

C.27

Loyn 1971

H.R. Loyn, *A Wulfstan Manuscript,* EEMF 17, Copenhagen 1971

B.2.2.8, 2.4.1-3, 13.2, 13.4, 14.4, 14.13, 14.16-7, 14.23, 14.26, 14.30, 14.51-4

Lumby 1876 [1964]

J.R. Lumby, *Be domes dæge,* EETS 65, London 1876 [1964]

A.17-21

Macalister 1929

R.A.S. Macalister, 'The Ancient Inscriptions of the south of England,' *Archaeologia Cambrensis* 84 [1929] 179-96

F.25

McAllister 1952-3
D.H. McAllister, 'An Edition of the Mercian Portions of the Rushworth Manuscript'
[Oxford B.Litt.] *Index* 3 [1952-3] no.129
C.8.2
McCabe 1969
L.L.R. McCabe, 'An edition and translation of a 10th-century Anglo-Saxon Homily'
[Minnesota diss.] *DA* 29 [1969] 3978A
B.3.2.40
McIntosh 1949
A. McIntosh, 'Wulfstan's Prose,' *PBA* 35 [1949] 129-30
B.1.9.8
MacLean 1884
G.E. MacLean, 'Ælfric's Version of *Alcuini Interrogationes Sigeuulfi in Genesin*,' *Anglia*
7 [1884] 1-59
B.1.6.1
Magoun 1945
F.P. Magoun, Jr, 'The Domitian Bilingual of the *Old-English Annals*: Notes on the F-
Text,' *MLQ* 6 [1945] 371-80
B.17.3
Malone 1933
K. Malone, *Deor,* MOEL, London 1933, 4th ed. 1966
A.3.20
Malone 1962
K. Malone, *Widsith,* Copenhagen 1962
A.3.11
Malone 1963
K. Malone, *The Nowell Codex,* EEMF 12, Copenhagen 1963
A.4, B.22.1-2
Manitius 1901
M. Manitius, 'Angelsächsische Glossen in Dresdner Handschriften,' *Anglia* 24 [1901]
428-35
C.71.2
Mann 1962-3
M.I. Mann, 'Ælfric's *De Veteri Testamento et Novo*' [Birmingham MA thesis] *Index* 13
[1962-3] no.153
B.1.8.4
Masi 1969
M. Masi, 'Three Homilies by Ælfric: The Lives of Saints Gregory, Cuthbert and Martin:
An Edition' [Northwestern diss.] *DA* 29 [1969] 4009A
B.1.2.10-1, 1.2.42
Mason and Valentine 1928
J.R. Mason and H. Valentine, 'Find of pre-Norman Stones at St. Michael's Church,
Workington,' *Transactions of the Cumberland and Westmoreland Antiquarian and
Archaeological Society,* n.s. 28 [1928] 59-62
F.54
Matthews 1965-6
P.M. Matthews, 'The Old English Life of Saint Pantaleon' [University College, London,
MA diss.] *Index* 16 [1965-6] no.235
B.3.3.30

Menner 1941
R.J. Menner, *The Poetical Dialogues of Solomon and Saturn,* MLA Monograph Series 13,
New York 1941
A.13
Meritt 1933
H.D. Meritt, 'Old English Scratched Glosses in Cotton Ms Tiberius C.II,' *American Journal
of Philology* 54 [1933] 305-22
C.45.1
Meritt 1934
H.D. Meritt, 'Old English Entries in a Manuscript at Bern,' *JEGP* 33 [1934] 343-51
B.16.3
Meritt 1945
H.D. Meritt, *Old English Glosses: A Collection,* MLA General Series 16, New York 1945
[1971]
C.31.3, 31.7, 32.6, 45-7, 51.4, 53.3, 55.1, 57, 61, 66.2, 66.4, 69.2, 71, 76, 78, 88, 92.1,
93, 94.3-4, 94.7, 97.2-4, 98.1, D.5, 18, 20, 32, 39-40, 42, 47, 51, 54
Meritt 1952
H.D. Meritt, 'Old English Aldhelm Glosses,' *MLN* 67 [1952] 553-4
C.31.2
Meritt 1957
H.D. Meritt, 'Old English Glosses to Gregory, Ambrose and Prudentius,' *JEGP* 56 [1957] 65-8
C.35, 70.2
Meritt 1959
H.D. Meritt, *The Old English Prudentius Glosses at Boulogne-sur-Mer,* Stanford Studies
in Language and Literature 16, Stanford 1959 [New York 1967]
C.94.1
Meritt 1961
H.D. Meritt, 'Old English Glosses, Mostly Dry Point,' *JEGP* 60 [1961] 441-50
C.31.2, 33.5, 51.2-3, 53.2, 63, 65, 77.1, 78.1, D.11, 16.2, 17, 19
Miller 1890-8
T.Miller, *The Old English Version of Bede's Ecclesiastical History of the English People,*
EETS 95, 96, 110, 111, London 1890-8 [1959-63]
B.9.6
Mone 1830
F.J. Mone, *Quellen und Forschungen zur Geschichte der teutschen Literatur und Sprache,*
Aachen and Leipzig, 1830
B.11.5
Morey 1937
Adrian Morey, *Bartholomew of Exeter, Bishop and Canonist,* Cambridge 1937
B.12.4.1
Morris 1868
R. Morris, *Old English Homilies, First Series,* EETS 29, 34, London 1868
B.1.3.17, 1.6.2
Morris 1871
R. Morris, *Legends of the Holy Rood,* EETS 46, London 1871
B.3.3.6
Morris 1874-80 [1967]
R. Morris, *The Blickling Homilies,* EETS 58, 63, 73, London 1874-80 [1967]
B.3.1.1

Morris 1874-80 [1967]
R. Morris, *The Blickling Homilies,* EETS 58, 63, 73, London 1874-80 [1967]
B.3.1.1
Mossé 1955
F. Mossé, 'Another Lost Manuscript of the Old English *Orosius?' ES* 36 [1955] 199-203
B.9.2
Musset 1965
L. Musset, *Introduction à la Runologie,* Bibliothèque de philologie germanique 20,
Paris 1965
E.2, 15, 28, 36, 38, 47-8
Napier 1883 [1967]
A.S. Napier, *Wulfstan,* Sammlung englischer Denkmäler 4, Berlin 1883, repr. with app.,
K. Ostheeren 1967
B.1.2.8, 1.6.3, 2, 3.2.40, 3.4.21-50, 11.1.5, 24.25.2
Napier 1887
A.S. Napier, 'A Fragment of Ælfric's *Lives of Saints*,' *MLN* 2 [1887] 377-80
B.1.3.4
Napier 1887
A.S. Napier, 'Bruchstück einer altenglischen Boetiushandschrift,' *ZfdA* 31 [1887] 52-4
B.9.3
Napier 1888
A.S. Napier, 'Ein altenglisches Leben des heiligen Chad,' *Anglia* 10 [1888] 131-56
B.3.4.51-2
Napier 1888
A.S. Napier, 'Altenglische Glossen,' *Englische Studien* 11 [1888] 62-7
D.21
Napier 1889
A.S. Napier, 'Altenglische Kleinigkeiten,' *Anglia* 11 [1889] 1-10
B.12.10, 20.8, 24.10-9, 24.26.3
Napier 1890
A.S. Napier, 'Altenglische Miscellen,' *Archiv* 84 [1890] 323-7
B.21.5.2, 23.1.18
Napier 1891
A.S. Napier, 'Bruchstücke einer altenglischen Evangelienhandschrift,' *Archiv* 87
[1891] 255-61
B.8.4.9
Napier 1893
A.S. Napier, 'Fragments of an Ælfric Manuscript,' *MLN* 8 [1893] 398-400
B.1.1.2
Napier 1893
A.S. Napier, 'Collation der altenglischen Aldhelmglossen des Codex 38 der Kathedral-
bibliothek zu Salisbury, ' *Anglia* 15 [1893] 204-9
C.31.14
Napier 1894
A.S. Napier, *History of the Holy Rood-Tree,* EETS 103, London 1894
B.3.3.5
Napier 1897
A.S. Napier, 'Two Old English Fragments,' *MLN* 12 [1897] 105-14
B.10.4.3, 18.3

Napier 1900
A.S. Napier, *Old English Glosses,* Anecdota Oxoniensia, Mediaeval and Modern Series 11, Oxford 1900
B.8.3, 27.2.2, 27.3.22, 27.3.29, C, D.9, 16.3, 21, 24, 46
Napier 1901
A.S. Napier, 'Contributions to Old English Literature 1. An Old English Homily on the Observance of Sunday' in *An English Miscellany presented to Dr. Furnivall,* Oxford 1901, 355-62
B.3.4.53
Napier 1901
A.S. Napier, 'Contributions to Old English Literature 2. The Franks Casket' in *An English Miscellany presented to Dr. Furnivall,* Oxford 1901, 362-81
A.42, E.2
Napier 1903-4
A.S. Napier, 'Notes on the Blickling Homilies,' *MP* 1 [1903-4] 303-8
B.3.3.17
Napier 1903-6
A.S. Napier, 'Contributions to Old English Lexicography,' *TPS* [1903-6] 265-358
D.28
Napier 1907-10
A.S. Napier, 'An Old English Vision of Leofric, Earl of Mercia,' *TPS* [1907-10] 180-8
B.4.2
Napier 1913
A.S. Napier, 'Two Fragments of Alfred's "Orosius," ' *MLR* 8 [1913] 59-63
B.9.2
Napier 1916
A.S. Napier, *The Old English Version, with the Latin Original, of the Enlarged Rule of Chrodegang,* EETS 150, London 1916
B.10.4.1, 10.6.2, C.5
Napier and Stevenson 1895
A.S. Napier and W.H. Stevenson, *The Crawford Collection of Early Charters and Documents,* Oxford 1895
15.3.10, 15.3.48, 15.6.11, 15.6.36
Needham 1966
G.I. Needham, *Ælfric: Lives of Three English Saints,* MOEL, London 1966
B.1.3.22, 1.3.26, 1.3.31
Nehab 1879
J. Nehab, *Der altenglische Cato,* [Göttingen diss.] Berlin 1879
B.7.1
Norman 1933
F. Norman, *Waldere,* MOEL, London 1933, 2nd ed. 1949
A.8
Norman 1848
H.W. Norman, *The Anglo-Saxon Version of the Hexameron of St. Basil ... and the Anglo-Saxon Remains of St. Basil's Admonitio ad Filium Spiritualem,* London 1848, 2nd ed. 1849
B.1.9.3

Noronha 1971
T.L. Noronha, 'Five Old English Verse Prayers: An Edition' [Stanford diss.] *DA* 32 [1972] 5748A
A.3.25, 20, 22, 28

Oess 1910
G. Oess, *Der altenglische Arundel-Psalter,* AF 30, Heidelberg 1910
C.7.5, 11.4

Okasha 1967
E. Okasha, 'An Anglo-Saxon inscription from All Hallows, Barking-by-the-Tower,' *Medieval Archaeology* 11 [1967] 249-51
F.31-2

Okasha 1971
E. Okasha, *Hand-list of Anglo-Saxon Non-runic Inscriptions,* Cambridge 1971
F.1-60

Okasha and Webster 1970
E. Okasha and L. Webster, 'An Anglo-Saxon Ring from Bodsham, Kent,' *AJ* 50 [1970] 102-4
F.6

Oliphant 1966
R.T. Oliphant, *The Harley Latin-Old English Glossary,* Janua Linguarum, Series Practica 20, The Hague 1966
D.16.1

Olsen 1930
Magnus Olsen, 'Notes on the Urswick Inscription,' *Norsk Tidsskrift for Sprogvidenskap* 4 [1930] 282-6
E.48

Oman 1930
C.C. Oman, *Victoria and Albert Museum, Department of Metalwork, Catalogue of Rings,* London 1930
F.39

Oman 1931
C.C. Oman, 'Anglo-Saxon Finger Rings,' *Apollo* 14 [1931] 104-8
F.59

Page 1959
R.I. Page, 'Language and Dating in OE Inscriptions,' *Anglia* 77 [1959] 385-406
385-406
E.10, F.10

Page 1960
R.I. Page, 'The Bewcastle Cross,' *Nottingham Medieval Studies* 4 [1960] 36-57
E.4

Page 1965
R.I. Page, 'A Note on the text of Ms. CCCC 422 [*Solomon and Saturn*],' *MÆ* 34 [1965] 36-9
A.13

Page 1966
R.I. Page, 'The Whitby Runic Comb,' *Whitby Literary and Philosophical Society Annual Report* 1966, 11-5
A.50

Page 1968

R.I. Page, 'The Old English Rune *Eoh*, *Ih* "Yew tree," ' *MÆ* 37 [1968] 125-36

E.8, 34

Page 1968

R.I. Page, 'The Runic Solidus of Schweindorf, Ostfriesland, and Related Runic Solidi,' *Medieval Archaeology* 12 [1968] 12-25

E.18

Page 1969

R.I. Page, 'Runes and Non-Runes' in D.A. Pearsall and R.A. Waldron, eds., *Medieval Literature and Civilization, Studies in Memory of G.N. Garmonsway,* London 1969, 28-54

E1, 29, 44, 53

Page in Wilson 1964

R.I. Page, 'The Inscriptions,' Appendix A in D.M. Wilson, *Anglo-Saxon Ornamental Metalwork 700-1100 in the British Museum,* London 1964, 67-90

B.25.4.4, E.25, 27, 33, 45-6, F.11, 24, 26, 30, 36, 41-4, 58

Page in Bowen 1967

R.I. Page, 'Note on the Inscription' in M. Bowen, 'Saxon Sundial in the Parish Church of All Saints, Orpington,' in 'Researches and Discoveries in Kent,' *Archaeologia Cantiana* 82 [1967] 289-91

E.37, F.35

Page in Addyman and Hill 1969

R.I. Page in P.V. Addyman and D.H. Hill, 'Saxon Southampton: A Review of the Evidence' Pt.II, 86-8 in *Proceedings of the Hampshire Field Club and Archaeological Society* 26 [1969] 61-96

E.44

Peers 1925

C.R. Peers, 'The Inscribed and Sculptured Stones of Lindisfarne,' *Archaeologia* 74 [1925] 255-70

E.32, F.28-9

Peers and Radford 1943

C.R. Peers and C.A.R. Radford, 'The Saxon Monastery of Whitby,' *Archaeologia* 89 [1943] 27-88

E.51, F.49-51

Peterson 1951

P.W. Peterson, 'The Unpublished Homilies of the Vercelli Book' [New York Univ. diss.] *ADD* 18 [1951] 227

B.3.1.2

Pheifer 1962-3

J.J.M.D. Pheifer, 'A new edition of the Epinal Glossary' [Oxford B.Litt.] *Index* 13 [1962-3] no.151

D.7

Phillips 1954

E.N.M. Phillips, 'Supplementary Notes on the Ancient Stone Crosses of Devon [4th paper,' *Transactions of the Devonshire Association for the Advancement of Science, Literature and Art* 86 [1954] 173-94

F.37

Plummer 1892-9 [1952]
C. Plummer, *Two of the Saxon Chronicles Parallel,* 2 vols., Oxford 1892-9, reissued
D. Whitelock 1952
B.15.1.1, 17.1, 17.4, 17.9

Pope 1967-8
J.C. Pope, *Homilies of Ælfric: A Supplementary Collection,* EETS 259, 260, London
1967-8
B.1.4, 1.8.6

Pope 1971
J.C. Pope, 'Ælfric and the Old English version of the Ely Privilege' in P. Clemoes and
K. Hughes, eds., *England before the Conquest, Studies ... presented to Dorothy White-
lock,* Cambridge 1971, 85-113
B.15.1.38

Priebsch 1899
R. Priebsch, 'The Chief Sources of some Anglo-Saxon Homilies,' *Otia Merseiana* 1
[1899] 129-47
B.3.4.54

Prou and Chartraire 1900
M. Prou and E. Chartraire, 'Authentiques de Reliques conservées au trésor de la
cathédrale de Sens,' *Mémoires de la société nationale des antiquaires de France* 59
[6 série IX] [1900] 129-72
B.16.17

Quinn 1956
J.J. Quinn, 'The Minor Latin-Old English Glossaries in Ms Cotton Cleopatra A.III'
[Stanford diss.] *DA* 16 [1956] 1902
D.8

Radford and Donaldson 1953
C.A.R. Radford and G. Donaldson, *Whithorn and Kirkmadrine, Wigtownshire,* Ministry
of Works Guide, Edinburgh 1953
E.40, 52

Raith 1933 [1964]
J. Raith, *Die altenglische Version des Halitgar'schen Bussbuches,* Bib. ags. Prosa 13,
Hamburg 1933 [Darmstadt 1964]
B.11.3.1-2

Raith 1956 .
J. Raith, *Die alt- und mittelenglischen Apollonius Bruchstücke,* Studien zur englischen
Philologie 3, Munich 1956
B.4.1

Raynes [Edwards] 1954-5
E.M. Raynes, 'Unpublished Old English Homilies' [Oxford D.Phil.] *Index* 5 [1954-5]
no.136
B.3.2.28, 3.2.32, 3.4.15

Rhodes 1889
E.W. Rhodes, *Defensor's Liber Scintillarum,* EETS 93, London 1889
C.6, 15, 20

Richards 1971
Mary J.P. Richards, 'An edition of the Old English *Of Seinte Neote*' [Wisconsin diss.]
DA 32 [1971] 3266A
B.3.3.28

Riehle 1966

W. Riehle, 'Ueber einige neuentdeckte altenglische Glossen,' *Anglia* 84 [1966] 150-5
C.77.2

Robertson 1956

A.J. Robertson, *Anglo-Saxon Charters,* Cambridge 1939, 2nd ed. 1956
B.15-16

Robinson 1965

F.C. Robinson, 'Old English Lexicographical Notes,' *Philologica Pragensia* 8 [1965]
303-7
C.31.7, D.44

Robinson 1972

F.C. Robinson, 'The Devil's Account of the Next World,' *NM* 73 [1972] 362-71
B.3.4.15

Roeder 1904

F. Roeder, *Der altenglische Regius-Psalter,* Studien zur englischen Philologie 18,
Halle 1904
B.7.3, 20.11.3, C.7.9, 11.9

Rosier 1960

J.L. Rosier, 'Old English Glosses to an epistle of Boniface,' *JEGP* 59 [1960] 710-3
C.10

Rosier 1962

J.L. Rosier, *The Vitellius Psalter,* Cornell Studies in English 42, Ithaca 1962
C.7.8, 11.7

Rosier 1963-4

J.L. Rosier, 'Contributions to OE Lexicography: Some Boethius Glosses,' *Archiv* 200
[1963-4] 197-8
C.9

Rosier 1964

J.L. Rosier, 'Instructions for Christians,' *Anglia* 82 [1964] 4-22
A.44

Rosier 1964

J.L. Rosier, 'The Stowe Canticles,' *Anglia* 82 [1964] 397-432
C.11.10

Rosier 1966

J.L. Rosier, 'Addenda to "Instructions for Christians," ' *Anglia* 84 [1966] 74
A.44

Rositzke 1940

H.A. Rositzke, *The C-Text of the Old English Chronicles,* Beiträge zur englischen
Philologie 34, Bochum-Langendreer 1940 [1967]
B.17.7

Ross 1935-6

A.S.C. Ross, 'Notes on the Runic Stones at Holy Island,' *Englische Studien* 70
[1935-6] 36-9
E.32

Rypins 1924

S. Rypins, *Three Old English Prose Texts,* EETS 161, London 1924
B.3.3.4, 22

Sanders 1878-84

W.B. Sanders, *Facsimiles of Anglo-Saxon Manuscripts,* Southampton, Ordnance Survey,

1878-84
B.15
Sawyer 1957-62
P.H. Sawyer, *Textus Roffensis,* EEMF 7, 11, Copenhagen 1957-62
A.52, B.14, 15.5.16-8, 15.6.28, 15.6.31, 16.16, 18.7, 23.1.6, C.59
Sawyer 1968
P.H. Sawyer, *Anglo-Saxon Charters, An annotated List and Bibliography,* London 1968
B.15
von Schaubert 1963
E. von Schaubert, *Heyne-Schückings Beowulf,* 18th ed. Paderborn 1963
A.4.1, 7
Schipper 1897-9
J. Schipper, *König Alfreds Übersetzung von Bedas Kirchengeschichte,* Bib. ags. Prosa 4,
Leipzig 1897-9
B.9.6
Schlutter 1909
O.B. Schlutter, 'Anglo-Saxonica,' *Anglia* 32 [1909] 503-15
C.89.1
Schlutter 1910
O.B. Schlutter, 'Anglo-Saxonica,' *Anglia* 33 [1910] 239-51
D.40, 43
Schlutter 1910
O.B. Schlutter, 'Zu den Brüsseler Aldhelmglossen,' *Anglia* 33 [1910] 232-8
C.31.1
Schlutter 1912
O.B. Schlutter, 'Altenglisch-Althochdeutsches aus dem Codex Trevirensis No.40,'
Anglia 35 [1912] 145-54
D.57
Schlutter 1912
O.B. Schlutter, *Faksimile und Transliteration des Epinaler Glossars,* Bib. ags. Prosa 8,
Hamburg 1912
D.7
Schneider 1968
K. Schneider, 'Six Old English Runic Inscriptions Reconsidered' in A.H. Orrick, ed.,
Nordica et Anglica: Studies in Honor of Stefan Einarsson, The Hague 1968, 37-52
E.9, 12, 15, 18, 21, 27
Schröer 1885-8 [1964]
A. Schröer, *Die angelsächsischen Prosabearbeitungen der Benediktinerregel,* Bib. ags.
Prosa 2, Kassel 1885-8, reprint with appendix H. Gneuss, Darmstadt 1964
B.10.3.1, 24.25
Schröer 1886
A. Schröer, 'De Consuetudine Monachorum,' *Englische Studien* 9 [1886] 290-6
B.10.5.2
Schröer 1888
A. Schröer, *Die Winteney-Version der Regula S. Benedicti,* Halle 1888
B.10.3.4
Scott 1956
F.S. Scott, 'The Hildithryth Stone and other Hartlepool Name-Stones,' *Archaeologia*

Aeliana, 4th series 34 [1956] 196-212

E.23

Sedgefield 1899 [1968]

W.J. Sedgefield, *King Alfred's Old English Version of Boethius' De Consolatione Philosophiae,* Oxford 1899 [Darmstadt 1968]

A.6, B.9.3, 12.4.7

Sievers 1877

E. Sievers, 'Bedeutung der Buchstaben,' *ZfdA* 21 [1877] 189-90

B.23.3.4

Sisam 1953

C. Sisam, 'An Early Fragment of the Old English Martyrology,' *RES* n.s. 4 [1953] 209-20

B.19.4

Sisam and Sisam 1959

C. and K. Sisam, *The Salisbury Psalter,* EETS 242, London 1959

A.50, C.7.13, 11.12, C.23.3

Sisam 1953

K. Sisam, *Studies in the History of Old English Literature,* Oxford 1953

B.1.1.40, 3.3.31, 6.1

Skeat 1871-87 [1970]

W.W. Skeat, *The Four Gospels in Anglo-Saxon, Northumbrian and Old Mercian Versions,* Cambridge 1871-87 [Darmstadt 1970]

B.8.4, C.8.1-2

Skeat 1881-1900 [1966]

W.W. Skeat, *Ælfric's Lives of Saints,* EETS 76, 82, 94, 114, London 1881-1900, reprinted as 2 vols. 1966

B.1.3, 3.3.7-8, 3.3.23, 3.3.34

Smith 1933

A.H. Smith, *Three Northumbrian Poems,* MOEL, London 1933, 2nd ed. 1968

A.32-4

Smith 1923

R.A. Smith, *British Museum: A Guide to the Anglo-Saxon and Foreign Teutonic Antiquities in the Department of British and Mediaeval Antiquities,* London 1923

F.17-9

Somner 1726

W. Somner, *A Treatise of Gavelkind,* 2nd ed. London 1726

B.15.7.2

Spindler 1934

R. Spindler, *Das altenglische Bussbuch,* Leipzig 1934

B.10.4.2, 11.1.1, 11.2.1-2, 11.6

Steinmeyer 1880

E. Steinmeyer, 'Angelsächsisches aus Rom,' *ZfdA* 24 [1880] 191-3

B.1.9.4

Steinmeyer and Sievers 1879-1922

E. Steinmeyer and E. Sievers, *Die althochdeutschen Glossen,* 5 vols., Berlin 1879-1922

D.31, 34-5, 37-40, 45, 47-50, 52-3, 55-6, 58

Stephens and Madge 1897

W.R.W. Stephens and F.T. Madge, *Documents relating to the History of the Cathedral Church of Winchester AD 1636-83,* Hampshire Record Society, London 1897

B.15.7.10

Stephens 1866-1901
George Stephens, *The Old-Northern Runic Monuments of Scandinavia and England*, 4 vols., London and Copenhagen 1866-1901
E, F.10, 14

Stevenson 1851
J. Stevenson, *The Latin Hymns of the Anglo-Saxon Church*, Surtees Society 23, Durham 1851
C.18.2

Stevenson 1912
W.H. Stevenson, 'Yorkshire Surveys and other Eleventh-Century Documents in the York Gospels,' *EHR* 27 [1912] 1-25
B.12.4.2, 16.24.4

Stevenson and Lindsay 1929
W.H. Stevenson and W.M. Lindsay, *Early Scholastic Colloquies,* Anecdota Oxoniensia, Mediaeval and Modern Series 15, Oxford 1929
C.1.2, 28

Stokes 1891
W. Stokes, 'Glosses from Turin and Rome,' *Beiträge zur Kunde der indogermanischen Sprachen* 17 [1891] 144-5
B.23.1.17

Storms 1948
G. Storms, *Anglo-Saxon Magic,* The Hague 1948
A.43, B.23.1, 25.4.3

Stryker 1952
W.G. Stryker, 'The Latin-Old English glossary in Ms Cotton Cleopatra A.III' [Stanford diss.] *ADD* 19 [1952] 230
D.8

Stubbs 1874
W. Stubbs, *Memorials of St. Dunstan,* Rolls Series 63, London 1874
B.14.19

Stüben 1939
W. Stüben, 'Nachträge zu den althochdeutschen Glossen,' *BGDSL* 63 [1939] 451-7
D.43

Swan 1968
W.J. Swan, '*Sermo de die iudicii*: An Ælfrician Homily' [Florida diss.] *DA* 29 [1968] 1221A
B.1.4.19

Swanton 1970
M. Swanton, *The Dream of the Rood,* Manchester 1970
A.2.5

Sweet 1871 [1958]
H. Sweet, *King Alfred's West-Saxon Version of Gregory's Pastoral Care,* EETS 45, 50, London 1871 [1958]
A.36-7, B.9.1

Sweet 1883 [1959]
H. Sweet, *King Alfred's Orosius,* EETS 79, London 1883 [1959]
B.9.2

Sweet 1885
H. Sweet, *The Oldest English Texts*, EETS 83, London 1885
B.18.2, 19.3, D.7, 36, E.11-2, 17, 20, 23, 27-8, 35, 41, 46, F.14
Taylor and Taylor 1961
H.M. and J. Taylor, 'The seventh-century church at Hexham: A new appreciation,'
Archaeologia Aeliana, 4th series 39 [1961] 103-34
F.20
Taylor and Taylor 1966
J. and H.M. Taylor, 'Architectural Sculpture in pre-Norman England,' *JBAA* 3rd series 29
[1966] 3-51
F.1, 5, 16, 22, 35
Thomas 1967
A.C. Thomas, 'An Early Christian Cemetery and Chapel on Ardwall Isle, Kirkcudbright,'
Medieval Archaeology 11 [1967] 127-88
F.3
Thompson and Lindelöf 1927
A.H. Thompson and U. Lindelöf, *Rituale Ecclesiae Dunelmensis,* Surtees Society 140,
Durham 1927
B.12.1.1, 12.5.5, 28.1.1, C.2, 13, 18.1, 21
Thorpe 1840
B. Thorpe, *Ancient Laws and Institutes of England,* 2 vols., folio ed. in 1 vol., Great
Britain Public Records Commission 28, London 1840
B.3.4.55, 10.6.1, 11.5, 11.10.1
Thorpe 1844-6
B. Thorpe, *The Sermones Catholici or Homilies of Ælfric,* 2 vols., Ælfric Society, London
1844-6
B.1.1-2, 1.9.6-7, 12.3.1-2, 12.4.1
Thorpe 1861
B. Thorpe, *The Anglo-Saxon Chronicle,* Rolls Series 23, London 1861 [1964]
B.17.3, 17.5-6
Thorpe 1865
B. Thorpe, *Diplomatarium Anglicum Ævi Saxonici,* London 1865
B.16.9.4, 16.10.3, 16.10.6, 17.12
Timmer 1952
B.J. Timmer, *Judith,* MOEL, London 1952, 2nd ed. 1961
A.4.2
Timmer 1954
B.J. Timmer, *The Later Genesis,* rev. ed. Oxford 1954
A.1.1
Torkar 1971
Roland Torkar, 'Textkritische Anmerkungen zum ae. Gedicht *Instructions for Christians,*'
Anglia 89 [1971] 164-77
A.44
Trahern 1964
J.B. Trahern, Jr, '*The Phoenix*: A Critical Edition' [Princeton diss.] *DA* 25 [1964] 458
A.3.4

Trask 1971
Richard M. Trask, 'The Last Judgment of the *Exeter Book*: A Critical Edition' [Illinois diss.] *DA* 32 [1972] 5753A
A.3.1

Tristram 1970
Hildegard Tristram [Paul], 'Vier altenglische Predigten aus der heterodoxen Tradition' [Freiburg i. Br. diss.] 1970
B.3.2.30, 3.2.45, 3.2.48, 3.3.2, 3.3.21, 3.3.24

Rose-Troup 1937
F. Rose-Troup, 'Exeter Manumissions and Quittances of the Eleventh and Twelfth Centuries,' *Transactions of the Devonshire Association* 69 [1937] 417-44
B.16.10.6

Tupper 1910 [1968]
F. Tupper, *The Riddles of the Exeter Book,* Boston 1910 [Darmstadt 1968]
A.3.22, 3.31, 3.34

Turner 1955
A.G.C. Turner, 'Some Old English passages relating to the episcopal manor of Taunton,' *Proceedings, Somersetshire Archaeological and Natural History Society* 98 [1953] 118-26
B.15.7.11

Ure 1957
J.M. Ure, *The Benedictine Office,* Edinburgh University Publications in Language and Literature 11, Edinburgh 1957
A.21-4, B.12.7

Varnhagen 1902
H. Varnhagen, *De Glossis Nonnullis Anglicis,* Erlangen 1902
C.71.2

Vickrey 1961
J.F. Vickrey, Jr, '*Genesis B*: A new analysis and edition' [Indiana diss.] *DA* 21 [1961] 3463
A.1.1

Vierck 1970
H. Vierck, 'Der C-Brakteat von Longbridge in der ostenglischen Gruppe' in K. Hauck, *Goldbrakteaten aus Sievern,* Münstersche Mittelalter-Schriften 1, Munich 1970, Anhang VIII
E.49

Vleeskruyer 1953
R. Vleeskruyer, *The Life of St. Chad,* Amsterdam 1953
B.3.3.3

Wanley 1705 [1970]
H. Wanley, *Librorum Veterum Septentrionalium Catalogus,* [vol. 2 of Hickes, *Thesaurus*] Oxford 1705 [Hildesheim and New York 1970]
B.1.2.8

Warner 1917
R.D-N. Warner, *Early English Homilies from the Twelfth Century Ms Vespasian D. XIV,* EETS 152, London 1917
B

Waterman 1959
D.M. Waterman, 'Late Saxon, Viking, and Early Medieval Finds from York,'
Archaeologia 97 [1959] 59-105
E.53
Wells 1970
D.M. Wells, 'A Critical Edition of the Old English *Genesis A* with a translation'
[North Carolina diss.] *DA* 31 [1970] 373A
A.1.1
Whitbread 1948
L.G. Whitbread, 'The Thornhill Cross Inscription,' *N & Q* 193 [1948] 156
E.47
Whitbread 1956
L.G. Whitbread, 'An edition of the Old English poem *Judgment Day II* with the Latin
source and prose adaptation' [London Ph.D.] *Index* 7 [1956-7] no.170
A.17
Whitelock 1930
Dorothy Whitelock, *Anglo-Saxon Wills*, Cambridge 1930
B.15.6
Whitelock 1939 [1963]
Dorothy Whitelock, *Sermo Lupi ad Anglos*, MOEL, London 1939, 3rd ed. 1963
B.2.4.2
Whitelock 1954
Dorothy Whitelock, *The Peterborough Chronicle*, EEMF 4, Copenhagen 1954
B.15.1.1, 17.9
Whitelock 1967
Dorothy Whitelock, *Sweet's Anglo-Saxon Reader*, 15th ed. Oxford 1967
B.16.6.5
Whitelock and Ker 1968
D. Whitelock and N.R. Ker, *The Will of Æthelgifu*, Roxburghe Club, Oxford 1968
B.15.6.15
Wildhagen 1910 [1964]
K. Wildhagen, *Der Cambridger Psalter*, Bib. ags. Prosa 7, Hamburg 1910 [Darmstadt
1964]
C.7.1, 11.1
Willard 1935
R. Willard, 'The Address of the Soul to the Body,' *PMLA* 50 [1935] 957-83
B.3.5.8, 3.5.14
Willard 1935 [1967]
R. Willard, *Two Apocrypha in Old English Homilies*, Beiträge zur englischen Philologie 30,
Leipzig 1935 [1967]
B.3.2.5, 3.2.30-1, 3.5.5
Willard 1936
R. Willard, 'On Blickling Homily XIII: The Assumption of the Virgin,' *RES* 12 [1936]
1-17
B.3.3.20
Willard 1949
R. Willard, 'The Blickling-Junius Tithing Homily and Caesarius of Arles' in T.A. Kirby
and H.B. Woolf, eds., *Philologica: The Malone Anniversary Studies*, Baltimore 1949, 65-78
B.3.2.14

Willard 1949

R. Willard, 'Vercelli Homily XI and its Sources,' *Speculum* 24 [1949] 76-85
B.3.2.36]

Willard 1960

R. Willard, *The Blickling Homilies,* EEMF 10, Copenhagen 1960
B.3.1.1

Williams 1914

Blanche C. Williams, *Gnomic Poetry in Anglo-Saxon,* New York 1914
A.3.13, 15

Wilson 1964

D.M. Wilson, *Anglo-Saxon Ornamental Metalwork 700-1100 in the British Museum,*
London 1964
E.25, F.40

Wilson 1896

H.A. Wilson, *The Missal of Robert of Jumièges,* Henry Bradshaw Society 11, London
1896
B.12.5.12, 24.4

Woolf 1955

R.E. Woolf, *Juliana,* MOEL, London 1955
A.3.5

Wormald 1934

F. Wormald, *English Kalendars before A.D. 1100,* Henry Bradshaw Society 72, London
1934
B.20.14, 24.4, C.88

Wrenn 1932

C.L. Wrenn, 'Late Old English Rune-Names,' *MÆ* 1 [1932] 24-34
B.25.1.3

Wrenn 1962

C.L. Wrenn, 'Magic in an Anglo-Saxon Cemetery' in N. Davis and C.L. Wrenn, eds.,
English and Medieval Studies presented to J.R.R. Tolkien, London 1962, 306-20
E.8

Wrenn 1965

C.L. Wrenn, 'Some Earliest Anglo-Saxon Cult Symbols' in J.B. Bessinger, Jr, and
R.P. Creed, eds., *Medieval and Linguistic Studies in honor of F.P. Magoun,* London and
New York 1965, 40-55
E.8, 34

Wright 1936

C.E. Wright, 'A Postscript to"Late Old English Rune-Names,"' *MÆ* 5 [1936] 149-51
B.25.1.3

Wright 1938

C.E. Wright, 'Two Ælfric Fragments,' *MÆ* 7 [1938] 50-5
B.1.1.4-5

Wright 1955

C.E. Wright, *Bald's Leechbook,* EEMF 5, Copenhagen 1955
A.43.7, B.21.2.1, 28.2

Wright and Campbell 1967

D.H. Wright and A. Campbell, *The Vespasian Psalter,* EEMF 14, Copenhagen 1967
C.7.7, 18.4

Wright and Halliwell 1841-3
T. Wright and J.O. Halliwell, *Reliquiae Antiquae,* 2 vols., London 1841-3
B.18.5
Wright and Wülcker 1884 [1968]
T. Wright, *Anglo-Saxon and Old English Vocabularies,* 2nd ed. R.P. Wülcker, 2 vols.,
London 1884 [Darmstadt 1968]
B.1.9.2, C.24, D.1-2, 8, 16.1
Wülcker 1882
R.P. Wülcker, 'Ueber das Vercellibuch,' *Anglia* 5 [1882] 451-65
B.3.2.43
Wynn 1961-2
J.B. Wynn, 'An edition of the Anglo-Saxon Corpus glosses' [Oxford, D.Phil.] *Index*
12 [1961-2] no. 149
D.4
Zandvoort 1949-50
R.W. Zandvoort, 'The Leiden Riddle,' *EGS* 3 [1949-50] 42-56, reprinted in *Collected
Papers I*, Groningen Studies in English 5, Groningen 1954, 1-16
A.34
Zarnecki 1953
G. Zarnecki, 'The Newent Funerary Tablet,' *Transactions of the Bristol and Gloucester-
shire Archaeological Society* 72 [1953] 49-55
F.34
Zimmermann 1916
E.H. Zimmermann, *Vorkarolingische Miniaturen,* Berlin 1916
B.16.13
Zupitza 1876
J. Zupitza, 'Englisches aus Prudentiushandschriften,' *ZfdA* 20 [1876] 36-45
C.26
Zupitza 1877
J. Zupitza, 'Kentische Glossen des neunten Jahrhunderts,' *ZfdA* 21 [1877] 1-59
C.29, 49, D.13
Zupitza 1878
J. Zupitza, 'Lateinisch-englische Sprüche,' *Anglia* 1 [1878] 285-6
B.7.2
Zupitza 1878
J. Zupitza, 'Zu den kentischen Glossen ZS. 21, 1ff.,' *ZfdA* 22 [1878] 223-6
C.29, 49, D.13
Zupitza 1880 [1966]
J. Zupitza, *Ælfrics Grammatik und Glossar,* Sammlung englischer Denkmäler 1, Berlin
1880, reprinted with intro. H. Gneuss 1966
B.1.9.1-2
Zupitza 1886
J. Zupitza, 'Drei alte Excerpte aus Älfreds Beda,' *ZfdA* 30 [1886] 185-6
B.9.6
Zupitza 1887
J. Zupitza, 'Altenglische Glossen zu Abbos Clericorum Decus,' *ZfdA* 31 [1887] 1-27
C.1.1

Zupitza 1888
J. Zupitza, 'Cantus Beati Godrici,' *Englische Studien* 11 [1888] 401-32
A.46
Zupitza 1889
J. Zupitza, 'Mercisches aus der Hs. Royal 2 A 20 im Britischen Museum,' *ZfdA* 33 [1889] 47-66
B.12.4.10, 12.8, 27.3.20, C.54
Zupitza 1889
J. Zupitza, 'Altenglische Glossen,' *ZfdA* 33 [1889] 237-42
D.15, 23
Zupitza 1890
J. Zupitza, 'Eine weitere Aufzeichnung der Oratio pro peccatis,' *Archiv* 84 [1890] 327-9
B.12.4.3.1
Zupitza 1890
J. Zupitza, 'Ein weiteres Bruchstück der Regularis Concordia in altenglischer Sprache,' *Archiv* 84 [1890] 1-24
B.10.5.1
Zupitza 1892
J. Zupitza, 'Kreuzandacht,' *Archiv* 88 [1892] 361-4
B. 12.4.4
Zupitza 1892
J. Zupitza, 'Kreuzzauber,' *Archiv* 88 [1892] 364-5
B.23.1.7
Zupitza 1882 [and Davis 1959]
J. Zupitza, *Beowulf,* EETS 77, London 1882, 2nd ed. N. Davis, EETS 245, London 1959
A.4

computational aids to dictionary compilation

RICHARD L.VENEZKY

DESIGN OBJECTIVES

The data processing system outlined here is seen as an aid to lexicography and not as a completely automated system. It will provide those clerical and editorial functions which the editors can use comfortably, within the constraints of a geographically distributed staff, an uncertain budget, and a projected life-span which most certainly will cross several generations of computing machinery. The relatively short time-periods envisioned for data collection and editing require that the most important data processing operations be as centralized as possible so that a steady flow of materials can be guaranteed. Computational operations which are logically distinct from this effort should be located wherever the most adequate funding and management can be found.

The most important criterion for the data-processing system is that it be based upon procedures which are already in use and which can be integrated smoothly into the normal editorial activities of the Dictionary staff. Experimentation on new methods will be done only in conjunction with the application of more standard procedures. Hence, attempts to extend the computational frontiers in the humanities will not impede the processing of Dictionary materials; yet on the other hand, the Dictionary will always be in a position to adopt improved methods as they become available.

A further desideratum for the data-processing system is that it produce usable output continually, rather than at the end of the data collection phase. This will enable the editors to monitor the quality and distribution of materials as they are processed, and to demonstrate progress at any point to all those associated with the project. However, such a procedure also imposes a burden upon the editorial staff, in that emendation and review will be required at each stage of the processing.

THE INITIAL SYSTEM

Introduction
The selection of initial functions for the system to perform have been derived from a number of meetings with the DOE editors and from personal visits to two other major dictionary projects, the *Historical Dictionary of Hebrew* in Jerusalem and the *Historical Dictionary of Italian* in Venice.[1] These functions are based upon existing computing systems and have been evaluated in terms of practicality and cost. They involve the encoding of Old English texts onto coding forms, card punching, and concording with the 1108 BIBCON system at the University of Wisconsin.[2] The printed concordance will give the context for each significant word (here called keyword) and the entire concordance will be followed by an alphabetized list of keywords, giving the frequency of occurrence

---

1 Various computer-aided dictionary projects, including the two mentioned here, are discussed by Richard W. Bailey and Jay L. Robinson, 'Computers and Dictionaries,' in Angus Cameron, Roberta Frank, and John Leyerle, eds., *Computers and Old English Concordances*, Toronto 1970, 94-102. (More detailed discussions of the methods used by each project are not generally available at present.) On other research related to computers and lexicography, see Harry H. Josselson, 'Lexicography and the Computer,' *To Honour Roman Jakobson: Essays on the Occasion of his Seventieth Birthday*, The Hague 1967, II, 1046-59; Carter Revard, 'On the Computability of Certain Monsters in Noah's Ark,' *Computer Studies in the Humanities and Verbal Behavior*, 2 [1969], 82-90
2 Richard L. Venezky, 'BIBCON: An 1108 system for producing concordances to prose, poetry and bibliographic references,' Computer Sciences Technical Report 134, University of Wisconsin 1971

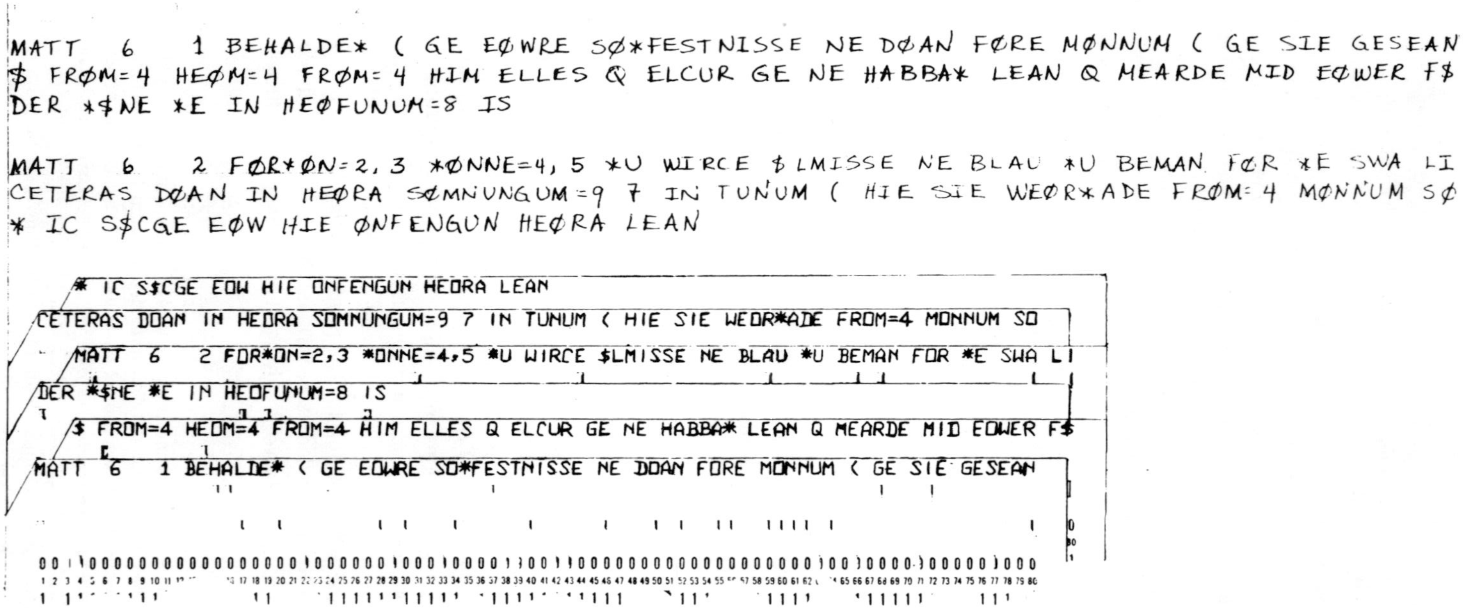

MATT 6 1 BEHALDE* (GE EÐWRE SÐ*FESTNISSE NE DÐAN FŌRE MØNNUM (GE SIE GESEAN
$ FRØM=4 HEØM=4 FRØM=4 HIM ELLES Q ELCUR GE NE HABBA* LEAN Q MEARDE MID EÐWER F$
ÐER *$NE *E IN HEØFUNUM=8 IS

MATT 6 2 FØR*ØN=2,3 *ØNNE=4,5 *U WIRCE $LMISSE NE BLAU *U BEMAN FØR *E SWA LI
CETERAS DØAN IN HEÐRA SØMNUNGUM=9 Ť IN TUŃUM (HIE SIE WEØR*ADE FRØM=4 MØNNUM SØ
* IC S$CGE EØW HIE ØNFENGUN HEÐRA LEAN

* IC S$CGE EØW HIE ØNFENGUN HEÐRA LEAN
CETERAS DØAN IN HEÐRA SØMNUNGUM=9 Ť IN TUNUM (HIE SIE WEØR*ADE FROM=4 MØNNUM SØ
MATT 6 2 FØR*ØN=2,3 *ØNNE=4,5 *U WIRCE $LMISSE NE BLAU *U BEMAN FØR *E SWA LI
ÐER *$NE *E IN HEØFUNUM=8 IS
$ FROM=4 HEØM=4 FROM=4 HIM ELLES Q ELCUR GE NE HABBA* LEAN Q MEARDE MID EØWER F$
MATT 6 1 BEHALIE* (GE EØWRE SØ*FESTNISSE NE DØAN FØRE MØNNUM (GE SIE GESEAN

FIGURE 1 Concordance input: *Rushworth Matthew*

of each within the concordance.[3] This system is now operating and has been used for several sample concordances. In addition, 5½" by 8" slips will be generated upon request for each concordance entry or for selected entries.

The printed concordances and slips will then be reviewed by the editor for transcription and keypunch errors, corrections entered, and if necessary the concordance re-run. Once a satisfactory copy of the text and concordance is obtained, the concordance and slips will be merged by hand into a master file, and the text (in machine-readable form) will be entered into an archive, from which copies can be generated upon request.

Concordance Program

The concordance program will generate concordances from input formats developed for 1/ prose and poetry, 2/ continuous interlinear glosses, and 3/ glossaries. Encoding standards for these formats are presented in the appendix to this chapter. Concordance output will always include a keyword-out-of-context listing and an alphabetized frequency list of keywords. Additional outputs which the editors may request are a list of keywords, ordered by frequency of occurrence, a list of keywords, spelled from back to front and alphabetized (a 'backwards' listing), and an alphabetized frequency list of stopwords.

Archive

The archive will serve as a distributable data base for linguistic and literary research.[4] It contains a text list and, for each text entered into it, a heading, reference table, and the text itself. These are described below.

TEXT LIST The text list contains the following entries for each text in the file:
1 text number (as listed in chapter 3 above)
2 short title[5]
3 date of composition (early, late, indeterminate)
4 location of composition (Saxon, Anglian, unknown)
5 date of entry into the file (or date of last correction to the text itself)
6 location of heading, reference table, and the text within the file.

The first five entries above can be queried, thus allowing users to obtain texts on the basis of any of these data, or any logical combination of them. For example, it will be possible to obtain a list of the short titles (or the texts themselves) for all Anglian prose texts entered into the archive before 10 March 1974. It will also be possible to obtain an index to the complete text list. The sixth item above is used internally by the system to determine the physical location where a particular text is stored.

HEADING The heading for each text will contain:
1 text number
2 full title and edition
3 text type
4 length of reference table
5 length of text.

The heading is formed from data supplied on control cards when a text is entered into

---

3 The editors can request that every word in a text be treated by the concordance program as a significant (key) word, or they can indicate that certain words should not be included in the alphabetized listing (e.g., 'seo,' 'in,' 'hwa'). Such words are called stopwords.
4 An archive for Older Scottish texts is described in A.J. Aitken and Paul Bratley, 'An archive of Older Scottish texts for scanning by computer,' *Studies in Scottish Literature*, 4 [1966], 45-7.
5 A list of short titles for OE texts is being prepared by R.B. Mitchell.

HEOFON

EAC SWYLCE ÆLIAS HINE GESSD (HIT NE KINDE OFER EORÞAN / HE MID HIS   3   15V   9
GEBEDUM *ONE HEOFON BELEAC *REO GEAR / SYX MONO+ •

7 EFT HE ADSD (SE HEOFON SEALDE RENAS / SIO EORÞE HIRE WÆSTMAS • •   3   15V   11

SIO SLMESSE GEORDFSR+ *ONE HEOFON 7 HIO CNYSSE+ HEOFONA RICES DURU •   3   16R   8

HEOFONA

DO+ HREOÞSUNGE=IU. FOR*AM HEOFONA NEALÆCE+ • • •   3   13V   5

HIT IS HEOFONLIC WORC 7 HEOFONA RICES DURU • / HIWUNG *SRE TOWEARDAN   3   14V   9
WORULDE •

SIO SLMESSE GEORDFSR+ *ONE HEOFON 7 HIO CNYSSE+ HEOFONA RICES DURU •   3   16R   8

HEOFONLIC

HIT IS HEOFONLIC WORC 7 HEOFONA RICES DURU • / HIWUNG *SRE TOWEARDAN   3   14V   9
WORULDE •

HEOFONLICAN

AGUSTINUS) CWÆ+ (FÆSTEN GEOPENA* *A HEOFONLICAN GERYNU • / UTASCYF+   3   14V   16
*A YFLAN LEAHTRAS • 7 *A SAWLE ONLYHTE+ •

MOYSES) GEFSSTE ON *AM WESTENNE *URH *SI HE GEEARNODE GEHYRAN *A •   3   15R   2
HEOFONLICAN GERYNU

HEOFONLICE

FOR*AM=6 HIE WIION (*SI NIS IDELLIC SR TO ARISENNE • / SR LEOHTE TO   3   14V   4
WACIENNE FOR*AM=6 DRYHTEN GENET *ONE HEOFONLICE BEAH *AM WACIENDAN •

HEOFONUM

*URH *A UFERHYGDE • OF HEOFONUM GEHREAS *SI WUNDORLICE ENGLA• • •   3   13R   4
GESCEAF1•

*AM HREOWSIENDAN IS SIO WSCCE WITODLICE TO BIGANNE • FOR*AM*E) HIO•   3   14R   3
HEOFONUM=6 UP AHEF+ *SS HREOWSIENDAN WÆSTMAS •

FIGURE 2 Sample concordance page: *Vercelli Homily 3*

1	AASLICE	1	ANDFENGEGE
1	A*WEGEN	1	ANDWEARDAN
1	A*WEGENE	1	ANFON
1	AB$D	1	ANGEAN
1	ABYRGDE	1	ANM
3	AC	1	ANNYSSE
3	AC)	1	APOSTOL
1	ADAM	1	APOSTOLUM
1	ADRIF*	1	ARISENDE
1	AFREMDOD	1	ARISENNE
1	AGENRE	1	ARLEAS
1	AGUSTINUS	1	ASCYF*
1	AGUSTINUS)	1	ASTREAHTE
1	AHEF*	1	AWEAHTE
1	AHSIAN	1	AWEC*
1	AHWYRFDE	1	AW*ER
1	ALYSDEFEN	20	*A
1	ALYSED	4	*A*E
1	ALYSE*E	1	*ACUMEN
1	AMEN)AE	1	*AD
7	AN	1	*ADA
1	AN*OHTE	1	*AGANNE
6	ANDETNES	1	*AGYTEND
8	ANDETNESSE	1	*ALLUHTE
1	ANDETTANNE	17	*AM
1	ANDETTEN	1	*AMAL
1	ANDETTNESSE	1	*AM*AM)
		1	*AM*E

FIGURE 3 Frequency list: *Vercelli Homily* 3

the archive and from data compiled by the updating program in processing the text.
REFERENCE TABLE The reference table contains an entry for each identifier which is
included within the text. An identifier most typically will be one of the following:

1 psalm and verse
2 page and line
3 homily or psalm, page and line.

With each identifier is the length (in computer characters) of the unit that it designates
and the physical location of that unit within the file. This table is used for locating contexts which are to be 1/ listed with concordance entries, or 2/ corrected, or 3/ processed
for linguistic or literary studies.
TEXT The text is stored as a continuous string of characters (including spaces) with all
identifiers removed. It can be listed in its entirety, or in part, or it can be used as input to
analysis programs.

Texts (with their headings and reference tables) are ordered according to the date on
which they are entered into the file. The text list is stored at the end of the file to
minimize the amount of data processing required when a new text is entered. With each
new text entered into the file or updated, a new text list is printed. A text may be
entered directly or may be entered in conjunction with the generation of a concordance.
Once a text is stored, concordances can be generated to that text directly from the file.
The text file will be available for distribution on magnetic tape, but will be stored on a
disk pack for use in the DOE system.

SYSTEM IMPROVEMENTS

Introduction

Once the initial data-processing system is implemented, pilot projects will be initiated on
a number of potential improvements. Included in these studies will be 1/ a pre-editing
scheme which could eliminate the need to transcribe texts onto coding forms, 2/ an
optical scanning procedure which might replace keypunching, 3/ a word-matching
program which would aid the editors in defining the entry form (lemma) for each keyword in a concordance listing, and 4/ a headword list in machine-readable form which the
editors could use in much the same manner as they would a shoe-box slip file. Outlines
of each of these pilot projects are presented below.

Pre-editing and Optical Scanning

Pre-editing involves the marking by an editor of identifiers, editorial changes, and encoding symbols directly onto a xerox copy of a printed text. This page would then be
typed, using a special optical character-reader fount, and read directly onto magnetic
tape. A sample of how this might be done is shown in figures 4 and 5. In the system
described here, the editor would mark all changes to the printed text except the replace-
ments for ð, þ, and æ, which would be done by the typist during typing. Similar systems
have already been used by Father Busa for parts of the *Aquinas Index* and by Professor
Schneider for the *London Stage* data bank.[6]

6 Private communication

(12ʳ)ʳ (4.) se eardað in heofenum bismerad² hie / 7 dryht́ hypeð ͘ hie / ðonne
QUI HABITAT IN CAELIS INRIDEBIT EOS / ET DNS SUBSANNABIT³ EOS. / 5. TUNC

spriceð · to him in eorre his / 7 in hatheortnisse his gedroefcð hie / ic
LOQUETUR⁴ AD EOS IN IRA SUA / ET IN FURORE SUO CONTURBABIT EOS. / 6. EGO

soðlice geseted ic eam cyning frō him ofer / sion mont ðone halgan his bodiende
AUTEM CONSTITUTUS SUM REX AB EO, SUPER / SION MONTEM SCM EIUS, PRAEDICANS

bibod dryht́ / dryht́ cwæð to me sunu min ðu earð / ic to dege ic cende ðec /
PRAECEPTŪ DNI. / 7. DNS DIXIT AD ME FILIUS MEUS ES TU / EGO HODIE GENUI TE. /

bide from me 7 ic sellu ðe ðeode erfeweardnisse / ðine 7 on æhte ðine
8. POSTULA A ME ET DABO TIBI GENTES HEREDITATE / TUAM, ET POSSESSIONEM TUAM

gemæru eorðan / ðu reces hie in gerde iserre / 7 swe swe fæt lames
TERMINOS TERRE. / 9. REGES EOS IN UIRGA FERREA, / ET TAMQUAM UAS FIGULI

ðu gebrices hie / 7 nu cyningas ongeotað bioð gelærde alle / ða ðe
CONFRINGES EOS. / 10. ET NUNC REGES INTELLEGITE, ERUDIMINI OMNES / QUI

doemað eordan / ðeowiað dryhtne in ege 7 wynsumiað him mid cwaecunge /
IUDICATIS TERRAM. / 11. SERUITE DNO IN TIMORE, ET EXULTATE EI CUM TREMORE. /

gegripað / / ðy læs hwonne eorsie dryht́ 7 ge forweorðen of
12. ADPRAEHENDITE DISCIPLINAM / NEQUANDO IRASCATUR DNS ET PEREATIS DE

wege / ðonne beorneð in scortnisse eorre his / eadge alle ða ðe getreowað
UIA IUSTA. / 13. CUM EXARSERIT IN BREUI IRA EIUS / BEATI OMNES QUI CONFIDUNT

in hine /
IN EUM. /

FIGURE 4 Pre-edited page for scanner typing

Psalm 2)


```
[2] (4) se earda+ in heofenum bismerad hie 7 dryht/ hyspe+
hie (5) +onne sprice+ to him in eorre his 7 in hatheortnisse
his gedroefe+ hie (6) ic so+lice geseted ic eam cyning fro/
him ofer sion mont +one halgan his bodiende bibod dryht/
(7) dryht/ cw$+ to me sunu min +u ear+ ic to dege ic cende
+ec (8) bide from me 7 ic sellu +e +eode erfeweardnisse +ine
 7 on $hte +ine gem$ru eor+an (9) +u reces hie in gerde iserre
 7 swe swe fât lames +u gebrices hie (10) 7 nu cyningas
ongeota+ bio+ gel$rde alle +a +e doema+ eordan (11) +eowia+
dryhtne in ege 7 wynsumia+ him mid cwaecunge (12) gegripa+
+y lâs hwonne eorsie dryht/ 7 ge forweor+en of wege (13) +onne
beorne+ in scortnisse eorre his eadge alle +a +e getreowa+
in hine
```

FIGURE 5 Typed page in optical scanner fount: OE portion of *Vespasian Psalter* Psalm 2

Word Matching

Word matching is a two-stage procedure by which each keyword generated by the concordance program has associated with it the form under which it will be edited for the Dictionary.[7] For example, 'fot,' 'fotes,' and 'fet' would all have the form 'fot' attached, while 'stanes,' 'stanum,' and the dialectal variants 'stanæs' and 'stanan,' would all be associated with 'stan.' The two stages involve 1/ automatic morphological segmentation and word matching in a wordlist, and 2/ entry of editorial corrections, additions, and homograph resolutions. Once each concordance keyword in a list is properly associated with an entry form, the entire list is merged into a headword list.

The wordlist associated with stage 1 will be compiled initially from *A Grouped Frequency Wordlist of Anglo-Saxon Poetry*, using the first 1000 most commonly occurring words.[8] A wordlist entry will contain a spelling, a suffix pointer which designates a list of legitimate suffixes for the spelling, a homograph indicator for each suffix which yields a homograph, and a code number for the entry form of the spelling (or, for homographs, the code number for each homograph). The entry forms are stored in a separate list and are retrievable by entry number only.

Forms which are orthographically unaltered with suffixation will require only a single entry in the wordlist (discounting dialectal and orthographic variants which have deviant base-form spellings). For example, 'scip' would appear as SCIP, with the suffix list #,[9] ES, E, U, A, and UM. (Several of these suffixes would be marked for homographs, as for example, for the northern form SCIP for SCEAP.)

Loss of 'h' (e.g., 'mearh,' 'meares') can be handled similarly by listing the base form without 'h,' and then including h in the suffix list as a pseudo-suffix. Thus, MEAR would appear in the wordlist, with the suffixes H, ES, E, AS, A, and UM. Parasitic vowels (e.g., 'fugol,' 'fugles') and syncopation of a medial vowel (e.g., 'halig,' 'halges') require two entries, one with and one without the varying vowel. Thus, for 'halig,' one entry would be HALIG, with the suffixes #, NE, RA, U, and RE; the other, HALG with ES, UM, E, A. Similar procedures will be used for listing words which undergo vowel harmony ('æ' → 'a' before back vowels) and certain other changes (e.g., 'here,' 'herges'). A sample from a word matching file is shown in figure 6.

The word matching procedure is roughly as follows.

1 The spelling of the concordance keyword is normalized, using at a minimum these substitutions:[10]

---

7 Word matching systems differing in operation from the one presented here are described for Modern English in E.J. Galli and H. Yamada, 'An automatic dictionary and the verification of machine-readable text,' *IBM Systems Journal*, 6 [1967], 192-207, and for Hebrew in James D. Price, 'An algorithm for analyzing Hebrew words,' *Computer Studies in the Humanities and Verbal Behavior*, 2 [1969], 137-65. Various computer techniques for organizing and searching natural-language word-lists are discussed in David Hsaio and Frank Harary, 'A formal system for information retrieval from files,' *CACM*, 13 [1970], 67-73; Sydney M. Lamb and William H. Jacobsen, Jr, 'A high-speed, large-capacity dictionary system,' *Machine Translation*, 6 [November 1961], 76-107; R. Morris, 'Scatter storage techniques,' *CACM*, 11 [1968], 38-43.

8 John F. Madden and Francis P. Magoun, Jr, *A Grouped Frequency Wordlist of Anglo-Saxon Poetry*, Cambridge, Mass, 1964. There is, however, a one-many relation between Madden-Magoun entries and entries for the wordlist required for word matching. For example, the first Madden-Magoun entry, accounting for 15,974 tokens out of a total corpus of 168,500-plus running words, includes all of the personal pronouns – a total of about 12 distinct forms.

9 # indicates no ending.

10 Some normalization of vowels may also occur, especially with the digraphs 'ea,' 'eo,' and 'io.'

BASE	SUFFIX LIST NUMBER	HOMOGRAPH INDICATOR	ENTRY CODES
HALG	7	0100	5960, 5965
↓	↓	↓	↓
Pseudo-base	List 7 contains 'es,' 'um,' 'e,' and 'a.'	Each bit corresponds to a suffix in the same ordinal position in the suffix list. A one bit indicates a homograph, a zero bit, no homograph. In this example, the addition of suffix 2 ('um') to 'halg' (= 'halgum') produces a homograph.	The first entry number refers to the entry spelling. Each succeeding number corresponds, in sequence, to the homographs indicated by the 1 bits in the homograph indicator.

FIGURE 6 Sample wordlist entry

    a/ ð, þ, th → þ
    b/ k → c
    c/ final geminate consonant → single consonant
    d/ ae, ę, æ → æ
    e/ cs, x, hs, hx, cx, etc. → cs.
2 Using the first letters of the concordance keyword, a wordlist section is located and each word in it compared against the keyword.
3 If no match is found, the first word in the wordlist section is compared again, using only as many letters as contained in the wordlist entry. If a match is found, the remainder of the keyword is compared to the suffixes associated with the wordlist entry.
4 Step 2 is repeated with each word in the section until either a match is found or the section exhausted.

After the matching procedure is completed, the keywords are printed, each keyword having next to it either one or more entry forms, or a series of question marks, indicating that no match was found. This list is then reviewed by the editorial staff, which checks for matching errors and undetected homographs, and enters the missing forms.

    The goal of the automatic segmentation and word matching procedures is to provide unique identification of 70 to 80 per cent of the concordance keywords. To do this will require a wordlist of approximately 10,000 entries (including multiple entries for the same word). The unidentified items will have entry forms marked by the editorial staff. After each concordance is run and the entry forms derived for each keyword, the editor will indicate modifications to the wordlist, including, *inter alia*, new entries, new homographs, and additional suffixes for particular lists.

Headword File
The headword file is an alphabetized list of the entry words which are derived from concording and word matching. Each entry word will have connected to it either a cross-reference to another entry word in the file, or an integer which indicates how many times

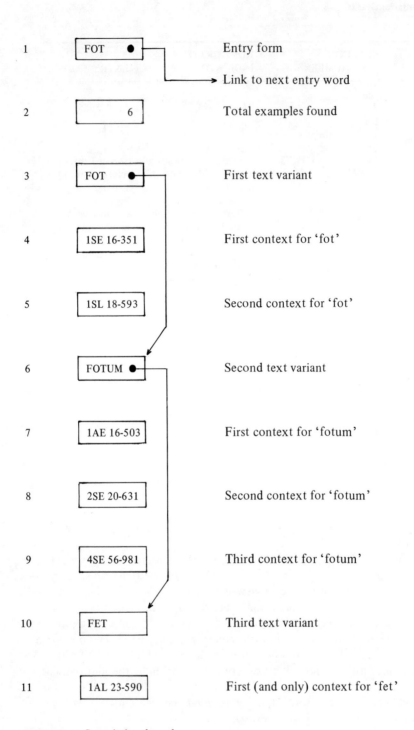

1	FOT ●	Entry form
		Link to next entry word
2	6	Total examples found
3	FOT ●	First text variant
4	1SE 16-351	First context for 'fot'
5	1SL 18-593	Second context for 'fot'
6	FOTUM ●	Second text variant
7	1AE 16-503	First context for 'fotum'
8	2SE 20-631	Second context for 'fotum'
9	4SE 56-981	Third context for 'fotum'
10	FET	Third text variant
11	1AL 23-590	First (and only) context for 'fet'

FIGURE 7 Sample headword entry

the word has appeared in input texts (for words which are always stopwords), or a list of text variants (that is, the actual orthographic and dialectal forms listed as concordance keywords). Each text variant in turn will have a list attached to it of identifiers for each context in which the particular variant was found. An identifier includes the text type, dialect, date of composition, and an address for locating in the archive the context in which it occurred. The entry words will be ordered alphabetically; the text variants, according to their date of entry into the file; and the identifiers, by text type (prose, poetry, or gloss).

An example of an abbreviated headword file entry as it might appear after a small number of texts has been processed is shown in figure 7. Each rectangular box represents an area of computer storage. Areas 1, 3, 6, and 10 contain OE words. Area 2 contains a count of the tokens of the entry found in input texts, and areas 4, 5, 7, 8, 9, and 11 identify specific texts (and locations within texts) where the variant forms of 'fot' have been found. In the first part of these areas is a code for the text type (1: prose, 2: poetry, 3: gloss), geographic location (S: Saxon, A: Anglian, U: unknown), and date (E: early, L: late, I: indeterminate). In the second part is the text number (corresponding to an entry in the reference table for the text).

Summaries for each entry word may be obtained, with totals for each text type, dialect, and date of composition. When the contexts for a word are desired, the addresses in the identifiers are used to retrieve them from the archive.

Implementation
The testing and implementation of these pilot schemes on the Univac 1108 will require approximately one man-year of work, assuming that each component outlined above proves to be useful for the Dictionary. If most of the system is written in Fortran, with marking during the programming stage of all coding which is dependent upon the Univac 1108, the cost of transferring the entire system to another machine of comparable size and configuration will be about one-third of the initial development cost. The most important subsystems which remain to be designed and tested are the word matching and the headword file programs. Word matching could be done by maintaining a list of every unique word encountered in the texts, rather than by storage of base forms with con-comitant morphological segmentation. Experimentation is required to determine whether or not the base-form approach is practicable for OE and less expensive than the unique word approach.

Design of the headword file involves primarily the selection of a data structure which will minimize the accumulated costs for updating and retrieving over the life of the file. Such a structure will be selected after estimates are made of 1/ the quantities of different types of data which will be entered, 2/ the structure of the data, and 3/ the expected frequencies of updating and retrieving.

COST ESTIMATES

Cost estimates for using all of the modifications just described are offered with full re-cognition of the uncertainties attendant on computers, decentralized management, voluntary labour, and a five-year time schedule. Computing costs, which make up the bulk of the expenditures forecasted here, will probably increase within universities over the next decade, primarily as a result of substantial decreases in direct computer centre

TABLE I

Costs for Processing One Million Words
(approximately seven million characters)

Typing, proofing, and correcting at .75 per 1000 characters	$ 5,250
Scanning at .09 per 1000 characters	$ 630
Typing paper and airfreight	250
Magnetic tape, disk packs, and other supplies	1,370
	$ 7,500
Concording and text file formation	10,000
Word matching and merging into headword file	10,000
Retrievals and reruns	2,500
total	$ 30,000

support by the U.S. and Canadian governments. (This trend has already forced retrench-
ment at a number of major North American universities.) Labour, the second largest
consumer of data processing funds, will undoubtedly also increase over the five-year
period projected for data collection and initial programming. To allow for these trends,
conservative estimates have been made, with margins up to 50 per cent above current costs.

The costs for transferring data into a machine-readable form using pre-editing and
optical scanning are based upon comparative studies done for the *London Stage Project*
at Lawrence University (Appleton, Wisconsin).[11] Processing, from published texts to
magnetic tape, will include:
1 marking of identifiers and textual irregularities on the printed text by members of the
   editorial staff,
2 typing of the text using an optical scanner fount,
3 proofing and correction,
4 optical scanning.
Typing, proofing, and correction estimates are derived by doubling the typing costs
charged by a professional data-processing firm. The optical scanning estimate is based on
an informal quotation obtained for the DOE materials from an optical scanner company.
Computing estimates have the largest margin of uncertainty; they are based upon costs
for running concordances to OE materials on the Univac 1108, plus costs published by
the University of Wisconsin Computing Center for the basic operations which underlie
the word matching and headword file processes. The total cost estimates, excluding the
editors' expenses, are shown in table I.

Assuming a total corpus of 3.5 million words and 80 per cent coverage of this volume,
the total data processing costs for five years would be $84,000, or approximately $16,800
per year. This estimate assumes that all words in the input texts will be concorded and
eventually merged into the headword file. If the more common function words, verbal
auxiliaries, and certain other high-frequency words like 'dryhten,' 'god,' and 'mann' are
excluded during the concording process, the yearly costs would probably be in the
neighbourhood of $12,000.

11 Private communication from Professor Ben Schneider

APPENDIX: ENCODING STANDARDS FOR OLD ENGLISH TEXTS

SECTION I: GRAPHEMIC ENCODINGS

A: Symbol substitutions
    ash $
    eth +
    thorn *
    wynn w
e-caudata –
uu is punched as a sequence of two U's, not as wynn; ae as a sequence of graphically separate letters is punched as two letters: AE.

B: Punctuation
For the Dictionary, two classes of punctuation marks should be distinguished: end punctuation (point, comma, colon, dash, double point, etc.) by a period; internal punctuation by a comma.

C: Abbreviations and contractions
Except for the conjunctive use of the 'and' sign (7), which should be punched as numeric seven, all contractions and abbreviations should be expanded. This applies to the 'and' symbol used in compounds (e.g., '7swarian'), as well as to the nasal stroke.

D: Runic characters
Runic characters, other than wynn and thorn in their roman roles, are punched as two slashes, //, followed immediately by the roman equivalents, and then followed by two additional slashes.
Examples
swaᚱ toglideð SWA //L// TOGLIDE+
ᚹ is geswiðrad //W// IS GESWI+RAD

E: Editorial alterations
Editorial alterations and emendations are indicated by a single slash placed at the end of the word without intervening space. (The type of alteration and the letters affected are not indicated.)

F: Word divisions
Word and particle divisions are normalized in accordance with lexicographic practices; prefixes, including the participial 'ge,' are written without following space or hyphen. Thus, 'gedon' is encoded GEDON, and not GE-DON or GE DON.

SECTION II: CONCORDANCE FORMATS

A: Prose and poetry[12]
Texts for concording are encoded into records, each record containing an identifier and a

---

12 For convenience of explication the discussion which follows is based upon 80-column punched cards. However, the concordance program will accept input from either cards or magnetic tape (7 or 9 channel); punched paper tape must be copied onto magnetic tape.

context. Records may be any length up to and including 400 characters, but all records for a single concordance must be the same length. Thus, the record length for a concordance should be based upon the longest context in the text. If the longest contexts with their accompanying identifiers exceed 400 characters, the overflow procedure described below should be followed.

The identifier, which must be the first entity of the first card of each record, contains the list number for the text[13] and an unambiguous index to the first word of the context, based upon MS position whenever possible. Usually, the index will consist of page (or folio) and line numbers. If line numbers uniquely identify each line in the text, the page or folio number may be omitted. For certain texts logical divisions are marked by numbering, capitalization, or other graphic devices (e.g., chapter and verse for gospels; psalm and verse for psalters). Identifiers based upon these divisions should use arabic rather than roman numerals. Titles should be treated as independent records and identified accordingly (e.g., verse zero for a chapter title in the gospels). Each component of the identifier must be in the same card location in each record. For alignment of components which vary in length, blank spaces should precede the component. For example, if the page number is placed in columns 10-12, a one-digit page number belongs in column 12; a two-digit number in columns 11-12. The length of the identifier field may vary from text to text, but must be constant within a text. Generally, 20 columns or less should be assigned to the identifier.

The context for both poetry and prose should be a citable syntactic/semantic unit. (In general, the verse line will not be an adequate context for poetry.) The context must begin in the same location on card 1 of each record. If more than 80 columns are required for identifier and context, column 1 of each succeeding card should be treated as adjacent to column 80 of the preceding card. Thus, if a word ends in column 80 of a non- final card in a record, column 1 of the next card must be left blank. (Words must be separated by at least one blank; excessive blanks are harmless and inconsequential.)

For long sentences which exceed the allowable space in a record, the following convention should be employed: terminate the sentence so that space remains for the sequence .n. (period number period), where n is 1 for the first such termination, 2 for the second, and so on. Then, begin the context segment of the next record with the same sequence (.n.), followed by the remaining context. (Since the .n. 'words' will be sorted into the same section in the keyword listing of the concordance, the editors will be able to link abnormally split clauses.)

B: Continuous interlinear glosses
For continuous interlinear glosses such as the *Lindisfarne Gospels*, a third field in addition to the identifier and context must be included in each record. This field, which must begin in the identical card and column position in each record, contains the Latin unit which is glossed. A suggested format is as follows:
card 1, cols 1-12: identifier
card 1, col 13 to card 3, col 46: Latin
card 3, col 47 to card 4, col 80: OE

C: Glossaries, occasional interlinear glosses, and text variants
For glossaries and related materials two related formats are available, one to be used

13 See chapter 3

when a cross-reference or source-reference is present and one to be used if neither of these is present. The basic format is:

Columns	*Contents*
card 1, cols 1-12	identifier
card 1, col 13 to card 2, col 80	lemma
card 3, col 1 to card 4, col 80	gloss
card 5, cols 1-59	cross-references
card 5, cols 60-80	source-reference

For no cross-reference or source-reference, only cards 1-4 are used; for cross- or source-references, cards 1-5. In the cross- and source-references fields, no spaces should occur within a single reference. If so, the parts separated by spaces will be treated as separate references. Therefore, a cross-reference to the *Corpus Glossary*, entry 1400, should be coded as CP1400 and not as CP 1400. And *Corpus* entry 400 should be coded CP0400 and not CP400, since the latter will be sorted into a position before CP1400. (In general, matching for alphabetization proceeds from left-to-right, character by character; where two entries are of different lengths, blanks are added on the right end to equalize the lengths.) The order of characters, from highest to lowest, for sorting cross- and source-references is: blank, A-Z, 0-9, special characters. For occasional interlinear glosses, only cards 1-4 are used. Text variants should be treated as occasional interlinear glosses (pseudo-glosses), with the lemma being the word or phrase from the text which is concorded, and the gloss, the variant from another text (which is abbreviated in the identifier field). Each variant word or phrase must be entered on a separate record.

The complete set of records for a text, once keypunched, proofread, and corrected, should – if at all possible – be transferred to magnetic tape.[14]

The concordance will contain an alphabetized list of words which occur in the contexts,[15] each word being followed by all the contexts (with accompanying identifiers) in which the word occurs. The collating sequence for keywords will place æ between 'a' and 'b,' and ð and þ between 't' and 'u.' Following the listing of words with contexts will be an alphabetized list of the same words, followed by the frequency of occurrence of each. For continuous interlinear glosses and glossaries, the keyword listing will contain only OE headwords; however, the other components of each record will be listed with the contexts.

---

14 For transfer from card to tape, blocking of records up to 10,000 characters per physical block is allowed. Either 7 or 9 channel tapes are acceptable.

15 Words will occur in the list in the same form as they occur in context, but minus any end-of-word encodings. Morphological and spelling variants will not be converted to canonical forms, nor will any attempt be made to separate homographs. For many concordances, certain high-frequency function words will be omitted from the alphabetized listing.

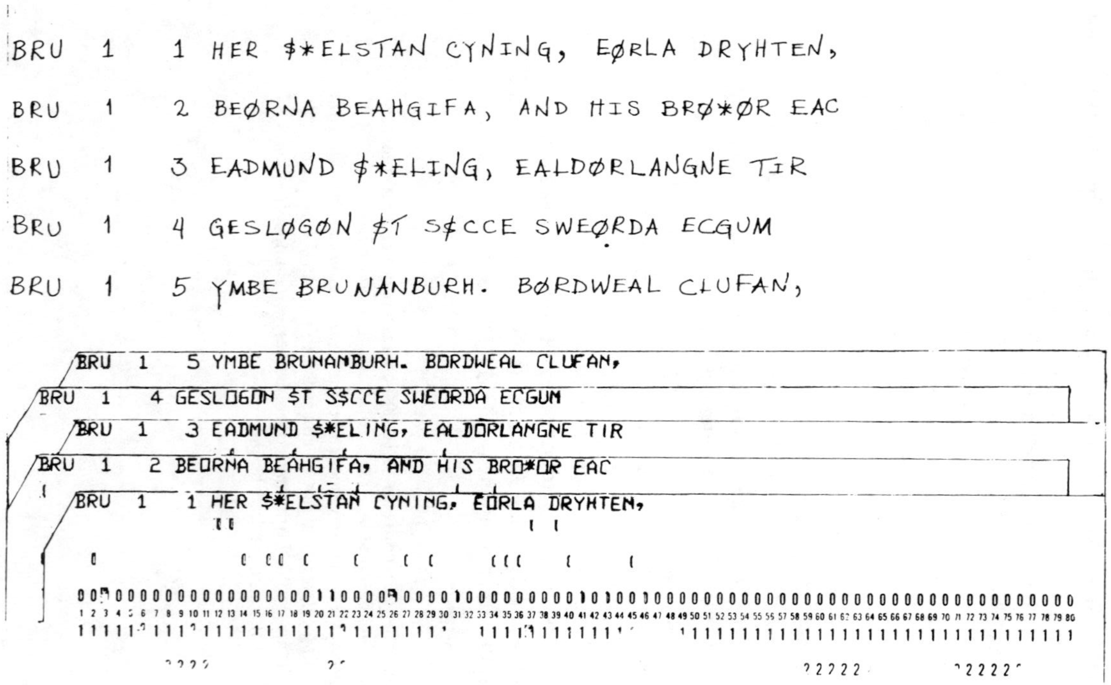

BRU 1   1 HER Þ*ELSTAN CYNING, EORLA DRYHTEN,

BRU 1   2 BEORNA BEAHGIFA, AND HIS BROÞR EAC

BRU 1   3 EADMUND Þ*ELING, EALDORLANGNE TIR

BRU 1   4 GESLOGON ÞT SÆCCE SWEORDA ECGUM

BRU 1   5 YMBE BRUNANBURH. BORDWEAL CLUFAN,

BRU 1   5 YMBE BRUNANBURH. BORDWEAL CLUFAN,
BRU 1   4 GESLOGON ÞT SÆCCE SWEORDA ECGUM
BRU 1   3 EADMUND Þ*ELING, EALDORLANGNE TIR
BRU 1   2 BEORNA BEAHGIFA, AND HIS BROÞR EAC
BRU 1   1 HER Þ*ELSTAN CYNING, EORLA DRYHTEN,

FIGURE 8 Encoded input, poetry: *Brunanburh*

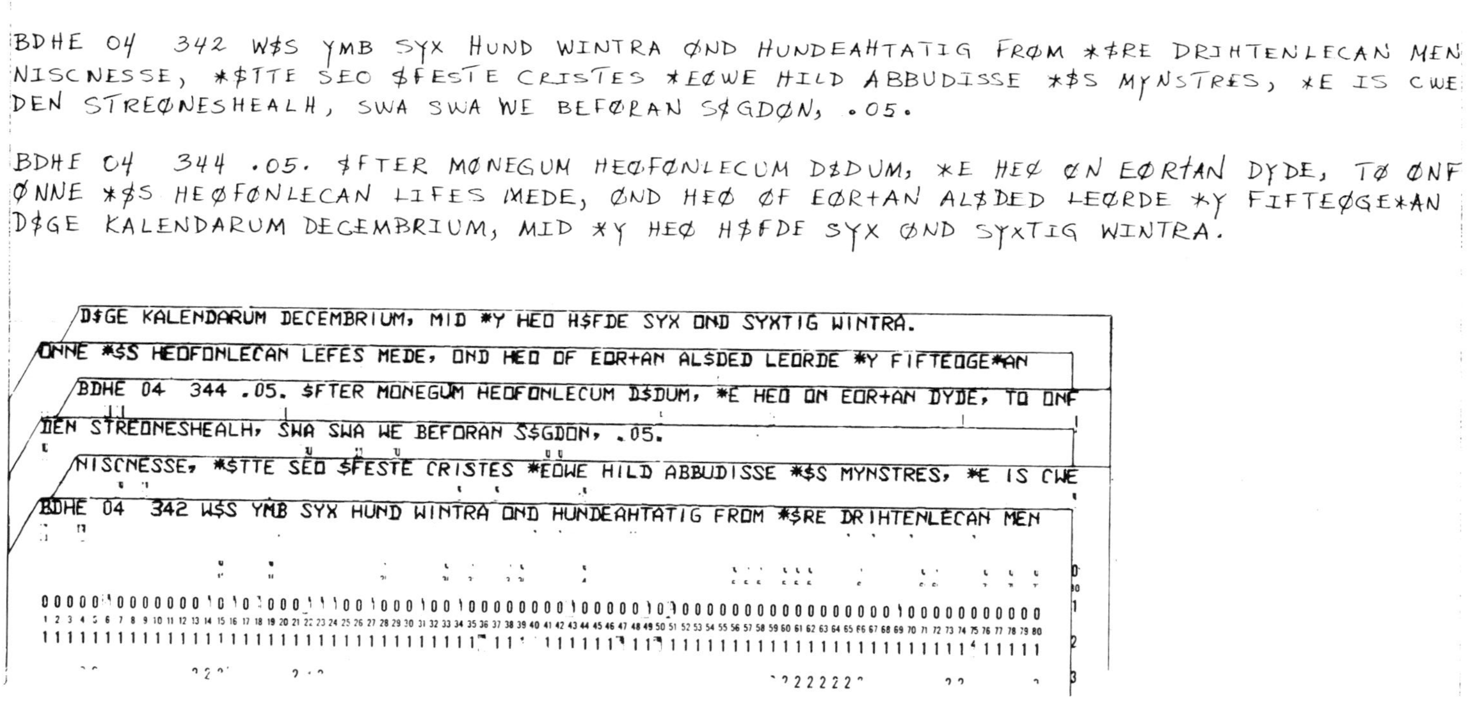
BDHE 04 342 W$S YMB SYX HUND WINTRA ØND HUNDEAHTATIG FRØM *$RE DRIHTENLECAN MEN
NISCNESSE, *$TTE SEO $FESTE CRISTES *EØWE HILD ABBUDISSE *$S MYNSTRES, *E IS CWE
DEN STREØNESHEALH, SWA SWA WE BEFØRAN S$GDØN, .05.
BDHE 04 344 .05. $FTER MØNEGUM HEØFØNLECUM D$DUM, *E HEØ ØN EØR+AN DYDE, TØ ØNF
ØNNE *$S HEØFØNLECAN LIFES MEDE, ØND HEØ ØF EØR+AN AL$DED LEØRDE *Y FIFTEØGE*AN
D$GE KALENDARUM DECEMBRIUM, MID *Y HEØ H$FDE SYX ØND SYXTIG WINTRA.
D$GE KALENDARUM DECEMBRIUM, MID *Y HEO H$FDE SYX OND SYXTIG WINTRA.
ONNE *$S HEOFONLECAN LEFES MEDE, OND HEO OF EOR+AN AL$DED LEORDE *Y FIFTEOGE*AN
BDHE 04 344 .05. $FTER MONEGUM HEOFONLECUM D$DUM, *E HEO ON EOR+AN DYDE, TO ONF
DEN STREONESHEALH, SWA SWA WE BEFORAN S$GDON, .05.
NISCNESSE, *$TTE SEO $FESTE CRISTES *EOWE HILD ABBUDISSE *$S MYNSTRES, *E IS CWE
BDHE 04 342 W$S YMB SYX HUND WINTRA OND HUNDEAHTATIG FROM *$RE DRIHTENLECAN MEN

FIGURE 9 Encoded input, prose: Bede's *Historia Ecclesiastica*

VP002 4 QUI HABITAT IN CAELIS INRIDEBIT EØS ET DNS≠2 SUBSANNABIT EØS.

SE EARDAT IN HEØFENUM BISMERAD HIE

⁊ DRY#T≠5 HYSPE꜀ HIE

VP002 5 TUNC LØQUETUR AD EØS IN IRA SUA ET IN FURØRE SUØ CØNTURBABIT EØS.

⁊ØNNE SPRICET TØ HIM IN EØRRE HIS

⁊ IN HATHEØRTNISSE HIS GEDRØEFE꜀ HIE

⁊ IN HATHEØRTNISSE HIS GEDRØEFE꜀ HIE

⁊ØNNE SPRICE꜀ TØ HIM IN EØRRE HIS

VP002 5 TUNC LØQUETUR AD EØS IN IRA SUA ET IN FURØRE SUØ CØNTURBABIT EØS.

⁊ DRYHT·5 HYSPE꜀ HIE

SE EARDA꜀ IN HEØFENUM BISMERAD HIE

VP002 4 QUI HABITAT IN CAELIS INRIDEBIT EØS ET DNS·2 SUBSANNABIT EØS.

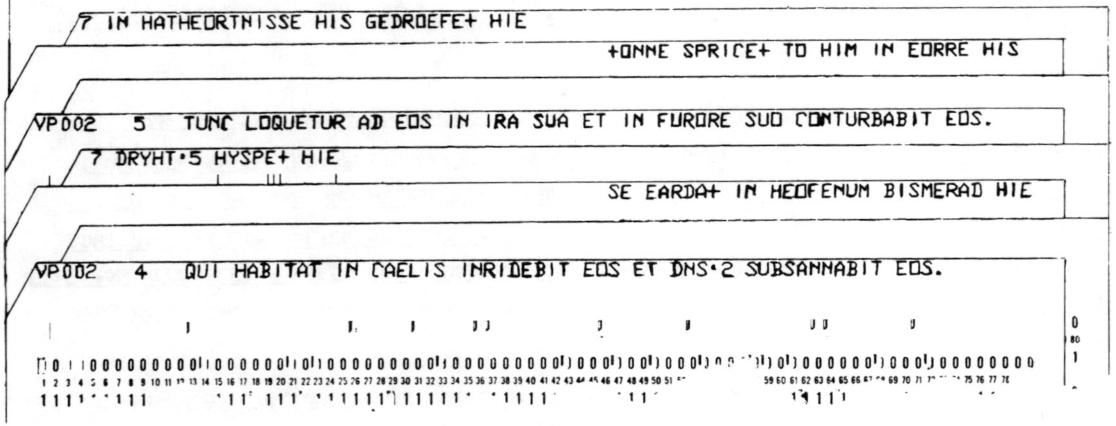

FIGURE 10 Encoded input, continuous interlinear glosses: *Vespasian Psalter*

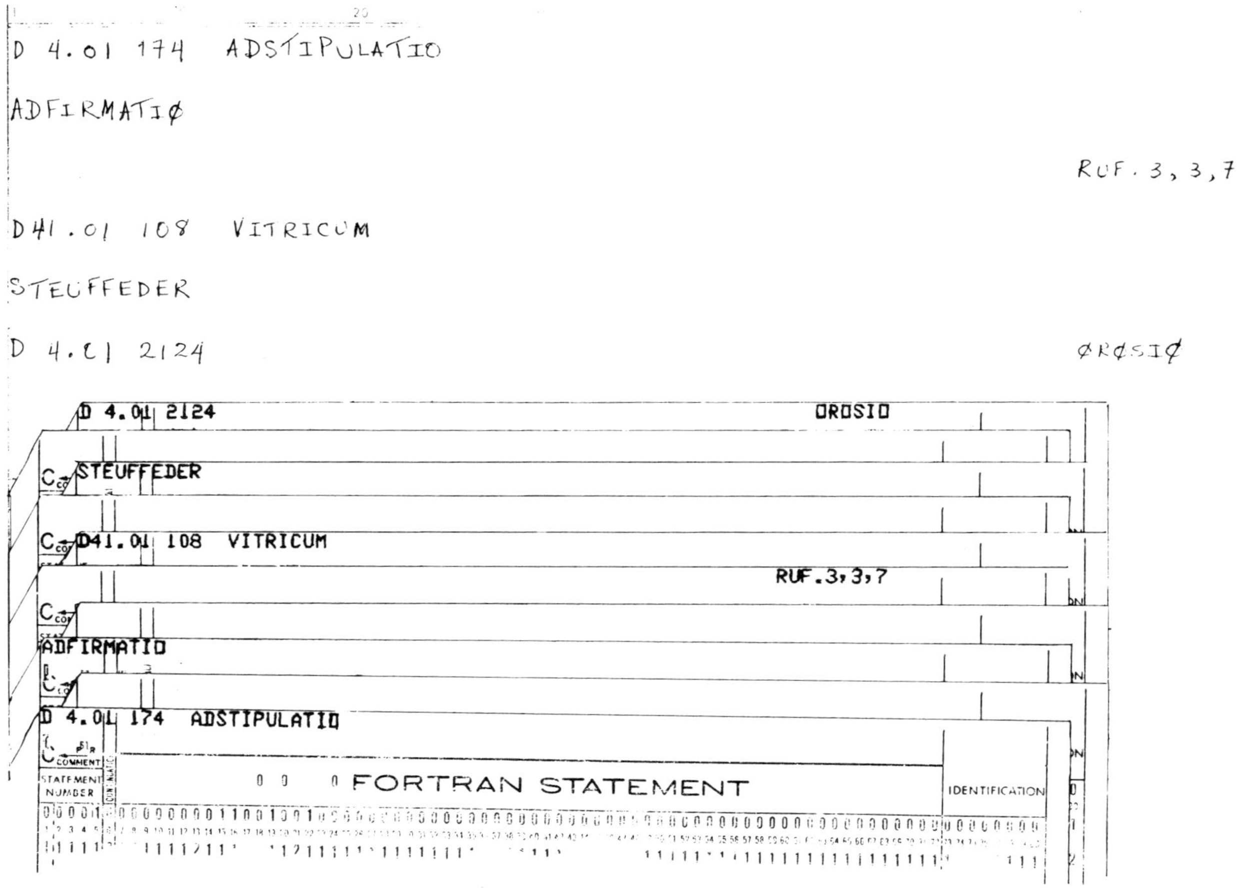

FIGURE 11 Encoded input, glossaries

some specimen entries
for the dictionary of old english

C.J.E. BALL AND ANGUS CAMERON

The purpose of this chapter is to sketch and discuss some specimen entries for the proposed new *Dictionary of Old English*. The editors wish to stress that at this stage none of the proposals is final, and most of them are merely tentative, or even speculative. Some decisions on the form of the dictionary entry must inevitably await the completion of the two earlier stages of the project (the preparation and the concording of the material). No detailed thought has yet been given to questions of layout and typography. We have experimented in the following pages with different formats for DOE entries and would welcome your comments on their relative effectiveness and any suggestions for possible improvement. A consistent and economical system of abbreviations and punctuation will have to be worked out at a later stage. Another major task which must be postponed for the present is the planning of a system of reference for the citations which will not become outdated and obscure before the end of the useful life of the Dictionary. In drafting this chapter the Dictionary editors have been assisted by a memorandum prepared by the International Advisory Committee. Dr R.B. Mitchell has advised on grammatical considerations. The material has been drawn from A.F. Cameron's thesis, 'The Old English Nouns of Colour: A Semantic Study,' presented for the degree of B.Litt. in the University of Oxford in June 1968.

PREFATORY NOTES TO THE SPECIMEN ENTRIES

The editors propose three types of entries: a full entry for common words, an exhaustive entry for rarer words (defined, perhaps, as those words which occur fewer than thirty times), and a special entry for grammar-words (effectively, all pronouns, conjunctions, and prepositions, together with some verbs, pronominal adjectives, and adverbs). Among the specimen entries on the following pages, 'bleo,' 'hiw,' 'hiwung,' 'hiwian,' and 'gehiwian' are examples of full entries; the remainder of the derivatives of 'hiw' and 'bleo' (suffixed +) are exhaustive entries; outline sketches are given of entries for a number of grammar words (see pp. 345-7), but these cannot be completed until all the material is available. The suffix + indicates that an exhaustive list of references is given in the entry, although all the examples of a word may not necessarily be cited (cf. 'bleo-fag,' 'hiwere,' 'scinn-hiw'). Consequently, some of the information given in the full entry can be dispensed with in the exhaustive entry (e.g., frequency of occurrence, distribution, typical collocations, Latin equivalents), since this can be easily deduced from a study of the citations and references. A full entry gives the following information: 1/ headword, 2/ variant spellings, 3/ grammatical details, 4/ derivational relationships, 5/ number of occurrences and any distributional restrictions, 6/ analysis of senses and illustrative citations, 7/ Latin equivalents, 8/ typical collocations, 9/ synonyms and antonyms, 10/ references to the appropriate entries in the MED and NED. It should be noted at once that there will be no entries for proper names, and that etymological and bibliographical information will be excluded, unless it is essential to the establishment of the meaning of the word in Old English. It is, however, hoped that three subordinate projects will be related to the main Dictionary, though published separately: an Old English onomasticon, an etymological dictionary, and an index of lexical studies arranged alphabetically according to the word discussed.

1 Headword
A headword is not a citation, so it is permissible to reconstruct the base form of a

paradigm where only oblique forms are extant (e.g., 'wundor-bleo'); but we will not normalize the headword (e.g., 'gebleoh'), unless merely erroneous spellings (as opposed to alternative spellings) survive. Where there is a choice, we will take the normal Late West-Saxon form (e.g., 'bleo,' 'hiw'), but there will be exhaustive cross references from alternative spellings, as indicated in the specimen entries.

2 Spelling
The spelling variants which are thus listed in the Dictionary will be repeated after the main headword (see 'bleo,' 'hiw,' etc.). This will be done in the case of all three types of entry. But no attempt will be made to give information about pronunciation beyond what can be deduced by the reader from the spellings. Vowel-length, however, will be marked on the headword, where appropriate, and not again within the entry. Runes will be transcribed according to the system established by Bruce Dickins (*Leeds Studies in English,* 1 [1932] , 15f). Except in cases of special interest (e.g., 'ðerh,' which is Northumbrian; 'end,' 'and,' which is an early form) the distribution of the various spellings will not be marked (e.g., 'hiu,' which is mainly Northumbrian; 'hif,' which is late).

3 Grammar
The grammar-words are a special problem, and it is probably unwise to try to lay down in advance too rigid a pattern for their treatment. But we would try to give the same sort of information about grammar-words as is provided for fully lexical words (e.g., variant spellings, derivational relationships, frequency and distribution, and Latin equivalents; the analysis of the various functions or uses of such words would probably be primarily syntactic and secondarily semantic (e.g., 'to,' 'þonne'). In addition, where possible, information would be given about overlap and contrast of grammatical function (e.g., the relations between 'se' and 'þes,' 'to' and 'fram,' 'þa' and 'þonne'). But even fully lexical words have grammatical peculiarities and require grammatical labelling. The word-class will be given for each entry, followed (where appropriate) by the inflexional subclass; in some cases (e.g., 'bleo-brygd') the latter information cannot be given because it is not known. Any morphological irregularities which are not treated in the standard Old English grammars will also be noted. How far we shall be able to give subtler grammatical information is not yet clear. In the case of nouns, 'ylde' must be marked 'only plural,' and 'here' 'collective' (since it colligates with singular and plural verbs). But it will require experimentation to establish the categories of the noun, adjective, and verb which can be labelled without leading us into constant difficulty with the distinction between those things which 'can't occur' and those things which merely 'don't occur.'

4 Derivational Information
The derivational relationships of compound words can easily be indicated by hyphenating the headword (e.g., 'wundor-bleo'), but affixed forms are more difficult to handle. It is suggested that (as in the case of 'gebleod,' 'hiwung,' 'gehiwian,' etc.) a reference be made simply to the source, which may be at one or more removes (cf. 'hiwung'), and to any further derivatives. In this way the Dictionary will dispense with entries for all elements below the level of the word, and no systematic information will be given about word-formation by means of prefixation and suffixation. In the case of simple words (e.g., 'bleo,' 'hiw') three types of derivatives must be distinguished: affixed forms, compounds in which the headword is first element, and compounds in which it is second

element. The number of items of each type, together with a full list of the items, will be given. Incompletely assimilated loanwords and loan-translations will also be referred to their source (e.g., 'plant(ian),' 'calic,' 'sancte'; 'ælmihtig,' 'welwillende,' 'godspell').

5 Frequency and Distribution

The number of occurrences of full entries will be noted, possibly to the nearest 100 in the case of very common words and grammar-words. As much information as possible will be given about distributional restrictions, although we cannot at this stage state precisely in how many ways it will be possible or useful to analyse the vocabulary. Certainly, the 'mode of discourse' in which words occur should be noted, perhaps as indicated in the full entries below where V = verse, P = prose, I = interlinear glosses, and G = collected glosses. But restrictions of date, dialect, and author will also be given, and it may be useful in some cases to state the 'field of discourse' in which a word typically occurs (e.g., the language of law, science, religion). For some words the frequency and distribution of particular senses may be notable (e.g., 'modig,' which means 'noble-spirited, brave' only in verse; 'hiwian,' which means 'to colour' only once); it seems useful, therefore, in such cases to indicate the number of occurrences of each sense and any special restrictions on its distribution.

6 Senses and Citations

This is, of course, the heart of the Dictionary and the part which it is most difficult to plan in advance. The analysis of the senses of a word may be done in a number of ways — historically, by genre, logically, syntactically, and so on. We would on the whole not wish to favour (or to exclude) any method of analysis and arrangement of senses in advance, but rather to treat each word in the way which produced the most informative results. It is clear that the Dictionary will not be primarily a historical dictionary; in this respect the editors feel more in sympathy with the introduction to the MED than that to the NED. We would prefer to aim for generosity of citation and reference than extreme complexity of semantic analysis: thus the sense 'complexion' could be distinguished for 'bleo' (in some of the examples under B), but we would prefer this to be implicit and to use the space for further quotations of examples or references. In the specimen examples we have intentionally varied the method of analysis to suit the particular example; most words are treated logically, but in some (e.g., 'hiwian') the syntactic analysis is important, and in others (e.g., 'hiw,' 'bleo') a distinction is made between the sense and the application of the word. This latter distinction seems to us fruitful in the case of many abstract words: e.g., 'ælmihtig,' which has a very limited application (it could not be used of Beowulf); or 'hleoþrian,' which can be used with both animate and inanimate subjects (note the crucial use in the *Dream of the Rood*, 26). The number of citations given for any entry will depend, of course, on the frequency of occurrence of the word and on its semantic complexity: in general, citations will be chosen to reinforce the information given about the distribution of the senses of a word.

7 Latin Equivalents

In the case of full entries it may be useful to gather together a list of typical Latin equivalents (in the specimen entries these are capitalized), but not errors (e.g., CALOR for 'bleo') or unique contextually determined equivalents. Of course, many of the citations will be given together with the Latin source.

8 Collocation

Where words contract habitual or typical collocational patterns these should be listed and the numbers of occurrences given. It is a matter of judgement where to stop in such listings: in the case of 'bleo,' should the unique example of 'bleo ... cyrran' be noted beside the relatively frequent 'bleo ... bregdan'? Probably some arbitrary figure will have to be accepted as a definition of a notable collocation. In the example given ('bleo ... bregdan') a cross-reference to 'bleo-brygd' is clearly in order, together with the appropriate reverse reference.

9 Sense Relations

We propose to give information, where possible, about the synonyms and antonyms of the entries. This will only be done where the information can be extracted from a study of usage: assumptions and guesses about sense relations will be excluded. This principle is exemplified in the lists of synonyms given for 'hiw' and 'bleo,' which are not co-extensive, although the headwords themselves are synonyms. It should perhaps be made clear that synonymy does not necessarily imply total equivalence in all senses and contexts: antonymy should similarly be qualified.

10 Cross-References to MED and NED

These references will be given wherever possible.

Finally, it may be worth noting that a number of appendices could well be attached to the Dictionary itself, or published separately: an index of New English-Old English equivalents; a thesaurus of Old English modelled on Roget and derived from the information given in the Dictionary about sense relations; a Latin-Old English dictionary; lists of sub-vocabularies of Old English (e.g., words restricted by date, dialect, genre, author, mode of discourse, field of discourse); lists of important derivational subclasses of Old English (e.g., abstract nouns formed with '-ung,' verbs formed with '-læcan,'); lists of important syntactic subclasses (e.g., verbs governing the dative case, nouns which colligate with singular and plural verbs).

blēo (*bleoh, bleow-, blio, blioh*)
Noun, neuter ja-stem. (4) *gebleod, gebleoh, unbleo, ungebleoh*; (8) *bleobord, bleobrygd, bleocræft, bleofag, bleofæstnes, bleomete, bleoread, bleostæning*; (3) *goldbleoh, twibleo, wundorbleo.* 53 (V 13, P 25, I 11, G 4). Not Anglian (but not so restricted in ME), not early, not Wulfstan.
a/ 'appearance'
b/ specifically 'colour'

A, as an attribute of the supernatural,
i/ of supernatural signs: Geseah ic þæt fuse beacen / wendan wædum ond bleom. *Dream of the Rood,* 22. Saturnus cwæð, 'Ac hu moniges bleos bið ðæt deofol and se Pater Noster ðonne hie betwih him gewinnað?' Saloman cwæð, 'Dritiges bleos.' *Prose Solomon and Saturn,* 168. Seo gastlice cwen, Godes gelaðung, is geglencged mid deorwurðre frætewunge and menigfealdum bleo godra drohtnunga and mihta. Ælfric, *Dedicatio ecclesiae,* 2, 586, 18.
ii/ of the devil and fiends: Mæg simle se godes cwide … manfulra heap / sweartne geswencan, næfre hie ðæs syllice / bleoum bregdað. *Solomon and Saturn,* 150.

B, as an attribute of man,
i/ of the soul: Hwilum he bið collsweart and gelice sio sawl hiwað on yfel bleoh, swa same swa se lichoma, and bið gyt wyrsan hiwes. *Vercelli Homily,* 4, 326. Heo is ungesæwenlic and unlichomlic, butan hæfe and butan bleo. Ælfric, *Nativity of Christ,* 177. We cwæden ær þæt heo wære butan bleo, forþan ðe heo nis na lichamlic. On lichaman bið bleoh, and seo sawul bið swa gewlitegod swa heo on worulde geearnode. Ælfric, *id.,* 208-9.
ii/ of the body: Ful oft þæt gegongeð, mid godes meahtum, / þætte wer ond wif in woruld cennað / bearn mid gebyrdum ond mid bleom gyrwað. *The Fortunes of Men,* 3. Glæd wæs ic gliwum, glenged hiwum, / blissa bleoum, blostma hiwum. *The Riming Poem,* 4. Þonne bryt se lichoma on manig-

fealdum bleon: ærest he bið on medmicles mannes hiwe, þonne æt nehstan on þam fægerestan manes hiwe. *Vercelli Homily,* 4, 173. and [Simon Magus] bræd hine on feala bleona þurh deofles þegnunga. *Blickling Homily,* 175, 5. Frecne bið eac, þonne þæs seocan mannes hraca bið maniges hiwes and bleo. *Bald's Leechbook,* 2, 46.

C, as an attribute of nature,
i/ general: ða ic þe on þa fægran foldan ge-sette / to neotenne neorxnawonges / beorhtne blædwelan, bleom scinende. *Christ,* 1391. and þingum eallunga bleoh gehwyrfþ [Rebusque iam color redit]. *Durham Hymn Gloss,* 21. Niht sweart gescæfta oferhelað eorþan bleoh ealra [Nox atra rerum contegit / Terrę colores omnium]. *id.,* 23. Hwi is þæt tacn on mislices bleos? On þam tacne is wæteres hiw and fyres, and þæt tacn þæt is se ren-boga cymð of þam sunbeame and of wætum wolcne, to þan þæt he sy middanearde to orsorhnysse mid þam wæterigan bleo, þæt wæter us eft ealle ne adrence. Ælfric, *Interrogationes Sigewulfi in Genesin,* 55. Men magon swa ðeah þa fyrwite beoð cepan be his bleo and be ðære sunnan oððe þæs roderes, hwilc weder toweard bið. Ælfric, *De Temporibus Anni,* 8, 12. Leort ða tacen forð, þær hie to sægon, / fæder, frofre gast, ðurh fyres bleo / up eðigean. *Elene,* 1105. Monan bleoh habban hynðe ḡ [Lunam colores habere damnum significat]. *Prognostics, De somniorum diuersitate,* 156.
ii/ of creatures: Se wifman se ne mæge bearn afedan nime þonne anes bleos cu meoluc on hyre handæ and gesupe þonne mid hyre muþe. *Lacnunga,* 171. Hrefen, þa hwile þe he gesihð his briddas hwites bleos, ne silð he him nane mettas. *Rule of Chrodegang,* 81. Hwilum brugdon eft / awyrgde wærlogan on wyrmes bleo. *Guthlac,* 911.
iii/ of plants: and heo hafað on ufeweardon þam stelan sæd ðistele gelic, ac hyt byð smælre and read on bleo. *Herbarium,* 134. and heo hafað sæd sinewealt and þæt byð

þreora cynna bleos. *id.*, 137. for þy þe is
geðuht þæt heo þone heofonlican bogan mid
hyre bleo geefenlæce se is on leden iris
gecweden. *id.*, 158.

iv/ of cloths and dyes: Ne seolocenra hrægla
mid mistlicum bleowum hi ne gimdon.
Boethius, 15. On ðæs sacerdes hrægle wæs
toeacan golde and iacincðe and purpuran,
dyrodine twegera bleo. *The Pastoral Care*,
14. Twegra bleo [bistinctus coccus].
Harley Glossary, B 264. bleo [blauum. color
est uestis] . *id.*, B 474.

v/ of gems and stones: swa þæt hi þær
gemetton ane mære þruh wið þone weall
standende geworht of marmstane eall hwites
bleos bufan þære eorðan. Ælfric, *Saint
Æthelthryth*, 81. and swaðeah ðæt bleoh
ðæs welhæwnan iacintes bið betera ðonne
ðæs blacan carbuncules. *The Pastoral Care*,
52. heo hæfð hwites marman bleoh.
Herbarium, 51. Þæt wæs swilce coriandran
sæd, hwites bleos swa cristalla. *Numbers*,
XI, 7.

D, of uncertain application,
bleoh [color] . *Ælfric's Glossary*, 306, 17.
anes bleos [unius coloris] , mislices bleos
[discolor] . *id.*, 306, 18-9. anes bleos [con-
color] . *Ælfric's Grammar*, 47, 16. anes bleos
[unicolor] , mislic bleo [discolor] . *Plantin-
Moretus Glossary*, 181, 13-4.

COLOR, CROMA.
mislic bleo (4); *bleo ... bregdan* (5) (cf.
bleobrygd).
= *hiw* (but cf. color [bleoh] , forma [hiw] .
Ælfric's Glossary, 306, 17-9); = *onlicnes*.
MED blē; NED blee.

blēo-bord +
Noun, neuter ja-stem.
'checker-board' (probably marked out for
the game of tables)
Swa missenlice meahtig dryhten / geond
eorþan sceat eallum dæleð / ... sumum tæfle
cræft, / bleobordes gebregd. *The Fortunes*

of Men, 71.
= *tæfl* (see H.J.R. Murray, *MÆ* 10 [1941]
57 f.)

blēo-brygd +
Noun.
'variation of colour'
Is se fugel fæger forweard hiwe, / bleo-
brygdum fag ymb·þa breost foran. *The
Phoenix*, 292. (cf. *bleo ... bregdan*)

blēo-fāg (*bleofah*) +
Adjective.
'coloured, many-coloured'
On þysne mislecan ymbhwyrft and bleofagan
[In orbem] . *Cleopatra Glossary*, 428, 10.
bleofah [uersicolor diuersos mutans colores] .
Aldhelm Gloss, Bouterwek 1853, 419.
Byrne is min bleofag. *Riddle*, 20, 3. Oferslop
bleofah habban ærende fullic ge [Byrrum
coloreum habere, nuntium fedum significat] .
Prognostics, De somniorum diuersitate, 33.
bleofage [multicolora] . *Prudentius Gloss*,
175, Meritt 1959, 19.

blēo-fāh see *bleofag*.
blēoh see *bleo*.
blēow- see *bleo*.
blīo see *bleo*.
blīoh see *bleo*.

geblēod (*gebliod*) +
Participial adjective. *bleo*.
'coloured'
and ða wyrta sona wynsumlice greowon mid
menigfealdum blostmum mislice gebleode.
Ælfric, *Hexameron*, 191. Cymeð wundorlic
Cristes onsyn, / ... on sefan swete sinum
folce, / biter bealofullum, gebleod wundrum,
/ eadgum ond earmum ungelice. *Christ*, 908.
gebliod reaf [stragulam uestem] . *Proverbs,
Kentish Glosses*, 86, 31.

geblēoh +
Noun, neuter ja-stem. *bleo.*

'appearance, colour'
swa ðeah þæs Ælmihtigan cystinys hi
geglencð mid swa wlitigum blostmum,
þæt hi oferstigað mid heora fægernysse ealle

eorðlice gebleoh. Ælfric, *Sixteenth Sunday after Pentecost,* 2, 464, 9.

geblīod see *gebleod.*

geheowian see *gehiwian.*
gehiowian see *gehiwian.*
gehiuian see *gehiwian.*
gehiwian (*geheowian, gehiowian, gehiuian, gehywian*)
Verb, Weak II: trans. (+ acc.) and intrans. *hiwian, hiw: gehiwung.* 75 (V 3, P 49, I 21, G 2).

a/ 'create, form, devise'; also in a bad sense
Swa on six dagum ærest god ealles middangeardes fægernysse **gehiwode** and gefrætwode. *Prose Saint Guthlac,* 5, 62, Gonser 1909, 125. and þa wuniað on wudum ða þe of þara treowa dropum **gehiwode** wæron. *Martyrology,* Herzfeld 1900, 46, 7. for þon þe he of þære eorðan selfre unmængedre ær gesceapen wæs and **gehiwad** þurh godes hand geweorc. *Biblical Note,* Napier 1889, 1, 10. and ic eom se ðe man of eorðan **gehiwode.** *Saint Eustace and his Companions,* 63, Skeat 1881-1900, 2, 194. Sec nu þinne þeow, Drihten, forþon þe þine handa me geworhtan and **geheowodan.** *Blickling Homilies,* Morris 1874-80, 87, 32. Ne mihte seo his swaðu næfre mid nænigre oðre wisan beon þæm oðrum florum geonlicod and gelice **gehiwad.** *Martyrology,* Herzfeld 1900, 74, 15. sio godcunde foretiohhung ... eall þing **gehiwað.** *Boethius,* 39, 6, Sedgefield 1899, 129, 9. he **gehiwige** dæda stranglice [Informet actus strenuos] . *Durham Hymn Gloss,* Stevenson 1851, 16, 1. Draca þes þone þu **gehiwodyst** to bysmriynne him [Draco iste quem formasti ad iludendum ei] . *Cambridge Psalter,* 103, 26, Wildhagen 1910, 261 (ðu **gehiwodes.** *Canterbury Psalter,* ðu **gehiowades.** *Vespasian Psalter,* ðu **gehiwodes.** *Junius Psalter*). Dracan þu þysne dædum ðinum / **geheowadest.** *Paris Psalter,* 103, 25. soðlice **gehiowades** [iam plasmaueras] . *Vespasian Hymn,* 13, Kuhn 1965, 159. and ealle lichamlicra þinga hiw heo mæg on hyre sylfre **gehiwian,** and swa **gehiwode** on hyre mode gehealden. Ælfric, *Nativity of Christ,* 225, Skeat 1881-1900, 1, 24. and ðara treowa æcyrfe and lafe ... on hwæthwuga fata **gehiwod** wæron. Bede, *History,* 3, 22, Schipper 1897-9, 291. Blodig wolcen ... on mistlice beamas wæs **gehiwod.** *Abingdon Chronicle (C)* 979, Rositzke 1940, 51. and heo nan þincg on hire næfð horses gecyndes, ac on eowrum gesihþum hit is swa **gehiwod** þurh ðæs deofles dydrunge. Ælfric, *Saint Swithhun,* 489, Skeat 1881-1900, 1, 470. Þa gesawen heo færlice an scipful manna þa wæron swiðe fægre **gehiwode.** *Saint Nicholas* (unpublished).

b/ 'disguise, pretend, dissemble'
dryhten ælmihtig ... hyne sylfne for ure þearfe to men **gehywode.** *Vercelli Homily,* 21 (unpublished). Þæt fyr com ufan ðe þa scep forbærnde, ac hit ne com na of heofenum þeah ðe hit swa **gehiwod** wære. Ælfric, *First Sunday in September,* Thorpe 1844-6, 2, 450, 33. he þa **gehywode** hine sylfne to næddran hiwe. *Monday in Rogationtide 1* (unpublished). Hwilon comon deoflu to sumum munuce ... and wæron **gehiwode** to heofonlicre fægernysse. *Rule of Chrodegang,* 84, Napier 1916, 99, 8. Þa **gehiwode** he hine sylfne to sumum ælþeodigum men. *Gregory's Dialogues,* 1, 10, Hecht 1900-7, 75, 4. and bæd þæt hi hyre fæx forcurfon on wæpmonna wysan, and mid wædum **gehiwodon,** swylce heo cniht wære. Ælfric, *Saint Eugenia,* 51, Skeat 1881-1900, 1, 28. Ne lufa þu þinne broðor mid **gehiwodre** heortan. Ælfric, *Admonitio,* 5, Norman 1849, 46, 4. he is

gehiwod to cristenum men, and is earm hæðengylda. Ælfric, *Circumcision*, Thorpe 1844-6, 1, 102, 16. and bið eac foroft swa gehiwod licetere swylce he wis sy. Wulfstan, *Gifts of the Holy Spirit*, 76, Bethurum 1957, 187. Þæt of gehiwudre eadmodnysse andetnysse stowe hi gemetan halignysse [ut ex ficta humilitate confessionis locum inueniant sancti-tatis]. *Liber Scintillarum*, 6, Rhodes 1889, 29, 5. gehiwedre [dissimulato, occultato]. *Aldhelm Gloss*, Bouterwek 1853, 517.

  c/ 'typify, symbolize'

Þurh myrran is gehiwod cwelmbærnys ures flæsces. Ælfric, *Epiphany*, Thorpe 1844-6, 1, 118, 3. Rihtlice wæs se bydel cristes æristes swa gehiwod. Ælfric, *Easter*, Thorpe 1844-6, 1, 222, 33. Her seo gytsung gehiwod wæs weorðlice on gegyrelan. *Prudentius title*, 61, Zupitza 1876, 42. gehiwudre spræce æfter gastlicre gebycnuncge [tropologiam]. *Ald-helm Gloss*, Napier 1900, 8, 15c. is gehiwot [figuratur]. *id.*, 11, 101.

  d/ 'depict, colour'

and gehiwode hire eagan and hire neb mid rude togeanes hieu. Ælfric, *From the Book of Kings*, 342, Skeat 1881-1900, 1, 404. and his forebreost fægre gehiwod swylce marmor-stan mærost cynnes. *De Sancte Iohanne*, 58-9, Kluge 1885, 478. Das twelf tacna sind swa gehiwode on ðam heofonlicum rodere. Ælfric, *De Temporibus Anni*, 4, 15, Henel 1942, 30. Quinqunx uel cincus þæt beoð þa fif dælas, beoð þus gehiwod. *Byrhtferth's Manual*, Crawford 1929, 190, 7.

(CON)FORMARE, (DE)PINGERE, (DIS)SIMULARE, FINGERE, (IN)FORMARE, PLASMARE, (TRANS)FIGURARE.

= *(ge)scyppan, gewyrcan, hiwian, geregnian.*

gehywian see *gehiwian.*

heo see *hiw.*

heow see *hiw.*

heowian see *hiwian.*

heowung see *hiwung.*

hiew see *hiw.*

hif see *hiw.*

hiow see *hiw.*

hiu see *hiw.*

hiung see *hiwung.*

hiw (*heo, heow, hiew-, hif, hiow, hiu, hyow, hyw*)

Noun, neuter ja-stem. (36) *æhiw, æhiwe, æhiwnes, æthiwian, anhiwe, behiwian, dimhiwe, frumhiwung, fyðerhiwe, geatolhiwian, geedhiwian, gehiwendlic, gehiwian, gehiwlæcan, gehiwodlice, gehiwung, gyldenhiwe, hiwere, hiwfæst, hiwian, hiwleas, hiwlic, hiwnes, hiwung, mænighiwe, oferhiwian, seofonhiwe, twihiwe, twihiwed, twihiwian, þrihiwed, þusendhiwe, ungehiwed, ungehiwedlic, unhiwe, unhiwed;* (2) *hiwbeorht, hiwfæger;* (3) *scinnhiw, spæceheow, wyrmhiw.* 278 (V 19, P 205, I 47, G 7).

a/ 'appearance' b/ specifically 'colour'

    A, as an attribute of the supernatural

i/ general: Ne ge næfre hys stefne ne gehyrdon, ne ge hys *hyw* ne gesawon. *West Saxon Gospels*, John 5, 37, Grünberg 1967, 213. Ne heora wlita ne awent to wyrsan *hiwe.* Ælfric, *Passion of Saint Cecilia*, 83, Skeat 1881-1900, 2, 360. Seo wyrd and sio *hiow* hie oft oncyrreð and on oþer hworfeð. *Alexander's Letter*, Rypins 1924, 11. *hiwum* [toraciclis, formis, imaginibus]. *Aldhelm Gloss*, Bouterwek 1853, 431 (*id.*, 416, 508, and Napier 1900, 1, 410, 1044, 4355).

ii/ of the Holy Spirit: Fer ræscendum leohte tungan *hiw* brohte [Ignis vibrante lumine

Lingue figuram detulit]. *Durham Hymn Gloss,* Beata nobis 2, Stevenson 1851, 94, 2 (also Gneuss 1968, 364). Leoht hafað *heow* and had haliges gastes / Cristes gecyndo. *Solomon and Saturn,* 410, ASPR 6, 37.

iii/ of the Son: þæs þu *hiw* lichoman geniman gemedemod þu wære [Cujus tu formam corporis Assumere dignatus es]. *Durham Hymn Gloss,* Rex æterne domine 3, Stevenson 1851, 31, 11 (also *Vespasian Hymn,* 13, 3, Kuhn 1965, 159). O eala þu crist halgena wlite and myht, lif and *hiw,* weg, leoht and ealdor [Christe sanctorum decus atque virtus Vita et forma via lux et auctor]. *Durham Hymn Gloss,* Christe sanctorum 1, Stevenson 1851, 69, 2 (also Gneuss 1968, 342). Ac se ðe is arwurðfol ofer ealle gesceafta, he gemedemode hine sylfne þæt he wære gesewen on ðam atelican *hiwe.* Ælfric, *Second Sunday after Pentecost,* Thorpe 1844-6, 1, 336, 35. Us is þonne mid mycelre gemynde to geþencenne þæt se ælmihtiga, se þe wæs on godes *hiwe,* god fæder efenece, onfeng þæt *hiw* ure tyddran gecynde. Geþencean we eac, gif oþer nyten wære to haligienne, and geteod to þon ecan life, þonne onfenge he heora *hiwe,* ac he wolde urum *hiwe* onfon. *Blickling Homilies,* Morris 1874-80, 29, 3-5. Þa he hyne gebæd þa wæs his ansyn oðres *hywes. West Saxon Gospels,* Luke 9, 29, Grünberg 1967, 182 (*id.,* Mark 16, 12, Grünberg 1967, 166). on oþrum *hiwe* [transfiguratus]. *Cleopatra Glossary,* Wright-Wülcker 1884, 481, 9. and in þam dæge bið dryhtnes onsyn swiðe egeslicu and ondryslicu and on þam *hiwe* þe he wæs þa hine iudeas swungon and ahengon. *Vercelli Homily,* 2, 10, Förster 1932, 44. And he geseah þa seofon candelstafas, and þæt *hiw* mannes bearnes þæt is þone god sylfa. *Easter Day 2* (unpublished).

iv/ of angels: Nat ic þeah heo beo biswicen þurh þæs engles *hiw. Nativity of Mary the Virgin,* 613, Assmann 1889, 134. Ic nan þing geseon ne mihte bute mines latðeawes scinende *heow* and gewæden. Ælfric, *Alia Visio,* Warner 1917, 117, 1. Hwilon he sceawæð hine seluen on engles *hywe* and bið þeahhweðere awariged gast swa swa he ær wæs. *Lent Homily,* Belfour 1909, 104, 1.

v/ of supernatural signs: Men gesawon ane hand on þam fægerestan readan *hiwe* of heofonum cumende. *Prose Saint Guthlac,* 1, 16, Gonser 1909, 105, 2. Heo is eac on onsyne utan yfeles *heowes. Blickling Homily,* Morris 1874-80, 197, 9.

vi/ of the sacraments: Se ðe forgymeleasige gehalgod husl on ðon þæt hit to lange licge, þæt him sy unsyfernes on oððe hit næbbe his *hiw,* fæste XL nihta. *Confessionale Pseudo-Egberti,* 24, Spindler 1934, 190 (also Mone 1830, 510; Raith 1933, 63). Micel is betwux þære ungesewenlican mihte þæs halgan husles and þam gesewenlican *hiwe* agenes gecyndes. Ælfric, *Easter,* Thorpe 1844-6, 2, 270, 12. Þæt þæt ðær gesewen is hæfð lichamlic *hiw,* and þæt þæt we ðæron understandað hæfð gastlice mihte. *id.,* 270, 29. Þeos gerynu is wedd and *hiw*; cristes lichama is soðfæstnyss. *id.,* 272, 6 (*id.,* 268, 27-35).

vii/ of the devil and fiends: Se hatte 'Lucifer', þæt ys 'Leohtberend', for ðære miclan beorhtnisse his mæran *hiwes.* Ælfric, *Letter to Sigeweard,* 79, Crawford 1922, 19. He nateshwon ne ondred heora deofellican *hiw,* ne he næs bepæht ðurh heora leasungum. Ælfric, *Martin,* Thorpe 1844-6, 2, 512, 22. Þa æt nextan comon cwelmbære deoflu swutellice gesewene, on sweartum *hiwe,* into ðam cilde. Ælfric, *Feria II in Letania Maiore,* Thorpe 1844-6, 2, 326, 12. Þa com her sæmninga micel weorud werigra gasta, and wæron swiðe on grislicum *heowe* and ondwliotan. Bede, *History,* 5, 13, Schipper, 1897-9, 638. Þa cwæþ se geeadcucoda, 'Me coman to silhearwan, atelices *hiwes* swa heage swa entes. Ælfric, *Saints Julian and Basilissa,* 286, Skeat 1881-1900, 1, 106. Þær hy mislice mongum reordum / on þam westenne woðe hofun / hludne herecirm, *hiwes* binotene, / dreamum bidrorene. *Guthlac,* 900 (*id.,* 909), ASPR 3, 75. Þa eode ut of þæs karcernes hwomme swiþe egeslic draca, missenlices *hiwes. Saint Margaret,* 3, Cockayne 1861, 43, 13.

B, as an attribute of man

i/ of the soul: Sume þing heo wyle, sume ðing heo nele, and ealle lichamlicra þinga *hiw* heo mæg on hyre sylfre gehiwian. Ælfric, *Nativity of Christ,* 223, Skeat 1881-1900, 1, 24. ealle hie sceolan þonne arisan and forþgan to þam dome on swylcum *heowe* swa hie ær sylfe gefrætwodan. *Blickling Homilies,* Morris 1874-80, 95, 18. And þonne cweð drihten to þam heah engle, 'Hwæt þeos sawul swyðe unfægeres *hiwes* is.' *Second Sunday in Lent* 2 (unpublished). and gelice sio sawl hiwað on yfel bleoh, swa same swa se lichoma, and bið gyt wyrsan *hiwes. Vercelli Homily,* 4, 326, Förster 1932, 101 (*id.,* 87-8, 100).

ii/ of the body: Se lichama ongan þa swætan and mislic *hiw* bredan. *Her is halwendlic lar,* Napier 1883, 141, 3 (*id.,* 140, 27). Ic wat ðæt þu eart wlitig on *hiwe. Genesis,* 12, 11, Crawford 1922, 115. Glæd wæs ic gliwum, glenged *hiwum,* / blissa bleoum, blostma *hiwum. The Riming Poem,* 3-4, ASPR 3, 166. He wæs lytel on his wæstmum and swiðe yfellices *hiwes* and forsewenlices. *Gregory's Dialogues,* 1, 5, Hecht 1900-7, 45, 31. þa heo þonon hwurfon þa wurdon þa twege cnihtæs al swa fægeres *hiwæs* swa heoræ fæderæs wæron and þa modra wæron alswa swearte swa heo ær wæron. *Invention of the Cross,* 1, Napier 1894, 18, 23. ond þæt ne gelyfdon, þætte liffruma / in monnes *hiw* ofer mægna þrym, / halig from hrusan, ahafen wurde. *Christ,* 657, ASPR 3, 21 (*id.,* 721, 725, ASPR 3, 23). þæs þe wealdend god / acenned wearð, cyninga wuldor, / in middangeard þurh mennisc *heo. Elene,* 6, ASPR 2, 66. þusend geara and eac ma is nu agan syððan Crist wæs mid mannum on menniscan *hiwe.* Wulfstan, *The Last Days,* 45, Bethurum 1957, 136. þæt is crist sylfa, se ðe of heofonum astah on eorðan, and hine geeadmedde menniscum *hiwe* to onfonne. *Easter Day 2* (unpublished). Crist com for us on þisne middaneard on þeowan *hiwe. Sunday Letter,* Priebsch 1899, 135, 28. And hwæt eart þu ... swa wunderlic on anes mannes *hywe* us to oferwinnanne. *Gospel of Nicodemus,* Hulme 1898, 507, 2. Drihten him æteowde his onsyne on fægeres cildes *heowe. Blickling Homily,* Morris 1874-80, 235, 29. ða ætywdon þær twegen godes englas on cæmpena *hiwe. Martyrology,* April 5 (St. Irene), Herzfeld 1900, 54, 24. Him com to godes engel on cuman *hiwe.* Ælfric, *Cuthbert,* Thorpe 1844-6, 2, 136, 25. þa gemette heo ænne deofol on mannes *hiwe,* se befran hwider heo wolde ... þa andwyrde se deofol on þam menniscum *hiwe.* Ælfric, *Stephen,* Thorpe 1844-6, 2, 30, 10. and hine þær deofla costodon mid ofermæte unclæne luste, efne swa þæt hi eodon on niht to him on geglengedra wifa *hiwe. Martyrology,* January 17 (St. Anthony the Hermit), Herzfeld 1900, 22, 3 (*id.,* 22, 10). Simon bræd his *hiw* ætforan ðam casere. Ælfric, *Peter and Paul,* Thorpe 1844-6, 1, 376, 11. deoful ætywde, / wann ond wliteleas, hæfde weriges *hiw. Andreas,* 1169, ASPR 2, 35. Wæs þis toscead hwæðere þætte fore missenlicre heora feaxes *hiwe* oðer wæs cweden se blaca Heawold, oðer se hwita Heawold. Bede, *History,* 5, 10, Schipper, 1897-9, 599. þa betwux hancrede læg se halga wer geedcucod, mid roseum *hiwe* ofergoten. Ælfric, *Feria III in Letania Maiore,* Thorpe 1844-6, 2, 334, 31. Na beseoh þu on wifes *hiw* and na gewilna þu wif on *hiwe* [Ne respicias in mulieris speciem et non concupiscas mulierem in specie]. *De vitiis et peccatis,* Ecclesiasticus 25, 28, Rhodes 1889, 223, 14 (*id.,* 225, 19). Forþam þe he oncneow *hiw* ure [quoniam ipse cognouit figmentum nostrum]. *Vitellius Psalter,* 102, 14, Rosier 1962, 252 (also *Tiberius, Regius, Blickling* and *Salisbury*; also see 44, 3; 44, 5; 44, 12; 46, 5; 49, 2; 49, 11). Genim þysse wyrte wos, syle drincan, heo agyfð þæt gecyndelice *hiw. Herbarium,* 141, Cockayne 1864-6, 1, 262, 14. frecne bið eac þonne þæs seocan mannes hraca bið maniges *hiwes* and bleo. *Bald's Leechbook,* 2, 46, Cockayne 1864-6, 2, 260, 13 (*id.,* 296, 7; 160, 15; 164, 7; 198, 21; 204, 10; 198, 4; 168, 13; 172, 4).

C, as an attribute of nature

i/ general: *Da he geðwæraðand wlitegað, hwilum eft unwlitegað, and on oðrum hiwe gebrengð. Boethius,* 39, 8, Sedgefield 1899, 131, 5. *Da gesceafta þe þæs an scyppend gesceop synden mænigfealde and mislices* hiwes *and ungelice farað.* Ælfric, *Nativity of Christ,* 50, Skeat 1881-1900, 1, 14. *ęlcum* hiwe *[omniformem]. Prudentius Gloss,* 459, Meritt, 1959, 48. *ætywdan feower circulas to þam mid dæge on butan þære sunnan hwites* hiwes. *Peterborough Chronicle* 1104, Plummer 1892-9, 239. *Þonne weorþeð sunne sweart gewended | on blodes* hiw. *Christ,* 935, ASPR 3, 29. *He sende þone ylcan gast on fyres* hiwe *ofer ða apostolas.* Ælfric, *First Sunday after Easter,* Thorpe 1844-6, 1, 232, 15 (*id.,* 1, 298, 4; 1, 312, 27; 2, 44, 4; 2, 202, 19; 2, 280, 5; 2, 472, 32). *Hwi com se halga gast ða on fyres* hiwe *ofer ðam apostolon, and ofer criste on his fulluhte on culfran gelicnysse? Nis ðæs halgan gastes gecynd oþþe micelnyss on ðam* hiwe *wunigende ðe he ða on gesewen wæs.* Ælfric, *Epiphany,* Thorpe 1844-6, 2, 44, 15. *ðam folce eode ætforan symle godes wolcn swilce ormæte swer, se wæs fyren geðuht on nihtlicere tide, and on gewunelices wolcnes* hiwe *on dæge.* Ælfric, *Midlent,* Thorpe 1844-6, 2, 196, 9. *and he wæs liðe on his menniscnysse swilce on wolcnæs* hywe. *id.,* 2, 200, 30. *Se giem iacinctus, se is lyfte onlicusð on* hiwe. *The Pastoral Care,* 14, Sweet 1871, 85, 5. *Nu cunne ge tocnawan heofenes* hyw, *wytodlice ge ne magon witan þæra tyda tacna. West Saxon Gospels,* Matthew 16, 3, Grünberg 1967, 90. *Heofon and eorðe gewitað, and ðeah ðurhwuniað, forðan ðe hi beoð fram ðam* hiwe *ðe hi nu habbað þurh fyr geclænsode, and swa ðeah symle on heora gecynde standað.* Ælfric, *Second Sunday in Advent,* Thorpe 1844-6, 1, 618, 4 (*id.,* 616, 35). *Ðises middaneardes* hiw *gewit.* Ælfric, *De Doctrina Apostolica,* 79, Pope 1967-8, 2, 626.

ii/ of creatures: *Geaf he and sealde þæt betste hors and þæs fægerestan* hiwes *Aidane þam bysceop.* Bede, *History,* 3, 14, Schipper 1897-9, 257 (*id.,* 258). *Wylle on anes* hiwes *cu meolce. Recipe,* Napier 1890, 326. *Þu nu earma wildeora and fugela and wyrma* hiw *ætywes. Prose Saint Guthlac,* 8, 16, Gonser 1909, 140 (*id.,* 139). *Ne geseah he witodlice on eallum þam dagum ær nane mennisclice gesihðe, ne nanre nytena oþþe fugela oððe wildeora* hiw. *Mary of Egypt,* 182, Skeat 1881-1900, 2, 12. *Hy habbaþ swelce swa græshoppan; hy syndon reades* heowes *and blaces* heowes. *The Marvels of the East,* Rypins 1924, 55 (*id.,* 52, 57, 19, 22, 24). *Dæt is wrætlic deor, wundrum scyne | hiwa gehwylces. The Panther,* 20 (*id.,* 25), ASPR 3, 69-70. *ða ða se halga gast, on culfran* hiwe, *uppon him gereste.* Ælfric, *Epiphany,* Thorpe 1844-6, 1, 104, 23. *he geseah þære ylcan his swustor sawle ut agane of hyre lichaman and on culfran* hiwe *gesecean þæs heofones digolnysse. Gregory's Dialogues,* 2, 34, Hecht 1900-7, 169, 8. *And him on read heow rudeð on þan hrynge. De Sancto Iohanne,* Warner 1917, 147, 25 (cf. Kluge 1885, 478). *On næddran* hiwe *beswac se deofol Adam.* Ælfric, *In Letania Maiore,* Thorpe 1844-6, 1, 252, 2. Hiwes, *bleos [coloris]. Aldhelm Gloss,* Napier 1900, 1, 529 (*id.,* 533).

iii/ of plants: *fleax ðæt bið hwites* hiwes. *The Pastoral Care,* 14, Sweet 1871, 87, 19. *Ne mænde ure drihten mid þisum wordum ða treowa þe on æppeltune wexað ... ac þurh heora* hiw *he gebicnode þa gesceadwisan men.* Ælfric, *Ninth Sunday after Pentecost,* Thorpe 1844-6, 2, 406, 11.

iv/ of cloths and dyes: *And þe biscop sealde heom alle godeweb to wæfenne of seolce and of mislice* hiwum *wahrift to þam temple. Nativity of Mary the Virgin,* 535, Assmann 1889, 132. *Feala* hiwes *hrægel [polimita]. Plantin-Moretus Glossary,* Kindschi 1955, 154, 12. *Se wolcnreada wæfels wislice getacnode ures Drihtnes deað mid ðære deage* hiwe. Ælfric, *Palm Sunday,* Thorpe 1844-6, 2, 254, 5.

v/ of sculptures and pictures: *Her amearcod is | haligra* hiw *þurh handmægen | awriten*

on wealle wuldres þegnas. Andreas, 725, ASPR 2, 23. hiwe *[simulacro, effigie, statua].*
Aldhelm Gloss, Bouterwek 1853, 460 *(id.,* 465, 495; Napier 1900, 1, 2285, 2530, 3784).
Se litigere þe lufeð ælces heowes lit. Honorius, *Elucidarium,* Warner 1917, 141, 10.

vi/ of gems, stones, and metals: *þa betstan meregrotu ælces* hiwes. Bede, *History,* 1, 1,
Schipper 1897-9, 8. *æþele gimmas, / hwite and reade and* hiwa *gehwæs. Meters of
Boethius,* 19, 23, ASPR 5, 176. *Is þæs* hiw *gelic hreofum stane. The Whale,* 8, ASPR 3,
171. *Eala, hwy is ðis gold adeorcad? and ðæt æðeleste* hiew *hwy wearð hit onhworfen?
The Pastoral Care,* Sweet 1871, 133, 11.

vii/ of liquids: *Na beheald þu win þænne hit geoluwað þænne scyð on glæse* hiw *his
[Ne intuearis uinum quando flauescit cum splenduerit in uitro color eius]. Liber
Scintillarum,* 28 (Proverbs 23, 31), Rhodes 1889, 105, 8.

D, of uncertain application
hio *[apricitas: color]. Corpus Glossary A,* 707, Lindsay 1921, 17. hiw *[species].
Plantin-Moretus Glossary,* Kindschi 1955, 166, 4. on hiwe *[effigiae]. Cleopatra Glossary,*
Wright-Wülcker 1884, 398, 36. hiw *[scema],* hiw *[specimen],* hiw *oððe anlicnys
[effigies],* hiw *[species]. Ælfric, Grammar,* Zupitza 1880, 33, 13; 41, 1; 82, 14; 233, 3.

c/ 'role, disguise'; also in a bad sense 'deceitful appearance'
þa bæd he ða ælðeodigan weras, ðe on cuman hiwe *him mid wunodon, þæt hi astodon.*
Ælfric, *Sexagesima,* Thorpe 1844-6, 2, 96, 35. *forþy þe mon meahte his lif tocnawan on
þan fyrste þe he on cuman* hiwe *on mynstre wunade. Benedictine Rule,* 61, Schröer
1885-8, 109, 16 *(id.,* 109, 5). *and swylce hie mid sceare and munuces* hiwe *God
ælmihtigne pæcen. Benedictine Rule,* 1, *id.,* 9, 14. *undernim ðu leorningcnihtes* hiw.
Ælfric, *Andrew,* Thorpe 1844-6, 1, 590, 21. *Wolde ðam cristenan genealecan on wær-
licum* hiwe. Ælfric, *Saint Eugenia,* 53, Skeat 1881-1900, 1, 28 *(id.,* 1, 36). *Forðan þe hi
ne sind na scep, ac sind wulfas on sceapa* hiwum. Ælfric, *Ninth Sunday after Pentecost,*
Thorpe 1844-6, 2, 404, 26 *(id.,* 404, 4, 9). *Feorðe cyn is þara þe hy under leasum* hiwe
ansetlan teliaþ. Benedictine Rule, 1, Schröer 1885-8, 135, 3 *(id.,* 136, 2). *On ðæm*
hiewe *ðe he sceolde his gielpes stieran, on ðæm he his striend. The Pastoral Care,* 8,
Sweet 1871, 55, 10 *(id.,* 51, 3; 301, 25). hiwe *[sub praetextu .i. sub defensione]. Aldhelm Gloss,* Napier 1900, 1, 2684 *(id.,* 3930, Bouterwek 1853, 469, 498).

d/ 'kind, species' (n.b. homonymic contact with *hiwan*)
And treow wæstm wyrcende and gehwilc sæd hæbbende æfter his hiwe. *Genesis,* 1, 12,
Crawford 1922, 82 *(id.,* 1, 21, 24, 25). *On ðam fiftan dæge he gesceop eall wyrmcynn
and ða micclan hwalas and eall fisccynn on mislicum and menigfealdum* hiwum. Ælfric,
De Temporibus Anni, 1, 14, Henel 1942, 8. *Manega synd mægena* hiw *[multę sunt
uirtutem species]. Liber Scintillarum,* 26, Rhodes 1889, 100, 11 *(id.,* 118, 10). on
seofum hiwum *[septem speciebus]. Aldhelm Gloss,* Bouterwek 1853, 479.

e/ 'symbol, type'
For ðam þæt fæsten ys halig þing ... and hyt ys hiw *þære toweardan worulde. Vercelli
Homily,* 20 (unpublished). *Nu berð petrus þæt* hiw *oððe getacnunge þære halgan
gelaðunge.* Ælfric, *Item de Sancto Petro,* Thorpe 1844-6, 2, 390, 14. hiw *[typum].
Aldhelm Gloss,* Napier 1900, 11, 6. *On ymbsnidenesse* hiwe *[in circumcisionis tipo].
Isidore Gloss, id.,* 40, 17.

f/ 'image, likeness'
þeahhwæþre on hiwe *ł on anlicnesse gindfærð mann [Verumtamen in imagine pertransit
homo]. Lambeth Psalter,* 38, 7, Lindelöf 1909-14, 63.

g/ a linguistic and rhetorical term: 'sign, form, class, figure of speech'
*lare witodlice on his se abbod apostolice sceall þæt he æfre hiwe healdan on ðam he
sægið [In doctrina namque sua abbas apostolicam debet illam semper formam servare in
qua dicit]. Interlinear Benedictine Rule*, 2, Logeman 1888, 14, 13. hiwum *[formulis].
Aldhelm Gloss*, Bouterwek 1853, 407 (*id*., 419, and Napier 1900, 1, 79, 536). *Boceras
habbað on heora cræfte wurðfulle* hiw *and tacna. Byrhtferth's Manual*, Crawford 1929,
182, 22 (*id*., 118, 1; 182, 31; 188, 8; 188, 10-4). *ælc stæf hæfð þreo ðing, Nomen,
Figura, Potestas, þæt is, nama and* hiw *and miht ... hiw, hu he gesceapen byð. Ælfric,
Grammar*, Zupitza 1880, 5, 5-6. *Figura is gecweden on englisc* hiw *oððe gefegednyss. id.,*
105, 20 (*id*., 87, 6-12; 217, 10; 91, 7-15; 17, 6-10; 92, 14; 211, 1-3, 5-6, 13; 9, 21).
Sum þæra dæla is metaplasmus, þæt is awend spræc to oðrum hiwe. *id.*, 294, 18. *On
þam boccræfte fela* hiw *synd amearcode, þa synd on Lyden figure, and on Grecisc
scemata gecweden. Byrhtferth's Manual*, Crawford 1929, 172, 13 (*id*., 172, 27; 172, 23;
96, 10). *Sume sind gehatene scemata þæt sind mislice* hiw *and fægernyssa on leden
spræce. Ælfric, Grammar*, Zupitza 1880, 295, 4.

COLOR, EFFIGIES, FIGURA, FORMA, FORMULA, PRAETEXTUS, SPECIES, TYPUS

manigfeald hiw, *manig* hiw *(mænighiwe), mislic* hiw, *missenlic* hiw; hiw ... *bregdan,*
hiw ... *cyrran,* hiw ... *hweorfan.*
= *(and)wlite*, = *bleo* (but cf. color [bleoh] , forma [hiw] . *Ælfric, Glossary*, Zupitza 1880,
306, 17-9), = *gelicnes*, = *hiwung*, = *(mæg)wlite*, = *onsyn*.
≠ *gecynd*.
MED heu, NED hue sb.[1]

hiwere (*hywere*) +. Noun, masc. ja-stem.
hiw.
'hypocrite'
Ac ateoh þu **hiwere** ærest þone beam ut of
ðinum eagan. *Ælfric, Dominica V Post Pentecosten*, 31, Pope 1967-8, 2, 498. **Hiwere** bið
se mann þe hogað ymbe þæt þæt he oðerne
gerihtlæce ær hine sylfne. *id.*, 175, Pope
1967-8, 2, 505. Wa eow bocerum and eow
Sunderhalgum, ge **hiweras** þe heofonan rice
ætforan mannum belucað. *Ælfric, Feria VI
in Secunda Ebdomeda Quadragesime*, 98,
Pope 1967-8, 1, 252. Wa eow **hiwerum**, ge
sind gelice gemettum ofergeweorcum. *Ælfric,
Ninth Sunday after Pentecost*, Thorpe 1844-
6, 2, 404, 17. And byð þonne **hiwere** þurh
þone heafodleahter and ranc on his gyrelum
and unrædfæst on dædum. *Ælfric, Second
Old English Letter*, 3, 173, Fehr 1914, 212.
And þa sum bisceop for his bilewitnysse
gelyfde þam **hiwere**. *Ælfric, Saint Martin*,
838, Skeat 1881-1900, 2, 272. **hiweras**,
wyrhtan [fabricatores] . *Aldhelm Gloss*,

Napier 1900, 1, 4244 (*id*., 2781, Bouterwek
1853, 471, 505). **hiwere** [simulator] .
Plantin-Moretus Glossary, Kindschi 1955,
203, 11.

hiwian (*heow-, hyw-*). Verb, Weak II: trans.
(+ acc.) and intrans. hiw: *æthiwian, behiwian, geatolhiwian, geedhiwian, gehiwian,
oferhiwian, twihiwian*; *hiwung*. 42 (V 0, P
25, I 12, G 4).
a/ 'create, form'; also in a bad sense
and ic þe **hiwode** to mines sylfes anlicnesse.
Vercelli Homily, 8, 53, Förster 1932, 153.
Se **hiwode** sienderlice hioræ heortæn [qui
finxit singillatim corda eorum] . *Canterbury
Psalter*, 32, 15, Harsley 1889, 52 (also
Tiberius, Vitellius, Regius, Stowe (hywode),
Salisbury. Also see 93, 9; 93, 20; 103, 26;
118, 73; 138, 5). **Hiwað** [confingat] . *Cleopatra Glossary*, Wright-Wülcker 1884, 381,
36 (*id*., 408, 26). Ic **hiwige** [fingo] .*Ælfric's
Grammar*, Zupitza 1880, 174, 13. And alle
lichamlice heow heo mæg on hire sylfæn
hiwæn, and swa **iheowed** on hyre mode

healden. Ælfric, *Christmas Day*, Belfour 1909, 94, 20. For þam ðe ðe deofel mæg felæ þingæ dwymorlice **hywiæn** before monnæ eagum, þonne him ilyfed bið. *Lent Homily*, Belfour 1909, 102, 33.
b/ 'disguise, pretend, dissemble'

i/ reflex. Gehwyrfde (**hiwede**) hine sylfne þa on anre næddran hiwe. *Second Sunday in Lent 1* (unpublished). And hine to oþrum men **hiwað**. *Seven Sleepers*, 692, Skeat 1881-1900, 1, 530. Sum fæmne hi facenlice **hiwode** sarlice seoce. Ælfric, *Martin*, Thorpe 1844-6, 2, 506, 5. Herodes **hiwode** hine sylfne unrotne. Ælfric, *Decollation of St John the Baptist*, Thorpe 1844-6, 1, 484, 26.

ii/ intrans. Ic eom eald to **hiwigenne**. Ælfric, *The Maccabees*, 94, Skeat 1881-1900, 2, 72. **hiwodan** ‡ liccetan [scematizarunt]. *Aldhelm Gloss*, Bouterwek 1853, 501 (*id.*, Napier 1900, 1, 4061). Ne hit ne **hiwað** mid wordum, þæt hit oðer ðence, and oðer sprece. Ælfric, *Dedicatio ecclesiae sancti Michaelis*, Thorpe 1844-6, 1, 512, 15. Ne **hiwa** þu, min bearn, swilce þu mid bilewitnysse mæge þe gan orsorh to mædena husum. Ælfric, *Admonitio*, 7, Norman 1849, 48, 9. Ne sceal he hit no yldan and **hiwian**, swilce hit him uncuð sy. *Benedictine Rule*, 2, Schröer 1885-8, 13, 16. Mænig wyrð þe gyt cimeð on uferan tidan þe ... namað hine sylfne and **hiwað** to gode, swylce hit crist sy. Wulfstan, *Matthew on the Last Days*, 41, Bethurum 1957, 120. **Hiwiende**, reoniende [musitantes i. fingentes]. *Aldhelm Gloss*, Napier 1900, 1, 2804 (*id.*, Bouterwek 1853, 472).

iii/ trans. and swa on mænige wisan he **hiwode** þurh drycræft fela leasbregda. *De temporibus Antichristi*, Napier 1883, 99, 16. þa forswelgað wydwyna hus **hiwgende** lang gebed. *Luke*, 20, 47, Skeat 1871-87, 198. se þe wæs swicolast and se þe litelicost cuðe leaslice **hiwian** unsoð to soðe and undom deman oðrum to hynðe. *To eallum folce*, Napier 1883, 128, 9. Idele and lease spel hi **hywiaþ** and mannum reccaþ. *Benedictine Rule*, 1, Schröer 1885-8, 135, 24. To ansyne follicre geþyld hi **hiwiað**, and on ge-

þance yrsunge attor hi behydað [Ad faciem publicam patientiam fingunt, et in animo iracundiae virus abscondunt]. *Liber Scintillarum*, 2, Rhodes 1889, 9, 12.
d/ 'typify, symbolize' (1)
þe **hiwedon** [obumbrabant]. *Aldhelm Gloss*, Napier 1900, 11, 104.
e/ 'colour' (1)
Hiwian [colorare]. *Plantin-Moretus Glossary*, Kindschi 1955, 224, 2.
(CON)FINGERE, (DIS)SIMULARE, FIGURARE, FORMARE
= *gehiwian, gehwyrfan, liccettan.*
    hiwuncg see *hiwung.*
    hiwung (*heowung-, hiung-, hiwuncg, hywung*). Noun, fem. o-stem. *hiwian, hiw: frumheowung, gehiwung.* 52 (V 0, P 38, I 11, G 3).
a/ 'image'
Ne hie ne ongytaþ þæt hi on fruman to godes **hiwunga** gesceapene wæron. *Blickling Homilies*, Morris 1874-80, 61, 7. Festen is swiðe god, hit is ... **hiwung** þare towearden weorulde. *Second Sunday in Lent*, Belfour 1909, 44, 30.
b/ 'creation'
forðon ðe he sylf oncneow **hiwunga** ‡ gescapennysse ure [quoniam ipse cognouit figmentum nostrum]. *Lambeth Psalter*, 102, 14, Lindelöf 1909-14, 162. And he lifde, adam, æfter þære menniscan **hiwunge** dcccc wintra and þrittig wintra, and þe sexteoþegan geare fram his **hiwunge** þæt he gegylte on neorxnawonge ungesælilice ofer godes bebod and ofer his hæse. *Biblical Note*, Napier 1889, 1, 13-6.
c/ in a bad sense 'fabrication, deception'
i/ general: **hiwunga**, lignes [figmenta i. plasmatio, mendacia, uaria figura, compositio]. *Harley Glossary F* 377, Oliphant 1966, 186. **Hiwunga** [frivola, ficta ‡ falsa aut inania]. *Aldhelm Gloss*, Bouterwek 1853, 451 (*id.*, Napier 1900, 1, 1929). **heowunga**, leasunge [nebulonis i. fallacis]. *Aldhelm Gloss*, Napier 1900, 1, 2238 (*id.*, Bouterwek 1853, 459). **hiwung** [scena, umbra]. Bouterwek 1853, 501 (*id.*, 501, Napier 1900, 1, 4057). **Hiwunge**, gedwimore [fantasmate i. simulatore]. Napier 1900, 1, 4059 (*id.*,

Bouterwek 1853, 501).

ii/ of the devil and fiends: þenne mihte he þeah alle weorldlice fegernesse togadere iseon þurð deofles **hywunge**. *Lent Homily,* Belfour 1909, 102, 33. Be þam þæt preostas hi warnien wyð þa scinlacan **hiwinga** deofla prettes. *Rule of Chrodegang,* Napier 1916, 7, 26. Hi woldon mid heora **hiwunge** þæs halgan weres mod awendan. *Prose Saint Guthlac,* 8, 10, Gonser 1909, 139.

iii/ of man: He getacnode þa leasan licceteras, ðe mid **hiwunge** god secað and næfre ne gemetað. Ælfric, *Epiphany,* Thorpe 1844-6, 1, 120, 2. Se ðe oðerne lufað buton **hiwunge**, nele he him hearmes cepan, ne his æhta him ætbredan. Ælfric, *Apostle,* Thorpe 1844-6, 2, 522, 20. And wæs ða geswutelod. his scincræft and **hiwung**. Ælfric, *Saint Martin,* 827, Skeat 1881-1900, 2, 270. And dyde swilce he æte of ðam offrungspice, and swa mid ðære **hiwunge** him sylfum geburge. Ælfric, *The Maccabees,* 93, Skeat 1881-1900, 2, 72. Nis nan asecgendlic oððe unasecgendlic fracodlicnysse **hiwung** þæs ic ne sih tihtende and lærende. *Mary of Egypt,* 383, Skeat 1881-1900, 2, 26. Se man þurh lease **hiwunge** deð swylce he rædfæst sy. Wulfstan, *Gifts of the Holy Spirit,* 83, Bethurum 1957, 187 (*id.,* 80, 121). Hu he arasode þa **hiwunge** Totillan cininge. *Gregory's Dialogues,* 2 (titles), Hecht 1900-7, 93, 5. He com hider mid **hiwunge**, cwæð þæt he wolde his man beon. *Abingdon Chronicle (C)* 1049, Rositzke 1940, 72 (also in *D*). Oft þurh **hiwunge** freondscype byð gegaderud [Sepe per simulationem amicitia colligitur] . *Liber Scintillarum,* 64, Rhodes 1889, 197, 10 (*id.,* 75, 4; 129, 12). þurh liccettunge and **hiwunge** [per adulationem et simulationem] . *Interlinear Prayer,* 19, 17, Holthausen 1941, 246.

d/ specifically '(the sin of) hypocrisy' Of ydelum gylpe bið acenned pryte and æbilignys, ungeðwærnys and **hywung**, and lustfullung leasre herunge. Ælfric, *Midlent: secunda sententia,* Thorpe 1844-6, 2, 220, 32. Gif he abryð on ðære ehtnysse, he ne bið þonne geleafa ac bið **hiwung**. Ælfric, *In*

Letania Maiore, Thorpe 1844-6, 1, 250, 21. þæt hluttre mod þe gode gelicað forsihð þa **hiwunga** and healt soðfæstnysse. Do þu feorr fram þe þa fakenfullan **hiwunge**. Ælfric, *Admonitio,* 5, Norman 1849, 46, 8.

e/ 'deceptive speech, lying' **Hiwung** oððe leasspel [figmenta] . *Cleopatra Glossary,* Wright-Wülcker 1884, 401, 18. þurh smicernesse and **hiwunge** [Hironiam] . *id.,* 416, 32. Ic sprece to him muðe to muðe and openlice, næs ðurh rædelsas ne ðurh **hiwwinge**. *Numbers,* 12, 8, Crawford 1922, 314.

DISSIMULATIO, FICTITIA, FIGMENTUM, FIGURA, MENDACIUM, SCENA, SIMULATIO, SPECIES. *deofles hiwung* (3), *leas hiwung* (3). = *gescapennes*; *leasung*; *gedwimor*, *leasspel*, *scuwa*. ≠ *soðfæstnys*.

hwonne (*hwænne, hwanne, ... *). Adverb and conjunction. *hwon*; *hwa, hwæt*. (n occurrences) (distribution). a/ indefinite adverbial uses ... b/ interrogative, introducing direct questions. c/ interrogative, introducing indirect questions. d/ temporal conjunction
  i/ 'when' ...
  ii/ 'whenever', 'until' ...
e/ conjunction introducing adjectival clause 'when' ... QUANDO, QUANDOQUE ... cf. *þonne*. MED (whan), NED when.

  hyow see *hiw*.
  hyw see *hiw*.
  hywere see *hiwere*.
  hywian see *hiwian*.
  hywung see *hiwung*.
  scin-hiu see *scinnhiw*.
  scin-hiw see *scinnhiw*.
  scin-hyw see *scinnhiw*.
  scinnhiw (*scinhiu, scinhiw, scinhyw*) +.
Noun, neuter ja-stem. 'apparition, evil spirit' Ne eom ic na **scinnhiw**, swa swa ge wenað. Ælfric, *Peter and Paul,* Thorpe 1844-6, 2, 388, 26. And hine gesewenlicne on manegum **scinhiwum** þam halgan æteowde. Ælfric,

Saint Martin, 712, Skeat 1881-1900, 2, 264. Forþan þe he wende þæt hit wære sumes gastes **scinhyw** þæt he þær geseah. *Mary of Egypt,* 170, Skeat 1881-1900, 2, 12. Fram heanysse **scinnhiwys** hys upahafyn ys [ab altitudine fantasie sue eleuatus est]. *Cambridge Hymns, Canticum Abbacuc,* 10, Wildhagen 1910, 382 (also *Vespasian Psalter,* scinhiowes his). Gewitan swefnu feor and **scinhyh** nihta [Recedant somnia procul et fantasmata noctium]. *Hymn Gloss,* Gneuss 1968, 277 (*id.,* 297). **scinhiw** [fantasma]. *Cleopatra Glossary,* Wright-Wülcker 1884, 400, 20 (*id.,* 400, 21; 466, 34; Meritt 1945, 60, 8; Oliphant 1966, 178). Wiccecræftas, **scinhiw** [Prestrigias]. *Cleopatra Glossary,* Wright-Wülcker 1884, 465, 15 (*id., Plantin-Moretus Glossary,* Kindschi 1955, 70, 12). deofles repe losede her reaflac gemah **scinhiw** forhtað [Demonis seva perit hic rapina pervicax monstrum pavet]. *Durham Hymn Gloss,* Stevenson 1851, 142, 6 (*id.,* Gneuss 1968, 406). Reþlic **scinhiw** [ferale monstrum]. *Harley Glossary F,* 183, Oliphant 1966, 179. mihtie **scinhiu** [portenta]. *Sedulius Gloss,* Meritt 1945, 28, 429.

sē (ðe ...), **sēo** (*sia, sie, sio, ðio* ...), **þæt** (*þet* ...). Demonstrative adjective; demonstrative and relative pronoun; adverb and conjunction. *þa; þær.* (n occurrences) (distribution).
a/ demonstrative adjective ...
b/ demonstrative pronoun ...
c/ relative pronoun,
  i/ combining antecedent and relative in one form ...
  ii/ with antecedent 1/ correlative with appropriate form of *se* ... 2/ some other word(s) ...
  iii/ in the case of the principle clause ...
d/ relative pronoun in immediate combination with *þe,*
  i/ when the *se* element is in the case of the principal clause ...
  ii/ when the *se* element is in the case of the subordinate clause ...
  iii/ when the case in both clauses is the same ...
  iv/ when the same form, but not case, is required in both clauses ...
  v/ combining antecedent and relative in the same form ...
e/ adverbial uses,
  i/ genitive ...
  ii/ dative and instrumental ...
f/ conjunction,
  i/ see s.v. *þæt* and *þætte*
  ii/ genitive, 1/ alone ... 2/ in combination with *þe* or *þæt* ... 3/ in prepositional formulae ...
  iii/ dative and instrumental, 1/ alone ... 2/ in combination with *þe* or *þæt* ... 3/ in prepositional formulae ...
IDEM, ILLE, IPSE, IS, QUI, ... cf. *he, þe, þes,* ...
MED (the), NED the, that.

tō (*te* ...). Adverb and preposition. (n occurrences) (distribution).
a/ adverb, with adjectives and adverbs,
  i/ comparison, 'too' ...
  ii/ litotes, 'not at all' ...
b/ separable prefix with verbs,
  i/ motion ...
  ii/ separation ...
c/ preposition,
  i/ + acc. ...
  ii/ + gen. ...
  iii/ + dat. or instr. ...
  iv/ with infin. ...
d/ with the appropriate case of *þæt,* conjunction,
  i/ with gen., *to þæs,* 'to the extent that, so that', 1/ without *þe* ... 2/ with *þe* ...
  ii/ with dat., *to þæm,* 'to the end that', introducing 1/ clauses of purpose with subjunctive, A without *þe* ... B with *þe* ...
e/ with the appropriate case of *hwæt,* interrogative,
  i/ with gen., *to hwæs,* 'whether' ...
  ii/ with dat. or instr., *to hwi, to hwon,* 'why' ...
AD, SECUNDUM, ... cf. *til; fram;* ...
MED (to), NED to, too.

þā (*tha* ...). Adverb and conjunction. *se, seo, þæt.* (n occurrences) (distribution).

a/ adverb, 'then' (usually followed immediately by the verb in prose),

  i/ alone ...

  ii/ correlative with *þa(þa)*; see **b** v/ below

  iii/ correlative with some other conjunction ...

b/ conjunction, 'when' > 'because', with pret. indic. of a single completed act in the past (usually with the word-order S (...) V in prose),

  i/ alone ...

  ii/ doubled, *þaþa* ...

  iii/ with *þe* ...

  iv/ in combination, 1/ *þa ... furþum,* 'as soon as' ... 2/ *þa ... ærest* ...

  v/ correlative with adverbial *þa* ...

TUNC, DUM, CUM, ... cf. *þonne,* ...

MED (tho), NED tho.

  þonne (*þanne, þænne* ...). Adverb and conjunction. *þon*; *se, seo, þæt.* (n occurrences) (distribution).

a/ adverb,

  i/ of time, 'then', 1/ past ... 2/ present ... 3/ future ...

  ii/ 'then, therefore' ...

  iii/ 'then, yet, but' ...

  iv/ correlative, 1/ with *þonne* (conjunction) ... 2/ with *gif* ...

b/ conjunction of time,

  i/ 'when, whenever' of single act in 1/ present ... 2/ future ...

  ii/ frequentative, 'whenever', in 1/ past ... 2/ present ... 3/ future ...

c/ conjunctive of cause, 'because' ...

d/ conjunction of concession, 'when, although' ...

e/ conjunction of condition, 'when, if' ...

f/ conjunction of comparison,

  i/ with a full clause following, 'than' ...

  ii/ with a contracted clause following, 'than' ...

  iii/ when two clauses are compared, 'than that' ...

CUM, DUM, QUANDO, TUNC, ... cf. *þa, hwonne,* ...

MED (than), NED than, then.

wundor-bléo +. Noun, neuter ja-stem. 'marvellous colour'
þæs temples scgl, / **wundorbleom** geworht to wlite þæs huses, / sylf slat on tu. *Christ,* 1139, ASPR 3, 34.